The Most Intensive and Top Secret Military Operations of Region Two

*By the Royal Laotian King and
U.S. CIA in Laos During the Vietnam Era.*

*Laos is a small, mountainous and landlocked country
surrounded by a lot more populous neighbors, going out of its
way trying to protect itself and find lasting peace.*

Former Colonel Vang Geu, The Author

Maiker Vang-Vue, Editor/Translator

Mai Joua Vang, Co. Editor

TABLE OF CONTENTS

INTRODUCTION

This book was meant for readers and researchers who are interested in finding how and why the more recent historical events have occurred in Laos, and why thousands of Lao people had to seek refuge in many countries around the world, deprived of their Lao citizenship, following the fight between the Lao groups where, in the end, no one won. The real winners were only foreigners. Please read all the records that might help improve your understanding of the situation, and serve as a lesson for all of us Lao natives in readjusting our views, changing our life plan and looking for new ideas, so that Laos' sad history does not repeat itself.

The book provides details on North-Vietnam's interference in Lao affairs and the dissension between the two Lao factions that resulted in several hundred thousands of the Lao being forced to become refugees living in several newly adopted countries across the world. It covers the records of various events that took place in Indochina and the kingdom of Laos, especially in Military Region II, which covered Houaphan and Xieng Khouang Provinces.

NOTES FROM THE AUTHOR

I, Vang Geu, was born at Ban Hom, Tasseng Phasay, Muang Pha, Xieng Khouang Province, Laos. A former military officer in Military Region II (MR-II), I served in the French Army during the Indochina War from 1953 to 1954. I have worked as a news broadcaster at the Lao National Radio Station in Vientiane, Laos and, during 1960-1964, was an employee of the National Bank of Laos in Vientiane. During 1968-1973, I was involved in the Vietnam War, fighting alongside the United States armed forces. My military assignments included serving successively as battalion commander, brigade commander, and division commander, fighting the enemy that invaded the kingdom of Laos. During 1973-1975, I served as chief of Economic and Development in MR-II, Laos.

I graduated from the Dong Dok Teacher's College in Vientiane with a teaching degree. I then completed a course in a foreign country, studying agriculture, cattle-raising and international development. I completed several military training programs, including national defense and high-ranking officer's duties. I have also received training in development, cooperation, conflict resolution, management, accounting, and psychology.

In 1975, I was forced to leave Laos and had to settle in several countries, including Thailand, France, and the USA, and worked as a leader of Lao refugees for several years. I worked in Northern France in low income housing, helping thousands of French find a place to stay at government-subsidized housing facilities. I also served as president of the Franco-Asiatique Association (1976-1980).

In March 1981, I made the decision to resettle in the United States where I reside to this day. I worked at the reception desk at the Minnesota department of agriculture, assisting refugees and teaching them how to grow plants, and worked as program associate-director at the University of Minnesota's Hospital. I was president of Lao Family, Inc. in Minnesota during 1982-1987 and, in 1987, decided to lead several thousands of Lao and Lao Hmong refugees in starting a new life in many eastern states, including Georgia, South-Carolina, and North-Carolina. During 1987-2011, I served as President of the Hmong-Lao Assistance Association, and have been working at McRae Industries as liaison officer from 1987 to date.

For the past twenty-two years, I have been residing with my wife, MayKao Thao Vang, in Samthong Village, a Southeast Asian American subdivision created in 1988 by the president of McRae Industries. We have six adult children and seven grandchildren who are members of Mt. Gilead First Baptist Church, where I teach a Laotian Sunday School class and serve on the Board of Deacons. On a typical day, I drive people to the Department of Motor Vehicles for driver license test, to the courts, to doctor's appointments, or to the bank. I can also be found interpreting at the parent-teacher conferences, assisting with immigration issues, talking with employers about their Asian staff, repairing plumbing leakages, preparing income taxes, etc.

In my free time, I started recording the various events of the past few decades in collaboration with the following friends and acquaintances:

1. Col. Thao Bone
2. Provincial Deputy-Governor Bounchanh Vouthisisombath
3. Agricultural Specialist Arya Lyfoung
4. Chaomuang (District Chief) Lao Thai Va Lue Vang
5. Police Maj. Dua Hang
6. Air Forces Capt. Vang Bee, T28 pilot
7. Col. Song Leng Xiong
8. School Principal Bouthalangsy Douangsavanh
9. Lt. Col. Chou Vang
10. Lt. Col. Ly Chao
11. Electrical Engineer Vang Yia
12. Maj. Sakon Keo Douangdy
13. Col. Vang Neng
14. Maj. Phothisane Vanh
15. Capt. Vang Xang
16. Col. Max Messnier
17. Maj. Pham Khamsouan
18. Col. Tou Fue Vang (Political Science Specialist)
19. Ms. Jennifer Moua, and
20. Catherine T. Hodges (who read, interpreted, and pre-edited the original version of the book at least three times).

I owe my greatest thanks to the people listed above, as well as many other folks who lent their helping hands on the side. Without their support, this book would not have been written. I was lucky to be able to collect the information and photos I needed because not many people were able to bring their personal possessions with them when they left Laos, an exit that was fairly sudden for most of us. This book should have been written much earlier, but the general environment did not permit its completion until now. Only time will tell whether the results of the changes that took place in Laos were good or bad in the long run for our country and its people or not. My intent was not to just recount the bad things of the past, but rather to help predict some of the likely changes that might occur in the future in Laos.

Every era had an end. Colonization ended after World War II, and communism ended after the Vietnam War, a war that gave good lessons to both sides --the Communist world and the Western world. For Laos, a new era has already started, with a new generation of children born in Laos and in foreign countries after 1977. These young folks are smart and speak many languages. They are the ones who will likely have a role in running the country of Laos, keeping it at peace with its neighbors in Southeast Asia and Northeast Asia, and staying open to tourists from around the world. Whether this new generation will actually have a chance to run the country or not will probably be in a large part up to mainland China and the United States of America. Asia countries need their umbrellas to maintain peace, promote friendly international cooperation, ensure internal integrity, and remain independent. We hope to see Laos in peace and in good harmony with other countries, and no more war in Indochina (Laos, Cambodia, and Vietnam). We have suffered more than enough during the Vietnam War. It is time for an era of peace and economic prosperity for the people of Indochina.

NOTE OF EDITOR/TRANSLATOR AND CO.

EDITOR/TRANSLATOR

I am Maiker A. Vang-Vue. I am the Editor/Translator of this book. I am now living with my husband and children in Eagan, Minnesota. I was born in Long Cheng, Laos during the Vietnam Era. I come from a military high rank in leadership family background and my father was a great leader during his time working under General Vang, Pao and The King of Laos. He was a Special Commando Leader. I like to have a special dedication to My father, a great leader and his brothers. I also like to thank my father in law, who was a great military leader during this war, too. I speak four languages. I graduated from NCSU, Raleigh, N.C.. I am a Crisis Victims Advocate. I wrote a children Hmong cultural story book. I am proud to have the honor to work with Former Lt. Col. Vang, Geu, The Author of this book. I studied Hmong History for a total of thirteen years taught by Dr. Xoua Thao, MD. and former President of Hmong Nationalities Organization. I also worked at Hmong Nationalities Organization as Hmong Human Rights Committee Chair, Social Media Planner and Anchor in Hmong Nationalities Organization for a total of thirteen years. I am now currently working at CNS as a Cultural and Society Commissioner. I had the opportunity to go back to Asia and taught English to KIS students in Vientiane, Laos. I love my Hmong peoples around the world. I'm thankful to all the great people and innocent people that sacrificed their lives for us. I am so honored to have this opportunity to be able to be part of this project and approved by Former Lt. Col. Vang, Geu. This book is about how leaders use intensive plans in strategy plans to protect innocent peoples and their country.

Joua Vang, The Co. Editor.

ENGLISH TRANSLATOR AND REVIEWER'S NOTES

According to Wikipedia, the Hmong ... "are an Asian ethnic group of people from the mountainous regions of Vietnam, Laos, Thailand and Burma. Hmong groups began a gradual southward migration (from China) in early of the 18th century due to political unrest and to find more arable land."

"A number of Hmong ... people fought against the communist-nationalist Pathet Lao during the Secret War in Laos. Hmong ... people were singled out for retribution when the Pathet Lao took over the Laotian government in 1975, and tens of thousands fled to Thailand seeking political asylum. Thousands of these refugees have resettled in Western countries since the late 1976s, mostly the United States but also Australia, France, French Guiana, and Canada." [http: // en.wikipedia.org/wiki/Hmong people].

The author is one of those Hmong fortunate to survive the Secret War in Laos and is perhaps the one person most capable of telling this story. Geu Vang has often compared the exodus of the Hmong and Laotian people to Moses as he led the Israelites out of Egypt. Since I met Geu Vang in 1987, I can say that he has continuously led his people—locally, statewide, and nationwide. I have never known anyone so devoted to helping others as Geu Vang is to the Southeast Asian American community. His compassion, commitment, generosity, sense of unselfishness, and love for his people are all factual evidences that his work is not yet completed.

It has been a blessing for me to have the opportunity to work with Geu Vang as he endeavors to help his people to assimilate into the American society. I am humbled as I see the seriousness with which Geu Vang and "his people" take the freedoms guaranteed in the United States Constitution and the traditional American values of family, freedom, God, and country. Working with the Southeast Asian Americans has changed my life and has allowed me to become a much better human being.

(Writer's note: I feel very fortunate to have met with Cathie Hodges, a retired teacher from West Montgomery High School in NC. Ms. Hodges has been instrumental in getting me on the right tract with the early English version of my book, which was originally written in Lao).

FORMER CAPTAIN, XAY (CHIA SHER) VANG, CO. BOOK REVIEWER NOTE

Former Captain Xay Vang,

I was involved with this war in Laos. I did my part. I was involved because I had to protect my people and my country. I believe in democracy and I did many military tasks in action at the frontier line in the Ho Chi Minh Trail zone in Laos. Lt. Col. Vang Geu's books provide great details of this war in Laos. Thank god that we survive and have the opportunity to live in the USA. Thanks to General Vang, Pao and the U.S. Government for being great leaders. He did not lose this war in Laos. It is the political decision and negotiation only. I like to honor all the great leaders and military officers that put their lives, lose their lives and sacrifice for all of us.

FORMER CAPTAIN TONG LOU VANG, VOLUNTEER AS A SUPPORTER FOR THIS BOOK PROJECT.

Former Captain Tong Lou Vang.

Volunteer to support this group. Thanks to Former Captain Tong Lou Vang, his time, his effort, and his leadership and having the plan of supporting to make the book possible.

CHAPTER 1

HISTORICAL EVENTS PRIOR TO 1945

The French officially entered Laos on November 10, 1861. In 1872, hordes of Chinese red flag, yellow flag, and multicolor flag troops invaded the northern part of Laos. The French leaders contacted the Hmong and recruited them to fight against the invaders. The successful operation increased French confidence in the Hmong. In May 1893, the French used their armed forces to remove Laos from Siam's control and put Laos under their own control as a French colony. They first named Chong Kai Mua as the first "Kaitong" (subdistrict chief) of the Hmong subdistrict of Nonghet, and then Lor Blia Yao (1913-1934). As administrators of Laos, the French next selected Touby Lyfoung to be the Nonghet subdistrict chief until 1945, during their war against Germany and Japan, and right before their war against North-Vietnam. After losing those two wars, the French were forced to move out of the Indochina peninsula per the Geneva Treaty.

TOULIA LYFOUNG'S MEMOIRS

On March 15, 1994, Toulia Lyfoung published his memoirs on the history of the Lao Hmong to remind the new generation about the past. Many parts of those memoirs are reproduced in the following sections. Throughout Laos's history, the Lao Hmong have always been part of the country's administrative, military, and police structure, especially when Laos was a French colony. During 1945-1954, the Lao Hmong have been fighting alongside the French in the Indochina war against the Vietminh and the Lao Issara.

During 1959-1973, the Lao Hmong collaborated with the Royal Lao Army and the US armed forces in the fight against the communists along the Northern Laos border. During the fight near the borders of the Soviet Union and Communist China, the former delivered tons of war material to North-Vietnam in 1970. From that point on, the US felt compelled to change their overall strategy in Indochina.

HISTORY OF THE LAO HMONG AND PAST DEVELOPMENTS

Around the year 1750, Hmong emigrated from China and settled around the highland mountains of Laos along border areas that were covered by forests and far removed from urban centers normally occupied by lowland Lao and other tribes that had resettled there before. They feared persecution from the Chinese. They also feared discrimination and violence from the Lao ethnic majority because they did not yet speak Lao and were not familiar with Lao leaders and Lao customs. The Hmong feared ghosts in the cities of Laos because many became sick and died after they returned home from venturing into town. In the mountains, the weather is cold, so mosquitoes rarely cause malaria. In the lowlands, however, the weather is warmer and contact with mosquitoes and ticks does cause deadly cases of malaria.

For all those reasons, only a few Hmong were able to live in the cities. Most of them would stay in the mountain areas away from cities, which prevented them from receiving an education and getting to learn Lao and French. During those times, the Lao who lived in the cities were more educated, could speak French, and often acted as representatives of the French Colonial Administration in making surveying contacts with the Hmong living in the mountains and the various villages. The French then set up taxation codes that created a lot of problems for the Hmong and eventually caused an armed resistance from them. The revolt was led by a Hmong leader named Paj Caiv Vwj at the village Pak Kha in between Houaphan Province and Xieng Khouang Province. The French dispatched Vietnamese soldiers to control the revolt in a very ferocious and barbarous way during 1919-1922. Paj Caiv surrendered to the French in 1922.

During the French persecution of the Hmong, the Lao leadership had little say in the conflict and, in fact, had to side with the French because they were under French control and because the Hmong had refused to pay the implemented tax. The Hmong did not have any fire-arms to fight against the French except for guns used for hunting; they relied only on Chao Fa's spiritual power for their protection and fought as isolated groups with the rest of their family members. For this reason, many people referred to this revolt as "Crazy War."

Tou Lia Lyfoung noted that anyone over eighteen years old must pay seventy-five brass coins in tax per year, but the Lao Leadership, who did the tax collection, did not exactly follow the tax code. They instead collected twelve more brass coins, for a total of eighty-seven brass coins. At the time, mostly the Hmong were poor people, had no income, and could not afford to pay the tax. To avoid jail detention, some Hmong had to sell their children to pay tax, which caused an uprising among most people. The French did not listen to the motives, sent in military forces to barbarously persecute the Hmong and caused many fatalities. Those who did not get killed were incarcerated, and many of them were later sent to the firing squad.

This news spread to the Hmong in China, who threatened to send the Chinese Hmong to help the Lao Hmong in Laos. Later on, Father Savina (a French preacher) came to intervene to stop the French from persecuting the Hmong. He was able to save the lives of about 100 people who were already handcuffed and waiting in line for a public execution at the sports stadium of Xieng Khouang. Father Savina also called for no more arrests and no more executions of the Hmong by the French. After that, the fight for justice led by Paj Caiv ended.

Not long afterwards, during that same year, 1922, Soob Ntxawm Lauj, a Hmong from Nonghet, led another fight for justice. This time, the French have just completed the construction of Highway #7 from Ban Ban to Nonghet and from Nonghet to Muang Saene in Central Vietnam. They gave Kaitong Lor Blia Yao the authority to recruit laborers for the road construction, and set the labor rate at 20 brass coins for the excavation of a one square meter hole, regardless of its depth. Even though the excavation had to be deeper than before, the daily labor rate still remained the same. When the project owner acted unfairly, the laborers stood up. Many people started screaming, "The crazy war is back!"

[Soob Ntxawm Lauj had a nephew named Soob Thaiv Lo, who is a refugee living in North-Carolina. During 1960-1970, Soob Thaiv Lo served as a member of the US-FAG in the Vietnam War. He flew backseat with the US pilot of the small airplane that flew in to locate enemy positions, reported that information to the US ground forces, and sent for air strikes. Soob Thaiv Lo was shot by the enemy's anti-aircraft during one of his flights. He was wounded in the head, but luckily, the pilot was able to bring him back to the airfield and transported him to the U.S. hospital in Thailand. He survived the good treatment at the US hospital and is now well-known among the Hmong people].

Tou Lia recorded that the French named Kaitong Lauj Blia Yao as a leader at the Kaitong level during 1913-1934 to replace Chong Kai Mua. After Lauj Blia Yao died, his son Chong Tou Lauj took his place as leader of the Hmong. During his term, several incidents took place within the Lee family. After Chong Tou Lauj died, his son Hnia Her Lauj replaced him as leader. After Hnia Her died, two brothers (Hnia Veu Lee and Ya Lauj Lee) and descendants of the Seng Lee family joined forces with the French to fight the Ho (Chinese) burglars who invaded and pilfered northern Laos in 1872, building themselves a good reputation within the Hmong and the French communities and enhanced the French's confidence in the Hmong. (Kaitong was a leadership position during the Annam's administration, similar to the position of Tasseng under the Lao administration). After the Seng Lee brothers, Ly Foung was named the next Hmong leader.

During the terms of Kaitong Blia Yao Lauj, Ly Foung served as his assistant and was his son-in-law. Ly Foung did great things for the Lee and other Hmong families. He was a smart man and could read and write Lao pretty well. However, his wife (the daughter of Kaitong Lauj) poisoned herself to death. Her father became very disturbed and had Ly Foung put in jail in Xieng Khouang for several months. These events forced Ly Foung, who did not know how to speak or write French, to send his four sons (Nao Chao, Touby, Tou Lia and Tou Geu) to school in Xieng Khouang. Kaitong Lauj did the same by sending Lauj Foung to school, where he later graduated as a teacher. As for Nao Chao, he was not able to complete any schooling and came home empty-handed.

Tou Lia graduated third of his class from a law school in 1941. While at school, he fell in love with Tiao Khampheng, a member of the Louang Prabang front royal lineage. The two got married and has three children together, all of them boys. Because of his good education, Tou Lia was assigned to work as a staff member of the Royal Office in Louang Prabang during 1941-1945.

Photo #1. *Kaitong Lo Bliayao, first Hmong Leader In Nong Het, Xieng Khouang*

Photo # 2. *Typical dress of a Hmong woman before 1920*

In 1946, Tou Lia returned to Xieng Khouang to join hands with Touby Lyfoung in leading the Hmong people to fight alongside the French, the Lao Issara and the Vietminh invaders. In 1947, Tou Lia was elected as Xieng Khouang's state representative and went to work in Vientiane until 1954, when he came back to Xieng Khouang for a break. In one of his personal records, Tou Lia noted that in 1941, he walked from Nonghet to Xieng Khouang, about 100 km, to meet with David Beaulieu, the French Commissaire (Administrator) of Xieng Khouang Province. The Commissaire invited Tou Lia to have breakfast with him at his official residence and asked him, "I've heard that you came to push the Hmong people against the French. Is that true?"

Tou Lia answered, "Where did you get this information?" and added, "I'm ready to face your informant." The French Commissaire did not answer the question but added another one, "What brought you down here in Xieng Khouang?" Tou Lia answered, "I am here to ask you for an official note to visit Hmong relatives at the border of Vietnam and Laos." After that, the Commissaire told Tou Lia, "Tomorrow, please come and meet with me in my office at 9:00 a.m."

Tou Lia wrote that when he entered Mr. Beaulieu's office as invited, many people were already sitting in the room, ready for a meeting. During this meeting, several personnel changes were made, involving some transfers and some dismissals as follows:

- Phoumi Vongvichit, the Chaomuang (District Chief) of Xieng Khouang, was moved to become the Chaomuang of Vientiane;
- Bouasy, the Xieng Khouang's legal officer, was reassigned as the assistant of the Chaomuang of Savannakhet (Southern Laos) and
- Thao Cham, the Muang Kham's legal officer, was discharged from his position because he was accused of being too self-centred in his duties performance. He was sent to early retirement in Savannakhet.

Tou Lia also wrote some notes about the Second World War and the Indochina War. During the Second World War, when Germany and Italy invaded several European countries, especially France that was heavily assaulted, towns and cities were badly damaged, and people fled everywhere. France almost did not survive. In Asia, Japan stood up to fight against the western powers and had its own plan to take power in Asia. Japan lost the war and left behind weapons in several Asian countries to help those countries in their fight to regain independence from their western conquerors.

During 1939-1954, the three countries in French Indochina (Cambodia, Laos and Vietnam) fought against French colonization. During this fight, French troops under the command of General de Lattre de Tassigny asked for US assistance and set up a defense stronghold at Dien-Bien-Phu in order to teach the Communists a lesson. Due to the lack of stronger US interest, France lost that war. The US has also agreed with Ho-Chi-Minh to hold a conference in Geneva, Switzerland, on May 21, 1954. The Communists and Ho-Ch-Minh needed a military victory before the scheduled conference and fought hard to defeat Dien-Bien-Phu on May 7, 1954. France thus lost the war and had to sign an agreement to grant independence to the three Indochina countries on July 20, 1954 (instead of May 21, 1954). For that very reason, the US did not sign the agreement--only 13 countries did.

During 1945-1954, the Hmong fought with the French. Even after the French pulled out of Indochina, the Hmong continued to fight relentlessly against the Vietminh. They disliked North-Vietnam's despotic regime and felt they had to protect their homeland in the mountains from being used as a hiding place or a military base for the North-Vietnamese troops. They knew the North-Vietnamese would just not let anybody who fought them alongside the French to continue to live in those areas.

Tou Lia went on to write the biography of Captain Bichelot (the local French leader), Chao Saykham, and Phagna Touby Lyfoung. These three leaders joined forces and led the fight against the Lao Issara and Vietminh in the liberation of Xieng Khouang, from the morning of January 25, 1956, until the evening of January 26, 1946. They initially ordered a retreat on the evening of January 26, 1946, based on a lack of food supplies and the fact that the Hmong, who took part in the operation, only had outdated guns that could not fire bullets very far. Immediately thereafter, Say Pao Vang, the leader of some 300 Hmong troops from Muang Pha and Na Vang, argued against the retreat order, "If we pull out, to reoccupy again the high positions on the mountains around Xieng Khouang later would not be easy. We need to continue one more day and see what happens."

One day later, on January 27, 1946, the calmness of the situation around Xieng Khouang prompted Captain Bichelot to send in a scouting team. The team found that the Vietminh and the Lao Issara had already left the area, leaving no one behind. The liberating troops then moved into the central part of the town of Xieng Khouang and later used it as the command center of the French, Lao and Hmong troops.

Say Pao said that from that point on, each time he made any suggestion, Touby always listened to him. At the battle to liberate King Sisavang Vong in Louang Prabang in 1946, the leaders of the anti-Lao Issara troops had Say Pao Vang dressed up as the king during a procession through town to announce that the (real) king had been freed. This make-up was for security reasons and did not prevent the by-standers to pay respect to the (fake) king.

[Say Pao had been the only surviving member of the Xieng Khouang liberators for a long time. He was born on May 5, 1919, in Xieng Khouang, Laos and passed away on May 15, 2011 in Georgia, USA].

In February 1945, Issara leader Prince Phetsarath appointed Phoumi Vongvichit, a high-ranking Chao Muang Grade 5 official, to replace Thao Lek Sengsathith as the Governor of Houaphan Province. Thao Lek was Phoumi Vongvichit's father-in-law and had been bestowed with the royal honorific title of Phagna Muang Khoua. Prince Phetsarath also instructed Thao Lek to liberate Xieng Khouang from the French and to serve as Governor of that province. Thao Lek and Colonel Sing Rattana Samay, a Lao Issara military officer, led a contingent of North-Vietnamese and Lao Issara troops in seizing Xieng Khouang on November 28, 1945. As mentioned earlier, less than two months later, Governor Chao Saykham and Phagna Touby Lyfoung led Hmong troops in the reoccupation of Xieng Khouang. This action angered the Lao Issara leadership --Tiao Phetsarath, Tiao Souvanna Phoumma, and Tiao Souphanouvong. After liberating Xieng Khouang, the pro-French troops arrested Phagna Muang Khoua and executed him at the Sanam Luang stadium in Xieng Khouang. It also pushed Phoumi Vongvichit to join the Vietminh and fight against the French and the Royal Lao Government.

During the Second World War, Japanese troops invaded Laos on March 9, 1945. Japan, the Lao Issara and the Vietminh mobilized troops to fight against the French to recover their independence. For his collaboration with the French, Touby Lyfoung was promoted to the rank of Nai Kong (district chief) of 4th class on August 28, 1946, to the rank of Oupahat of 1st class in July 1947, and to the rank of Chaomuang of 4th class soon afterwards. Lao and Hmong leaders who fought with the French against the Lao Issara in Houaphan and Xieng Khouang Provinces in 1946 included Touby Lyfoung, Chong Toua Moua, and Chao Saykham Southaka Koumane.

On November 1, 1949, Touby Lyfoung was promoted to the position of deputy governor in charge of Hmong affairs within Xieng Khouang Province and was conferred the honorific title of Phaya Damronglithikay ("the trusted guardian of high power and authority") by H.M. the King of Laos. Later on, he also got several high-level medals and decorations from the French and the Lao authorities.

Photo #3*. Mr. Lyfoung and his family in 1928 at Nong Het, Xieng Khouang, Laos. Mr. Lyfoung was born in 1888 and died on December 12, 1939. He was the son of Mr. Lypao (Ly Dang Pao). Front row, left to right: 1. Touby (3rd son); 2. Tougeu (4th son); 3. Toulia (5th son); 4. Mr. Lyfoung (head of the family), 5. Nang Mao No (daughter, who later was married to Mr. Tou Ly, Gen. Vang Pao's older brother. After Tou Ly died in a car accident, she remarried with Col. Mua Su, son of Col. Cher Pao Mua. Nang Mao No died in Georgia, USA, in 2006.); 6. Kue Choua Lyfoung (Mr. Lyfoung's 3rd wife, carrying her son Chou, died in 1929); 7. Mr. Lyfoung's daughter Mao Song (she later became Mrs. Vang Nkaj Zeb. She was the mother of Col. Vang Neng, from France. She passed away in 2006 in the US). Second row, left to right: 1. Ly Chao (first son of Mr. Lyfoung); 2. Yang Tongxeng (brother-in-law, married to Phauj Zuag); 3. Ly Pobzeb (2nd son of Mr. Lyfoung, served as Tasseng, later died falling off a horse saddle; his wife then became his brother Touby's second wife); 4. Thoj Blia (wife of Mr. Ly Chao); 5. Mrs. Lyfoung, born Yang Va (Mr. Lyfoung's first wife, died in 1945); 6. Mrs. Tongxeng Yang, nee Mao or Paj Zouag. This picture was taken by Prince Phetsarath during his visit to Xieng Khouang during 1927-1928. Lt. Col. Vang, Geu's photos collections.*

In 1939, the Second World War exploded and then raged in France and throughout Europe. The French suffered heavy casualties and were the obvious losers. As a result, the French troops in Indochina had no real backup to fight against the Japanese. Many got killed, and the rest sought refuge among their local supporters --especially low-land Lao and Lao Hmong, who put them into hiding in the forest areas. During that war, the Lo Kaitong family chose instead to join the Japanese, the Viet Minh and the Lao Issara in the fight against the French, but ended up being the victims of the Vietminh who were using them. The Lo Kaitong family made that decision because the French had picked the Lyfoung family to lead the Hmong in the Nonghet area in replacement of the Lo family. They wanted to regain their dignity among the Hmong people. Unfortunately, luck was not on their side due to the Vietminh's ploy.

During 1945-1946, many changes took place as a result of the Japanese occupation. The Ly family, who used to side with the French, had to flee into the jungle with the French troops, who were pursued everywhere by the Lao Issara, the Hmong Lo, Vietminh, and the Japanese.

Photo # 4. Mr. Lyfoung's wife and the mother of Phagna Touby Lyfoung (to the left, resting her right hand on the head of a kid) and her three sisters in 1923. Lt. Col. Vang, Geu's photos collection.

During the Second World War, Vang Pao was still a teenager of, about fourteen years old. Touby, Chao Saykham and the French used Vang Pao as a messenger and informant operating

5

around the mountains of Nonghet and Xieng Khouang. He performed his duties exceptionally well and ended up being a very reliable secret agent. By the time he was eighteen, the French recruited him into the French military service. In 1951, he went to the Army officer training school Dong Hen, Savannakhet Province, where he graduated with the rank of aspirant. Vang Pao was a well-behaved cadet, very smart in military tactics, a sharpshooter with excellent health, and a fast runner. One of Vang Pao's close friends at the Cadet School was Col. Koka Phonsopha, who now resides in North- Carolina.

The Japanese invaded Laos on March 9, 1945. The first atomic bomb hit Hiroshima on August 6, 1945, and the second bomb hit Nagasaki on August 9, 1945. Those two dates were, respectively, August 7 and 10 --Japan's local time.

The Japanese surrendered to the Allies on August 14, 1945 (August 15, Japan's time). They withdrew their troops from Indochina and left behind their arms and ammunitions to the Vietminh, the Lao Issara and the Thai for use in the fight against the French and the English -- who used to control several Asian countries for a long time. Another part of their war materials was delivered to the Nationalist Chinese (Kuo-Minh-Tan), who dispatched Division 913 from Yun-Nan to disarm the Japanese. The Lao Issara and the Viet Minh rose up to fight against the French using that equipment.

Photo # 7. *Tiao Khammanh Vongkot Rattana and his third daughter visited Xieng Khouang between February 25, 1951 and July 3, 1951. From left to right: 1. Touby Lyfoung, 2. Tougeu Lyfoung, 3. Tiao Khammanh Vongkot Rattana (born on May 7, 1889 in Louang Prabang, died on January 22, 1972 in Louang Prabang, Laos; oldest son of Tiao Vongkot andPrincess Rattavadee), 4. Tiao Khamphoui Vongkot (born July 10, 1923 in Louang Prabang, died of old age on December 12, 2002 in Clermont-Ferrand, France at the age of 79; was a Lt. Col. in the Royal Lao Army, Social Service), and 5. Toulia Lyfoung (born on March 14, 1922 in Xieng Khouang, died of old age on October 5, 1996 at Aulnay-Sous-Bois, France at the age of 74; was elected representative of Xieng Khouang Province during 1947-1950, and a member of the legal committee until 1975). Photo taken on February 27, 1951. Lt. Col. Vang, Geu's photos collection. Source see in reference page.*

In 1946, the Lao Issara and the Hmong Lo troops were wiped out by the French and had to seek refuge in Thailand and in areas along the Vietnam/Laos border, first in Sayabouri Province and later in Champassack Province. That same year, the French forced Thailand to return those two provinces back to Laos. The Lao Issara then escaped to Phongsaly Province in northern Laos and to Nge-Anh Province, along the North-Vietnam/Laos border, north of Yiep Son. During 1945-1954, the French emerged from the German occupation and started showing renewed interest in the Lao and Lao Hmong ethnics. This was an opportunity for France to regain power and a sizeable amount of natural resources that were lost during the armed conflicts. Besides, France still considered Indochina as its colonial territory and wished to come back and reenergize the economy of those naturally rich territories to help reshape its own economy.

In September 1945, the French started flying military equipment from Calcutta, India, to Laos and dropped it from the air to spots where their troops were still in the hiding. Hiding spots included several southern Lao provinces led by Prince Boun Oum Na Champassak, Louang Prabang Province led by Tiao Kindavong, and Xieng Khouang and Houaphan Provinces led by Chao Saykham, Touby Lyfoung and Chong Toua Moua. As mentioned earlier, the fight against the Lao Issara and the Vietminh in the Nonghet and Xieng Khouang areas made Lao Issara leader Phoumi Vongvichit unhappy with the French, Lao and Hmong leaders because they had captured Phagna Muang Khoua, Khamlek (the brother of the national head monk Bounthan and the father of Dr. Khamsengkeo Sengsathit) and summarily executed him.

Photo #8 (left). Chaokhoueng Chao Saykham Soukthaka Koumane (born in 1918, immigrated to France and died in Perpignan; fought the war against the Viet-Minh together with Touby Lyfoung and against the Vietnamese communists with Gen. Vang Pao during 1960-1975 before immigrating to France; a real Phuan prince who loved his family, his people and his country, and did a lot for the Hmong population – see his biography in Chapter 20). Photo #9 (right). Touby Lyfoung (born in 1919, died of an agonizing death at the Vieng Xay re-education camp, Houaphan Province). Both Chao Saykham and Touby Lyfoung were Lao leaders who fought

the Lao Issara and the Viet-Minh alongside the French during 1945-1954. Phagna Touby never left the country. Lt. Col. Vang, Geu's photos collections. Source, see in reference page.

In December 1945, Tou Lia and Pa Cha Ly mobilized around 300 Hmong in the Navang and Phou Phaxay regions (south of Xieng Khouang Province) and gave them basic military training. During the mobilization and training, one company of the Lao Issara and Viet Minh moved in to attack Sane Ho but got ambushed by a platoon of Hmong. Because the Hmong were only armed with shotguns, the outcome was not as good as expected. Later on, Tou Lia and Pa Cha Ly took the 300 or so armed Hmong to join hands with Touby and Chao Saykham in the successful liberation of Xieng Khouang. From there, they gathered a 600 Hmong contingent and headed out to the Plain of Jars, Muang Soui, Phou Vieng, and Sala Phou Khoune. From Sala Phou Khoun, the original contingent was split into two groups of 300 people each.

The first group took Highway 13 to Luang Prabang, led by Tou Lia. Its mission was to release the King who was confined at the royal palace by the Lao Issara. By the time Tou Lia and his troops were about to reach Louang Prabang, the Lao Issara had already left town. This first contingent then provided security surveillance and protection for the king. The second contingent, led by Pa Cha Ly, followed Highway 13 in the other (southward) direction, heading toward Kasy, then followed the high mountain trail to Muang Phoune and Vang Vieng. Its mission was to help liberate the capital city of Vientiane, which was then under Lao Issara's control. When they arrived in Vang Vieng, they had a quick fight with Lao Issara soldiers and were ordered to pull back. By the time they reached Muang Phoune on April 25, 1946, the Lao Issara had already left Vientiane.

––**Photo # 10.** *Mrs. Touby Lyfoung, her children and relatives. Front row boys: 1. Touvu Lyfoung, 2. Touxa Lyfoung, 3. TouXoua Lyfoung, and.4. Toulong Lyfoung. Back row: 5. Lyvang Lyfoung, 6. LyXu Lyfoung, 7. Lykhoua Lyfoung. Girls: 8. Gaoly Lyfoung (on her mom's arm), 9. Mrs. Touby Lyfoung (born Song Yang Tongseng), 10. Tiao Khamphoui Vongkotratana, third daughter of Tiao Khammane Vongkot Rattana and sister of Tiao Khampheng Vongkot Rattana, former wife of Toulia Lyfoung), 11. unknown, 12. Mao*

SongYang, and 13. Nang Song. The photo was taken in front of the residence of Mr. Touby Lyfoung in Xieng Khouang in February 1951. Lt. Col. Vang, Geu's photos collections.

When he got back to Xieng Khouang, Say Pao Vang, commander of the recruits from Muang Pha and Phou Pha Say said, "Only an educated person can be a leader. I know that because I don't have an education and am having a problem doing anything. I was scared when Phagna Touby made me a military commander." For that reason, in February 1947, he moved to Dong Danh (near Lat Houang, not too far from Xieng Khouang) with his children and younger brothers so they could attend school. [The author was one of those who started school in 1947]. They were part of the very first Hmong family in Xieng Khouang Province to get a chance to learn about Jesus Christ, a Christian family that led many others to convert to Christianity.

Photo #11. *The first Team Hmong Leaders First Row, left to right: 1. Tswv Choj Lis (Nai ban Phakvene); 2. Txiajvaj Xyooj (Tasseng Phousane Noi); 3. Ntsuab Txos Xiong (tasseng Phou Phaxay); 4. Suavtuam Lis (tasseng Keng Khoui). -Second Row, left to right: 1. Neejtswb Vaj (Gen. Vang Pao's father, Photong Nong Het); 2. Txiajvaj Xyooj (Tasseng Phak Leung); 3. Paj Lwj Lee (Photong Phak Boun); 4. Nomyis Yang (Tasseng Phou Fa); 5. Txoovtuam Muas the first Hmong Naikong Phoudou). -Third Row: left to right: 1. Phagna Damrong Rithikay Touby Lyfoung; 2. Ly Chao Lyfoung; 3. Tiao Khammane Vongkot Ratana; 4. Xaiv tshob Yang (Naiban Hine Tang); 5. Nchaiv Pov Vang (Tasseng Na Vang); 6. Lao Officer; and 7. Toulia Lyfoung. Lt. Col. Vang, Geu's photos collections.*

Tou Lia wrote in his Memoirs, "The recruitment of the Hmong for the fight against the Lao Issara and the Vietminh this time allowed the Hmong to get to know each other a lot better, and made them feel they are part of the same unified ethnic group. This is different from the past when

9

the Hmong first emigrated from Mainland China to resettle in Laos. They then did not know each other, lived in small groups, and made little progress in thinking and ideology. But once they were involved in a common fight, the Hmong and the Lao collaborated better with each other and appreciated each other more."

When the Lao Issara fought against the French, Laos was still a French protectorate. This led to the creation of two factions or two political parties as follows:

o The Lao Issara led by Prince Phetsarath, the losing faction, and
o The Pro-French faction, with several leaders from north to south, the faction with an edge in the fight against the Lao Issara and the Vietminh.

In Vientiane, Prince Phetsarath was the leader who set up the government and, on October 12, 1945, named Phagna Khammao Vilay as Prime Minister of an 11-member Cabinet. See Chapter on Government Formation. He issued a proclamation dismissing King Sasavang Vong from the throne.

By the end of 1945, in the war that raged between the two sides across Laos, the Lao Issara side ended up being the losers, compelling one of its groups to retreat across the Mekong River into Thailand. While crossing the Mekong River on a boat in the Thakhek area, Prince Souphanouvong got seriously injured by gunfire from a French fighter plane. The Vietnamese living in Thailand were able to help him escape from danger. After he recovered from his injury, Prince Souphanouvong reported back to his boss Ho-Chi-Minh, in North Vietnam, along with the following Issara party members: Phoumi Vongvichit, Soth Phetlasy, Keo Viprakorn, Nouhack, Kaysone Phomvihan, Quinim Pholsena, Fay Dang Lo, Lo Foung, and a few others. Another Lao Issara group went back to Vientiane to join hands with the Royal Lao Government.

The government structure in Vietnam under the French regime was similar to the government structure in place in Laos. The French put Prince Nguyen Vinh Thuy, the son of the former emperor, on the throne under the name of Emperor Bao-Dai. They also divided the country into three regions for easier administrative control--Tonkin (North Vietnam), Annam (Central Vietnam), and Cochinchine (South Vietnam). There were indeed plenty of reasons why the people of Indochina chose to fight against the French.

Ho Chi Minh (alias Nguyen Ai Quoc), according to known sources, was born in 1890 and died on July 20, 1969, in Hanoi, North Vietnam. He studied Communism in France and traveled to Russia in 1927 for further studies. He went to Thailand in 1928, traveled to Oudorn Thanee, Sakon Nakhorn, and Nakhorn Phanom, and stayed in hiding in the village of Ban Na Chok, motivating Vietnamese residents to rise up to help recover independence from France. At that time, Thailand was implementing a policy different from France's policy.

In 1931, Nguyen Ai Quoc went to Hong Kong to contact North Vietnamese residents but was arrested by the English authorities, who arrested and put him in jail. To reduce French pressure for extradition, the British fakely announced in 1932 that Quoc had died. They then quietly released him in January 1933. In 1934, Nguyen Ai Quoc went back to Russia and, starting around 1940, began regularly using the name "Ho-Chi-Minh". In 1941, he returned to North Vietnam to work with the Thai Nong, Thai Dam, Thai Khao, and Hmong ethnics in seeking military support from the US for the fight against the Japanese. But the weapons he got were used against the French instead in an effort to free Vietnam from French domination. The French then were faced with many challenges due to the Second World War.

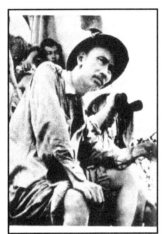

Photo#12 (left). Ho Chi Minh (born in 1890, died on July 20, 1969 in Hanoi, North Vietnam) went secretly aboard a French ship on the way to France where he completed his communism training. In this picture, he was observing and planning how to wipe out the French's positions in Dien Bien Phu, in March 1954

Photo#13 (right). Kaysone Phomvihane had met with Ho Chi Minh earlier in 1951. Source see in reference page.

In 1945, Ho Chi Minh and the Lao Issara began to form national liberation fronts. On August 15, 1945, Ho-Chi-Minh led armed attacks on several French positions in Vietnam. On August 27, 1946, situational changes made it possible for France to regain power in Indochina. This forced Ho-Chi-Minh, along with Vietminh and Lao Issara troops, to flee to the jungle and start guerilla operations. These operations expanded by the day and caused the French to use military forces to fight the Vietminh and the Lao Issara. The fighting unavoidably caused loss of lives and material damage and, as a result, increased Vietnamese resentment and their hate for the French.

In 1949, China went from a democratic regime to a communist regime, from Chiang Kai-Shek to Mao Zedong. In 1950, war erupted in Korea between the Western and the Eastern powers, including mainland China, which supported North Korea. In 1950, fighting in Indochina intensified and gave an opportunity for Ho-Chi-Minh to decide to join the camp of communist mainland China and use the China-Vietnam-Laos border area as training centres for the Vietminh. This development caused serious concern to the French and US governments about the growth of communism which could potentially spread over other parts of south-east Asia. The French and the US then decided to set up the Dien-Bien-Phu military base to counter communist expansion, along with other programs as follows:

- In Phongsaly Province, set up the garrisons of Muang Khoua and Muang Ngoy, under the command base of Nam Bak, Louangprabang Province, and
- Establish thousands of grass-root, village-level armed guards in preparation for the fight against the Vietminh in North Vietnam. Recruits were to include several ethnic groups, including especially Hmong (under Vang Chong's command), Thai Dam (under Deo Van An's command), Thai Khao and North Vietnamese.

Photo #14. *The group that fought the war against the Lao Issara and Viet Minh, 1945-1954. From left to right: front row: 1. Paj Lwj Lis, 2. Neej Tswb Vaj, 3. Touby Lyfoung, 4. Nom txos Lyfoung, 5. Ly Xiong, 6. Tsuab Txos Xyooj. Second row: 1. Ntsuab Pov Yang, 2. Ntxoov Vws Tsab, 3. Lis Vaj Tooj Pov, 4. Tswv Choj Lis , 5. Xaiv Tshob Yang, 6. Txiaj Xab Mua, 7. Nom Yis Yang, 8. Suav Tuam Lis, 9. Txiaj Vaj Xyooj, 10. Tooj Kais Xyooj (Tasseng Phou Sane Noi). This photo was taken in 1948 in Xieng Khouangwhen Phagna Touby Lyfoung was appointed the first Hmong district chief in Laos. Lt. Col. Vang, Geu's photos collections and source, see in reference page.*

Photo#15 *(left). Naikong Chong Toua Mua and Sergent Haze, a Frenchman of German descent and a farmer at Phou Dou after his discharge from the French Army stationed at the Khang Khay Camp. He was a close friend of the Naikong of Phou Dou and was active in supplying vegetables to the French troops in Khang Khay. Naikong Chong Toua died in early 1952 by car accident, due to his lack of car driving experience.*

Photo # 16 *(right). From left to right: Tasseng Say Pao Vang, Chay Dang Vang and Col. Cher Pao Mua.Say Pao Vang was the one whoasked Phagna Touby not to retreat from Xieng Khouang on January 26, 1946. Col. Cher Pao Mua was the commander of LS 32 at Bouam Long with no less than 12,000 soldiers attached to Regiment 28. He immigrated with his family to Thailand as a refugee but refused to leave his troops behind. He went back to fight in Laos where he died in 1994. Lt. Col. Vang, Geu's photos collections. Source, see reference page.*

During 1951-1954 French war in Indochina, fierce fighting occurred between the French and the communist troops. In the end, France lost Indochina and created thousands of refugees (most of them educated people) who had to leave North-Vietnam to resettle in Laos, Thailand and France. Lt. Vang Chong, a Hmong leader, was one of those who had to leave North-Vietnam to resettle in Laos. Lt. Vang Chong was a Hmong leader who left North-Vietnam and resettled in Laos.

Photo #17. *Lt. Vang Chong, a Hmong leader in Dien-Bien-Phu in 1952. He immigrated to Laos in 1955 and died of illness at Long Cheng in 1973.*

Photo # 18. *Mr. Deo Van An, a Thai Dam leader in Dien-Bien-Phu in 1954. He immigrated to France in 1955.Lt. Col. Vang, Geu's photos colltions*

Photo # 19. *Thai Khao Leaders (from left to right): Ong Sang, Ong Dzeng and Ong Dzin. : Lt. Col. Vang, Geu's photos collections.*

BIOGRAPHY OF LT. VANG CHONG (OR VANG CHONG TOUA)

Lt. Vang Chong was born in August 1919 in Ban Houei Xane, Tasseng Dien-Bien-Phu, in the Province of Lai Chau, North Vietnam. He died in Laos' Military Region II at Long Cheng, Xieng Khouang Province, in April 1973. When Vang Chong was ten years old, his uncle Liaj Vam Vang sent him to school at Dien-Bien-Phu, where he lived with the family of one of his uncle's friend, a Thai Dam native, to be closer to school. In 1936, his uncle Dang Seng Vang, a district chief, pulled him out of school to perform some record filing work, as his secretary was not experienced enough in that area.

In 1944, French Maj. Imfeld nominated Vang Chong to be the deputy-Chaomuang of Dien-Bien- Phu and exercise administrative control over some 18,000 Thai Dam, LaoTheung, Hmong

2

and Thai Khao. In 1945, Vang Chong was arrested by the Japanese and detained for about a month. The Japanese wrote to District Chief Dang Seng Vang to ask him to collect three thousand silver coins as bail payment for Vang Chong's release. This was right before the atomic bombs hit Japan. As a result of those incidents and Japan's surrender, Vang Chong was released from prison without having to pay anything. Later that year, deputy-district chief Vang Chong led a group of forty Hmong to Yunan Province in southern China to look for French families who sought refuge there during the Japanese occupation and bring them back to the French garrison of Lai Chau, North Vietnam and set up the Dien-Bien-Phu military base.

In November 1947, two companies of Thai Khao troops attacked many Hmong villages and burned them down. The French were not able to do anything to prevent this type of attack. Therefore, Vang Chong felt compelled to lead Hmong troops to mount a revenge attack against the Thai Khao. In December 1949, the French ordered the Hmong to resettle in Muang Khoua, Phong Saly Province in northern Laos, and get ready to support the French in their fight against the Vietminh. The Muang Khoua garrison was then under the command of Capt. Vigauche.

By the end of 1950, the French had Vang Chong and several Hmong soldiers take a two-month military training. Once the training was completed, Vang Chong was promoted to the rank of Sergeant, put in command of a Hmong company, and deployed to the garrison of Ban Anh, Muang Ngoy, close to the Nam Bark garrison. His assignment was to secure the area around Nam Bark and protect the northern part of Laos. Sergeant Vang Chong was a very well-disciplined commander who knew how to fight, judging from the hundreds of enemy troops he put out of action and the sizeable amount of arms and ammunition he was able to collect. He got a citation from the Muang Khoua French commander and, based on his outstanding achievements, was promoted to the rank of Lieutenant and deployed to the Muang Khoua garrison to clear the Vietminh from the banks of the Nam Ou River.

In August 1953, Capt. Mason invited Touby Lyfoung to visit Lt. Vang Chong and his troops at Muang Say. The French also promised to send a radio dispatcher and a nurse to assist Lt. Vang Chong's troops and get them ready to support the French base of Dien-Bien-Phu. All these promises were fulfilled. In February 1954, Vang Chong advanced his troops toward Dien-Bien-Phu. As they were 30 kilometers away from the Camp, many problems arose, including gradually intensified attacks from the Vietminh and diminishing food supply and ammunition. He had the radio dispatcher send a message to the Dien-Bien-Phu commander but got no replies. Not a single supply airplane was in sight. This was close to the end of February. Vang Chong had no choice but to order a 40-kilometre retreat and wait for airplanes to drop them some supplies. The retreat was painful, with the enemy on their tail every step of the way and the Hmong troops running out of ammunition.

Before Lt. Vang Chong began to move his troops toward Dien Bien Phu, he had about thirty of his men sent to Saigon/Ho-Ch-Minh City, South Vietnam, for parachute training. Although these men had not yet completed the training, the French dropped them off at Dien Bien Phu. All thirty of them were killed while still floating down on their parachutes. Because they had access to state-of-the-art anti-aircraft weapons, the Vietminh were also able to shoot down several French airplanes.

French officers operating in the Dien-Bien-Phu area in North Vietnam since 1937, including S/Lt. Navan, S/Lt. Beagent, Maj. Imfill, Maj. Delling, and Maj. Salan. A few others were there even earlier. Those stationed in the Phongsaly area in Laos at the same time as Lt. Vang Chong included Lt. Vally, Capt. Vigauche, Major Fournier, Capt. Mason (GCMA) and Gen. Rene Cogny (who provided the names of the officers to Lt. Vang Chong). During his fights in northern Laos, Lt. Vang Chong got citations from the French and King Sisavangvong. He decided to resettle in Laos in 1955.

Photo #20. *Lt. Vang Chong's troops were about to be dropped by parachutes to Dien-Bien-Phu (where they all got killed). Lt. Vang, Geu's photos collections.*

The preceding paragraphs were excerpted from the notes recorded by Maj. Nao Chue Vang, son of Lt. Vang Chong, who resetlled in Laos and participated in the 1960-1975 fight alongside Gen. Vang Pao and the US. Maj. Nao Chue Vang noted that his father and his uncle, Liaj Vam Vang, told him the Dien-Bien-Phu war was a modern-age battle that used airplanes and firearms that were never seen before, a very scary episode indeed. This war led more than 40,000 refugees to resettle in Laos and eastern Thailand in 1954. These were Hmong who used to live in the following provinces of northern Vietnam: LaiChau, Laokay, Hazang, Dien Bien Phu, and Songla. *[Note from the author: My personal thanks to Major Nao Chue, a high-ranking officer in the Royal Lao Army during 1960-1975, for sharing his personal notes.]*

Photo #21. *Important Thai Khao leaders who fought alongside the French during 1950-1954 and resettled at Lat Houang, Xieng Khouang Province. From left to right: Lt. Nguyen Dinh Tan (died in Toul, France), Lt. Pham Van Duon (immigrated to Metz, France, where he died in 1980), and an unknown officer. Several thousand of refugees from different ethnic groups in North Vietnam resettled in the Lao provinces of Xieng Khouang, Sayabouri, Vientiane and Savannakhet. Lt. Col. Vang, Geu's photos collections.*

At the end of 1955, the French totally withdrew from Indochina per the Geneva Accords. The Vietminh, however, stayed on in the border areas, using these areas as trails and hiding spots for their troops as part of an ultimate plan to invade South Vietnam and unify the country of Vietnam. This was the main reason behind the US-Vietnam war during 1959-1975. Starting in 1955, the US sent many agents to provide assistance to the kingdom of Laos. The US observer in Xieng Khouang Province was Pop Buell, working for USAID.

In 1947, Phagna Touby Lyfoung got the high honor of being named the first Hmong Chaomuang (district chief) of Xieng Khouang Province, and Chong Toua Mua was named the first Hmong Naikong (semi-district chief) with administrative responsibilities over the Hmong in the Phou Dou area. That same year, Toulia Lyfoung was elected representative of Xieng Khouang Province, the very first one of Hmong ethnic origin. On May 11, 1947, Toulia Lyfoung was seated as a member of the National Assembly in the capital city of Vientiane. He later sponsored legislation that established equal rights among all ethnic groups living in the kingdom of Laos.

During 1949-1958, Touby Lyfoung served as deputy-Governor of Xieng Khouang Province. At that time, the literacy rate for the Hmong living in urban areas was about 20 percent. Later on, Youa Pao Yang was promoted to the position of deputy-Governor in charge of the Hmong affairs, replacing Phagna Touby Lyfoung, and Txiaj Xab Mua was promoted to the position of Hmong district chief, replacing Youa Pao Yang. In 1949, Touby Ly foung decided to choose Youa Pao Yang to replace him as the Chaomuang Hmong. This made Beechou Lor unhappy and pushed him to join the Lao Issara, but in 1955, he came back to work for Touby Lyfoung. In 1961, Kong Le occupied Xieng Khouang, and Beechou joined Kong Le. In 1963, Beechou was assassinated in the Plain of Jars by Kong Lae troops for unknown reasons.

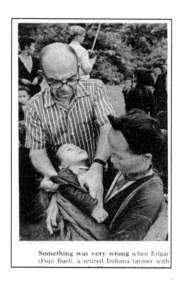

Something was very wrong when Edgar
(Pop) Buell, a retired Indiana farmer with

Photo # 22. *Pop Buell from USAID diagnosed a sick child in Xieng Khouang in 1960.*

Les peuples
de la montagne

4 : Jeune femme thaï blanche
au travail dans la rizière.
Fonds 11ᵉ Choc

Photo #23. *An old Thai Dam riffle*

Photo #24. *A Thai Khao woman working on her water-activated rice mill Lt.Col. Vang, Geu's photos collections. Source see in Reference.*

In June 1958, Touby Lyfoung got elected representative of Xieng Khouang Province at the complementary elections open to the Neo Lao Hatsat Party. After the elections, Touby then moved to Vientiane.

In 1949, Phagna Tougeu Lyfoung (see more details in the Biography section) got married to Nang Sisamone Thammavong, the daughter of Nha Phor Thip Thammavong. *(Mr. Thip Thammavong helped Gen. Vang Pao set up a joint Lao-Lao Hmong radio broadcasting program in Long Cheng, Military Region II. He later resettled in Canada and died in that country).* In

1975, Tougeu Lyfoung and his family resettled in France. He later came to the USA, where he died on February 10, 2004, of natural death.

Photo #25(left). Phagna Toulaprasith Tougeu Lyfoung.

Photo #26 (right). Tougeu Lyfoung and his wife Sisamone Lt. Col. Vang, Geu's photos collections. Source, see in reference page.

Between 1750 and 1958, about 600,000 Hmong have resettled in the following provinces in northern Laos: Phongsaly, Luang Namtha, Luangprabang, Sayabouri, Houaphanh, Xieng Khouang, and Vientiane. *[During that time, Bokeo was part of Luang Namtha Province, and Borikhamxay was part of Vientiane and Khammouane Provinces. As a result of territorial subdivisions made after the change of regime in 1975, Laos is now divided into 17 provinces, including Metropolitan-Vientiane, whose statute is a Prefecture].* As for the Hmong population in Xieng Khouang Province, the survey conducted by USAID in 1973 in territories under the Royal Government's control revealed no less than 400,000 Hmong were living in that province.

On August 27, 1946, France signed a Modus Vivendis that granted the kingdom of Laos independence within the confines of the French Union. On July 19, 1949, France granted full independence to Laos' King Sisavangvong while still providing financial support and assuming defense responsibilities vis-à-vis Laos' neighboring countries.

In 1949, changes in the political and administrative arenas that took place after the end of the Second World War led to serious conflicts between the democratic world and the socialist-communist world. Regime changes resulted in a world split into two blocks: a communist Eastern Block and a democratic Western block. Ho-Chi-Minh was given an opportunity to become a member of the Eastern bloc starting in 1950, as he needed logistic and military support and assistance from the other communist countries for his fight to expulse the French army from Vietnam and the entire Indochina peninsula.

Photo #27. *– On July 19, 1949, King Sisavangvong signed the Treaty of "Independence within the French Union" with French President Vincent Auriol. Vang, Geu's news documentations records. Source, see in reference page.*

In 1951, Communist China allowed Ho-Chi-Minh to mobilize his troops along the China-Vietnam and Vietnam-Laos borders to get ready for the fight against the French. In 1952, upon becoming aware of Ho-Chi-Minh's plan, France initiated a request for support and assistance from the US in preparation for a fight against Ho-Chi-Minh's troops. With the same objective in mind, France also set up several military bases, including Dien-Bien-Phu in North Vietnam, Plain of Jars in Xieng Khouang Province, Xieng Ngeun in Louangprabang Province, and Seno in Savannakhet Province. The French wanted to be ready to fight against Ho-Chi-Minh's army.

In December 1952, Ho Chi Minh sent Division 312 to attack Laos for the first time, aiming at cutting French reserve forces in Houaphan and Phongsaly Provinces and liberating those territories to serve as strongholds for the Lao Issara. At the same time, the Vietminh sent two of their regiments to Xieng Khouang Province with the following assignments:

- Regiment 148, moving from Samneua to attack Ban Bane and
- Regiment 195 (including Vietminh and Hmong Lor soldiers), moving from Muang Sene in central Vietnam to attack Nonghet and use it as a Hmong Lor military base.

Regiment 195 captured all the members of the Hmong Lee families and some of the Lao families as well and detained them at Muang Sene in central Vietnam. This detention created dissension within the Hmong community and caused them to split into two groups. From that point on, some sided with the Viet Minh, and others sided with the French.

Touby's first wife died as a result of the Lor military invasion of Nonghet. May See Xiong was one of the captives who were detained for years in Muang Sene. She married Ly Doua about two months before the Lor's attack on Nonghet and was taken prisoner. After she was released in 1955, she came back to live with her husband. She now resides in St. Paul, Minnesota. She said, *"The hot climate in Muang Sene caused many of the women and children to catch malaria. They later spent their captivity in Sumou, at the Laos/North-Vietnam border").* The attack of Nonghet by the Lor and Viet Minh forced many Hmong to leave Nonghet for Lat Houang, Xieng Khouang, and Dong Dane.

Vietminh Division 308 headed to southern Laos, cleaned up French troops in Savannakhet and Saravane Provinces and used jungles and mountainous sites in those provinces as military bases and training camps for the Viet Cong from South Vietnam in preparation for the fights against South Vietnam.

During August 13-15, 1950, Prince Souphanouvong announced his registration as a member of the Indochina Communist Party (Vietminh), apparently as an ignition cord to get the Vietminh involved in the armed fighting in Laos. He became the Trojan horse that helped the deployment of Vietminh troops into Laos. Not long afterwards, on August 20, 1953, the Lao Issara announced its political formation in the town of Samneua in preparation for the fight against the French and the Vientiane Royal Lao Government.

April 12, 1953, marked North Vietnam's second invasion of Laos. Army deployments included the following:

- Division 312 was to attack Louang Prabang and destroy the Xieng Ngeune airbase.
- Division 304 and Division 306 were to attack Xieng Khouang and Houaphan Provinces, including destroying the French airbase at the Plain of Jars.
- Division 308 was to attack SavannaKhet and destroy the Seno airbase in central Laos.

Fighting in those areas occurred at the same time but did not cause too many losses to the French troops. The main objective of the Vietminh attacks was to demoralize French, South Vietnamese and Lao troops and to immobilize troops that were about to be sent to reinforce Dien-Bien-Phu. The French had to counter-attack the Vietminh everywhere to keep them away from the various airbases and ensure safe flights. Their troops operated on the highway from Xieng Khouang to Dien-Bien-Phu, from Louang Prabang to Houaphan and Dien-Bien-Phu, and from Louang Prabang to Nam Bak and Phongsaly. Because Dien-Bien-Phu was prematurely taken over by the Communists, the latter highway ended in the Nam Bak area.

Mr. Nouane Dam Inthivong, a former civil servant in Houaphanh Province, wrote, "As Dien Bien Phou was being encircled by the Vietminh and Communist China, the French ordered the Houaphanh Province civil and military officers to move to the Plain of Jars, Xieng Khouang Province, for safety reasons. Those evacuees left on April 13, 1954, heading for the mountain range of Thieng Khay. On April 14, 1954, the North Vietnamese communists caught up with them, arrested them at Ban Na Muang, and put them in prison at Phu Thieng Khay for around six months. Some of them were released on September 14, 1954.

The communists set up a people court to decide on the fate of the remaining detainees. On April 14, 1953, the following five people were sentenced to death at the <u>First condemnation</u> issued at Phu Thieng Khay:

1. Mr. Khampane Bounyarith, Governor of Houaphanh Province;
2. Mr. Xieng Khammy, Chaomuang of Xieng Kho;
3. Mr. Phommasy, leader of village security guards in Samneua;
4. Mr. Ba Boua, a military officer stationed at Muang Pua; and
5. Mr Ba Thong is a military officer (and a native of Lat Bouak, Xieng Khouang Province).

On November 2, 1953, death sentences were issued at the <u>Second condemnation</u> at Ban Khang Khek, Muang Samneua, for:

1- Mr. Xieng Kanya Bounlutay, Chaomuang of Samtay;
2- Mr. Xiengthoune Bounlutay, deputy-Chaomuang of Samtai;
3- Lt. Kham Phieo, a military officer stationed at Xieng Kho;
4- Mr. Bao Boua Heme Inthavong, Tasseng Pao of Muang Samtai;
5- Mr. Chanta, a military officer stationed at Muang Phat Samtai;
6- Sergeant Xieng Gna, stationed at Ban Tao, Muang Samtai.

At the <u>Third condemnation</u> on November 03, 1954, at Kenglith Muang Kang and Muang Soy Houaphan Province, death sentences were issued for:

1- Mr. Ba Theng, Naikong of Muang Soy;
2- Mr. Pham Ba Theu, Chao Muang of Kaya (the father of Col. Khamtai So Phabmisay);
3- Lt. Lo Khamdao, military officer and interpreter stationed at the 23rd Company of 8th Battalion BCL (the younger brother of Mr. Lo Khamthi Nokanya and the older brother of Lo Kham Dae or Nouane Dam Inthivong who wrote these notes) and
4- Mr. Khampha, Naiphong (Naikong) of Muang Kang at Muang Soy.

Finally, at the <u>Fourth condemnation</u> at an undisclosed site in the jungle, the following individuals were sentenced to death:

1- Mr. Oudom Phiphat, Chao Muang of Parkseng;
2- Mr. Phiakham, Tasseng of Muang Sone, Houaphanh Province;
3- Mr. Phengkeo, Naiphong of Sopsay;
4- Mr. Bathene, a French soldier stationed at Ban Xiengkhor;
5- Mr Batoup, Naiban of Nongkieng;
6- Catholic Priest Rev. Thao Tieng, stationed at Muang Soy; and
7- Mr. Deo Van Peung was a French soldier stationed at Muang Seunela (a Thai Dam minority native).

Mr. Nouanedam Inthivong added that the Vietminh secretly executed thousands of people in Houaphan Province and that they did everything to eradicate the Lao people with "no regret, no justice, and very inhumanely." Their objective was to "kill the owner to get his property", meaning the Lao territory.

Mr. Nouanedam is now a US citizen. (Thank you so much for giving this information).

After the Kong Lae's Coup d'état, the US reinforced the military camp of Nam Bak. Starting in 1962, Vietminh and Red China troops mounted ferocious attacks against this camp, causing great losses to the Royal Lao Army and causing more serious concerns to the US. President Eisenhower, who took office in 1953, used to declare, "If Laos were to fall, the door would be wide open for the Communists to invade the entire South-East Asia region (SEA)." This was the reason that convinced President Kennedy to send troops to set up defensive positions in Thailand in 1962.

An ex-military parachute jumper also noted in his memoirs that, by the end of April 1953, France sent two battalions of Lao and Lao Hmong soldiers for parachute training. The Lao contingent went to Seno, Savannakhet Province, and the Lao Hmong contingent went to Chinaimo, Vientiane Province.

In mid-April 1953, France had two divisions of French Foreign Legion troopers chasing the Vietminh away from the Plain of Jars as follows:

o One company of French Foreign Legion troops coming from Europe, together with South Vietnamese soldiers, to cleanse the enemy along Highway 4 from the Plain of Jars to Lat Houang, to Dong Dane, and liberate the town of Xieng Khouang and remain there until further order, and

o Another division of French Foreign Legion troops also came from Europe to cleanse the enemy along Highway 7 from the Plain of Jars to Khang Khai, to Phou Dou, to Tat Peub Falls, and liberate Ban Bane and stay there until further order.

By the end of June 1953, two battalions of Lao and Lao Hmong troops who had just completed parachute jumping training returned to Xieng Khouang with the mission to cleanse the Vietminh troops at various sites within Xieng Khouang Province and be ready for deployment to reinforce Dien-Bien-Phu troops. The cleansing operations that started in June 1953 were performed by the following army units:

o One Lao Hmong battalion under the command of Sergeant Major Youava Lee moved from the Plain of Jars heading toward Xieng Khouang to be combined with the French Foreign Legion troops stationed in the outskirts of Xieng Khouang. This battalion took the lead in the cleansing operation in the eastern region, between Xieng Khouang and Muang Mork, and all the way close to the border with Vietnam near the town of Muang Sene and

o Two battalions of Lao and Lao Hmong parachute jumpers, respectively under the command of Sergeant Major Deuane Sounnarath and Sergeant Major Nengchu Thao, and the overall command of Lt. Max Mesnier and assistant-commander Lt. Vang Pao. Other military assistants included Sergeant Emery and Sergeant Langlade. These two battalions started the Vietminh cleansing operation in the Phu Dou and San Tior area and then joined forces with three battalions of Hmong local villagers-guards commandos already stationed at San Tior. Those three battalions were respectively under the command of Naikong Vakai Yang, Naikong Tongpao Ly, and another Hmong Vang Naikong.

From San Tior, the two battalions of parachute jumpers did the Vietminh cleansing operation in the direction of Ban Bane as planned, in cooperation with the commander of the French Foreign Legion troops waiting at Ban Bane. Once they have reached Ban Bane, those two battalions attacked the Vietminh camp of Ban Phou Nong, where about one enemy battalion was stationed. The attack occurred in the morning, when the enemy was still unprepared, and lasted for several hours. We lost two soldiers, one Lao and one Hmong, and had two injured –one Lao and one Hmong, including Sergeant-Major Deuane Sounnarath. Damages suffered by the enemy were not known because the two sides went their separate ways, but the enemy must have for sure suffered more damage than our troops -- since they were caught unaware and were fighting back from a lower elevation. Our troops retreated to Ban Bane for a one-week rest. The Hmong battalion then returned to San Tior, while the Lao battalion remained at Ban Bane because their commander had been injured.

Once they were back at San Tior, the Hmong battalion of parachute jumpers was merged with the three battalions of local villager guards under the overall command of Lt. Max Mesnier and Lt. Vang Pao. The combined battalions moved from San Tior to Ban Houei Kinin and got ambushed by the enemy mid-way, resulting in the loss of two villager guards and the death of five Vietminh soldiers. Our troops moved on and were able to read the enemy's position, only a few kilometers away from Ban Houei Kinin. Lt. Vang Pao led a quiet attack without the enemy's knowledge, killing 20 of them on the spot, injuring several troopers and forcing the rest to run away. Our troops suffered no casualties.

The reinforced battalions moved on toward the old village of Lor Blia Yao (the Kaitong) by the name of Ban Keng Khouay and ran into some enemy resistance. The French commander ordered his troops to keep moving ahead toward Ban Phak Lak, where some fighting occurred with the enemy stationed at that village. Our troops stayed at Ban Phak Lak for a short while, waiting for further orders, resupply of food and ammunition, and headcount updates. Once everything was ready, the troops moved out according to a secret plan, i.e., at first, moving toward Nonghet during the day time and then at night moving in a different direction –toward Ban Keo Patou, the village of Lt. Vang Pao's father and the headquarters of Vietminh's Regiment 195. Before positioning the troops for the attack, the French commander asked for time to allow for Sergeant-Major Youava Lee's battalion to arrive. The plan of attack was based on the following deployments:

o   Sergeant-Major Youava Lee's battalion, combined with one battalion of Hmong Commandos, was to deploy from south to south-east toward Ban Keo Patou and

o   Lt. Vang Pao's battalion of parachute jumpers, combined with one battalion of Hmong Commandos, was to deploy from southwest to northeast to Ban Keo Patou, with the overall mission to attack the enemy at Ban Keo Patou.

The fight was extremely furious, lasted for almost three hours, and resulted in the following results for our troops:

o   Lt. Vang Pao's battalion and the Commandos battalion: no losses;

o   Sergeant-Major Youava Lee's battalion: one soldier killed and another injured (Bliayao Xiong).

The Vietminh forces filled the whole village and paid little attention to the surrounding mountain range. The allied troops used that opportunity to occupy the mountain range and fought from those higher elevations. The enemy's losses were uncertain, although the villagers later reported that these losses were quite heavy because the enemy was at a lower elevation and unprepared. The allies did not go in and verify the accuracy of the villagers' report. Lt. Vang Pao pulled his troops for several days of rest at Ban Pha Boun and then moved them to Ban Phak Khet to continue the cleansing operation in that region. At that point, the Vietminh changed their tactics. They then realized that the French were successful in using Hmong soldiers for guerilla fights, so the Vietminh started to use the same strategy –recruiting pro-Vietminh Hmong to serve in their guerilla units to fight against the French.

During September-October 1953, the fight against the Vietminh got more complicated as a result of this new Vietminh's strategy of using their Hmong supporters (who were familiar with the area) as guides and informants. Between Phak Khet and Nam Matt, the battalion of parachute jumpers recorded several fatalities when it was ambushed by the Vietminh. Naikong Mong Va, a very important leader in the Phak Khet area and the commander of the Commandos troops, was one of the fatalities. The fight lasted for several days before fizzling out.

On November 16, 1953, the airborne battalion and three commando battalions were deployed to Nonghet. When they arrived at Ban Phou Nong Samchae, those troops (under the command of Lt. Mesnier and his deputy, Lt. Vang Pao) surrounded the village at around 4 a.m., took position at one of the mountains near the village, and got ready to attack Ban Nong Samcherr. The troops operating from the mountain did not pay attention to the other higher mountains located about one kilometer away. But Lt. Vang Pao led one company and headed toward the highest mountain around. As they were about to reach the top of that mountain, Lt. Vang Pao discovered fresh enemy footpaths that suggested new enemy maneuvers and decided to wait until dawn to better identify the enemy's positions. At dawn, the enemy shouted twice in Vietnamese and once in Hmong at the French troops on the lower mountain, "Are you guys over the hill, friends or enemy?" They then fired at the troops on the lower mountain and inflicted several injuries on our soldiers.

When the Vietminh were shouting, Lt. Vang Pao was not too far away from them, which allowed him to launch two BV bombs in their direction and caused several fatalities and injuries. These were bombs that could be fired from special guns. One enemy soldier, who was seriously injured and could not run away, chose to hide in a cave near the high mountain and left behind a blood trail. Lt. Vang Pao ordered his nephew, Thong Vang, to go after the injured escapee.

Photo #28 (left). *Lt. Vang Pao, standing in front of his nephew Thong Vang (with a white hat, died at Phou Nong Sam Cher on November 16, 1953).*

Photo #29 (right). *The Hmong Commando Battalion cleaned up the Viet-Minh in the Nong Het area in 1953. Lt. Col. Vang, Geu's photos collections. Source see in reference and https://www.unforgettable-laos.com/*

The latter was hiding in the cave and shot and killed Thong Vang on the spot. *(Thong Vang was the soldier with a white cap shown walking behind Lt. Vang Pao in Photo #28).* Sergeant-Major Emery tried to recover Thong Vang's body, but he, too, got seriously injured. Lt. Vang Pao tried to do the same. He fired at the escapee in the cave, who fired back and wounded him fairly badly. Two of Lt. Vang Pao's soldiers tried to help him, but one got killed, and the other one (Mua Cha) got seriously injured. The allied troops stopped the shooting until 4 or 5 p.m. before resuming it. At that point, they got no firing back from the enemy, who must have escaped. Our troops then went in to haul out the bodies of dead soldiers and buried them after rituals.

In 1957 Laos was granted independence by France. The two sides had a chance to meet and talk. That's how it was found out that the guy who shot Lt. Vang Pao was a Hmong native by the name of Seng Yang, a long-time Vietminh recruit. He got hit by a BV bomb, fainted due to severe hemorrhage, could not flee and had no choice but to fight to the death. Fortunately for him, the clouds were then all over the area, limiting the visibility range to 20 meters and allowing him to eventually escape.

After the attack of Ban Phou Samcherr, the airborne battalion and three commandos battalions went for a rest at Ban Pha Boun. Lt. Vang Pao went for an injury treatment, got promoted to the rank of Captain, and returned to his former Hmong regiment command position (where his marching order was still to cleanse the Vietminh from the North-Vietnam/Laos border area). This caused a lot of damage to the enemy because Capt. Vang Pao was using a different strategy – attacking at night, using trails the enemy was incapable of guessing. This brought scores of good points for him that eventually reached Ho-Chi-Minh's ears and prompted the Vietminh leader to say, "Vang Pao is a great fighter." Indeed, Capt. Vang Pao was able to liberate several critical military posts, including,

- o Nam Kanh camp, an old military post that Chaomuang Tongpao Lee left in 1952 when the Lao Issara, the Vietminh and the Hmong Lor attacked Nonghet. This post was staunchly defended by the enemy but was still conquered by Capt. Vang Pao. *(In 1977, North Vietnam moved its border to the Nam Kanh camp, about 20 kilometers westward from the original borderline).* Ban Nong Khieo was an important village for the Hmong Lee (Naikong Va kai Ly's village) that was attacked by the Hmong Lor and the Vietminh, forcing several thousands of Hmong living in that area to resettle at Lat Houang and in Xieng Khouang; and
- o The eastern area of Nonghet, near the Laos/North-Vietnam border, is close to Pak Kha (the village of Col. Lee Naokao Lyfoung's mother). After the Vietminh trail between Nonghet and Ban Keobone (the village of Kage Vang and Lt. Col. Vang Foung) was liberated, Capt. Vang Pao pulled his troops back to the French garrison of Nonghet.

Please read the book written by Lt. Col. David regarding the importance of the establishment and duty performance of the Lao and Lao Hmong military under the leadership of Phagna Touby Lyfoung and Chao Saykham Southakakoumane.

Absent those two leaders, the 1944-1945 military operation by the Ayrolles contingent would not have been possible, and Capt. Bichelot would not have been able to sustain the fight against the Japanese and the Vietminh troops. Later on, a new leadership was in place under Mr. Defarges (during 1950-1952) and Mr. Haze (during 1953-1954), who was well-known to many Hmong. Mr. Haze gave a jeep to Naikong Chongtoua Moua, who was the first Hmong who could drive a car. For lack of driving experience, the Naikong pulled the wrong shift-gear when he was driving uphill, forcing the jeep to move backward and roll into a small stream, seriously injuring himself. Mr.

Haze sent him for medical treatment in Hanoi, North Vietnam, but he died on the way in. His body was brought back to Phou Dou for burial. This accident occurred in the beginning of 1952.

DUTY PERFORMANCES OF COL. MESNIER

Mr. Mesnier was a special member of the GCMA organization (Groupement de Commandos Mixtes Aeroportes – airborne Commandos). Following his graduation from the military cadet school in France, S/Lt. Mesnier was sent to duty in Indochina. In 1953, he was part of the GCMA operating in Saigon, South Vietnam, and, in July of the same year, was reassigned to Khang Khay, Xieng Khouang Province, to work with Capt. de Bazinde Bizons, the number one specialist in mountain gureilla warfare. S/Lt. Mesnier replaced Lt. Devaux as the commander of GCMA 201, which included 900 Hmong soldiers under Lt. Vang Pao and about 1,000 Lao soldiers. Sergeant Major Deuane Sounnarath was the commander of the second Lao airborne battalion.

There were no less than 20 Lao and Lao Hmong officers and two French officers, Sergeant Langlade and Sergeant Emery. Sergeant Emery got injured during the Phou Samcherr attack. The marching order for GCMA 201 was to cleanse the Vietminh in the Nonghet region, take over the Keo Patou region, and defend the Nonghet area, Xieng Khouang Province. Lt. Vang Pao and his Hmong subordinates were in charge of collecting news and monitoring the enemy movements. All this information was critical to the success of the enemy cleansing operation.

Photo #30. Col. Matt Mesnier with his wife Francoise   in France, May 8, 2008, Lt. Col Vang, Geu's photos collections.

Photo #31. Lt. Matt Mesnier in Laos, August, 1954

COMBAT USING SIGNALS

On November 16, 1953, a major fight against the enemy took place at the Nong Samcherr mountain range. At that time, Lt. Vang Pao was the operational commander, assisted by two French officers, Sergeants Emery and Langlade. The end results from the allies' side included two dead soldiers and several injuries affecting Lt. Vang Pao, Sergeant Emery and two soldiers. The enemy lost 15 soldiers on the spot. The airborne battalion, the GCMA and the Marquis ceased all operations before the beginning of December 1953. Three medics landed on parachutes to administer chicken pox injections to the troopers following the earlier deaths of several soldiers. From October 1953 to March 1954, the airborne battalion and the Marquis contingent attacked Viet-Ming Division 195 and Battalion 81 in the Nonghet area and inflicted heavy losses on the enemy.

NORTH-VIETNAM INVADED LAOS

(Please read the Agreement Kaysone signed with North Vietnam).

In the last 10 years or so, Vietnam had a population of over 50 million people who were having a hard time supporting themselves. The Vietnamese government then decided to invade several resourceful regions of Laos, especially the Bolivian Plateau which was a rich agricultural region crossed by several streams. Fortunately for the Communist Vietnamese, luck was on their side in the form of faithful Lao followers, which led to the signing of a Lao-Vietnam agreement, which allowed no less than 5 million Vietnamese people to rush into Laos. Furthermore, the Communist Vietnamese also forced the Lao and the Lao Hmong from the Plain of Jars and the southern part of Laos to leave their lands and properties in an extremely painful and barbarous way, especially for the Lao Hmong. The lowland Lao were able to force themselves to live with the North Vietnamese, although some of them had to move somewhere else.

Some of the Hmong took shelter in several mountain ranges and tried to survive very summarily. Over the last few decades, thousands of them have been killed on the battlefields and/or forced into jail. Even worse, the Lao red communist government had granted Lao citizenship to North Vietnamese and let over two million of them legally live in Laos. Those new citizens have the same rights as the Lao natives, are under the control of the North Vietnamese army, and pretend they are here to help the Red Lao fight against the Lao rightists who want their country back in their hands. This removes the need for the Lao communist government to have an army of its own because North Vietnam is already taking care of all of Laos's national defense needs. The only thing left for the Red Lao government to do is to maintain a police force and local surveillance teams consisting of villager recruits to watch for any misdeed committed by Lao natives —the real owners of the country. These government forces are only equipped with light firearms like AK's weapons with limited firing range. Therefore, the management of the country, in the eyes of observers from around the world, has always been perceived as being grossly deficient in terms of human rights. Yet, no other countries in the world had stepped in to try to discourage such a practice. What they have done, if anything, was mostly to assist in other areas because the communists are very good at hiding their long-term goals.

In August 2004, the Vietnamese communist government claimed there were many deep jungles in Laos that served as shelters for the anti-government forces. For this reason, they have sent teams to go out and clear up Lao forests, hauling away all species of trees that are of use for any purpose to their people. Forest destruction made Laos an empty and dry land. Starting in 2006, development projects in Laos helped confirm that communist Vietnam had taken over Laos, including the various Lao government agencies that had been infiltrated by North Vietnamese informants. Vietnamese men and women who roam the streets to sell hand-carried merchandises and Vietnamese contractors who bid for construction jobs are all communist spies and informants. As for the Lao communist police and security guards, they are just secret agents looking for news to pass on to the Vietnamese communists.

The Lao Red government does not try very hard to lead its people. It would rather just let them live like beggars and often look for jobs in the neighboring countries or wait for the money to be sent in from relatives living abroad to survive on a day-by-day basis. Young kids are without caretakers and lack education; many of them are insubordinate and drug addicts. This is the result of a plan to eradicate the Lao people faster to leave room for the Vietnamese to fill. All of the above observations came from an educated individual who loves the Lao people and is eager to reveal the truth about things happening in Laos to the Lao readers. That person is none other than Col. Max Mesnier.

The French promoted Capt. Vang Pao to the rank of Major and, in March 1954, put him in charge of the airborne battalion and the three commando battalions that had been resting at the Khang Khay garrison for one month. By the end of April 1954, the French mobilized an army division under the command of Maj. Vang Pao, consisting of two Hmong airborne battalions, two Hmong commando battalions, three Lao battalions, two battalions of French Foreign Legion, and one combined Lao and Lao Hmong battalion from Louangprabang. The division moved from Lat Bouak, near Khang Khay, crossed the Nam Khan Khao River, and went past Bong Tha, Na Khang, and Samtai. It was close to reaching Phou Leui Mountain when Dien-Bien-Phu surrendered to communist North Vietnam on May 7, 1954.

Before the Dien-Bien-Phu camp was established, President Dwight D. Eisenhower, who took office in the beginning of 1953, used to say, "If we lose Laos, it would be as if we open the door of Southeast Asia and India to the Communists." For that reason, the US and the French governments agreed to teach a lesson to the Communists at a time when the Communists were expanding tremendously in Asia. However, the US misread the meaning of the fight against North Vietnam; it felt it was against its policy of not assisting any country or any party that was fighting another country in an attempt to colonize that country. For the US, taking part in the Vietnam War would mean helping France regain power in Vietnam, Laos and Cambodia and making them French colonies again.

Based on that stand, the US tried to contact Ho-Chi-Minh to persuade him not to attack Dien-Bien-Phu, arranged a conference in Geneva, Switzerland and set the May 21, 1954 date for that meeting. But Ho-Chi-Minh and the rest of the communist world wanted to impose their military and political power; they seized this opportunity to attack and capture Dien-Bien-Phu before the scheduled date for the Geneva Conference in an attempt to spread their influence across the entire world. The US let the French fight the communists by themselves, although many countries on the communists' side were fighting against the French.

While the Vietminh were attacking the French garrison of Dien-Bien-Phu, Ho-Chi-Minh learned that Maj. Vang Pao was the commander of an army division consisting entirely of Hmong recruits on its way to reinforce the embattled French garrison. He was deeply concerned by this news and ordered his own troops to intensify their efforts to seize Dien-Bien-Phu before Maj. Vang Pao's forces arrived.

The fall of Dien-Bien-Phu sent the word "Communist" resonating throughout the entire world. The US then realized that Ho-Chi-Minh was not trustworthy in the Indochina peace negotiations at the July 20, 1954, scheduled conference in Geneva. Thus, the US did not sign the agreement; only 13 other countries did.

Photo #32. Lt. Col. Sang, Maj. Vang Pao, Chao Saykham Southakakoumane and Phagna Touby Lyfoung in Lat Bouak, west of Xieng Khouang in, the end of April 1954, inspecting Hmong Commando troops ready for deployment to support French troops in Dien-Bien-Phu. Vang, Geu's photos collections. Source, see in reference and see in in Unforgettable Laos.

Photo #33. French Foreign Legion Troops Troopsunder the command of Sgt. Leugeux.

Photo #34. French Foreign Legion under the command of Sgt. Paris.

Lt. Col. Vang, Geu's photos collections and source, see in Unforgettable Laos.

In 1954, Tou Lia Lyfoung came back for a break in Xieng Khouang in preparation for the next representative elections. He married for the second time with the adopted daughter of the Chaomuang Phuan in order to increase his popularity among the Xieng Khouang Province's voters. Tou Lia was a noted personality, smart, and full of many good ideas to help his constituents. Instead of just staying relaxed, he tried hard to inspire many young Lao and Lao Hmong to attend training courses on family affairs and sanitation. The results of the courses were not as good as expected due to lack of instructors and teaching materials.

In 1957, Tou Lia Lyfoung was invited to take another position in Vientiane as a member of a committee to review Laos' legal matters. He stayed in Vientiane until the day he went to France as a political refugee. He passed away in France in 1996. While still living in Vientiane, Tou Lia took one of Lauj Faydang's sons, Lauj Xauv, to live with him in 1958, when his protégé returned to Xieng Khouang and got married to Nang Say Her in Dong Dane. On May 18, 1959, Lauj Xauv and other Hmong Lor went back to Vietnam, refusing to be part of the Vientiane government.

Phagna Damrong Rithikay Touby Lyfoung *(see his resume in Chapter 20)* did not leave Laos because he had agreed with Prince Souvanna Phouma that they would stay together through thick and thin until the last day of their lives. However, Prince Souvanna Phouma has not been sent to jail like Touby was. Instead, he was able to stay peacefully at the house of his brother, Prince Souphanouvong, in Vientiane. Some believe that the two princes had supported the Neo Lao Haksat in delivering Laos on a golden plate to communist North Vietnam. Because Prince Souvanna Phouma did not read between the lines, Laos ended up being divided into three parties that fought and self-destroyed each other. In the end, communist North Vietnam came out as the winner and was able to take Laos as a North Vietnam colony.

In 1955, the two Lao political parties started negotiations on national unification. On June 10, 1956, the National Assembly met in a special session to discuss government restructuring and power sharing. During August 1-8, 1956, Prince Souphanouvong led his delegation to Vientiane to negotiate with the Vientiane faction. On November 2, 1957, the two parties signed an agreement to form the first two-party coalition government team on November 19, 1957.

The two parties agreed to have the Lao Communists regroup their troops as follows:

o Dispatch one battalion consisting mostly of Hmong recruits to resettle in the Plain of Jars, Xieng Khouang Province (under the command of Lt. Col. Tou Ya);
o Dispatch one Lao Issara battalion to resettle in Samneua, Houaphan Province, and
o Allow several Lao Issara companies to serve in the capital city of Vientiane and the royal city of Louangprabang and treat those two cities as neutral and unarmed centres.

In March 1958, the two sides started having some disagreements. The Pathet Lao were unhappy with their assigned role and refused to put the two provinces they had been controlling back under the control of the coalition government. There were too many things they did not trust. Therefore, King Savang Vatthana decided to ask Prince Souvanna Phouma to serve as Prime Minister with Prince Souphanouvong as his deputy. At any rate, political conflicts still continued to linger.

As a result of the 1957 political changes, Maj. Vang Pao was transferred to Muang Peunh, Houaphan Province, to work on the defense of northern Laos. The communist party then agreed to be part of the new royal Lao government. In 1959, Gen. Phoumi Nosavan ordered the transfer of Maj. Vang Pao back to Xieng Khouang. In the beginning of that year, Maj. Vang Pao had ordered Capt. Leepao to pursue the Lao Issara troops who had fled the Plain of Jars on April 18, 1959, when Maj. Vang Pao was under the direct command of Gen. Ouan Rattikoun. In 1960, many issues surfaced, prompting Gen. Phoumi Nosavan to name Maj. Vang Pao as commander of the battalion in charge of the airbase at the Plain of Jars. Two weeks after Kong Lae staged his coup d'état in Vientiane, Maj. Vang Pao himself was the subject of an assassination attempt by his deputy, but he safely escaped.

In November 1957, Capt. Kong Lae was named director of the Commandos training school at the Chi Nai Mo camp in Vientiane Province. He used that opportunity to meet with Prince Souphanouvong every night at the prince's residence at Pak Passack on the Mekong River bank, off Khoun Bourom Avenue, Vientiane. This was reported on page 49 of the book on national heroes of the Lane Xang, authored by Douangsay Louangphasy. The August 9, 1960, coup d'état and the jail escape of Prince Souphanouvong and his followers proved that Kong Lae might have a planning role in those events, making the jail escape so easy. There were many other new developments piling up during that period, developments that needed to be clarified by Gen. Kong Lae (or Capt. Kong Lae). For example, since he was a supporter of Prince Souphanouvong, why did he later choose to fight against the Lao communists again? What caused the Plain of Jars to fall, and what forced him to retreat to Muang Phanh? And, after the fall of Muang Phanh, why did he decide to move to Muang Soui and finally to Muang Kasy, Vientiane Province (where he did not stay very long)? After Kong Lae went abroad, the only thing left from the Neutralist Party was a name. The Lao civilian, military and police officers, for the most part, were not aware of the communists' strategy and, therefore, became easy victims.

Mr. Tou By Lyfoung - Mr. Fai Dang LO
Hmong Coalition 1959 Xieng Khouang

Photo#35. *The first Hmong Coalition in Xieng Khouang Province. Front row L to R: Touby Lyfoung; Fai Dang Lo; Thao Tou Yang; Lo Foung. Second row: Youa Pao Yang; Mr. Toui Tounalom (Dr Khammeung's father). Mrs. Touby Lyfoung, Mrs. Fai Dang Lo, Mrs. Lo Foung, Mr. Txiaj Xang Mua Chao. Third Row: # 1 unknown, #2 unknown, # 3 Ly Doua (former nurse, died in Thailand), #4 Mr. Seuang Sourinthavong, #5 and #6 unknown, # 7 Ly Khoua Lyfoung, # 8 unknown. Fourth Row: #1 Mr. Bounmy Thiphavong (Col. Sisavath's father), #2 unknown, #3 Nao Yeng Ly, #4 Thao Hong Saycocie (chief of the post office in Xieng Khouang), #5 with a black hat Blong Ly, former nurse, #6 Mr. Siphanh Sihanath (Xieng Khouang treasurer). The rest of the people are unknown. Lt. Col. Vang, Geu's photos collections and source, see in Unforgettable Laos.*

Mr. Chong Koua Vue, The Province Commissioner of Bolikhamxay province, Laos, led by Mr. Touby Lyfoung in the mid 50's up to the late 1960 (Mong Mour and Mong Nqha) and Authorized by Chao Sisavan Vathana, Royal Lao King, Laos.

Lt. Col. Chong Neng Vang was The Province Commissioner of Bolikhamxay province, Laos, led by Mr. Touby Lyfoung in the mid. 60's up to 1970. (Mong Mour and Mong Nqha)and Authorized by Chao Sisavan Vathana, Royal Lao King, Laos.

Mr. Chai Vang Yang, Xah Cheh District Commissioner of Sai Somboung province of Laos from 1967-1975 under the leadership of Touby Lyfoung and Authorized by Chao Sisavan Vathana, Royal Lao King, Laos.

In December 1957, one Pathet Lao battalion was stationed at the Plain of Jars, another one in Houaphan Province, 250 soldiers in the city of Vientiane and 250 soldiers in the city of Louangprabang. Starting in 1958, the two political parties were faced with many issues. The Lao communists complained that they had been ranked unfairly, that things were not implemented as agreed, and that there were too many gameplays. On May 14, 1959, Gen. Ouan Rattikoun flew up to Xieng Khouang to try to resolve misunderstandings with the Pathet Lao at the Plain of Jars, but he was stopped and asked a gunpoint not to meet with anybody. The General had to fly back to Vientiane and, on May 17, 1959, ordered three of his battalions to lay siege to the Plain of Jars camp occupied by Lt. Col. Tou Ya. On May 17, 1959, the Pathet Lao promised to collaborate with the Vientiane faction within the next 24 hours. Because of this promise, Vientiane's troops did not pay close attention to the surrounded Pathet Lao troops. On May 18, 1959, heavy rain fell on the ground at midnight, allowing the Pathet Lao Battalion to escape, unbeknownst to the Vientiane surroundings. The following day, Gen. Ouan ordered his troops to trail them to no avail. He then ordered Maj. Vang Pao to get Hmong troops in the pursuit.

The leader of the pursuing team was Capt. Leepao. His unit caught up with the fleeing Pathet Lao near Muang Mork and engaged in a fight in which the commander of Pathet Lao Battalion 2, Tou Ya, got shot in the leg. Capt. Leepao reported to Maj. Vang Pao that most of the Pathet Lao troops were teenagers and women. Maj. Vang Pao ordered Capt. Leepao to stop the attack and let the enemy walk away. As for the Pathet Lao battalion stationed in Samneua, they did not run away. About 100 soldiers of various ethnic groups dropped their guns and went home. The rest, over 300 lowland Lao recruits, were moved to Saravan Province by the Vientiane government and regrouped as a new battalion without any further complications.

Photo # 36. Capt. Kong Le (Vientiane 1957) when he met Tiao Souphanouvong every evening at Pak Pasak Khounboulom Road.

Photo #37. The first Coalition Government (Vientiane Party & Communist Party) 1957 Front left: Souvanna Phouma and right: Souphanouvon. Lt. Col. Vang, Geu's photos collections and source, see in Unforgettable Laos.

During this entire period, Tougeu Lyfoung, Toulia Lyfoung and Touby Lyfoung resided in Vientiane as members of the National Assembly. No big problems occurred, just minor ones, if anything. The two factions kept talking to each other through the International Control Commission set up by the Indochina Peace Accord signed in Geneva in 1954.

VIETNAM WAS DIVIDED INTO TWO PARTS

In 1954, Vietnam was divided into two parts: North Vietnam and South Vietnam.

- North Vietnam –the Democratic Republic of Vietnam—is a communist, socialist regime led by Ho-Chi-Minh as President, with Hanoi as the capital city and
- South Vietnam –the Republic of Vietnam—is a democratic regime under Emperor Bao-Dai, with Saigon as the capital city. (Currently, Saigon is named Ho-Chi-Minh City).

The dividing line was the 17th parallel between Vinh-Linh and Quang-Tri. In 1955, Ho-Chi-Minh had planned to fight to pull the two parts of Vietnam into one. This resulted in the invasion of Laos by the North Vietnamese Army, who used the Lao Issara as a mask so they could use part of Laos as a trail to South Vietnam for their fight to unite their country. They built a road on the Lao territory stretching from the 17th parallel to Saravan and Quanh-Tri to the Laos border with Cambodia, a road named Doan 559 or Ho-Chi-Minh Trail starting in 1959. They took over part of Laos' eastern border, from north to south, and used it as hiding shelters and training camps for their troops. At present, the Vietnamese communists are occupying both the land along the borderline and the Ho-Chi-Minh Trail and treating them as their rightful properties without giving anybody any chance to protest.

After Vietnam regained its independence from France, Emperor Bao-Dai announced his abdication from the throne, citing the fact that Vietnam still remained a French colony as before. He then went to meet with Ho-Chi-Minh, forcing the South Vietnamese to elect Ngo-Dinh-Diem as President in his place. Emperor Bao-Dai did not feel safe living in Vietnam and, therefore, sought political refuge in France, where he died on July 31, 1997 in Paris.

Following the communists' defeat of the French at Dien-Bien-Phu on January 6, 1956 the Lao Issara changed their name to Pathet Lao.

In 1957, the two Lao factions started working together but ran into many issues, causing the Royal Lao Government (headed by Phoui Sananikone) to arrest on May 25, 1959, key members of the Lao communist party. Those arrested and detained at the Police Camp of Phone Kheng in Vientiane included 1) Prince Souphanouvong, 2) Phoumi Vongvichit, 3) Nouhak Phoumsavanh, 4) Phoune Sipraseuth, 5) Sithon Kommadam, 6) Xiengma Khaikhamphithoune, 7) Meunh Somvichit, 8) Sisana Seusane, 9) Singkapo Sikhot Chounlamany, 10) Khamphay Boupha, 11) Phao Phommachan, 12) Bouasy Chareunsouk, 13) Khamphet Phommavan, 14) Somboun Vongmor Bounthan, 15) Phoukhao and 16) Mana. The reasons for the arrests were as follows:

- The presence of communists in the royal Lao government has led the US to cut its assistance to Laos;
- The communists refused to let their troops and the two provinces under their control have anything to do with the Vientiane government. In addition, the Pathet Lao military unit stationed at the Plain of Jars had vacated the camp and went into hiding.

These were the reasons cited by the Phoui Sananikone Government. Foreign embassies in Vientiane were concerned and unhappy about this development.

On October 29, 1959, King Sisavangvong passed away. The situation in Laos worsened as a result of many issues, including plots used by the Lao communists to assassinate rightist politicians, high-ranking officials, businessmen, and religious preachers. All these reasons raised concerns within the US government, which then sent in more observers and instructors to train Lao police and military. The training received by Kong Lae's Second Battalion of parachute jumpers was an example. Because of that training, nobody paid much attention to what Kong Lae might be doing during that period. Besides, the royal Lao government was busy making funeral arrangements for the deceased king and was too distracted to watch the political detainees as closely as it should. This gave those detainees a good opportunity to easily run away from prison at midnight on May 23, 1960. Thongsy Khotvongsa, the military guard in charge of the prison surveillance, served as the lead person in the jailbreak.

When Prince Souphanouvong and his followers were still in detention, the Vietnamese communists sent an agent to try to contact Capt. Kong Lae and the prison surveillance staff. At that time, Saly Vongkhamsao, a member of the Indochina Communist Party, was tasked with building a political base in the plain of Vientiane. Capt. Kong Lae was the one who contacted Prince Souphanouvong and Saly Vongkhamsao to lay out a plan to help Prince Souphanouvong and his team run away from the jail and find a temporary hiding place in the Vientiane area. He was looking for the right opportunity, and shooting for the funerals of King Sisavangvong scheduled for August 1960. On August 9, 1960, Capt. Kong Lae staged a coup d'état in Vientiane, allowing Prince Souphanouvong and his team to travel safely to Samneua.

After the Kong Lae's coup d'état, military fighting intensified day by day, not only in Laos but also in Vietnam. This created a lot of problems for the Lao people, who suffered and got scared -- something that has not happened very often before.

In 1954, the Indochina Peace Accord made it clear that foreign troops must leave Laos and for France to fully implement the Accord by withdrawing all of its troops. By contrast, the number of North Vietnamese troops in Laos kept growing, in flagrant violation of the Accord. On the surface, this seemed to enhance the success of Prince Souvanna Phouma's neutral government. In reality, the Khang Khay camp in Xieng Khouang Province was full of communist troops and embassies of communist countries, and not a single embassy of a free world country. Because of that situation, the US decided to step in and support Chao Boun Oum Nachampassack Gen. Phoumi Nosavan and South Vietnam in order to prevent communist expansion into Southeast Asia.

After Prince Souphanouvong was put in detention, national elections took place that provided the majority of representative seats to Tiao Somsanith's party. Tiao Somsanith then replaced Phoui Sananikone as Prime Minister and named Gen. Phoumi Nosavan as deputy prime Minister and Minister of Defense. Gen. Phoumi Nosavan then created the department of National Coordination to replace the multitude of overlapping departments in Vientiane with a single office. Gen. Siho Lanephouthakoun (then an Army Colonel) became director of the new department.

In 1959, complementary national elections were scheduled to fill holes caused by the lack of communist participation in the previous elections. Moua Chia Sang was a candidate who ran for election to become a representative of Xieng Khouang Province. On his way to Nonghet, he was shot and killed in the car he was driving at Ban Phak Khet, near Nonghet, Xieng Khouang Province, in the beginning of May 1959.

CHAPTER 2
THE FIGHTINGS OF THE 1960S

Source:

chrome-extension://efaidnbmnnnibpcajpcglclefindmkaj/https://media.defense.gov/2019/Jul/02/2002153035/-1/-1/0/B_0156_CELESKI_SPECIAL_AIR_WARFARE_%20AND_THE_SECRET_WAR_IN_LAOS_AIR_COMMANDOS_1964_1975.PDF

Region two military based headquarter, Long Cheng, Laos

source:

https://www.commondreams.org/news/2008/08/22/film-reveals-cias-most-secret-place-earth

Starting in 1958, the US got involved in the military and economic assistance programs to Laos in the aftermath of the French war. On August 9, 1960, Kong Lae staged a coup d'état to bring down Tiao Somsanith's government that included Gen. Phoumi Nosavan as deputy-Prime Minister. The plotters asked Prince Souvanna Phouma, who had just started his term as Laos Ambassador to France, to come back and form a new government. Kong Lae used a helicopter to fly to Muang Kasy and bring back the Pathet Lao leaders who ran away from jail a while ago so they could be part of Souvanna's cabinet. Those leaders included Nouhak Phoumsavan, Phoune Sipraseuth, Sisana Sisan, Singkapo Sikhot Chounlamany, and Phoumi Vongvichit.

Most of the Lao people were hoping and thought that Prince Souvanna Phouma's neutral government was going to seek assistance from France. They were disappointed because the Coup's leaders joined hands with the Pathet Lao and the communist world instead, thereby flooding Vientiane with North Vietnamese troops. Only a few days after the coup d'état, the deputy commander of the Plain of Jar airbase working under Maj. Vang Pao tried to assassinate his boss one night, but Maj. Vang Pao managed to escape safely. It was possible that this assassination attempt might have been ordered by the Coup leaders in Vientiane. This incident might have a role in Maj. Vang Pao's decision to fight Prince Souvanna Phouma's neutralism.

About one week later, Maj. Vang Pao was able to mobilize his troops and retake control of the Plain of Jars. A few days later, Prince Souvanna Phouma sent Gen. Amkha Soukhavong to Xieng Khouang to collect rice to feed communist troops stationed in Vientiane. Maj. Vang Pao captured Gen. Amkha and delivered him to the Counter-Coup leaders in Savannakhet. Prince Souvanna Phouma then sent Touby Lyfoung as, the government's Minister of Justice, to Xieng Khouang to pacify the population and advice them to stay put. Maj. Vang Pao detained Touby Lyfoung to prevent him for collaborating further with Prince Souvanna Phouma's government.

On September 10, 1960, Gen. Phoumi Nosavan announced the formation of a Counter-Coup d'état group in Savannakhet, under the leadership of Prince Boun-Oum Na Champassack with the goal of liberating Vientiane from Kong Lae's Coup d'état group.

On December 8, 1960, Col. Kouprasith Abhay, commander of Military Region II, led his troops to retake Vientiane but without success because the coup d'état group had the support of the North Vietnamese troops. *[Before 1962, there was no Military Region V, just four military regions. Xieng Khouang, Samneua and Vientiane Provinces were part of Military Region II]*. These developments forced Prince Souvanna Phouma to fly out to and seek refuge in Phnom-Penh, Cambodia where he stayed for a couple of months. On February 11, 1961, the Prince flew to Xieng Khouang to join Capt. Kong Lae and the North Vietnamese troops who had already occupied the Plain of Jars on December 31, 1960, and used it as their stronghold.

On December 13, 1960, the first airborne battalion parachuted at Tha Na Leng, near Tha Deua, joined forces with Military Region II (MR-II) troops in Chi Nai Mo, and moved in to fight the troops of Kong Lae's coup d'état. Several battalions of ground forces of the Savannakhet Counter-Coup d'état group made their way from Savannakhet along Highway 13 from Paksane to Vientiane. This was to reinforce MR-II's troops and the first airborne battalion who were fighting the Coup d'état battalion and the North Vietnamese troops in Vientiane.

December 16, 1960, was the last day of the fight between the two adversaries, the day Vientiane was liberated from the coup d'état troops. Kong Lae retreated from Vientiane along Highway 13 to Sala Phou Khoune. Phoumi Vongvichit, in his memoirs, wrote, *"We did not want to fight in Vientiane because of the risk of inflicting too much damage to the residents and the city. So we decided to take the Plain of Jars and continue our fight from there."* The Pathet Lao troops were waiting for Kong Lae's troops in Vang Vieng. Upon Kong Lae's arrival, North Vietnamese airplanes dropped arms, ammunition, and food supplies to Kong Lae's troops, along with canons, light tanks, and handguns. Kong Lae moved his troops toward Muang Kasy, Sala Phou Khoune and then took over the Muang Soui's airbase in Xieng Khouang Province on December 25, 1960.

The situation was in big turmoil because of Capt. Kong Lae's Coup d'état. Maj. Vang Pao lost contact with his commanders and did not get any policy guidance from the government. This confusion prevented him from getting better prepared to defend the Plain of Jars. The Kong Lae and Vietnamese troops attacked Ban Bane and opened up Highway 7 from Vietnam to the Plain of Jars as follows:

- o The first contingent, consisting of Lao communist and North Vietnamese troops, moved from Samneua to Ban Bane;
- o The second contingent, consisting of Lao Hmong communists and North Vietnamese, moved from Nonghet to Ban Bane and
- o The third contingent, consisting of Kong Lae's and Lao communist troops, moved from Muang Soui to Ban Bane.

After they took over Ban Bane, Kong Lae and North Vietnamese troops moved next toward the Plain of Jars. The troops that took Muang Soui were deployed, along with light tanks, to guard the steel bridge over the Nam Ngum River on the highway leading to the Plain of Jars. The North Vietnamese used several hundreds of Russian Ilyushin aircraft to fly into Muang Soui from dawn to dusk --two planes at a time-- to drop off all kinds of arms and ammunition to Kong Lae. Some of the planes even landed in Muang Soui. The air supply operation lasted only four days. Kong Lae then attacked the Plain of Jars with tremendous assistance from the communist world, designed to wipe out the entire Lao population.

On December 29, 1960, Gen. Phoumi Nosavan deployed one airborne battalion to reinforce Maj. Vang Pao's troops --about one battalion strong stationed in the Plain of Jars—to help defend the Plain of Jars against North Vietnamese and Kong Lae troops. As the allies' troops set foot on the Nam Ngum River steel bridge, they were immediately surrounded by the enemy, who fired 12.8 mm and 14.6 mm guns from their light tanks. Several allied troopers were killed on the spot, and some of them had to jump to their death from the bridge. Officer Nao Her Vang reported later that it was really scary and extremely demoralizing to hear the thundering noise of the big guns.

Photo #38. *Maj. Vang Pao (left hand resting on his belt) is shown with many Hmong leaders, ready to retake the Plain of Jars airport. Photo taken in 1960. Col. Tou Lu Mua was shown with both hands on his belt. Col. Song Leng Song and Col. Cher Pao Mua, Bouam Louang commander, are shown to the right of Maj. Vang Pao. Lt. Col. Vang, Geu's photos collections and source, see in Unforgettable Laos.*

The 105 mm machine gun squads that accompanied Gen. Phoumi Nosavan's airborne reinforcement battalion did not even have the time to line up their weapons. Instead, they had to leave almost everything behind at the last second. On December 31, 1960, the airbase at the Plain of Jars and the town of Xieng Khouang were entirely in the hands of the enemy. The troops of Maj. Vang Pao and Gen. Phoumi Nosavan retreated on wheels toward Xieng Khouang, abandoned their vehicles around Ban Sam Khone, south of Xieng Khouang, and continued on foot toward Tha Vieng and Tha Thom. At that point, Maj. Vang Pao flew in on a helicopter and met with Gen. Phoumi Nosavan. He also had a chance to run into US Agent James W. Lair, who was responsible for the US military assistance to Laos until 1967. *[This job was next handled by Pat Landry until*

1969 and by Jerry Daniels until 1975. Later on, from 1975-1982, the job covered refugee resettlement in Thailand].

On January 5, 1961, Maj. Vang Pao went up to Phou Bia, established his command center at Ban Padong (Lima Site LS 05), and called on the people of Xieng Khouang and Samneua Provinces to set up military defense units and accept weapons provided by the US. Once he had armed units in place, he deployed them to retake various sites between Xieng Khouang and Samneua from the enemy.

The US set up intelligence units and put in place defensive plans for the northern part of Laos (Phonsaly) and Houaphan Province, prompting Red China to heavily attack the Nam Bak camp in 1962. The US then decided to set up an Air Forces base in Thailand. As the military situation intensified, North Vietnam deployed troops into South Vietnam in 1963. Once the US decided to put South Vietnam under Ngo-Dinh-Diem, the Vietnam War erupted.

Maj. Vang Pao was the first Hmong officer of the Royal Lao Army to be promoted to the rank of Lieutenant-Colonel. In 1962, he was a full Colonel and the commander of Military Region II (which covered Houaphan and Xieng Khouang Provinces). *Please refer to Gen. Vang Pao's biography in Chapter 20.* Between 1961 and 1965, several Red Lao soldiers deserted their units to join Gen. Vang Pao after realizing that the Red Lao were dictatorial and were simply serving North Vietnam's causes. During that time, there were no less than 40 Vietnamese battalions in Laos, compared to less than 50 Lao battalions. *(Each of the military regions had no more than 10,000 soldiers, and there were only four of them. Also, the defense budget was very limited. The first US Agent who came in to help provide military assistance to Military Region II was James W. Lair. The US Ambassador was then William Sullivan].*

In 1961, Touby Lyfoung lived in Savannakhet following his detention by Maj. Vang Pao in Xieng Khouang. He later had the opportunity to go back to Vientiane to join Prince Boum Oum's government (as the Minister of Social Welfare and Public Health).

In 1961, about 10,000 Hmong and lowland Lao in Xieng Khouang and Houaphan Provinces enrolled in the Laos army thanks to US assistance. They received military training at several garrisons, including Pa Dong, Ban Sanh Hor, and Sam Thong. The military instructors were mostly Thai, and some of them were Americans. Other training sites were added, including the following:

o Southern and western regions: Ban Padong (LS05), Ban Na (LS15), Ban Pha Pong, Ban Xieng Dett (uphill Lao village, LS26), Ban Tham Sonn (LS47), Ban Phou Fa, Ban Phou Vieng and Ban Phou Nong Phi (Lt. Col. Touvang Yang's village); and

o North and northwestern regions (LS05): Bouam Long Camp (LS32). Col. Cheupao Moua was the commander of this 12,000-soldier camp that had never been occupied even once by the enemy from 1961-1975. But, in the end, this camp fell to the communists once the US pulled out of Indochina. Those living in this camp suffered extremely heavy losses.

SAFELY RUNNING AWAY FROM BOUAM LONG (LS32)

In 1976, one soldier left his family behind and fled across the mountain ranges into Thailand. When he later met his friends and bosses, he said that as soon as his commanders fled abroad, he and his colleagues almost fainted, ran out of breath, and did not know what to do. Some dropped on their knees, started invoking the holy spirits, and put their hands on the ground, desperately praying for divine advice. When Col. Cherpao Moua, commander of the Bouam Long, was informed of the situation, he decided to go back to Laos to see whether he should bring his troops out of the country or continue fighting. They took a vow to do everything together --leave together or die together. They fought together because they did not like the communist regime that lied to people and used them. Col. Cherpao went back and fought until 1994 and died in the jungle of Laos.

The military bases in the northern part (LS05) of MR-II included the following:

o Keo Bone Camp (the birthplace of Lt. Col. Vang Foung and a military base under his command), which fell to the enemy on April 30, 1970;
o Phou Saboth Camp (the birthplace of Col. Nhia Lue Vang and Lt. Col. Vang Koua) under the command of Col. Nhia Lue Vang. In 1969, this base was heavily attacked by the enemy as it was located near Laos/North Vietnam, near Samneua, the headquarters of the Lao Communists.
o San Tior Camp (LS02), located mid-way between Xieng Khouang and Nonghet, has always been a critical obstacle for the enemy that used Highway 7 between the Plain of Jars and North Vietnam. This base has been very effective in controlling enemy movements and was the main target for the enemy before 1969. The allied forces lost an important military officer, Lt. Col. Lysao, the younger brother of Col. Ly Tou Pao. In the beginning of 1970, all the military bases in the northern part of MR-II fell into the hands of the North Vietnamese communists. Seventy percent of the total MR-II land area was lost, including the entire Houaphan Province.

The military bases in the eastern part (LS05) of MR-II included:

o Muang Mork Camp (LS46), an important base for the defense of MR-II and MR-V, was equipped with several tens of thousands of military and civilian personnel. This camp had been heavily attacked and occupied several times by the enemy but was taken back each time. The allied troops were stationed here until 1975 before retreating into the jungle following the US cut in military assistance. Its commander, Col. Chong Koua Vue, did not have a chance to leave the country and was killed in the Laos jungle in 1981. Muang Mork Camp was surrounded by three supporting camps --Khay Ampeu, Khay Meh, and Khay Phou Louang Noi.
o Phou Ka Bork Camp, located on top of the highest mountain range close to the town of Xieng Khouang, created a lot of danger to the enemy operating around Xieng Khouang. It was heavily attacked by artillery and rockets and fell to the enemy in 1968.

The many changes that took place in Southeast Asia (including the China war, the Korean War, the Indochina War, the fall of Dien-Bien-Phu and Kong Lae's coup d'état) had caused concerns to the US. President Kennedy, who took office on January 21, 1961, decided to provide military assistance to Laos in 1961 and to South Vietnam in 1963 to limit communist extension. He believed Ho-Chi-Minh did not comply with the agreement on Dien-Bien-Phu reached under the Geneva Accord of 1954.

During 1961-1964, the US was interested in setting up intelligence teams to monitor the enemy's movements in northern Laos (Phonsaly and Houaphan Provinces) as Priority One and Xieng Khounag Province as Priority Two. The US helped the Royal Lao Government establish a military camp at Nam Bark, Phongsaly Province and several other sites in Houaphan Province.

On September 27, 1962, following the creation of the Laos Tri-Party Government, US Ambassador Leonard Unger paid a visit to the Kong Le's forces at the Plain of Jars. On November 22, 1962, the US provided supplies and equipment to the Neutralist Army by plane. This created a problem that caused Col. Deuane Sounnarath, an avid communist follower, to dislike and disagree with US assistance. Col. Deuane led neutralist forces under his command and North Vietnamese troops to attack the smaller Kong Lae's forces that had to retreat to Muang Phann on June 4, 1963. On October 4, 1963, the US increased its airborne assistance to Kong Lae and Gen. Vang Pao in the fight against communist North Vietnam. The US also provided T-28 pilot training and several T-28 aircraft to the Royal Lao Government.

On February 27, 1963, King Sisavang Vatthana and the Royal Lao Government, which proclaimed itself as being neutral, paid a visit to the US and listened to US President Kennedy's briefings. The US became involved in the war that broke up in Laos and South Vietnam in the beginning of 1963 and lasted until 1975. In the end, the parties that joined forces with the US suffered heavy losses because of the cut in US assistance in the final phases of the conflict.

Photo #39 *(left). US President Kennedy explained that the fall of Dien-Bien-Phu was a great concern to the US and led to the Vietnam War.*

Photo #40 *(right). US President Kennedy went over the various events that happened in Laos as a result of the Vietnamese violations of the previously signed agreements. Lt. Col. Vang, Geu's photos collections and soure, see in Unfortable Laos.*https://jfk.artifacts.archives.gov/peopl e/2012/king-savang-vatthana

Photo #41. US President Kennedy invited the Lao King and members of his neutralist government to pay a visit to the USA on February 27, 1963. After the visit, the Vietnam War broke out on March 2, 1963 and lasted until May 1975. From left to right: Pres. Kennedy, King Savang Vattana, Tiao Souvanna Phouma, Ngone Sananikoke, Phoumi Vongvichit, and other guests. Lt. Col. Vang, Geu's photos collections and source, see in Unfortable Laos.

https://jfk.artifacts.archives.gov/people/2012/king-savang-vatthana

MILITARY BASES IN HOUAPHAN PROVINCE

In 1962, several military bases were established in Houaphan Province, with headquarters located at Na Khang Camp (LS36) as part of a sub-military region under the command of MR-II commander Gen. Vang Pao. Many officers served as the commander of this sub-military region, the last one being Col. Phanh Siharath, who fought until he was killed at the camp in 1969. In March 1966, the Na Khang Camp was heavily attacked by the enemy. Gen. Vang Pao flew in for inspection on a US helicopter and landed at the camp's airbase to meet with the commander of the sub-military region. He was met with heavy enemy fire that caused several severe injuries. The day before that inspection, as airplanes were dropping food supplies at the Na Khang Camp, the enemy fired canons at the airbase to prevent collecting the supplies. At night, the enemy went in to steal some of the rice supplies and rearranged the empty bags to make them look full from afar.

The next day, when Gen. Vang Pao landed on the runway and people were jumping to the ground, the enemy, who was hiding inside the rice bags, immediately fired at the helicopter. One bullet hit the aircraft and skidded onto one of Gen. Vang Pao's shoulders. His guards fired back and killed the shooters hidden inside the rice bags. The helicopter took off immediately to leave the scene momentarily. A few minutes later, after Gen. Vang Pao was carried to a safe place, the helicopter came back and picked him up. The General was later flown on a Caribou aircraft to Oudone, Thailand and then to Hawaii for medical treatment that lasted about one month. He returned to Laos after his wound was healed.

In the beginning of 1967, James Lair and Gen. Vang Pao went to Houaphan Province to assess the feasibility of establishing a radar station at Phou Phathi to be called LS85.

Photo # 42. *Col. Bill met Gen. Vang Pao at LS 367 to discuss the establishment of LS85 at Phou PhaThi in 1966. Lt. Col. Vang, Geu's photos collections and source, see in Unforgettable Laos.*

In February 1969, the enemy deployed enormous forces to lay siege to Na Khang Camp and attack it heavily. This caused the loss of the Na Khang Camp and the death of Col. Phanh Siharath. Several other officers also either got killed or were taken prisoners. Phou Koum Camp (LS50), which served as a backup support base for Na Khang Camp, was also captured by the enemy at about the same time.

Other military camps in the vicinity of Phou PhaThi Camp (LS85) to the east included Muang Lab, Houa Muang, Houei Tong Khor, Houei Mar, and Ban Houei Savian --the birthplace of Maj. Kiatou Walu Vang, who was the camp's commander and the strategic planner for the defense of Phou PhaThi.

Military camps to the west of Phou PhaThi included Houei Kham Moune, Phou Dene Dinh, Pak Kha, Ban Phia Kham and Houei Loyh. All of those camps fell to the enemy at about the same time, on March 9, 1968. Phou PhaThi Camp was seized on March 11, 1968.

DIEN-BIEN-PHU AND PHOU PHATHI WERE THE TWO MOST CRITICAL BASES

Phou PhaThi Camp was the most important base in the war against communist North Vietnam because it was located on a high mountain that stood by itself, was hard to get to, and was not too far from the Laos/North Vietnam border. The US decided to install a radar station at the camp to 1) monitor the enemy's movement in northern Laos, 2) provide intelligence support for the US air missions over North Vietnam, especially around Hanoi, and 3) facilitate the search for missing aircraft and pilots shot down in North-Vietnam.

Many circumstances led to the loss of Phou PhaThi. First, there was some misunderstanding between the commander of the troops stationed on top of the mountain and the commander of those stationed at the foot of the mountain. Those commanders did not coordinate their work too well when they mapped out the defense plans for the region. Even the regional command center was not informed about that plan. Second, there was a lack of intelligence gathering and monitoring of enemy movements. Third, surveillance at the foot of the mountain was rather lamed and had many loopholes. The enemy's elite daredevil units had no problem using the only trail that led to the top of the mountain to attack the allied troops. Fourth, there was a lack of backup troops and US air forces support. This greatly affected the morale of the allied troops, given the fact that the enemy was equipped with more powerful firearms and was in greater numbers than the allies. This resulted in the loss of Phou PhaThi and 60 percent of the MR-II's land area on March 11, 1968.

MORE FACTS ABOUT THE PHOU PHATHI CAMP LS 85

Phou PhaThi was an isolated high mountain with steep slopes and only one trail leading to the mountain top. If that trail was better defended and patrolled more frequently, the enemy would not have been able to get to the top of the mountain, which was what the enemy daredevil troopers did. *[See the red map containing the enemy's plan of attack].* Before the attack, North Vietnam sent in three old AN2 airplanes to fly over Phou PhaThi Camp, take photos, and drop several bombs made of 120 mm mortars. The allies used choppers to chase the AN2 airplanes and shot down two of them. The third one, which flew in first, was able to escape with the pictures that were used later in the plan of attack.

In November 1967, the enemy mobilized massive armed forces to attack the allied posts in MR-II, especially in Houaphan Province. All the military camps around Phou PhaThi were heavily attacked at the same time, making it impossible for the allies to help each other. The enemy then converged on Phou PhaThi with troops ten times stronger than the allied troops in the beginning of March 1968. Every day, between 5 p.m. and midnight, they would fire all kinds of heavy weaponry, e.g., 122 and 130 mm artillery, 122 mm rockets, and bombs of various sizes at the allied troops on top of the mountain and at Maj. Kiatou Va's military base at the foothill. This heavy bombardment from the enemy forced Col. Soua Yang to flee to Houei Tong Khor Camp, leaving his troops behind at the top of the mountain without any commanding officer. Maj. Kiatou Vang, commander of the foothill base, also decided to pull his troops out, given the heavy bombardment, the 360-degree attack, the lack of reinforcement, and the fact that his soldiers were trained as guerilla fighters ("fight and run") and did not know how to defend ground positions ("fight and defend").

The allied troops assigned to the defense of Phou PhaThi included the following:

o At the top of Phou PhaThi, about 250 Hmong soldiers, about 100 Thai recruits, 17 radar specialists, and 2 CIA agents. Of the 19 radar specialists and CIA agents, 11 of them disappeared, and the remaining 8 were safe. Of the 8 initial survivors, 7 were lifted to safety on helicopters, and 1 was killed by enemy fire when he was being pulled up to the aircraft. No information was available on the Hmong and Thai survivors. Many of them apparently jumped to their death or got killed because the enemy left no prisoners behind.
o At the foothill, about 800 soldiers under the command of Maj. Kiatou. All of them fled in all directions and were subject to unknown losses. The enemy's losses were also undetermined since they were the victors. It was reported later that once the helicopters had evacuated all the allied troops, T-28 airplanes and jet fighters flew in several times to drop bombs on the deserted camps.

In 1965, the enemy attacked Nam Bak Camp (in northern Louangprabang Province), Saravan Province in southern Laos, Sepone, and Savannakhet Province and deployed several army divisions to Laos. Because of those attacks, the US decided to set up an Air Forces base at Oudone, Thailand, to provide air support to ground forces in Laos and Vietnam and to drop bombs on North Vietnam.

In 1965, the political situation in the US was in turmoil due to student protestations against the war in Vietnam, for which the government was recruiting young Americans and sending them to fight the war in Vietnam. The tension continued to worsen as a result of new developments in South Vietnam. In 1967, the US deployed important forces to reinforce the defense of Khe-Sanh and Hue, which were the targets of heavy attacks by North Vietnam. Phou PhaThi was also attacked during that time, which explained the lack of air support from the US. The enemy that took part in the Phou PhaThi attack consisted mainly of Chinese ethnic soldiers, while the attackers of Khe-Sanh and Hue were North Vietnamese and Viet-Cong troops.

The first attempt to destroy the radar site came on Jan. 12, 1968, as two Russian-built An-2 Colt biplanes, such as the one shown here, dropped converted 120 mm rounds on the installation.

Photo #43 (left). A view of Phu PhaThi and the steep way up.

Photo #44 (right). North Vietnam's AN2 aircraft. Lt. Col. Vang, Geu's photos collections and source, see in Unforgettable Laos.

The fall of Phou PhaThi affected in many ways the political and military situations in Laos because the communists used massive forces and received tons of ultra-modern warfare equipment from the Soviets. This resulted in Laos losing 60 percent of its territory to the enemy and in MR-II losing 90 percent of its Houaphan war zone and 60 percent of its Xieng Khouang war zone in 1968. This was very scary and nerve pinning for the entire country.

Three sides of Phou Pha Thi were nearly vertical; the fourth was heavily fortified. Lima Site 85 perched on the very top of the bluff. (Joint Task Force-Full Accounting photo)

Since 1994, Joint POW/MIA Accounting Command has made trips to Laos and Vietnam, gathering information about the fate of Americans at Phou Pha Thi. In this photo, a JTF-FA investigator rappels down the sheer face of the mountain. (JTF-FA photo)

Photo #45 (Left). The top of Phou Pha Thi is a steep and high mountain top where the US installed a radar station in 1967 to monitor US air operations over North Vietnam around Hanoi.

Photo #46 (right). 1994 US MIA Mission to search for the body of lost American specialist at LS85. (Thank you, Steve Vogel, at The Washington Post, for sharing this news about LS 85). Lt. Col. Vang, Geu's photos collections and source, see in Unforgettable Laos.

A new painting by aviation artist Keith Woodcock, "An Air Combat First," depicts a confrontation in 1968 in which two North Vietnamese aircraft crashed. (Courtesy Of Keith Woodcock)

Photo #47(left). An Air America Bell 212 helicopter chased an enemy's AN2 aircraft and shot it down.

Photo #48 (right). An AN2 aircraft was being exposed for public viewing at Long Cheng. Lt. Col. Vang, Geu's photos collections and source, see in Unforgettable Laos.

In 1965, US jets undertook flying missions to bombard North Vietnam and one of them got shot down by the enemy. At that time, Col. Thong Vongrasmee, commander of the Houaphan military sub-region headquartered at Na Khang Camp, was on a chopper looking for the fallen jet. The chopper was able to save the jet pilot's life. However, Col. Thong himself was killed by a sniper while hanging on the rope that was being pulled up to the aircraft. His body was flown to Vientiane for burial.

Photo #49. *Gen. Vang Pao on top of Phou Pha Thi looking at the surrounding area and making defensive plans in early 1967. Lt. Col. Vang, Geu's photos collections and source, see in Unforgettable Laos.*

The day after the fall of Phou Pha Thi, Maj. Kiatou flew on a chopper and circled the mountain in search of the troops under his command who were hiding in the surrounding area, as Maj. Kiatou was watching the ground from the air during several air rounds. The enemy located him on their telescope and shot him to death on the chest. The fall of Phou Pha Thi led to Gen. Vang Pao losing his confidence in Col. Soua Yang. From that point on, the Colonel was never assigned any of his normal important missions -- just general inspection duties in MR-II and an advisory role, if anything.

Photo #50. *Left to right: Col. Thong Vongrasamy (successfully rescued a US pilot shot down in North Vietnam but got himself killed), CIA Pop Buell, Col. Khamsao and Col. Douangta Norasing (who now resides in Georgia, USA). Lt. Col. Vang, Geu's photos collections and source, see in Unforgettable Laos.*

Dien-Bien-Phu was a critical strategic element that led to the regional war in Indochina and a painful lesson for the US who decided to listen to Ho-Chi-Minh rather than its allies. It created a vibrant picture of the free world that was afraid of communism. Eventually, the US became involved in the fight against communist expansion into Southeast Asia and sent aircrafts to bombard North Vietnam. The Phou Pha Thi radar base was established to monitor and improve the efficiency of those air strikes.

Likewise, Phou Pha Thi (LS85) was also the most important strategic installation close to the Laos/North-Vietnam border and Hanoi. This military base created a psychological threat to the North Vietnamese, in addition to the US air operation that was already going on over North Vietnam. Ho-Chi-Minh had to find every possible means to destroy the base to ease his army's worries. However, the US considered the war in South Vietnam to be more important than defending Phou Pha Thi. It also felt it should faithfully implement the agreement that made Laos a neutral country, which was just the opposite of what North Vietnam was doing. This is where history is repeating itself. Like Dien-Bien-Phu signaled the end of the French era, the fall of Phou Pha Thi, which resulted from the lack of air support from the US, was also the precursor of another communist victory over a western power.

By getting involved in the Indochina war, the US was pursuing several objectives, including testing new military equipment and teaching a lesson to the communist world on how bad a war would be. Indeed, as a result of that war, the dominant communist country disintegrated on its own, and several other communist countries were able to regain their independence and/or reshape their power structure. Through the Vietnam War, the masks of the dictatorial communist leaders had been removed.

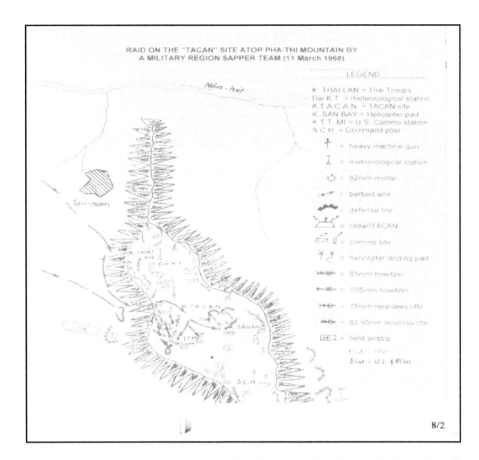

Photo# 51. *North Vietnamese sappers attacked LS85 after heavily bombarding the site from 5:00 p.m. to midnight on March 11, 1968, and focusing on Thai and TACAN troops. The Hmong and Thai troops faced a lack of air support from the US. Lt. Col. Vang, Geu's photos collections and source, see in Unforgettable Laos.*

4

CHAPTER 3

MILITARY EXPANSION AFTER THE FALL OF PHOU PHA THEE

A great hero sacrificed his life at The CIA Radar Site, Phou Pha Thi, Xeneoung Province, Laos.

Major Pao Vang Zaxue Nhia Dang was The only one as The 105 Pao Vang and the only one who sacrificed his life during the Fall of Phou Pha Thi in 1968. Major Pao Vang Zaxue Nhia Dang R 204. Lt. Col. Pao Vang Zaxue Nhia Dang participated in the Intensive Special Commando Military Training in Phitsanulok, Thailand, by The CIA and Thai Royal Military along with the Royal Lao King from 1961-1964. In 1965, he was assigned to the Major status in the military as his task was to be The 105 MM Leader at the Phou Pha Thi mountain, The CIA Radar Frontier Site, Samneung Province, Laos from 1966-1969. Photo collection of Former Captain Xay Vang, his younger brother.

In the middle of 1968, Gen. Vang Pao had a plan to recover the lost MR-II territories for the first time from the enemy. The plan was called Kou Kiat (Honor Recovery) and involved the following deployments:

o One regiment to seize the Xieng Khouang area
o One regiment to seize the Plain of Jars
o Two regiments to seize Phou Pha Thi (LS85)

In July 1968, during the rainy season, Gen. Vang Pao mobilized his troops and moved them out to attack various targets as follows: move from Phou Khae to the town of Xieng Khouang, seize the old camp of Phou Ka Boh on top of Phou Chong Vorng mountain, occupy the town of Xieng Khouang and destroy the arsenal (37 mm anti-aircraft and several 120 mm artillery), seize tanks and enemy food supplies, and destroy the enemy troops at the Tham Kap cave. The allies killed 374 enemy soldiers and discovered a sizeable amount of medical supplies hidden in the cave near

5

Xieng Khouang airport. After the recapture of Xieng Khouang, Plain of Jars and Muang Soui, Gen. Vang Pao relocated about 20,000 refugees from Xieng Khouang to Tha Lath, near the Nam Ngum Dam in Vientiane Province. He also had weapons taken from the enemy shown at a public exhibition at Long Cheng, where newsmen were invited to come and see and spread the news around the world on what the communists used to invade Laos.

PLAIN OF JARS ATTACK PLAN

In 1968, to recapture the Plain of Jars, Gen. Vang Pao used Thai recruits to reinforce Kong Lae's troops at Muang Soui (LS108) in the defense of that town. At that point, Kong Lae had moved his command centre to Muang Kasy (LS18), mounted an attack from Sam Thong to Phou Louang Maat, Ban Na, Phou Xeu toward Muang Phann and then the Plain of Jars.

At first, the battalion that led the attack was a Lao Theung battalion under the command of Maj. Thao Lu was a former French soldier during 1950-1954. Maj. Lu was able to seize Phou Louang Maat but made the bad decision to allow his troops to use alcoholic drinks to celebrate their victory. That same evening, while they were having fun and getting mildly intoxicated, the enemy deployed a guerilla unit for a swift attack on the camp and killed the Major and 120 of his troopers. This signaled the end of the Lao Theung battalion for lack of leadership. Gen. Vang Pao deployed another army unit to replace the decimated battalion and allow it to move on to the Plain of Jars. He recaptured several old posts and destroyed arsenals and several 37 mm anti-aircraft and 122 mm artillery weapons.

Gen. Vang Pao took three jars and sent the first one to the governor's office in Samthong, the second one to the Royal Palace in Luang Prabang, and the third one to the US National Museum in Washington, DC. He also moved several thousands of Xieng Khouang residents to resettle at Tha Lath, Vientiane Province.

The recaptured posts did not stay very long in the allies' hands. They were seized at the end of the year by the enemy, who deployed tanks, vehicles and huge armed forces. In the beginning of 1969, North Vietnam's Division 312 and several Dak Cong battalions started attacking the allies on three fronts:

o They seized the strip between Xieng Khouang Pha Khao and Long Cheng,
o They attacked the allies stationed at the Plain of Jars and trailed them all the way to Phou Louang Maat, Phou Pha Say, Samthong, and Hinh Tang (LS74). They seized Samthong by the end of 1968. Starting in January 1969, they attacked Long Cheng, and
o They attacked the Thai units that were defending Muang Soui. The Thai units had to retreat for lack of reinforcement and support when facing a stronger enemy force. In any fight that lasts longer than six months and no rest, most soldiers would be tired, discouraged and have low morale. Furthermore, in this case, the enemy was equipped with better weapons, including tanks, various kinds of artillery, and rockets with a greater firing range than the allies' rockets.

Biography of Tom Lum (CIA agent/military advisor)

Photo #52 (left). *Col. Tom Lum and young Hmong kids dressed as soldiers in 1968.*

Photo #53 (right). *That Dam is an ancient tower monument located in the town of Xieng Khouang. Lt. Col. Vang, Geu's photos collections and source, see in Unforgettable Laos.*

Tom Lum was born in St. Louis, MO, the son of a Chinese American. After graduating from college in 1960, he was sent to military training at Ft. Benning, GA, where he was trained as a parachute jumper and military pilot. Following his 1962 graduation, he was assigned to the 82nd Airborne Division at Ft. Bragg, NC and then deployed to South Vietnam to serve for one year as a propeller aircraft pilot, fighting the enemy and providing air transportation to ground troops. After his return from his Vietnam tour, Tom Lum worked as a trainer for propeller aircraft pilots at Training Center 11, Ft. Benning, GA. He later quit his trainer job but kept his military role, and then joined the CIA. In 1968, he was sent for duties in Laos, where he worked for two years as an intelligence gathering pilot and military adviser for Regiments 25 and 26 in MR-II, along with Lao officer Vang Leng. Tom Lum completed University-level military training in 1987. He retired as a Colonel in 1993 and received a retirement pension from the CIA.

Photo #54. *Col. Tom Lum standing in front of a damaged North Vietnamese military vehicle in Xieng Khouang 1968. Lt. Col. Vang, Geu's photos collections and source, see in Unforgettable Laos.*

Photo #55. An aircraft just dropped a bomb over the Tham Kab cave (white smoke). The Xieng Khouang airfield was close by. Lt. Col. Vang, Geu's photos collections and source, see in Unforgettable Laos.

Photo #56. Dropping bombs on the Tham Kab cave caused hundreds of fatalities to the enemy troops and offered them a good lesson. Later on, instead of using the cave as a hiding place, the enemy then just dug holes in the ground and hided in those ground holes. According to more recent news, it appears that, starting in 1976, North Vietnam has been maintaining this cave as a memorial for the 375 soldiers killed there in 1968. Lt. Col. Vang, Geu's photos collections and source, see in Unforgettable Laos.

Photo #57. Col. Tom Lum was on his way to investigate how damages to the cave occurred. Lt. Col. Vang, Geu's photos collections and source, see in Unforgettable Laos.

Photo #58. Col. Tom Lum inspecting weapons and ammunitions captured in 1968.

Lt. Col. Vang, Geu's photos collections and source, see in Unforgettable Laos.

Photos # 59, 60, 61 and 62. *Several hundred of North Vietnamese troops were killed at the Tham Kab cave in 1968 due to air bombardments. These pictures only revealed Vietnamese soldiers, no local population. The Lao PDR is using this cave as a memorial for the remembrance of the killed people ---mostly the communist soldiers who died in this cave. The North Vietnamese later stopped using the cave and hided themselves in individual ground holes instead... Lt. Col. Vang, Geu's photos collections and source, see in Unforgettable Laos.*

Photo #63. *37 mm guns captured in 1968 in Xieng Khouang close to the stadium and Tham Kab cave.*

4

Lt. Col. Vang, Geu's photos collections and source, see in Unforgettable Laos.

Photo #64. *BV 24 Regiment under the command of Vu May (holding a piece of white paper in his hand and wearing a red beret) on its way to attack Xieng Khouang in 1968. In 1975, he immigrated to Thailand but did not go to a third country. Instead, he decided to lead a group of refugees back to Laos and work with the Lao communists under the North Vietnamese. He died soon afterwards for unknown reasons and under unknown circumstances in the communist hands. Lt. Col. Vang, Geu's photos collections and source, see in Unforgettable Laos.*

Photo #65. *Several types of ammunition were captured from the North Vietnamese enemy at their hiding place in Tham Kab cave near Xieng Khouang in 1968 during the Honor Recovery battle led by Maj. Gen. Vang Pao.*

Photo #66 (left). Because of their badly damaged houses, the people of Xieng Khouang had no place to live and had to escape danger. In 1968, Gen. Vang Pao had to move about 20,000 people to Tha Lath near the Nam Ngum Dam, Vientiane Province.

Photo #67 (right). People were waiting for the airplanes to take them to safer places in the flat area of Vientiane Province in 1968. Lt. Col. Vang, Geu's photos collections and source, see in Unforgettable Laos

Lt. Col. Vang, Geu's photos collections and source, see in Unforgettable Laos.

Photo #68 (left). A group of T-28 aircrafts are getting ready to move the allied refugees anytime.

Photo #69 *(right). Xieng Khouang airfield, not far from Tham Kab Cave, which was destroyed by air raids in 1968. Lt. Col. Vang, Geu's photos collections and source, see in Unforgettable Laos.*

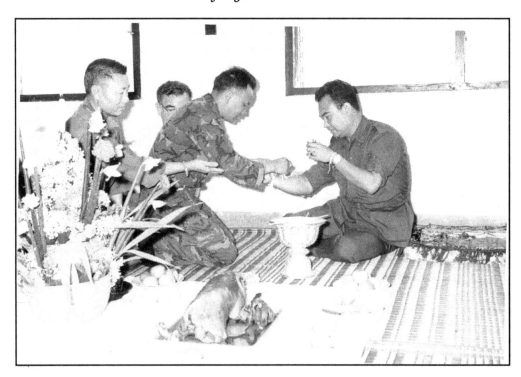

Lt. Col. Vang, Geu's photos collections and source, see in Unforgettable Laos.

Photo #70. *Col. Neng Chu Thao and Gen. Vang Pao welcoming H.E. Tiao Sisouk Nachampasak during his visit to MR-II to congratulate Gen. Vang Pao for his victory at the Kou Kiat battle in 1968.*

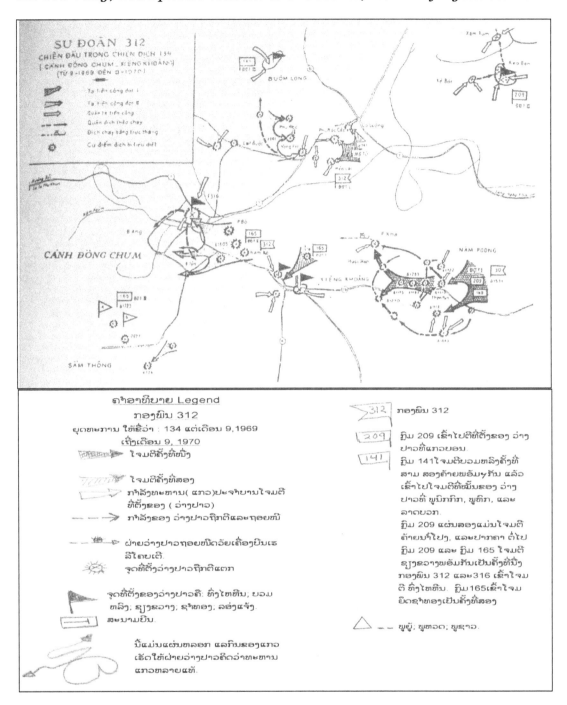

Photo #71. *The enemy deployed Division 312 and many other regiments to attack Gen. Vang Pao's MR-II troops, who suffered heavy human and territorial losses, including Xieng Khouang, Ban Na, Khang Kho, Pa Dong, and Phou.*

Lt. Col. Vang, Geu's photos collections and source, see in Unforgettable Laos. Pha Say, Phou Louang Matt, Hine Tang and Samthong. Long Chengw was also heavily bombarded by 130 mm artillery.

Photo #72 (left). Col. James W. Lair paying a visit to Long Cheng.

Photo #73 (right). Burr Smith leaning on a stone jar. Lt. Col. Vang, Geu's photos collections and source, see in Unforgettable Laos.

Photo #74 (left). Destroyed Vietnamese 76 mm artillery.

Photo #75 (right). North Vietnamese 82 mm and 61 mm weapons were captured in 1968. Lt. Col. Vang, Geu's photos collections and source, see in Unforgettable Laos.

In July 1968, during the rainy season, Gen. Vang Pao requested the help of several battalions of the Thai Army to ensure the defense of the area around Long Cheng and Samthong. In August 1968, Gen. Vang Pao sent two regiments by air to Houei Tong Khorr to push the enemy toward Phou Pha Thee, encircled and attacked it with air support from the US and T-28 aircraft from the

Royal Lao Air Forces to recapture Phou Pha Thee. The fighting reached the top of the mountain but could not proceed further because the enemy put in place formidable, ready-to-fight-to-death defense units along the uphill trail. Several anti-aircraft weapons were also in place at the top of the mountain, firing continuously to prevent helicopter landings. Several helicopters did get shot, and one jet aircraft was shot down. This fight to recapture Phou Pha Thee was not successful because the enemy was stronger and capable of firing at the allies from all directions and at the same time. All the posts that were recaptured were soon seized back by the enemy.

Photo #76. *North Vietnamese AK 47 and 40B guns and ammunitions captured in 1968.*

Lt. Col. Vang, Geu's photos collections and source, see in Unforgettable Laos.

The enemy extended its cleansing operation to Na Khang (LS36), the command center of the Houaphan military sub-region. Using an impeccable siege and heavy attacks, they seized Na Khang Camp in February 1969, gained full control of Houaphan Province, and caused the death of a very important military officer in Na Khang Camp, Col. Phanh Siharath.

Between 1961 and 1965, MR-II received assistance from the US in several areas, including

- o Military advisor James W. Lair was the coordinator for all weapons needed for the fight against North Vietnam.
- o Civilian advisor Pop Buell was the coordinator for all equipment, food supplies and basic tools needed by refugees to survive after they had lost everything.

Between 1967 and 1970, US advisors included:

- o Military advisor Pat Landry –who later died in December 2005 in Texas, USA
- o Civilian advisor: USAID staff as usual until May 14, 1975.

Starting in 1970, Jerry Daniels was the US military advisor. Once the three Lao factions agreed to form a joint Lao government, US assistance was redirected to post-war development, e.g., agriculture, livestock, and mining in MR-II. From May 15, 1975, to 1982, Jerry Daniels was in charge of MR-II refugees resettled in Thailand. He died at his Thai residence in 1982.

On July 23, 1963, the Lao neutralist forces, combined with communist North Vietnamese troops, attacked the camps of Phou Pha Xay and Khang Kho (LS204) —the village of Chaomuang Yuatong Yang. Lt. Col. Vang Pao deployed forces to recapture those two bases. He was promoted to the rank of Colonel of the Royal Lao Army and then became the commander of MR-II until May 14, 1975.

Photo #77. *H.M. King Sisavang Vatthana conferring medals to MR-II high-ranking civil servants and military officers at Long Cheng in 1965. Col. Phan Siharath was shown in the middle, next to Chaokoueng Chao Saykham (in black suit). Lt. Col. Vang, Geu's photos collections and source, see in Unforgettable Laos.*

Photo #78. *Thai Army Officers Burr Smith and Gen. Vang Pao at Long Cheng in 1968.*

Lt. Col. Vang, Geu's photos collections and source, see in Unforgettable Laos.

In 1963, Lao neutralists and North Vietnamese attacked Pa Dong (LS05), Khang Kho (LS204) and Phou Pha Xay and captured Khang Kho and Phou Pha Xay while still shelling Pa Dong with heavy weapons. This led Col. Vang Pao to start a new base at Phou Pha Khao (LS14). He was then promoted to the rank of Brigadier General of the Royal Lao Army. In 1964, realizing that the Phou Pha Khao's runways were too short and too dangerous for the pilots at take-off and landing, BG. Vang Pao took US experts with him to Long Cheng to look at the feasibility of building an airbase at that new location. With the US experts' green light, he then had the construction of the new airport started in 1964 and named it L20A.

Photo #79. *Pat Landry (with red necktie), Vang Geu, and Vince Shields (CIA, signing a letter) at Long Cheng in 1970. Lt. Col. Vang, Geu's photos collections and source, see in Unforgettable Laos.*

4

Jerry Daniels, Long Cheng, 1973 (Mouasu Bliaya collection).

Photo #80. *Jerry Daniels at Long Cheng in 1973, by Mouasu Biliaya photo collection*

AIR STRIPS AND LIMA SITES

The Long Cheng airbase (L20A) was located in Xieng Khouang Province, halfway between Xieng Khouang and Vientiane Provinces, and north of the Nam Ngum Dam. The flight between Vientiane and Long Cheng took about 30 minutes. Long Cheng is south of the Plain of Jars and only 15-minute flight away. The airport was about 500 meters wide and 1,500 meters long, with a total surface area of 750,000 square meters limited by three mountain ranges --Middle Long Cheng or Long Cheng Airport, North Long Cheng or United Lao Radio Station, and South Long Cheng or Long Cheng to the east of the Lao Theung ethnics.

Photo #81. *Pha Khao Airfield (LS 14) in 1964*

5

Photo #82. *Long Cheng Airfield (LS20A) in 1971 and Lt. Col. Vang, Geu's photos collections and source, see in Unforgettable Laos.*

The various Lima sites that provided reference points to pilots included the following airports: Wattay (Vientiane L08), Muang Kasy (LS18), Muang Hongsa (LS65), Nambak (LS54), Long Cheng (L20A); Samthong (LS20B); Plain of Jars (LS22); Muang Soui (LS108); Na Khang (LS36); Bouam Long (LS32); Phou Koum (LS50); Sanh Chor (LS02); Muang Mork (LS46); Muang Chaa (LS113), a station that changed its name to Muang Desa when the Lao king visited it in 1970, and then to Muang Xaysomboun (current Lao PDR name); Phakhao (LS14); Padong (LS05); Khang Khor (LS204); Ban Na (LS15); Ban Hinh Tang (LS74); Namfene (LS224); Phou Hae (LS255); Phak Khae (LS353); Phou Kang (LS337); Phou Sanh (LS240); and Muang Phoune (LS37), the village of Chaomuang Touxia Tao. The big sign above Phou Mork from west to east read as follows: CG, CC, CE, CB, CW, CA and CT (which stand for Charles George; Charles Charles; Charles Echo; Charles Bravo; Charles Wisky; Charles Alfa and Charles Tango).

The highest peak to the west was called Skyline One, and the highest peak to the east was Skyline Two. The peak east of the Long Cheng airbase was named Appolo. East of Long Cheng airbase was the Long Cheng Tai or Ban Lao Theung and a stream flowing to the west called Nam Ngoua Creek. The whole mountain range north of the Long Cheng airport was the Phou Mork range. The lower hill south of the Long Cheng airport was named Phou Phra Rassavang. Based on the above, the airport was located in a valley, and one could only take off or land here by flying in from the east. A mountain range formed the airport's west end.

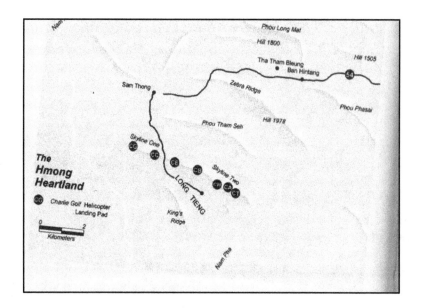

Photo #83. Critical defensive points around Long Cheng Airfield on the Phu Mork Mountain Range (CG, CC, CE, CB, CW, CA) Lt. Col. Vang, Geu's photos collections and source, see in Unforgettable Laos.

Photo #84. North Vietnamese tanks destroyed by Gen. Vang Pao's troops in 1970 at the Plain of Jars

Lt. Col. Vang, Geu's photos collections and source, see in Unforgettable Laos.

AGREEMENT BETWEEN THE THREE LAO PRINCES

In 1962, the three Lao princes decided to form a tri-party government to bring peace to the Laos kingdom. This development gave every Lao citizen great hope for peace and no more war. Gen. Vang Pao laid out a post-war reconstruction plan for MR-II, focusing on construction, road repairs, public health, education, and management. He built new offices for provincial and district management, a new hospital, and a new school for provincial Governor Chao Saykham Southakakouman. He also built a royal resort for use by the king during his field visits to the Province.

Once the building construction was completed, the General invited King Savang Vatthana to visit MR-II during 1965. The king then promoted BG. Vang Pao to the rank of Major General and conferred him the honorific title of Phagna Nora Pamok (The Courageous King Lion). Soon afterwards, the situation changed drastically when the Neutral Party was divided into two neutralist factions, one led by Kong Le and one led by Deuane Sounenarath.

Photo #85. *H.M. King Savang Vatthana and high-ranking officials paying a visit to Long Cheng in 1965 andLt. Col. Vang, Geu's photos collections and source, see in Unforgettable Laos.*

Communist North Vietnam fought the Kong Le neutralists and the Vientiane rightists. This led the US to increase its air strikes over several targets in Laos, causing a scary development because North Vietnam was mobilizing massive military forces in northern Laos, Phongsaly, Houaphan, Xieng Khouang, and in MR-III, MR-IV in southern Laos.

Photo #86. *H. M. the King during a visit to MR-II in 1970 to celebrate the Hmong New Year after the second recapture of the Plain of Jars. This was his last trip to MR-II. Lt. Col. Vang, Geu's photos collections and source, see in Unforgettable Laos.*

Photo # 87. *The Laos Crown Prince, on his visit to Long Cheng in 1973, being welcome by high-ranking MR-II military officers (shaking hands with Col. Vang Geu and followed by Gen. Vang Pao). He never left the country and was detained at a re-education camp, where he died. Communism is a regime that destroys monarchy. Lt. Col. Vang, Geu's photos collections and source, see in Unforgettable Laos.*

CHAPTER 4

GOVERNING SYSTEM IN MILITARY REGION II

PRIMARY EDUCATION

At first, the General Inspector of primary schools in Xieng Khouang Province was Mr. Vanheuang Vongsavanthong, and his assistant was Chao Say. The next General Inspector was Thao Tou Bounmasanoun and his assistant, Mr. Mua Lia. Starting in 1967, Mua Lia was the General Inspector, and his assistant was Mr. Bouthalangsy Douangsavanh until May 14, 1975.

The various schools and school principals were as follows:

School Districts:	Principals:
Muang Kham (Ban Bane)	Phia Pheng Vinaiya
Muang Pek (Phonesavan)	Boun Boulom, then Phoui Phongsavath
Muoung Khoune (Xieng Khouang)	Khamsay Norasing
Muang Ngane	Somthong Mang Mohmek
Muang Tha Thom	Chanh Phasayasith
Muang Lat Houang	Kila Mounivong

Following the changes in the political scene in 1961, the US started providing assistance in education and made it possible for the Hmong and the Lao in MR-II to receive a modest level of education.

Notes: Assistant Inspector General of Xieng Khouang Province's Primary Schools, Bouthalansy Douangsavanh, wrote, "Education has helped the Lao people become more alert, more knowledgeable and more conscious in many areas. When the various ethnicities get together, schools are built in every village, big and small. In the past, only those who had money had a chance to get an education. Nowadays, anywhere the refugees show up, teachers will be sent there, thanks to the US assistance and the support from Gen. Vang Pao."

Starting in 1968, Mua Lia and Boutharangsi Dounagsavanh kept expanding the education system by assigning school principals to many school districts (SD) as follows:

1. Pha Khao SD: Bouthalangsy Douangsavanh (now lives in Texas), followed by Chantho Pakdy Monivong.

10

2. Samthong SD: Ly Lo. After it was attacked in 1968, the school moved to Phak Khe.
3. Long Cheng SD: Yang Ying, followed by Xiong Kao (when Yang Ying was reassigned to Bouam Long SD). School Principal Yang Ying was later moved successively to Long Cheng South, Long Cheng Middle, Phou Sanh, and back to Long Cheng until the day he left Laos for the USA. He died in July 2007 in Minnesota.
4. Bouam Long SD: Xiong Kao. He later moved to Long Cheng, SD and then to Phou Vieng, SD. He resettled in Iowa, USA.
5. Ban Na SD: Lo Toua and his deputy, Chanh Phasaiyasith. Lo Toua now resides in Morganton, North Carolina, raising chickens. After Ban Na was attacked, Lo Toua moved to Nam Yone SD to replace Chanh Phasaiyasith, who was reassigned to Nam Pounh Desa SD at Muang Desa.
6. Phou Soh, Phou Sanh Nhai (Song Lai) SD: Yang Yi. He later moved to Pak Meuy, SD.
7. Na Luang SD: Yang Bee
8. Thong Mieng SD: Toumoua Lee. (Resettled in the USA, where he died not long after arrival).
9. Nam Mo SD: Lem Thong
10. Muang Cha (Muang Desa) SD: Khamla Khamphavong
11. Phou Xane Luang SD: Khambay Vongthongchit
12. Muang Soui SD: Khamkone Douangsadeth. He later moved to Phak Kherr/Phou Tao SD.
13. Muang Om SD: Khamphi Sisaket
14. Khoua Lek/Huei Pa Chark SD: Chanepha Chanthalangsy

In 1972, there were over 400 primary schools, 161 male teachers, 4 female teachers, 4,788 male students, and 1,054 female students. Based on those numbers, one could notice there was a severe shortage of teachers in Xieng Khouang Province. There were clearly not enough educated teachers with formal degrees from teacher training colleges. The war that erupted in every corner caused risky conditions and discouraged teachers from teaching in MR-II schools.

SAMTHONG COLLEGE

The first principal was Prof. Khamleck, followed by Prof. Toufue. In 1969, Samthong was attacked by the enemy, forcing the Samthong College to reopen in Vientiane, next to the Fa-Ngum College. When Toufue enrolled in the Army, Lechard Daniel, a French native, replaced him as principal. In 1973, Samthong College reopened at Muang Cha (Muang Desa), where Prof. Lychao served as principal until his move to the USA in 1975. Lychao died on October 3, 2009, in Soouth-Carolina.

After the battle of Dien-Bien-Phu, the situation in Laos changed drastically, with Houaphan and Phongsaly Provinces falling entirely under the control of the Lao Communists. Most of the population who disliked the communist regime had to move into the jungle to fight the enemy or resettled as refugees in other provinces, especially in cities, for security reasons. This created a lot of problems for administrative and educative programs. People faced a lack of leadership and many other complicating security issues as a result of the many facets of communist interference that had never been experienced before.

After the French left Indochina, hundreds of thousands of refugees from North Vietnam resettled in several provinces of Laos, such as Xieng Khouang, Vientiane, Savannakhet and

Sayabouri. After Kong Lae staged his coup d'état, people across the country rushed to the urban centers to flee the fighting that took place in rural areas in provinces like Houaphan, Phongsaly and several other southern provinces. This created administrative confusion and disruptions and made it difficult for people to communicate and to regroup, except possibly under very rare circumstances. A good example related to the Houaphan part of MR-II where Sim Vichitvongsa served as the school principal, followed by Mountri Sophabmixay.

POLICE STRUCTURE

The chief of police person was Pol. Col. Bounthong Sengkhamyong, and his deputy, Pol. Maj. Yang Chao. Lao ethnic policemen performed their police duties starting in 1949, the year France conferred within-the-French-Union independence to Laos. Police was separated from the military. From 1950 onward, training programs were provided to form police officers and policemen throughout the Laos kingdom. As for the Hmong, police training started in 1955 and produced the following Xieng Khouang Hmong Policemen (by promotion/class):

o First promotion: Hang Sao, Yang Chao, Kue Chia, Vang Tou, and Xiong Foua
o Second promotion: Hang Doua, Yangchao Noi, Lo Xang, Moua Chou, Moua Bee, Kue Chia, Heu Doua, and Heu Cheu
o Third promotion (Army officers reclassified as police officers): Vang Tou, Vang Xang, Yang Toua, Chaki Yang, Faydang Thao, Ly Lue and Yang Cheu.

Later on, many Hmong policemen were trained in Xieng Khouang and other Lao provinces (including Vientiane) following the Kong Lae's coup d'état. No official records are available on the composition of those promotions.

There were a total of about 200 policemen in Xieng Khouang Province.

Please read Pol. Maj. Hang Doua's biography in Chapter 20.

ADMINISTRATIVE SYSTEM

Before 1945, Laos had no provincial governors -- only deputy governors, because it was still a French colony. At the district chief level, some districts were under direct French control. After 1949, the year Laos regained its independence from France. Laos started seeing native Lao serving as provincial governors. In each of the 12 provinces that were created, the administrative structure consisted of one Chaokhoueng (governor), several Chaomuang (district chiefs), Nai Kong (mini district chiefs), Tasseng (county chiefs), and Nai Ban (village chiefs). Each of those provinces was represented at the National Assembly by its elected "deputies". MR-II, created in 1962, covered two provinces: Xieng Khouang and Houaphan.

XIENG KHOUANG PROVINCIAL GOVERNMENT

In 1949, the Governor of Xieng Khouang was Chao Saykham Southakakoumane. There were two deputy governors: one Hmong and one Lao. The first Hmong deputy governor was Phagna Touby Lyfoung, who was succeeded by Youapao Yang and, in 1975, by Mua Chia. The Lao deputy-governor was Thongsavath Vongsavanthong, who was succeeded by Chao Khong when Mr. Thongsavath was named governor of Pakse Province. Chao Khong was succeeded by Khamsing and, in 1975, by Bounchan Vouthisisoumbath. *(Both Mua Chia and BounChanh were resettled as refugees in France).*

Over the years, several people served as Xieng Khouang representatives for fixed terms. The Hmong representatives included Toulia Lyfoung (elected in 1947), Tougeu Lyfoung (elected in 1951), Touby Lyfoung (elected in 1958), and Touyia Lee (the last one before the communist takeover of Laos. The last elected representatives from Xieng Khouang Province were Ly Tou Yia (a Hmong who died in France), Bounthanh (a LaoTheung who died in France.), and Chao Sopsaysana Southakakoumane (a Lao refugee to France where he died on March 16, 2009).

Provincial Service Departments

(Public Health, Primary School, Justice, Military, and Police)

Xieng Khouang Province was divided into 5 districts as listed below (with the names of the successive district chiefs):

Muang Khoun   Van Tanovan, Thone Nettavong, Doua Kham Phengthirath (1961)

Muang Perk   Bounpheng Norasing (1961)

Muang Kham   Kham-Ouan, Bounmy Thiphavong Khamheuang (the father of Col. Sisavath), and Khammane Vorasane (1961)

Muang Mork   Oui Chanthivong

Muang Hmong   Touby Lyfoung, followed by Mr. Youa Pao Yang and Txiaj Xang Mua

In 1949, when Touby picked Youapao as the Muang Hmong district chief, Bichou Lo became unhappy and decided to change sides and go and work with the Pathet Lao. Bichou Lo felt he was much better educated than Youapao Yang, did not like Toulia Lyfoung for personal reasons, was unhappy because his father got jailed in Muang Kham, and got very little support from his relatives, most of whom were on the Pathet Lao team. His father was put in jail because, as a Tasseng (county chief), he mismanaged the tax collection system by not implementing Chaomuang's instructions. As taxpayers did not have the money to pay taxes, his father made advance payments for them and later came back to recover his advance payments. The Chaomuang deemed this was illegal and put him in prison. These were the reasons for Bichou Lo's desertion in 1949. However, in the end, Bichou Lo came back to Touby's camp in 1957 when the Lao factions were at peace.

On December 13, 1960, Kong Lae's forces captured Xieng Khouang. Bichou Lo fled to join the neutralists in 1961. But in 1963, the communists captured and killed him barbarously at the Plain of Jars, Xieng Khouang Province. The Kong Lae's presence brought complications to the province's administration. To improve the management system, Gen. Vang Pao and Chaokhoueng Saykham decided to recommend breaking the provincial set-up into 10 districts, as shown below with the names of the district chiefs and Police chiefs:

1. Muang Nonghet: Ly Neng Thong (Hmong)/Pol. Maj. Xiong Fua (Hmong)
2. Muang Kham: Bounchanh Vouthisisombath (Lao)/Pol. Maj. Thong Thep (Lao)

3. Muang Pangxai: Paul Moune (Lao)/Pol. Maj. Khamsene (Lao)
4. Muang Ngat: Ly Xiong (Hmong, now resides in Minnesota)/Pol. Maj. Khampoune

(Lao)

5. Muang Mork: Khamsing, followed by Khamsouane Sananikone and Oui

Chanhthivong (Lao)/Pol. Maj. Samingkham Aphayavong (Lao)

6. Muang Houng: Xao Chia Thao (Hmong)/Pol. Maj. Hang Doua (Hmong)
7. Muang Khoun: Samingkham Aphayyavong (Lao)/Pol. Maj. Hang Chue
    (Hmong)
8. Muang Perk: Khamtanh Thiphavong Khamheuang (Lao)/Pol. Maj. Xieng Mounty
9. Muang Viengfa: Muageu Mua Nou Tua (Hmong)/Pol. Maj. Heu Doua (Hmong)
10. Muang Viengsay: Youa Tong Yang (Hmong)/Pol. Maj. Yang Chao Noi (Hmong)

Please read the biography of Mr. Bouchanh Vouthisombath, former Chaomuang of Muang Kham and deputy-governor of Xieng Khouang Province, in Chapter 20.

PERSONAL RECOUNT OF HISTORICAL EVENTS

(by Bounchan Vouthisombat)

On March 9, 1945, the Japanese troops entered the town of Xieng Khouang, arrested several French colonial employees, and closed the local schools. At the time, I was still a student along with other classmates that included, as far as I can remember, Lytou Lyfoung (Phagna Touby Lyfoung's brother, the future Public Works chief engineer of Savannakhet), Khampheui (a native of Muang

Xieng Dett, the future Public Works chief engineer of Pakse), and Khammeung Tounalom (future medical doctor).

One day, after the school term, I and one of my friends, Bounta (a native of Ban Na Ou, Tasseng Xieng, 5 kilometers away from the town of Xieng Khouang), made a trip by foot to Lath Houang. We left Xieng Khouang at 8 a.m., went past an unknown Hmong village, and headed toward Muang Kha. After a 5-kilometer walk, once we realized that we were on the wrong trail, we back-tracked and took a different route that led us to Muang Kha, where we arrived at 9 p.m. The next morning, we left Muang Kha and walked along the highway between Nam Hoy Nou and Bouak Kob. When we reached the highway, we saw military vehicles on the road carrying scary and fully armed French soldiers. At the time, the Japanese have not yet seized the French camp of Khang Khay. We continued our trek until we reached Ban Chom Thong and then Ban Tong, near Muang Kham (which was still Japanese-free).

When the Japanese troops first arrived in Muang Kham, 300 of them were temporarily stationed at Ban Tong, with about 15 to 20 of them staying at my house. This Japanese battalion was building the road toward Houaphan Province, using French and Moi Kouang Toum prisoners for ground digging on the Ban Bane to Sop Lao-Nam Neun stretch. The road construction, including ground digging and tree cutting, was a truly cooperative effort that everybody, regardless of rank and status, contributed to. There were no slaves, no bosses. Soldiers and officers alike were part of the labor force. Good discipline was strongly enforced; people worked and ate together. Local villagers were not disturbed, and there was no discrimination toward women. Those who crossed the line were punished, e.g., they had to stand in front of the officers and be subject to body punishments commensurate with the severity of their wrongdoing.

This battalion was in place for about three months until the Japanese surrendered in 1945 following the dropping of the US A-bombs. The Japanese stopped the war and went home through Vietnam. Seven Japanese battalions retreated from Houaphan Province and headed toward Vietnam and, ultimately, Japan. Each of them stayed overnight at Ban Tong, one battalion at a time. Each night during those seven days, some 20 Japanese troopers spent the night at my house. All of them were very disciplined and well-behaved.

In 1946, I took part in the creation of Muang Phonesavan. At the time, I was serving at the district office at Houei Kham, a Vietnamese village located between Khang Khay Camp and Phonesavan. The Chaomuang of Muang Perk was Thao Khampheng Thongkham, and then Thao Van Tanovan. The latter was the district chief who led the administrative officers and the local residents in clearing up an old forested area in Tasseng Kat and started building the current town of Phonesavan. Once the new town was ready, the Muang Perk district office was then moved from Ban Houei Kham to Phonesavan. Before deciding on using this name, Chaomuang Van Tanovan recommended several alternative names to Chaokhoueng Saykham. The Chaokhoueng officially wrote back, "You are Thao Van; the town you created should be named Phonesavan." Therefore, from 1946 on, the new town was called Phonesavan. (Mr. Van Tanovan and his family resettled in Portland, Oregon, USA. Very few people of his age are still alive today. For that, he was indeed very lucky).

Photo #88. *District Chiefs of Xieng Khouang Province in 1972 (photo taken on September 30, 1972). Front row from left to right: Samingkham Aphayvong, Ouy Chanthvong, Mua Yeu Noutoua, Yang Dao, Bounchan Vouthisombath, Douakham and Phomoune. Back row from left to right: Xao Chiay Thao, Neng Thong Lee and Ly Song.*

Lt. Col. Vang, Geu's photos collections and source, see in Unforgettable Laos.

Photo #89. *Nhaluang Bounchan Vouthisombath, deputy-governor of Xieng Khouang Province and his wife. Photo taken in 1997 in France. Lt. Col. Vang, Geu's photos collections and source, see in Unforgettable Laos.*

INVOLVEMENT IN THE INDOCHINA WAR

On April 12, 1953, the Vietminh deployed three divisions to invade Laos for the second time. Division 312 attacked French troops between Samneua and Louangprabang; Divisions 304 and 306 attacked Xieng Khouang to destroy the Plain of Jars airport; and Division 308 attacked southern Laos. This led to severe losses to military camps in Houaphan Province and forced the troops from northern Laos to retreat in the jungle and find some ways to get to the Plain of Jars. The Plain of Jars became a strong French military camp that was set up to control the Vietminh's invasion. Not long afterward, French Foreign Legion troops, consisting of soldiers from the Arabic countries of Morocco and Algeria and South Vietnam, also came to the rescue. Once they arrived at the Plain of Jars, the Vietminh army started its attack but was not able to seize the camp because the area was very flat, and aircrafts were dropping flares all night that identified the exact enemy's positions. The Vietminh then moved their troops on Highway 4 toward Xieng Khouang, with French troops on their tails until they reached the Dong Darn area. The Vietminh stayed between Dong Darn and Xieng Khouang for less than a month before they were pushed away and retreated toward Sanh Noi/Thaene Phou.

In 1953, once Xieng Khouang was recaptured, I stayed there for 10 days before returning to the Plain of Jars to be with the South Vietnamese battalion and the Hanoi parachutist battalion. Ten days later, I was reassigned to the French Foreign Legion contingent under the command of Capt. Max Blin. The contingent was deployed from the Plain of Jars on foot and spent the night at Ban Khang Mone. On the second day, we walked along Highway 7 past the Tat Peub Falls and were ambushed by the Vietminh at a narrow and steep section of the road near the diversion to Ban

Dene Dinh, about 11 kilometers north of Ban Bane. The fighting lasted for about an hour before the enemy retreated toward Ban Bane.

The attack of Ban Bane, Muang Kham took place according to the following plan:

o One battalion deployed toward Muang Kha from Muang Thaer and entered Ban Bane,
o One battalion approached Ban Bane from the north, along Nam Say Creek, then moved on to the Ban Bane flat area and
o One battalion (the French Foreign Legion contingent under Capt. Max Blin's command) to which I was assigned approached Ban Bane from the middle road along Highway 7.

The troop movement was under the constant air surveillance of a small Moral airplane. When there was a fighting, B4 and T4 black and very fast one-engine aircrafts were there to drop bombs and fire on the enemy. Sometimes, B26 airplanes also joined the air attack, flying four at a time.

It took fifty days to liberate Ban Ban from the Vietminh. Before entering Ban Bane in May 1953, I used to tell Capt. Max Blin at Tat Peub that, "Our people out here live by themselves, away from the Vietnamese. By and large, they would not want to be with any Vietnamese." After chatting about this and other subjects with me, Capt. Blin told his commanding officers by radio and by microphone, "Before we enter the town, make sure to tell your troops not to get into people's houses. Don't take anything from them, not even a single fruit, because their leader is here with us."

From 1953 to 1954, the French battalions stationed in Muang Kham behaved themselves extremely well, did nothing to harm the local citizens, raised not a single complaint, and maintained an excellent relationship with the public. Members of the French Foreign Legion came from several countries, such as Italy, Germany, Algeria and Morocco. None of them was allowed to be ranked higher than an "Adjudant-Chef" because they were treated like mercenaries. All the officers higher than an "Adjudant-Chef" had to be French.

After recapturing Ban Bane, several French regiments returned to the Plain of Jars, leaving only the French Foreign Legion contingent in Ban Bane, with the mission to fortify the Sam Phou camp and to cleanse the Vietminh between Ban Bane and Phak Khaer. This contingent stayed in Ban Bane for a year and was later sent back to the Plain of Jars to get ready for deployment to Dien-Bien-Phu. It was replaced in Ban Bane by Battalion 6 of the Royal Lao Army under the command of Maj. Bounleuth Sanichan.

Before the Vietminh attacked the Plain of Jars in 1953, I was recruited in the military rank and sent to Vientiane, supposedly to later attend the Officer Training School in Pakse. For some reason, I did not get to go to Pakse and, instead, was sent back to the Plain of Jars to serve as an aide to the French Foreign Legion contingent stationed there. Five other individuals were with me at the Plain of Jars, including Sattasinh (Ms. Mou Soua's husband), Col. Bounnoi Noymani, Kongsadeng (a teacher and the son-in-law of Mr. Louis Lescure), and another person whose name I forgot. I served with the French Foreign Legion in Muang Kham for a year before Muang Kham was captured by the enemy.

During the retreat from Muang Kham, I served as a guide to the French regiment under the command of Capt. Rebour and Roland Selbe (the brother-in-law of Chao Saykham and the husband of Chao Phengdi) took them up to the Phou Sanh mountain range. We spent the night at the Hmong village of Ban Ham Kheu, near Ban Bouam Long (the village of Mr. Jeupao Moua) and, the following day, descended to Ban Nalam and walked our way to the Plain of Jars.

In 1953, I took my family to seek refuge in Hanoi, making that trip along with Phagna Touby's family. Capt. Max Blin warned me before that, "The Vietminh will attack the Plain of Jars in 1953. They will attack all the strategic roads and all the airbases." He said it would be wise to put my family in a safe place for a while.

On the day I was supposed to come back to the Plain of Jars from Hanoi, Hanoi's airport was attacked by the Vietminh. I saw French tanks moving around the airport.

Upon my return from Hanoi, I rejoined the French forces and participated in the reoccupation of Ban Bane. Shortly afterwards, Vietminh troops deployed from Tham La caves were poised to attack the military camp in Ban Bane, coming from Ban Chior and Ban Xieng Khoune. However, they were ambushed by the allies' Battalion 6 at Tat Peub Falls and Ban Xieng Khoune, had many soldiers killed in action, and were forced to retreat back to the Tham La cave. After this failed attack, the entire French Foreign Legion's Battalion 6 moved out of Ban Bane and was replaced by the Royal Lao Army's Battalion 6.

In 1955, I traveled to Bangkok, Thailand and met with a Lao delegation headed by Mr. Oun Sananikone. He took a group of villages and Tasseng elders, including tens of Hmong natives of Xieng Khouang, on an observation tour of several sites in Thailand, looking at rural development projects. From Bangkok, we visited Ayouthaya and Lopburi. While in Lopburi, we were told that many residents of that province, in Ban Mee District, were mostly Thai Phuans who came generations ago from Xieng Khouang and still spoke with a Lao Xieng Khouang accent. Back in Bangkok, Gen. Phao Srianon, Minister of the Interior of the Royal Thai Government, invited us to a dinner at the Erawan Hotel in honor of the Lao visitors.

In 1957, Prince Tiao Phetsarath returned from Thailand and went to visit Muang Kham. The Chaomuang of Muang Kham, along with his staff and the district elders, gathered together and held a welcome and well-wishing party for him at the Chaomuang's office. That same year, a Vietnamese delegation came from Hanoi to negotiate border issues at Ban Nam Kanh, Muang Nonghet. The negotiation was fruitless and had to be rescheduled in Hanoi. In September 1957, the delegates met there for several days but did not reach any agreement --just the agreement to meet again sometime in the future. I kept the documents on the border negotiations in my files until the day I left the country. I forwarded the photo of the Lao delegation to North Vietnam, along with the document that nominated them and the map of the contested border area, to Gen. Vang Pao in the USA via TouXoua Lyfoung (Touby Lyfoung's son), when he went to the USA for Phagna Tougeu Lyfoung's funeral in 2004.

In November 1957, I attended a meeting of the World Youth Association in Tokyo, Japan, along with H.E. Chao Sopsaysana, H.E. Inhpeng Souryathai, Mr. Pha Pholsena (a Ban Keunh's native), Tiao Sisa Ngouane (the wife of Pol. Gen. Vattha Phanekham), Mr. Bounketh, and Mr. Thao Ngo (President of the Vientiane Chinese Association). We flew from Vientiane to Saigon and then to Manila, The Philippines, where we stopped over for a short while. I was sitting on the same seat row as H.E. Inhpeng Souryathai on the flight to Tokyo.

On August 9, 1960, Capt. Kong Lae staged a coup d'état in Vientiane. At about the same time, the Chaokhoueng of Xieng Khouang was taking H.E. Bouavan Norasing on a trip to Muang Kham. After they overheard Kong Lae's coup d'état announcement over the radio, they then decided to hurry back home.

In December 1960, Kong Lae's troops and the communists attacked Muang Kham in three directions as follows:

o Kong Lae and Pathet Lao troops moved from the Plain of Jars to Ban Bane via Tat Peub Falls,
o Hmong Lor and North Vietnamese troops moved in from Nonghet and
o Vietnamese communist troops moved in from Tham La cave. When they arrived at Ban Chor, Ban Ban Xieng Khoune, they began heavy artillery fire on Muang Kham.

The allied troops did not know what to do because the attackers were firing from all directions. They then chose to retreat toward Muang Thae and then to Muang Phan. Before the communists attacked Ban Bane, Gen. Vang Pao and I led Hmong troops from Xieng Khouang to fight the Vietnamese and Pathet Lao in the flat area north of Ban Bane, near the road to Ban Kang Na and Ban Sop Ma. When I heard about Kong Lae's coup d'état and asked Gen. Vang Pao about it, he told me, "Kong Lae will come to Xieng Khouang for sure!" He had trees cut along the highway and disposed of them across the road to prevent traffic movement. But when Kong Lae retreated from Vientiane, he was still able to easily bring his troops to Muang Soui and seized Ban Bane, Muang Kham, the Plain of Jars, and Xieng Khouang successively very easily.

I left Muang Kham in the company of a military construction unit under the command of Lt. Oneta Phanivong. From Ban Ban, we spent the night in the forest up in the Muang Therr mountain range and then continued uphill in the direction of Ban Pha Phaat. We ran into Battalion 23, under the command of Capt. Ka Viphone, which was retreating from Samneua and Tham La and heading toward Muang Kham. From Ban Pha Phaat, I joined the regiment commanded by Lt. Nengchue Thao and Lt. Ly Naokao at Ban Tha Lin Noi and moved out with them at night to enter the highway between Dong Dane and Ban King, and headed toward Phou Khae. From Phou Khae, we walked across the plain around Ban Pha and headed up toward Ban Khang Khay (Chaomuang Youatong Yang's village).

Once we reached Ban Khang Kay, Gen. Vang Pao sent an HT-34 Helicopter to fly us to Padong LS05. At Padong, we led villagers in building an airstrip. Once the airstrip construction was over, I informed Gen. Vang Pao I was going to go to Vientiane and then to Savannakhet to meet with the governor of Xieng Khouang. At that time, the Xieng Khouang provincial office was temporarily located in Savannakhet, right behind the Savannakhet provincial office. I stayed in Savannakhet for several months and had a chance to gather the payroll records of Xieng Khouang administrative personnel. I actually went out to pay salaries to all the Xieng Khouang administrative officers working with the lowland Lao Battalion under Col. Chansom Pakdy Monivong and stationed at Phou Pha Khao, Xieng Khouang Province. After that, I came back to work at the Xieng Khouang temporary provincial office at the Department of Interior in Vientiane until 1962. That year, I rejoined Gen. Vang Pao at Long Cheng to make arrangements for the election of Xieng Khouang representatives. The General let my family and I stay in a house in front of his Long Cheng's residence.

In 1963, Chaokhoueng Saykham delivered the document that he wrote in French on the history of the Muang Phuan to Mr. Archambault in Bangkok. In 1965, after Gen. Vang Pao completed the construction of Samthong, I moved in there from Long Cheng.

I moved to France in 1976. Chao Sayasouk Southakakoumane (Chao Saykham's son), who studied in France, showed me Chao Saykham's document on the history of Muang Phuan and a tutorial book on oriental culture compiled by the Ecole d'Extreme Orient (Far-East Institute). The tutorial book went as far back as Chao Chetchieung and his son Khoun Boulom, who came from Muang Thene in the 7th or 8th century to establish the Muang Phuan princedom. I found out that the book contains several pages of Lao quotes from Chaomuang Thao Phane of Muang Kham, as excerpted from the letter he wrote to Prince Phetsarath on the same subject.

WORKING FOR GEN. VANG PAO (1962 -1975)

n 1965, Gen. Vang Pao took me to Phou Pha Thee, Houaphan Province, with him. We spent the night at Ban Pha Thi --located in the foothill near the trail to the top of the mountain—with Lt. Kia Tou Va Lue Vang, commander of the regiment in charge of the defense of Phou Pha Thi. The purpose of the visit was to have an open discussion with the elders, administrative leaders, and Hmong constituents about the election of the Hmong Chaomuang (district chief) by the name of Lao Thai. The discussions were quite lengthy and lasted from early evening to 11 or 12 p.m. After the town hall meeting, we ate a late dinner with pork tartare as the main dish. This dish was very tasty, especially when we were a little bit hungry. After that night, I became sick while on the way from Phou Pha Thi to Samthong and had to stay at the Samthong's hospital. The Philippine physician, Dr. Jany, gave me some medicine and asked me, "What did you eat over there?" I said, "I had some pork tartare and suspect the meat might not be well cooked." He said, "Yes, eating uncooked pork meat would certainly make you sick. In the future, never eat uncooked meat again."

Photo #90. *Vientiane's Wattai Airport under flood water in 1966 -- –an omen that the situation would get worse and that many changes would take place in the country. Lt. Col. Vang, Geu's photos collections and source, see in Unforgettable Laos.*

When I was stationed in the Samthong-Long Cheng area, each time Gen. Vang Pao visited a military camp, he would almost always take me along with him. I saw him fire artillery quite a few times. In 1966, we went to Ban Hai, near Ban Kang Na and Ban Houa Na (Sopna), a flat area around Ban Bane, right before the North Vietnamese and the Pathet Lao seized Muang Kham and Xieng Khouang. We visited the battle field of Tha Vieng –Ban Kieo Manang, Muang Omm--, Tha Vieng and Tha Thom –headquarters of Regiment 13, which, under the command of Col. Chansom Pakdymonivong, just occupied the town. We went to Muang Ngarn and visited the important base at the top of the Hom Chong Mountain overlooking Muang Ngarn. We went to the battle field of Houa Muang and the Phou Thong Lott Mountain, near Kiew Famut, where our troops were stationed before they seized Kiew Famuth. We stayed in Na Khang and then went to the Plain of Jars, Lat Houang and Phongsavan. When we were in Lat Houang, we climbed the nearby mountain top overlooking Ban Na Nou. When our soldiers saw the North Vietnamese troops running across the village, they fired artillery in the enemy's direction. Pretty soon, the enemy fired back. Fortunately, their shell hit a tree near where we were standing. Had it not hit that tree, one wonders what would have happened to us. This was really a sign of miraculous protection provided by the angels.

In 1966, the year Vientiane was flooded by the Mekong River flows, we visited the construction site of the future Nam Ngum Dam, as well as other similar dam sites in Thailand. Following a favorable site inspection by the Japanese experts, the Chaomuangs from all over the Lao kingdom paid a visit to the site of the dam to be built on the Nam Ngum River. Material excavated from the ground was stored in a big building at the dam site.

In Thailand, we went to the site of the already completed Oubolrat Dam in Khone Kaen Province. Following that visit, the Thai authorities invited all the Lao guests to stop by Ban Xieng, a village where Thai Phouan refugees were resettled after being forced out of Xieng Khouang before Khone Kaen Province was created. Upon our arrival, local leaders, elders and Ban Xieng residents offered a splendid Baci welcoming ceremony, complete with flowers and candles and floor cultural dances, to the visiting Lao Chaomuangs. After the Baci ceremony, the host elders confided that they were descendants of Phuan immigrants and said they were not sure how they ended up there.

But once they were here, they wasted no time rebuilding their lives and living conditions, forging friendships, taking care of each other, and setting the base for trading and commodity exchanges. They said they did not practice the same exchanges with residents who moved in from other areas, did not know them, and, in the end, could not stay on for those reasons. The Ban Xieng residents grew mulberry, raised mulberry silkworms, and worked together very well as a closely-knit team. After the visit to Ban Xieng, we went to the office of the Governor of Oudorn Province. The Governor gave the Lao Chaomuangs a one-hour briefing on his province's agriculture, cattle raising, social development, and natural resources programs. He then took them to the national library, a newly completed 7-story building in Khon Kaen Province. The tour guide explained that this library had to be able to store at least 1.2 million books to cover all the needs. At that time, only 600,000 books were in the library.

ACTIVITIES PERFORMED AFTER THE CREATION OF SAMTHONG

In cooperation with Gen.VangPao, XiengKhouang Governor ChaoSaykham Southakakoumane and military and civilian leaders invited King Savang Vatthana, the Queen, and members of the Royal Lao Government led by Prime Minister Prince Souvanna Phouma, and Royal Lao Army generals to visit Long Cheng. Provincial military and civilian leaders welcomed the King and the Queen with a Baci welcoming ceremony at the officers' club in Samthong. At the end of the ceremony, the King thanked the General, the Provincial Governor, the military and civilian provincial leaders and the general population who attended the event. He said, "No matter where we are, do not forget to look after each other. We are all the descendants of Khum Boulom."

Before the Baci ceremony, Mr. Lo Khamthi had the opportunity to ask Prince Souvanna Phouma a question at Chaokhoueng Saykham Southakakoumane's residence. He said, "Your Highness, I'm concerned about our country since you and your brother have brought in North Vietnamese to fight a war in Laos. After the war, I'm afraid we will never have enough time to fully replay them with our blood. What do you think?" Prince Souvanna Phouma answered, "Don't worry. I have already talked with North Vietnamese Prime Minister Pham-Van-Dong. He told me that once the Americans leave Indochina, the North Vietnamese see no further need to keep their troops in Laos. That's what he said." Mr. Lokhamthi reacted, "Nothing to worry about, really? Your Highness, when our rice crops are ripe, please do not let the North Vietnamese come in and pick them up!" Prince Souvanna Phouma remained speechless.

After the North Vietnamese seized Samthong, the Governor's office was relocated to the mouth of Pak Meuy River, a tributary of the Nam Ngum River. I got a malaria fever that lasted for several months and almost took my life. One night, I stayed at Gen. Vang Pao's residence and tried to get an intravenous antibiotic shot from Dr. Khammeung. The doctor told me that malaria could never be cured regardless of how many drugs I was taking because its germs were deeply entrenched in my body. The only way out is through the infusion of salt water and repeated injections over several days to allow salt water to seep through the whole body and kill all the germs. Another guest at Gen. Vang Pao's house was Mr. Thip Thammavong, the father-in-law of Mr. Tougeu Lyfoung. That same night, the enemy came through the Phra Rassavang Mountain and fired mortar shells at Long Cheng. Aircrafts flying in from an unknown spot also dropped bombs over the area between Long Cheng and Nam Ngoua and caused several fatalities among the population in 1971.

In 1973, I was admitted to Mong Kout Kao Hospital in Bangkok, Thailand, along with Col. Khamhoung Pravonviengkham, who was there for intestinal disease treatment. Gen. Ouane Ratikoun, Commander of the Royal Lao Army, was also there for kidney stone surgery. He said the stone was the size of a small fingertip and that this was his third kidney operation. This was the same year when Gen. Thao Ma and Col. Bounleuth Saycocie dropped bombs on Chinaimo and Phon Kheng camps in August. Gen. Thao Ma was caught and killed following the air raid.

The ongoing negotiations between the communist and the Vientiane factions ran into several problems and caused the Vientiane faction to distrust the communist faction. Because the half-Vietnamese Lao leader Kaysone Phomvihane brought thousands of communist troops into Laos, the Vientiane faction had to ask Gen. Thao Ma and Gen. Phoumi Nosavan to set up a coup d'état. This was made without the knowledge of MR-V Commander, Gen. Kouprasith Abhay, who then put up a strong defense because of previous episodes of conflicts in 1965 when he himself organized a coup d'état and forced Gen. Thao Ma and Gen. Phoumi to flee to Thailand. The 1973 bombing was the second air operation Gen. Thao Ma performed. This time, he could not escape; his plane was shot down, and he had to make an emergency landing, got arrested and was killed on the spot at the Wattai Airport by Gen. Kouprasith. This event might have played a role in Gen.

22

Bounpone Marktheparak's decision not to leave the country. He was eventually put into jail by the communists and died under extremely excruciating conditions at the Vieng Xay re-education camp.

Gen. Vang Pao and Chaokhoueng Saykham were both great leaders who understood and were sensitive to each and every need of the population. They implemented assistance programs that allowed their constituents to become self-sufficient, get some education, stay well-informed, have a good future, and practice religions because religions teach people to be honest. They did everything they could, but their intentions were not completely fulfilled because of the political insecurity that prevailed all over the region.

THE FEBRUARY 21, 1972 EVENT

This was the day President Nixon, his wife, and selected members of his cabinet visited Peking in mainland China. That same night, Gen. Vang Pao, one US journalist, Col. Tou Fue, several troopers, and I flew on a powerful helicopter to the top of Phou Bia to spend the night. I was not quite sure which mountain peak we landed on, but the whole mountain range looked so grandiose and had many summits. The wind was blowing around the clock, even when we were asleep. This was indeed a high-elevation spot covered with unfrozen ice. It was so cold we could not sleep, had to keep burning wood to stay warm, and spent time chatting all night with the US journalist. We listened to the radio broadcast from Peking about the reception provided by the Chinese Government, just one battalion of honor troops that greeted President Nixon and escorted him to the hotel in downtown Peking. China did not mount a huge reception like it did for Prince Sihanouk, the King of Cambodia, when he visited China earlier and was greeted by a big crowd of Chinese who threw flowers on the ground in his honor all the way from the airport to the hotel.

[Thank you, Nha Luang Bounchanh, for sharing your notes on your personal involvements in the 1945-1975 events with all our younger readers].

HOUAPHAN PROVINCE'S ADMINISTRATIVE SYSTEM

The governor of Houaphanh Province in 1947 was Kinim Pholsena, followed in 1949 by Van Tanovan. Chaokhoueng Van Tanovan's deputy, Khampane Boungnarith, was later executed by the Pathet Lao Communists after they seized Houaphan Province. Later on, Thongsavath Vongsavanthong became the provincial governor, with Champa as his deputy. The situation in Houaphan Province has often been in turmoil as a result of the communist invasion, leading to the nomination of military officers as acting provincial governors and forcing many military families to move to other out-of-province locations. The first acting military governor was Col. Khamsao Keovilay, followed by Col. Thong Vongrasamy (who died in 1965 while trying to rescue an American pilot who was shot down by the enemy). His replacement, Col. Phanh Siharath, was killed in action in 1969. The next acting governor was Col. Boun Noi, with Ounkham Outhaythani as deputy. In 1973, the acting governor was Col. Chansom Pakdy, with two deputies --Sim Vichit Vongsa and Thongsonh Sophamixay. *(Thongsonh graduated from the Law School in Vientiane, went on a training program in France, and was assassinated in 1973 at Ban Son for political reasons)*.

The Police Department was led by Col. Khampheng Sophamixay.

Houaphanh Province consisted of 7 districts, as listed below with the names of the district chiefs:

- o Muang Samneua: Phia Sene Phomma Nivong (Lao);
- o Hua Muang: Phomma (Lao);
- o Muang Xiengkhor: Eng Phouangsavath (Lao);
- o Muang Sone: Phanthavong Pavongvieng Kham (Lao);
- o Muang Sui: Theng Soyavong (Lao); followed by Outhone S. Phabmixay
- o Muang Sam Tay: Bouaket Bounlutai (Lao); and
- o Muang Hong Nonh: Lao Thai Va Lue Vang (Hmong).

Photo #91. The Buddhist temple was built in Long Cheng in 1972 with a golden anchor under the direction of Xieng Khouang provincial about Phra Maha Khamphan Nanthavong (currently living in France, who later brought in a large Buddha statue from Thailand in 1973). Lt. Col. Vang, Geu's photos collections and source, see in Unforgettable Laos.

In 1975, Col. Phan Ene was the Commander of the Houa Phanh Military sub-region until May 14, 1975. Elected provincial representatives were Mua Xeu, Phom Bounlutay and Sim Vichitvongsa.

24

Photo #92. *Chaomuang Lao Thai Va Lue Vang*

Lt. Col. Vang, Geu's photos collections and source, see in Unforgettable Laos.

[Thanks to Chaomuang Lao Thai Va Lue Vang, School principal Boudtharangsy Bouasavann, Pol. Maj. Hang Doua, and deputy-Governor Bounchanh Vouthisisombath for sharing these historical records with all our younger readers and helping them understand why the Hmong and the lowland Lao had to seek political refugee in several countries around the world. Please read the biography of Chaomuang Lao Thai Va Lue Vang in Chapter 20].

HEALTH DEPARTMENT OF MILITARY REGION II

The first Medical Commander was Col. Dr. Khammeung, assisted by Lt. Col. Bounthanh. In 1972, when Col. Dr. Khammeung was transferred to Vientiane, his replacement was Lt. Col. Dr. Bounthanh, assisted by Lt. Nang Leua. Eighty percent of the population living in the territories ruled by Gen. Vang Pao received adequate modern health care thanks to the US, who provided medical supplies and set up the Senesouk Clinic in Samthong – a clinic that was destroyed by the Communists in early 1969. All the medical equipment at the clinic was lost, but the medical staff was safely relocated to Ban Xone-Naxou (LS272) and stayed there until May 14, 1975.

CHAPTER 5

MILITARY PILOTS IN MILITARY REGION II

In early 1966, Gen. Vang Pao asked for US help in training Hmong pilots to fly T-28 aircraft. Lowland Lao T-28 pilots got their training in 1965 but, once they graduated, were rather reluctant to be deployed to MR-II, partly because of dialect linguistic problems. Therefore, Gen. Vang Pao was asking for special training that focused on the Hmong recruits who would be willing to serve in MR-II, knowing very well that, practically, almost none of them spoke any English.

THE FIRST GROUP OF HMONG T-28 PILOTS

The first group of Hmong T-28 pilots included Vang Toua, Vang Chou, Vang Ge and Ly Lu. Following his graduation in 1966, Vang Toua flew a T28 aircraft with two Lao pilots to drop bombs on the enemy along the Ho Chi Minh Trail near Thakhek. All three pilots disappeared. It was possible their plane might have hit the mountain during a cloudy day of the rainy season that severely limited the pilot's visibility. Another possibility was that their planes could have been shot down by the enemy when they were flying at a low altitude. Vang Chou and Vang Ge did not complete the training, only Vang Toua and Ly Lu did.

In 1966, Ly Lu was asked by Maj. Gen. Vang Pao to come and work closely with him at MR-II. Lao and Hmong pilots also took turns serving in Long Cheng. Ly Lu led his Hmong and Lao colleagues in fighting the enemy whenever allied troops were being deployed. He was a courageous pilot who dropped bombs with extreme precision, even on ground holes where the enemy was hiding. In 1967, 1968 and 1969, the North Vietnamese Communists were demoralized by the bombing raids flown by Ly Lu and other Lao pilots. Wherever the enemy dare-devil troops were stationed, it was almost certain that all of them would be buried at that same location.

In the middle of 1969, Maj. Gen. Vang Pao started the "Thanong Kiat" (Safeguarding Honor) Operation between the Plain of Jars and Muang Soui, pushing the enemy out of the area. There were two major enemy resistance points located over two mountains east of Muang Soui that were equipped with 12.8 mm and 14.6 mm machine guns and 122 mm artilleries firing at the allies when there were no aircrafts flying in the air. Therefore, Maj. Gen. Vang Pao ordered Ly Lu and two other Lao pilots to drop 500-pound bombs to create at least one meter-deep cavities. The bombs were dropped one by one along the mountain ridges from east to west. Ly Lu fully executed the order, but his aircraft was heavy due to the weight of the bombs and the two pilots on board. The back-seat pilot, Lor Neng, was there to learn how to drop bombs from Ly Lu.

The first flight was a non-event, but during the second flight, when the aircraft was climbing up, it was fired from the rear by the enemy using 12.8 mm and 14.6 mm anti-aircraft guns. The T-28 airplane got shot, was inflamed and fell to the ground. No pilots were seen jumping off on parachutes. Gen. Vang Pao was very sad and went home with tears in his eyes. The next day, the allied troops captured the mountain camps and searched for the bodies of Capt. Ly Lu and Lt. Lo

Neng to bring them back for a funeral in Long Cheng. Pilot Ly Lu was a great and courageous fighter, who was never afraid to go on missions and fully executed his duties performance. He was a pilot who went on flying missions daily and had more flying hours to his credit than any other pilot in the world. He was well-known and highly regarded by US military experts.

Photo #93*. From left to right: Vam Ntxawg Tsheej (Backseat of Raven), Ly Tou xiong T28, Xiong Kuam T28, Gen. Vang Pao MR-II Commander, Yang Xiong T 28, Raven Pilot & Commander of Chao Pha Khao MR-II, Yang Bee T28 pilot. Photo taken in 1971, the year of the heaviest enemy attack on Long Cheng. Lt. Col. Vang, Geu's photos collections and source, see in Unforgettable Laos.*

After Capt. Ly Lu's class, there were many other pilot classes as listed below.

THE SECOND GROUP OF HMONG T-28 PILOTS

The second group in 1967 included the pilots listed below, along with a quick summary of their duties and how they survived/died:

1. **Lo Neng** was killed with pilot Ly Lu in 1969;
2. **Ly Yeng:** killed in action in 1970 when the aircraft he was flying was shot down and fell on a big tree near the Plain of Jars;
3. **Nhia Thao** was shot down in the Plain of Jars in 1970. His body was never found;
4. **Mua Teng** was shot down in the Phou Hinh Tang Mountain in 1971 after the enemy recaptured the Plain of Jars;
5. **Vang Dao** landed short on the wrong airstrip at Long Cheng, could not put the brakes on time, hit a storehouse and died on the spot;
6. **Heu Ying** died during training in a plane accident. The flight instructor was able to safely jump off the aircraft, but not the student pilot;

7. **Yang Xiong** a clever pilot fully involved in air operations against the enemy. His aircraft got hit many times by anti-aircraft guns, but he always closely escaped danger. He flew Raven 01 aircraft for a little over a year, locating enemy positions, and became the commander of the Chao Pha Khao pilots in Military Region II. He immigrated to the US and died in Minnesota in 2005 from illness;

8. **Vang Seng** performed air operations against the enemy for about two years. He lost his life due to bad weather conditions, as described in the following paragraphs. Col. Cher Pao Mua, commander of the allied forces in Bouam Long (LS 32), asked Gen. Vang Pao for air support just the night before the enemy heavily attacked them around the mountain range west of the Bouam Long airport. The enemy was also digging a tunnel toward the allies' military post and was about to reach it while also continuously firing big guns at the camp. This prevented the allied forces from performing their enemy-cleansing operation and prompted them to ask for air support. Vang Seng volunteered to fly solo to help Col. Cher Pao Mua, who also happened to be his father-in-law.

Photo #94 (left). T-28 pilot Capt. Vang Seng was sent to LS 32 to give air support to his father-in-law. The mission was successful, but the weather was bad. He planned to fly low in order to land at L20A but hit a tree, crashed and died in December 1971.

Photo #95 (right). High-ranking civilian and military officers marching behind Capt. Vang Seng's coffin to the burial site. Photo taken in 1971 at Long Chenng, XiengKhouang, Laos. Lt. Col. Vang, Geu's photos collections and source, see in Unforgettable Laos.

According to Col. Cher Pao Mua's testimony, about one hour before Vang Seng reached his bomb-dropping target, several strange phenomena occurred. The Lao flag that hung on top of a pole in the middle of the field fell to the ground without any wind blowing around. The thick clouds that used to cover the mountain top surrounded by the enemy suddenly lifted off, allowing Vang Seng to easily spot the enemy's bunker. Vang Seng dropped bombs on the enemy's tunnel and killed all the soldiers in the bunker. This also silenced all enemy's heavy gun firing.

The allied forces were then able to continue their cleansing operation. Col. Cher Pao Mua was very satisfied with the results and asked Vang Seng to go back for one more round to finish off the enemy's artillery close to the camp. However, Vang Seng disappeared from the sky and never returned. What actually happened was that when Vang Seng flew back from Bouam Long to Long Cheng, thick clouds prevented him from accurately locating the airport. This forced him to fly at a lower altitude to go through the clouds and try to land at the airport. In the process, he had to fly over Phou Mork Mountain, which was covered with tall trees. Unfortunately, his airplane hit the trees, broke into two pieces, and fell to the ground. *[I personally flew in to look for the aircraft and was able to locate its dislocated pieces as well as Vang Seng's body. I took the body back to Long Cheng for religious rituals in early December 1971].*

9. **Vang Su** performed his air pilot mission extremely well. He flew over several enemy camps and was able to drop bombs very accurately on enemy targets, very much like pilot Ly Lu. He got shot twice by the enemy's anti-aircraft guns. The first time, he survived thanks to the help from a US helicopter and suffered no wounds. But the second time, Vang Su got shot by the enemy's 37 mm anti-aircraft guns and didn't realize they created a big deadly wall in front of him.

In 1972, the allied forces recaptured the Plain of Jars from the enemy and were in action all the way to Lath Sene. The enemy left behind a tank in the middle of a courtyard at Lath Sene as they rushed out to hide from the aircraft and had no time to drive the tank away. That morning, Lytou Xong was the Raven 01 pilot who helped locate the enemy's position and asked T-28 pilot Vang Be to destroy the three tanks that were on the highway. Two of the tanks were damaged, but the third one did not get hit too badly as the aircrafts were running out of bombs. That's how the tank was left behind. Gen. Vang Pao then ordered pilots Vang Su and Mua Chue to go back and finish it off.

When Vang Su arrived at the scene, the situation had changed. The enemy was already well prepared to protect the tank and pick it up as soon as ordered to do so. The first bomb that Vang Su dropped did not hit the target. Pilot Mua Chue, who followed him in a north-to-south direction, dropped a bomb that also missed the target. Vang Su called Mua Chue and told him, "Be, watch me. If I still miss my target this time, you can call me Doggie!" Vang Su made his second attempt, flying again from north to south, but the enemy had installed two 37 mm anti-aircraft guns at Ban Tone, west of Lath Sene, and fired them at Vang Su, putting a big blackboard in front of him. When hit by the bullets, Vang Su's aircraft fell to the ground at Lath Sene. Mua Chue veered up high in the sky and dropped the bombs he had left on the enemy's anti-aircraft artilleries. A loud explosion ensued, bringing tears to Mua Chue's eyes –these are Mua Chue's own words. He then flew back to Long Cheng.

As sunset was approaching, this was not the right time to pick up Vang Su's body. The next day, the allied forces attacked the enemy and reached the area where Vang Su's aircraft fell to the ground. As Commander of the Second Division, I ordered a contingent of 50 soldiers to plough the field, looking for Vang Su's body. They did find pieces of the aircraft but not his body. I then did the field ploughing myself, walking along the banks of the Nam Sene Creek. I detected a bamboo stem floating in the middle of the stream with a scarf wrapped around it. I was intrigued and asked the soldiers to bring that stem in. Sure enough, Vang Su's body was there, attached to the bamboo stem. We took it back to Long Cheng for the funeral.

2

Photo #96 (left). *Capt. Vang Sue, T-28 Pilot. He was assigned by Gen. Vang Pao to finish one of the enemy tanks in the plain of Lat Sene, Xieng Khouang Province. He was hit by the enemy's 37mm anti-aircraft. His plane blew up and killed him in July 1972.*

Photo #97 (right). *Pilot Vang Seng's funeral. L to R. Vue Neng, Vang Sue (T28 pilot), Yang Xiong (T-28 & Raven 01 pilot) and Vang Bee (HT 34 pilot). Photo taken in 1971 at Long Cheng. Lt. Col. Vang, Geu's photos collections and source, see in Unforgettable Laos.*

10. **Vue Ger** was only on duty for a short period when he was hit by the enemy's anti-aircraft. The enemy was using ultra-modern anti-aircraft weapons to shoot at T-28, an aircraft of World War II vintage, rather slow-moving and more suitable for training purposes than for actual air operations. T-28 was still very effective in supporting troop movements. Whenever the enemy chooses to fight to death, that place will end up being the site of their burial.

Photo #98. T-28 pilot Vue Ger in 1970 . Lt. Col. Vang, Geu's photos collections and source, see in Unforgettable Laos.

THE THIRD GROUP OF HMONG T-28 PILOTS

The 1968 class T-28 pilots graduated in 1970 and included the following:

3

1. **Ly Teng:** flew T-28 and C-47 aircrafts and immigrated in 1975 to California, USA;
2. **Vue Long:** was killed in 1971 near Phou Lieng Kai Mountain (between Phou Pha Xay and Phou Hinh Tang);
3. **Vang Bee:** a T-28 pilot who had more flying hours than any other pilot. Here are some more pertinent details:

- 1970-1973: flew T-28 aircraft. 1973-1975: flew Baron aircraft
- 1974-1975: flew Cessna and Baron Airplanes as Gen. Vang Pao's personal pilot
- 1973: flew T-28 to support allied forces at Muang Mork. His aircraft was shot down by the enemy at LS46, but he was rescued by US and Lao pilots
- On March 13, 1973, Gen. Vang Pao offered a spiritual, well-whishing ceremony on the same day for both pilots Vang Be and Mua Chue.

Photo #99. T-28 pilot Vang Be in 1973

Lt. Col. Vang, Geu's photos collections and source, see in Unforgettable Laos.

[**Notes from the author**. I remember what pilot Vang Be once said, "The North Vietnamese fire according to plan and with great accuracy. They also used ploys. If you don't pay attention, you will be the loser. When we are in the air, we are strategically ahead. But we have to watch the enemy's reaction, be familiar with the ground, be aware of the weather conditions that were predicted to occur during the planned operation, and know how to fly up into the sky and down onto the ground. Unless it was deemed necessary, the enemy would not fire at an aircraft." Vang Be added, "Each time the allies asked for air support and warned that the enemy is equipped with anti-aircraft guns, the pilots should attack the anti-aircraft positions first…. The enemy is normally more afraid of T-28 than a jet aircraft."]

In 1971, the allies used the following forces to attack the Plain of Jars:

- Regiments 21 and 26, with the mission to seize Lath Bouak and Phou Houat and use them as strongholds
- Regiments 24 and 22, along with some of Cher Pao Mua's forces, with the mission to seize Nongpet and Tatpeub in an attempt to cut Highway 7 behind the enemy line.

Pilot Vang Be used to say, "Bomb dropping to support allied troops' movement during the Lath Bouak's operation revealed that the enemy was not afraid of T-28 aircraft at all. They just went out screaming at T-28s and even fired small guns at them. We can drop bombs over them as if they were chickens or pigs." After the allies seized the area's mountain range, they discovered that the enemy had left hundreds of dead bodies in the valley and ground holes.

For more details, please read Air Forces Capt. Vang Be in Chapter 20, Selected Biographies.

It was noticed that the dead bodies were from both men and women who were still fairly young. This was an enemy ploy. Also, since their anti-aircraft artillery was installed near Khang Khay, each time an aircraft flew through the valley in a south-to-north direction to drop bombs, the enemy would always be able to shoot it down. This was within the 10,000+ foot shooting range of their 37 mm anti-aircraft guns were good at. By comparison, the T-28 aircraft's flying range was only about 8,000 feet during up and down maneuvers before and after the bomb dropping.

Pilots made their attack plan based on the topography and the enemy's movement. Nongpet was located in a narrow valley to the east and the west. This caused the enemy to believe for sure that the pilots, in order to drop bombs on the valley, would have to fly in a south-to-north direction. Furthermore, at the time, the pilots did not fly very high –just slightly above the mountain top, dropped their bombs, moved toward the allies' bases, and came back to the targets over and over again. Pilot Vang Be said, "Bomb dropping during that air operation had caused more enemy damages than during any other previous air operations."

Pilot Vang Be was a very capable and extremely courageous man. While almost all the Hmong and Lao military officers quickly immigrated to other countries, pilot Vang Be chose to flee into the jungle and continued his fight against the communists from 1975 to 1984. Later on, he crossed the Mekong River to Thailand and went on to start a new life in the US as a result of political changes and the absence of international assistance.

4. **Xiong Koua:** after training, served duties for several months at Long Cheng. When he came back from one of the missions and tried to land at Long Cheng airport, a Charlie Green Helicopter flew in front of him and blew his T-28 off the airstrip. Xiong Koua jumped from the plane, but when the parachute opened, part of its strings hit one of his eyes. After losing an eye, he stopped flying the T-28. He is now a US Citizen living in Chicago, Illinois, USA.

5. **Mua Chue:** was a smart T-28 pilot with good decision-making skills and warm friendships with his peers, very keen at performing his duties, and a pilot who shot targets more accurately than many other pilots. At one point in August 1972, the Second Division led by Col. Geu Vang moved to Lath Sene to liberate the Plain of Jars. He called pilots Mua Chue and Vang Bee to help because so many enemy troops were stationed on the nearby mountain. Vang Bee was the first to land; with Mua Chue and Yang Bee providing cover. As soon as Vang Bee landed, anti-aircraft shells were sprayed over him, forcing him to take off. Mua Chue called him and said, *Look at me and see how it works.* He then flew up as high as possible --around 10,000 feet or more-- then flew vertically down around 8,000 feet above the enemy position and dropped all six bombs in one trip. Two anti-aircraft guns were completely destroyed. Vang Bee and Yang Bee did exactly the same. They dropped all

their bombs as well. The other two antiaircraft guns were destroyed, too. The ground troops later occupied the position and saw the dead bodies of many North Vietnamese Communists. Four of them were chained to their 14.6 mm anti-aircraft guns, with no way to run away from the bombs.

Mua Chue, Vang Su, Yang Bee, and Vang Seng were very brave pilots that year but, Vang Su, Vang Seng were later killed in the battle. In 1973, when the North-Vietnamese communists came closer to Long Cheng, Mua Chue was ordered to destroy their 12.8 mm machine guns near Phou Mok (Skyline II). His plane was hit and caught on fire. He jumped out and landed near the airport in Long Cheng. This was a couple of weeks before Vang Bee's plane was shot down in LS46. In 1976, Mua Chue's brother-in-law (who then lived in France) petitioned his family members to go to France from the refugee camp at Nam Phong, Thailand. Mua Chue passed away in France in 2000, due to depression, because he badly missed the rest of his family and friends.

6. **Ly Tou Xiong:** a well-groomed person. He liked to joke and was somewhat of a playboy. He was a good T-28 pilot but could not strike the targets accurately. He flew the T-28 for two years. In 1972, Gen. Vang Pao assigned him as a Raven 01 pilot to locate enemy targets support and guide the movements of ground troops. In May 1972, Ly Tou Xiong and Yang Xiong were given the mission to cover Division II in their operation to reoccupy the Plain of Jars. In early June 1972, at dawn, Yang Xiong located Lt. Col. Vang Youa, Commander of Regiment 23, who was badly wounded in battle the night before and could not walk. The enemy surrounded him and his guard. Yang Xiong called the HT34 to rescue him. The HT34 was led by Col. Geu Vang, Commander of Division II, who asked Yang Xiong to shoot a smoke rocket to identify Lt. Col. Vang Youa's location. Lt. Col. Vang Youa and his guard had killed several North Vietnamese around them before dawn and were almost captured by the enemy. Yang Xiong arrived on time and covered them, and called HT34 to rescue Lt. Col. Vang Youa. The rescue by the HT34 was a success, but by the time the HT34 flew out, it was repeatedly shot at by the enemy. Miraculously, none of the bullets hit the HT34.

The mission to rescue Lt. Col. Vang Youa was a suicide mission because the North-Vietnamese had completely surrounded the area. As the HT34 returned to the base at Long Cheng, the HT34 pilot Lt. Sisavanh Vongnaphone looked over his plane and said, *"It was God who saved us and the plane from being hit."* [Sisavanh Vong Naphone immigrated to Elgin, Illinois USA. He died in 2001, and was survived by his wife Nang Bounheuang Vong Naphone and children]. At Lath Sene, early in the morning before Lt. Col. Vang Youa was hit, three North-Vietnamese communists' destroyer tanks were in the pursuit of Division II's ground troops.

In early June 1972; in response to the Commander of Regiment 23's call for air support, Ly Tou Xiong flew a Raven 01 in and suddenly appeared in the sky. When the enemy saw the Raven, they jumped out of their tanks and ran away in the open field to hide under the tall grass. Ly Tou Xiong launched anti-personnel rockets to the enemy soldiers instead of trying to destroy the tanks, and did kill many of the fleeing soldiers. He also called the T-28 pilots to fly in and destroy the tanks. One tank was left unscathed and still parked near the middle of the plain at Lath Sene. Gen. Vang Pao ordered Vang Sue and Mua Chue to destroy this last tank, which was equipped with 37 mm anti-aircraft gun that was then used to shoot down Vang Sue's plane and kill him.

4

In 1973, Ly Tou Xiong was flying a Cessna at Gen. Vang Pao's order, because the war had already practically ended. He flew the general to many places to visit the population in Military Region II. In December 1973, Ly Tou Xiong flew him to Nam Fene (LS223), and then flew back to Long Cheng with Vang Chong. It was cloudy and Ly Tou Xiong tried to fly low, at about 500 feet above ground. While following the road near Phak Khet Mountain, Ly Tou Xiong hit a tree and both pilots were killed instantly at 8 a.m. Vang Chong, who died with Ly Tou Xiong, was a HT34 pilot. He completed pilot training in 1973, just a few months before his death.

7. **Yang Bee** was a T28 pilot and a sharp shooter. He immigrated to San Diego, California USA.

8. **Yang Pao** was a T28 pilot for a few months and was assigned the mission to destroy the enemy's 12.8 mm and 37mm anti aircraft guns at Nam Sene Valley. His plane was too slow for 37 mm and 14.6 anti-aircraft guns. He was shot down on March 23, 1972. He jumped out and was captured by the North-Vietnamese communists, but was released in 1978. Vang Bee went to help him and guided him to Thailand. He was a refugee in California.

9. **Vang Seng Khang,** after graduation as a T28 pilot, flew only two missions. He saw many anti-aircraft guns and was scared to death. He fell sick and could not carry out any more flying missions. Gen. Vang Pao had a doctor give him a physical exam. The doctor diagnosed nothing wrong with him, so he was instructed to go home and recover, but he never returned to duty.

10. **Bounchanh,** the first Lao Theung minority T-28 pilot, flew missions for about one year. On June 23, 1972 Gen. Vang Pao ordered him to destroy the 86 mm artillery in Ban Hine Tang (LS 74). His plane was shot down during that mission and he was rescued by fellow HT34 pilots. He immigrated to California USA. *[Many young Lao Theung ethnics had undergone training to become T-28 pilots, but many of them did not pass the tests because of the English language barrier]*.

11. **Sau Thao and Nhia Thao** were twin brothers. Sau Thao was a T-28 pilot. He flew several missions and was shot down. His body was never recovered.

12. **Nhia Thao** was greatly upset about his brother's death. On April 3, 1972, Gen. Vang Pao ordered Nhia Thao and a Lao Pilot to drop bombs near Ban Ban, close to the Laos/Vietnam border. The two pilots disappeared, and their bodies have never been recovered.

THE FOURTH GROUP OF HMONG T28 PILOTS

The fourth group of Hmong T28 pilots finished their training at the end of 1972. This group included the following:

1. **Vang Tou,** who flew several missions. On his last mission, as he was landing, he landed short on the airstrip and found no way to fly out. He hit the building nearby and broke his nose. He stopped flying and immigrated to the US where he now lives in North-Carolina.
2. **Vang Teng,** who flew a few missions in 1972 and some in 1973. He came as a refugee to St. Paul, Minnesota, USA where he still lives. He has a heart problem and is very weak in 2009.
3. **Ly Yang,** who flew only a few missions. He is a refugee now living in Mississippi, USA.
4. **Yang Phong,** who flew few missions. He is also a refugee living in St. Paul, Minnesota, USA.
5. **Ly Mua,** who flew few missions. He is a refugee in the USA, at an unknown location.

THE FIFTH GROUP OF HMONG T-28 PILOTS

The fifth group of Hmong T28 pilots, who completed training in 1973, included the following:

1. **Vang Foua:** completed training just as Laos fell to the Communists. He immigrated to the USA and now resides in Georgia, USA.
2. **Mua Soua:** had not served in Laos. He immigrated to the USA and now resides in California, USA.
3. **Yang Ge:** nicknamed "Cheu Tha," immigrated to the USA and now resides in Ohio.
4. **Yia Khang:** immigrated to the USA and now lives in Narvon, Pennsylvania.

THE ROLE OF A T-28 AIRCRAFT

One T28 plane could carry six bombs of 250 pounds each, or four bombs weighing 500 pounds each, and two 12.7mm machine guns holding cartridges for about 1,000 rounds. It could carry CBU Bombs (Cluster Bomb Unit) and many rockets. The T28 could fly about four hours and was efficient in helping ground troops to mount offensive or defensive attack against enemy troops. Without air support, our troops would not be able to fight the North-Vietnamese communists. In addition, the North-Vietnamese were strongly supported by the Communists around the world, especially USSR and Communist China. This made the North-Vietnamese military personnel and equipment many times stronger than their Royal Lao Government counterparts --who could only survive thanks to air support from the US. The air support received by Laos was limited to the support from the US, the only party that respected Laos's Political Neutrality compared to North-Vietnam (who openly violated the neutrality agreement by sending military and war equipment to support Kong Le's coup d'état in 1960 in Vientiane).

HMONG HT-34 PILOTS

The following were trained HT-34 Pilots:

1. **Vang Bee** graduated in 1973 and flew air operations for a year. The May 1975 regime change prompted him to immigrate to California, USA, where he died in 1994.
2. **Vang Chong:** shortly after graduation, served as HT-34 Pilot. He flew a Cessna airplane to Nam Fene (LS 223) with Cessna pilot Ly Tou Xiong and, on the way back to Long Cheng, ran into a mechanical failure and was killed in December 1973.
3. **Vang Kha:** flew for almost a year. He later immigrated to Pennsylvania, USA.

Photo #100. *Helicopter carrying heavy weapons and vehicles. Lt. Col. Vang, Geu's photos collections and source, see in Unforgettable Laos.*

Photo #101. *HT34 Pilot Maj. Vang Kha in 1973, standing near a Chopper Helicopter. Lt. Col. Vang, Geu's photos collections and source, see in Unforgettable Laos.*

HMONG DAKOTA C-47 PILOTS

The first two Hmong C-47 pilots were **Xiong Kou** and **Mua Va**. In 1970, Mua Va crashed on the mountain below the Long Cheng airport while transporting food from Vientiane to Long Cheng. They both died on site.

7

In 1973, Gen. Vang Pao sent T-28 pilots **Ly Teng** and **Mua Chue** for training on C-47. **Ly Teng** graduated in 1973 and flew only a few missions before he immigrated to USA. **Mua Chue** also graduated in 1973 and flew a few missions with Ly Teng; then Mua Chue immigrated to France where he died in 2000 from depression.

HMONG AIRPLANE MECHANICS

Lo Ge, **Mua Xiong**, and **Ly Ying:** both completed training as airplane mechanics in 1971.

Raven 01

The first promotion of Raven operatives included **Mua Chue, Txiaj Vang Xiong, Vang Chou and Seng Foung**. As back-seaters, their mission was to seat in the rear of US aircrafts referred to as Raven (planes that flew in the air looking for military targets such as anti-aircraft guns, tanks, troops movements, etc.) and translate messages for the pilots to ensure they were correctly stated and correctly interpreted. There were several other operatives serving in this back-seat role whose names are not well-known, except for **Yang Heu** (killed in Xieng Khouang in 1968), **Ly Mua, Chia Va Song, Ly Nou, Phab Qig, and Vam Ntxawg Tsheej.**

Photo #102. Raven 01 is a small plane used to locate enemy targets and call in air strikesto support ground troop operations. Lt. Col. Vang, Geu's photos collections and source, see in Unforgettable Laos.

Photo #103. *Backseater Wa Jer Cheng (also known to US Raven pilots as "Mr. Scar" in 1968. Lt. Col. Vang, Geu's photos collections and source, see in Unforgettable Laos.*

VamNtxawg Tsheej's face was marked by a big scar caused by a landing accident when he landed a Raven plane at Muang Soui. Many US agents operating in MR-II called him Mr. Scar. This was a "Do or Die" event because the US pilot of the Raven was killed in the air, and Ntxawg Tsheej had to take over but missed the landing strip. The plane flipped and heavily injured his back and his front head. Ntxawg Tsheej did not leave Laos long because of those injuries and died in that country.

Lor Thai was shot by enemy anti-aircraft guns during one of his sorties in the Plain of Jars and suffered a serious wound on his forehead. Fortunately, the US hospital staff was able to save his life. Lor Thai immigrated to the US and now lives in North Carolina.

The American Raven 01 pilots who came to help the Hmong in Military Region II included Raven 20, Raven 21, Raven 22, Raven 23, Raven 24, Raven 25, Raven 26, Raven 27, and Raven 28. Their leader was Capt. **Art Cunillius,** a Raven 01 pilot who also flew Raven 20 in MR-II. He is now a General in the United States Air Forces. [*Thanks from the author to Maj. Vang Chou for providing the information*].

HATS OFF FOR THE PILOTS

Starting from 1972, Air Force Maj. Yang Xiong was the commander of the MR-II military pilots, named "Foung Bin Pha Khao" (Pha Khao Pilots). The group consisted of two units, the Yellow Pha Khao Unit and the Green Pha Khao Unit. Each unit had between 3 and 5 airplanes to use interchangeably in air raid missions against the enemy.

Lao military pilots in other military regions were shot at and usually got killed when they inadvertently hit the mountain because of cloudy weather that limited their visibility range. In MR-II, the problem was even more complicated because of this region's higher mountain ranges.

A team of Lao T-28 pilots from MR-I once spent the night in the same house and left at 9 a.m. on their bomb dropping mission. In the way back, their plane was flying at low altitude and accidentally hit a mountain near Long Cheng. All those on board were killed, with their bodies broken into pieces and unrecognizable. It was found out later that the pilot was Thao Khamphat, a native of Sayabouri Province. Three or more fatalities occurred that same day in the battle front as a result of enemy firing.

In retrospective, it can be stated unequivocally that the Lao and Lao Hmong ethnic pilots accomplished their mission with courage, determination, and deep sense of nationalism. They loved Laos and its people who were fighting together in all corners of the country to defend its national independence. They truly deserved our warm and eternal recognition their personal sacrifices and dedication.

CHAPTER 6

MILITARY STRUCTURE OF MILITARY REGION II

There were several high-ranking military officers in Military Region II. The Region's Commander was Maj. Gen. Vang Pao from 1962 until May 14, 1975, when the Pathet Lao seized power. Gen. Vang Pao immigrated to the US and died in that country on January 6, 2011.

Gen. Vang Pao had two deputy commanders, one lowland Lao deputy and one Hmong deputy. Brig. Gen. Tiao Monivong Kindavong was the lowland Lao deputy from 1968 until 1973 when he was reassigned to Vientiane. He was the second son of Tiao Kindavong, a member of the Vang Na royal lineage. His replacement, between 1973 and 1975, was Col. Anamay, a low Lao officer. The second deputy commander was Col. Neng Chue Thao, a highland Hmong native.

Photo# 104 (left). Maj. Vang Pao in January 1961, at the top of Pa Dong Mountain. He named this site LS05 and used it as the regroupment center for armed forces to fight against the Lao and Vietnamese communists and the Lao neutralists who had just captured Xieng Khouang Province.

Photo# 105 (right). Maj. Gen. Vang Pao in 1973, as Commander of MR-II. Lt. Col. Vang, Geu's photos collections and source, see in unforgettable Laos.

When the Pathet Lao came to power, Brig. Gen. Tiao Monivong was named Commander of MR-II, replacing Gen. Vang Pao who had left for Thailand. Brig. Gen. Tiao Monivong stayed with the Pathet Lao but could not work with them too well, left the country for a while before he was arrested and sent to a re-education camp. He was released in early 1992, chose to self-exile in

France by the end of that year, and later died on October 4, 2005 in Bordeaux, France. As for Col. Anamay, after the communist take-over, he immigrated to Australia where he passed away.

Photo # 106. *From left to right: Niam Song Mua, Me La, Gen. Vang Pao, and Niam Ntxhiav Thao (Niam Ntxhiav Thao, died in 2007 in California). Photo taken in 1973 at Pak Khe. Photos by National Geographic, 1973 and also see source in source, see in Unforgettable Laos.*

Photo #107. *Gen. Vang Pao with his family in 1971 at Long Cheng. From left to right: 4 children on the front row: Ying Vang, Chareunesouk Vang, Mayka Vang & Maykia Vang. Second row from left to right: Gen. Vang Pao, Xia Thao (Gen. Vang Pao's wife), Sisouk Vang, Cha Vang, Chai Vang, Ze Vang, Somsanouk Vang, Lu Vang, & Vanou Lyfoung (Tougeu Lyfoung's son). Third row from left to right: Chia Moua (Gen. Vang Pao's wife), Kia Vang in front of her mom, Nang Lay Vang, Me Lab (Gen. Vang Pao's wife, remarried after she came to the USA), May Kao Vang, May Kao Lyfoung (Francois's wife), Nang Sisamone Lyfoung (Tougeu Lyfoung's wife), Mr. Francois Vang, Pai Lor (Gen. Vang Pao wife, separated after*

HIGH RANKING HMONG OFFICERS

COL. NENG CHUE THAO

He was the Hmong deputy commander of MR-II. During 1950-1954, as a member of the French Army, he fought the war against the Communists in Indochina. He was also Gen. Vang Pao's brother-in-law. He attended the military school in Dong Hene in 1952 and became sergeant upon graduation. He fought the Vietminh along with Lt. Vang Pao during 1953-1954 (until the beginning of the US war in Indochina). As commander of Battalion 2, he once attacked the Vietminh at Nonghet. During 1961-1965, he was the Commander of Regiment BV 21. From 1965 to 1973, he was the military advisor of MR-II. During 1973-1975, he was deputy commander of MR-II. He immigrated to Texas, USA, where he passed away in 1995 due to old age illness.

COL. LY TOU PAO

From 1961 to 1964, LyTou Pao was Gen. Vang Pao's assistant. From 1964 to 1969, he was the Chief of Staff of the Joint Operation Center (JOC) of the Special Guerilla Units (SGU) in Military Region II (MRII). From 1969 to 1975, he was the commander of the Xieng Khouang military sub-region. On May 14, 1975, he immigrated to France and, in 1984, moved to the US, where he lives in California. He passed away in September 2017 in California, USA.

COL. YOUA VA LEE

Photo #108. *Col. Youa Va Lee (with big hat) fought the "Honor Restoration" war in 1970 in*

3

the Plain of Jars under the command of Gen. Vang Pao (holding the radioset). Also shown on the photo was Tiao Mangkhala, Prince Souvanna Phouma's on (with big pipe). Geu's photos collection and see in source of The Unforgettable Laos.

In 1953, Youa Va Lee was the Commander of the Hmong Parachutists Battalion who led the French regiment in the pursuit of the Viet Minh in Muang Ngat and Muang Mork in eastern Xieng Khouang Province. He remained in the French Army until 1954 and was in the same officer graduating class as Col. Neng Chue Thao. In 1961, he became Commander of the First Battalion responsible for the security of Long Cheng. In 1966, he became military advisor to Gen. Vang Pao and, in 1975, immigrated to southern France where he died in 1982.

COL. SHOUA YANG

From 1961 to 1962, Shoua Yang was the Commander of the Second Battalion and, during 1962-1964, was in charge of Zone 11 and Commander of Battalion 24 at Sane Chor (LS02). During 1965-1968, he was named military advisor of the allied troops stationed at Phou Pha Thee (LS85) and the Houaphan sub-military region. From 1962 to 1963, he became Commander of all military bases in northern Xieng Khouang Province. In 1969, he was named MR-II Chief of Staff but resigned less than a month later for lack of training. Since that time, he did not get any significant assignments except for the position of military general inspector of MR-II until May 14, 1975, when he immigrated to France, where he died on April 12, 2007.

Photo #109. *Col. Shoua Yang, MR-II Adviser, in 1969, at the start of the "Honor Restoration" war at the Plain of Jars. Geu's photos collection. Lt. Col. Vang, Geu photos collections and see in source of The Unforgettable Laos.*

COL. KHAM HOUNG

From 1968 to 1975, Col. Kham Houng was the Chief of Staff of the Lao troops in MR-II. He immigrated to France and died in Paris due to illness.

COL. NHIA XOU YANG

From 1961 to 1967, Col. Nhia Xou Yang was Commander of Battalion 203 at Phou Fa-Phou Vieng. He led his battalion in several battles in the Plain of Jars, and was in charge of military reorganization of MR-II. In 1970, he asked to be put on leave of absence and, in 1975, immigrated to the US where he now lives in Minnesota.

COL. CHER PAO MUA

From 1961 to 1975, Char Pao Mua was the Commander of the Bouam Long Camp (LS32). He has been fighting the Communists with great courage and has never surrendered this camp. Col. Cher Pao Mua had about ten thousand (twelve thousand, including families) soldiers under his command, some of whom deserted to join the Lao and Vietnamese communists and literally disappeared from the scenery without anybody knowing anything about their whereabouts and destinies. Those who survived in the forests had to continue to fight to avoid being killed like animals by the Lao communists, to defend their country with honor, and to avoid incarceration and extreme suffering at the Vieng Xay re-education camp in Houaphan Province. They had been seeking understanding and support from the free world and the US during the Vietnam War. The main reason for their taking sides with the US was to fight against the communists, prevent the expansion of the red virus in western countries and Southeast Asia, and save democratic processes from exposure to the red peril and red cancer. For all these reasons, Col. Cher Pao Moua decided to go back to his troops to lead them to safety, and he did so at the expense of his own life, which he lost in Laos in 1994

COL. YONG CHUE YANG

From 1968 to 1969, Yong Chue Yang was the commander of Battalion 201 stationed in Ban Na (LS15) and was later replaced by Col. Toulong Yang. During 1969-1972, he was the military advisor of MR-II. In 1972, he was for three weeks the acting Commander of Division II for Col. Vang Geu, with the command center located on top of a bare mountain between Phou Bia and Phou Pha Xay. Col. Yong Chue Yang coordinated with the Commander of Regiment 33 (Col. Boualiane, who came from MR-III in Savannakhet) in instructing T-28 pilots to drop bombs on enemy positions near the allied post of Phou Pha Xay. The bombs were dropped on the wrong positions and hit Regiment 33's Battalion 3 instead, causing some fatalities and injuries. The error was in part caused by the steep mountain that made it difficult for the pilots to see their targets. Besides, the enemy was also firing anti-aircraft shells at the north and west sides of the mountain. Therefore, rather than dropping one bomb at a time, the pilots dropped all six of them at the same time. Col. Yong Chue Yang immigrated as a refugee to Wisconsin, USA, and died there in 1992 from natural causes.

COL. NHIA LUE VANG

From 1961 to 1968, Col. Nhia Lue Vang was commander of the military base at Phou Saboth, north of Ban Bane-Muang Kham, which was lost to the enemy in early 1970. The base was later regrouped as Battalion 228 under the command of **Lt. Col. Vang Kua**, who led that battalion in supporting MR-IV's attack of a communist post in Paksong, Champasak Province. That post was attacked several times by the MR-IV troops but unsuccessfully. Lt. Col. Vang Kua was able to seize two mountain positions in MR-IV, making Gen. Soutchai Vongsavanh, Prince Boun-Oum Na

Champassack and several MR-IV leaders very happy. Col. Nhia Lue was an advisor to Lt. Col. Vang Koua and MR-II until 1975, when he immigrated to the refugee camp of Nam Phong, Khong Kene Province, Thailand. He died at the camp that same year from malaria.

LT. COL. VANG KOUA

As mentioned earlier, in 1970, Lt. Col. Vang Koua led Battalion 228 to reinforce Military Region IV (MR-IV) to liberate Pak Song with good success and was well recognized by Gen. Soukchay, Commander of MR-IV and the people of Pakse Province. Col. Vang Koua died in North Carolina, USA, on October 4, 2002. He was killed by his son-in-law during a family dispute.

COL. TOU LONG YANG

From 1961 to 1965, Col. Tou Long Yang was the commander of Phou Phi camp, west of Phou Fa - Phou Vieng. He served as officer liaison with Military Region I for several years, immigrated to France then to the USA, where he now lives in Michigan and runs a fairly large restaurant business.

COL. TOU LU MUA

From 1952 to 1960, Col. Tou Lu Mua was the chief of the Hmong district of Phou Dou. From 1961 to 1967, he served as the MR-II's Financial Officer, working directly under Gen. Vang Pao. In 1967, he was replaced by Lt. Col. Vang Neng and, during 1967-1969, became Chief Military Inspector of MR-II. During 1969-1975, he served as lead-secretary and military advisor to Gen. Vang Pao with his deputy, Lt. Col. Mua Kao. Col. Tou Lu Mua immigrated to France and, in 1989, came to the US to resettle in Colorado. Because he did not have adequate medical insurance coverage, he went back to France in 2007.

COL. WA SENG VANG

From 1950 to 1963, Col. Wa Seng Vang fought with the Neo Lao Hak Xath against the French in the Muang Mork area (LS46). In 1963, he chose to fight with the allies, knowing that Gen. Vang Pao was the Commancer of MR-II. In 1965, he attended military officer school in Long Cheng and was later appointed Commander of Battalion 2. In 1968, he was seriously wounded and was put on sick leave. During 1968-1975, Col. Wa Seng Vang served as military advisor in Military Region II until the day he immigrated to Wisconsin, USA.

COL. LUE VANG (LUE DAM)

From 1950 to 1954, Lue Vang served as Commander of the first Company of Parachutist Battalion with the mission to pursue (along with then Lt. Vang Pao) Viet Minh troops who had attacked the Plain of Jars earlier and were then retreating toward Nonghet. From 1961 to 1966, he was named Commander of the Battalion in charge of security at Long Cheng. From 1966 to 1968, he was Commander of the Battalion that protected Pha Khao (LS14). From 1968 to 1975, he became advisor to Military Region II (MR-II). He immigrated to Denver, Colorado, USA and then moved to Minnesota, where he died in 2004.

COL. VANG THAI

From 1961 to 1968, Vang Thai was Commander of Battalion 211. From 1969 to 1975, he was Commander of MR-II Training Center and, on May 14, 1975 immigrated to California, USA. From 1975 to 2005, he was President of the Hmong-Lao Veteran Association, Inc. in the USA.

COL. LY XANG

In 1959, Ly Xang graduated from the Teacher's College in Vientiane and taught at a primary school in Phonsavan during 1960-1961. Because of the political changes in the country, he enrolled in the Royal Lao Army and was later appointed training officer at several military camps to get troops well prepared for the fight against the enemy. In 1968, after Houaphan Province fell to the enemy, Col. Ly Xang went back to serve at positions behind the front line. In 1975, he immigrated to California, USA. He later took a trip back to Thailand and died there on August 25, 1995. His body was brought back to the USA and buried in Saginaw, Michigan next to the tomb of his wife (who died in 1983).

Ly Xang was the son of Chao Muang Tong Pao Lee, a native of Ban Nam Kanh, Nonghet, near the important French military camp of Phan Nieng (that was established during the Vietminh era). In 1952, the Vietminh fiercely attacked Phan Nieng Camp in order to seize Nonghet. Hundreds of them died during the attack. Chao Muang Tong Pao performed very well for the French. In 1975, he immigrated to France to live with his daughter-in-law, the second wife of Col. Ly Xang, and a native of Pakse by the name of Nang Boutsady. Chaomuang Tong Pao died in France in 1984.

COL. XAY DANG XIONG

From 1968 to 1975, Col. Xay Dang Xiong was Commander of the training center with Col. Vang Thai. He was a well-disciplined and strict officer. He immigrated to Milwaukie, Wisconsin, USA, and now lives in Florida, USA.

Photo #110. Col. Xay Dang Xiong and George (alias Digger), CIA GM 21 (1070-1971)

Passed away 3/20/2018

Lt. Col. Vang, Geu's photos collection and see in source of The Unforgettable Laos.

COL. LY TENG

Col. Ly Teng is Gen. Vang Pao's brother-in-law. In 1961, he served as an officer with Volunteers Battalion 21. From 1961 to 1962, he went on military and leadership training in Thailand. From 1963 to 1965, Ly Teng was Commander of SGU Battalion 202. In 1966, he became chief of the training center in Long Cheng. From1966 to 1968, he served as officer liaison in the capital city of

Vientiane. During 1968-1969, he was the Chief of the Third Bureau working on plans to recapture Phou Pha Thee (LS85) with duty station in Long Cheng. During 1970-1971, he received a military staff training course in Vientiane, taught by a French instructor. During 1971-1972, he served as chief of staff of the Joint Operation Center (JOC) for MR-II Logistics. From 1972 to 1973, he was Commander of SGU Regiment 23. From 1973 to 1975, Col. Ly Teng was MR-II deputy-chief of staff responsible for logistics. He immigrated to Thailand on May 14, 1975 and, in 1976, to Minnesota, USA.

COL. LY XEE BLONG LYFOUNG

Col. Ly Xee Blong was the step-son of Touby Lyfoung. He served as the main liason officer between the Ly family and the Vang family. He immigrated to France where he died in 1996. *(Col. Ly Xee Blong was the son of Phagna Touby Lyfoung's older brother. When his brother died, Touby married his sister-in-law).*

COL. LY NAO KAO LYFOUNG

Col. Ly Nao Kao was the third son of Mr. Lyfoung and his third wife, Nang Kue Chua, all of whom were from the Keo Park Kha Hmong family living in the eastern part of Xieng Khouang Province, close to the Laos/North Vietnam border. From 1953 to 1954, he served as a French soldier assigned to the Hmong Parachutist Battalion in the pursuit of the Vietminh to Nonghet. From 1961 to 1969, he was the Commander of Artillery Battalion in Military Region II (MR-II), a position assumed by Lt. Col. Yang Chue in 1969. From 1969 to1975, he was the military advisor of MR-II). He immigrated to France and then to Minnesota, USA. He died on May 5, 2010 in Minnesota.

COL. MUA SU

Col. Mua Su, the son of Col. Cheu Pao Mua, served as MR-II representative in the Sayabouri, Louang Namtha, Nam Gnou and Luang Prabang operational areas. He used to attend Military Staff Training at Long Cheng. During 1972-1973, he replaced Col. Ly Tou Pao as SGU Chief of Staff in MR-II. Between 1973 and 1975, he was appointed Commander of Division II responsible for military security in the Sala Phou Khoune area, near the junction of Highways 13 and 7. His deputy was Lt. Col. Vang Neng. Col. Mua Su immigrated to Thailand and did not go anywhere else.

COL. TONG WA LOR

From 1967 to 1969, Col. Tong Wa Lor was Commander of Battalion 221 that occupied Nam Mai Camp near Hine Tang (LS74). He was killed in Hine Tang in 1969 during a Vietminh attack.

COL. LY PAO

From 1950 to 1954, Ly Pao was a French soldier serving in the Hmong Parachutist Battalion led by then Sergeant-Major Youa Vang Ly in the pursuit of the Viet Minh from Muang Mork to Nonghet. In 1959, Maj. Vang Pao ordered Capt. Ly Pao to pursue the Pathet Lao troops that fled from the Plain of Jars under the command of Lt. Col. Tou Ya. His battalion caught up with the Pathet Lao troops and was engaged in a short fight near Muang Mork. From 1963 to 1967, he was named regional field Commander at several operational theaters in Sayaboury, Luang Prabang and Luang Nam Tha. In 1975, Col. Ly Pao immigrated to France and died there in 2005.

COL. YOUA PAO SONG

Col. Youa Pao Song served as battalion and regiment commander in the Long Cheng area. He later immigrated to Colorado, USA.

COL. LO SENG

Lo Seng started fighting the enemy alongside Gen. Vang Pao when the French were still in power. He attended the officer school together with Neng Chue Thao and Youa Va Ly. He eventually got to the rank of Colonel but then resigned to go back to grow rice like a common citizen in a farm located 52 kilometers away from Vientiane. No news was available from him, as he never left Laos.

COL. LY LO

Col. Ly Lo was an important Hmong army officer in Houaphan Province. In 1971, he was the Commander of Regiment 26 that attacked the enemy in the Song Hack-Muang Kheung and the Plain of Jars areas. In May 1975, he immigrated to Thailand and initially refused to move to a third country. Eventually, he immigrated to the USA, where he died on December 23, 2007 in Hickory, NC.

COL. SONG LENG XIONG

Song Leng Xiong was born in 1940 at Phou Sane, Muang Perk, Xieng Khouang Province. In 1947, he attended school at Phou Dou. From 1953 to 1955, he enrolled in the French Army as a commando trooper with the mission to secure Phou Vieng area.

In 1960, during the Kong Lae's coup d'état, Song Leng Xiong rejoined the army as a sub-Lieutenant and was named Commander of Company 4, Battalion 201 stationed near Phou Vieng. From 1967 to 1968, he attended military staff training in Long Cheng, MR-II tought by Thai military instructors. During 1968 - 1969, he was appointed Commander of Battalion 209 and during 1969 - 1972, the Commander of Regiment 23. In 1974, when the SGU was removed, he became an officer in the Royal Lao Army. During 1972-1975, Col. Song Leng Xiong became Commander of the Operating Battalion in MR-II. On May 14, 1975 he left for the refugee camp of Nam Phong and in 1976 moved to Soune Vinay Center. In 1993, he immigrated to Minnesota, USA and, in 2005, moved to Florida. He said, *"When I arrived in Florida, the atmosphere was happier and livelier than in Minnesota. I also feel healthier."* When asked why he felt that way, his answer was, *"It is cold in Minnesota. I don't have any chance to do any outdoor exercice like in Florida. The weather here is also not too different than in Laos."* But in 2008, he suffered a stroke and moved back to Minnesota for medical treatment. Apparently, Florida offered less health assistance to refugees than Minnesota. At the time, translation service was also almost non-existent in Florida.

High Ranking Lao Officers

Col. Chansom Pardimonivong

From 1973 to 1975, Col. Chansom Pardimonivong was Commander of the Houaphan military sub-region and Governor of Huaphan Province until the day he was sent to the re-education camp in Vieng Xay. He was released from the camp in 1988 and immigrated to France where he died in January 2006.

Col. Thao Chai

During 1960-1976, Col. Thao Chai was MR-II Military Liaison Officer stationed in Oudone Thani, Thailand. He did not leave the area, and later died in Thailand.

Photo #111. From L to R: Hang Xao: (chief of MR-II Second Bureau), Burr Smith (US Military Attache), Soua Yang (MR-II Military Commander) and Thao Chai (MR-II Representative in Oudone, Thailand). Picture taken on February 27, 1963 during their US visit at President Kennedy's invitation. Lt. Col. Vang, Geu's photos collection and see in source of The Unforgettable Laos.

Col. Thong Vongrassamy

From 1964 to 1965, Col. Thong Vongrassamy was Commander of the Huaphan Military sub-region and the Governor of that province, replacing Col. Khamsao Keovilay. Col. Thong died in the battle front while on a mission to rescue an American pilot whose plane had been shot down. The American pilot was safely rescued but, unfortunately, Col. Thong was shot and killed by an enemy sniper while holding on to the rope that was dropped to rescue the American pilot. His body was later sent to Vientiane for funeral.

Col. Phanh Siharath

From 1965 to 1969, Col. Phan Siharath replaced Col. Thong Vongrassamy as Commander of MR-II Huaphan sub-region, and Chaokhoueng of Houaphan Province. In February 1969, the enemy mounted a massive attack against the Na Khang camp (LS36). In the absence of outside military support, the camp fell into the enemy's hand. Col. Phanh Siharath and most of his troops were either killed or injured.

COL. DOUANGTA NORASING

Col. Douangta was in charge of the Support & Benefits ("Sawatdi Karn") services in Military Region II. He immigrated to California, USA in 1975 and then moved to Georgia.

COL. PHIMPHA AND COL. KHAMSAO KEOVILAY

Both of them served as Liaison Officers in Vientiane to follow up with the news and report back to the MR-II's military chain of command. Col. Khamsao was a Samneua native who has fought in the allies' rank for years.

COL. KHAMKAB AND LT. COL. THAO NA

During 1967-1971, Col. Khamkab was the Commander of the Engineer Battalion of MR-II and was later reassigned to Vientiane. He then lost all contacts with his former colleagues. During 1971-1975, he was replaced by Lt. Col. Thao Na, who never left the country. After the communist take-over, Thao Na was deployed to a construction site in the Plain of Jars. Since then, no more news was received from him.

COL. TOU SENG-AROUN

During 1965-1969, Col. Tou was the military advisor for MR-II, following the death of Col. Phang Siharath at the Na Khang camp (LS36). No news was received from him after the refugee exodus.

COL. BOUNNOI PHAOPHONGSAVANH

During 1969-1973, Col. Bounnoi was the Commander of Huaphan MR-II sub-region and Governor of Houaphan Province, following the death of Col. Phang Siharath at the Na Khang camp (LS36). No more news about him since the refugee exodus.

COL. BOUALOY

During 1972-1975, Col. Boualoy was named Commander of the Psychological Operations Battalion. No more news about him since the refugee exodus.

COL. SISAVATH VONGKHAMHEUANG

Col. Sisavath was sent to the Sam-Tai re-education camp and later released in 1979. He immigrated to France, where he stayed with his family until his death.

POL. COL. PHIMPHONE

Pol. Col. Phimphone was MR-II Chief of Police and died in that military region.

COL. VATTHA

Not enough information is available.

COL. BOUNCHAN

Not enough information is available.

COL. PHAN-ENH INTHAVIXAY

Not enough information, except that he did immigrate to France with his family.

GEN. AI-TAM SINGVONGSA

Gen. Ai-Tam, a native of the Huaphan Province, served as Chief of the Second Bureau of the Royal Lao Army. He and his family first immigrated to France and then moved to Australia.

OFFICERS OF THE RANK OF LT. COL.

Lt. Col. Chong Koua Vue.

Lt. Col. Chong Koua Vue sacrificed his life in Long Cheng, Laos, in 1973. Chong Koua Vue was a Province Commissioner under the leadership of the Praya Touby Lyfoung in Xieng Khouang Province and King Chao Sisavatthana in the mid 50's in Mueng Nqah and Mueng Morh zones, Xieng Khouang province, Laos. He worked closely with General Vang Pao from 1961 to 1973 in region two military projects from 1961 to 1973, mostly in Moung Nqha zoning in the Khong 22 in region two.   Under General Vang, Pao's leadership, he was assigned to create seven military based camp military training and four military airports in different villages in Bolikhamxay province. Furthermore, he and his team observed the Ho Chi Minh trail in different zoning based on General Vang Pao's assigned authority in the military project action plan.   He sacrificed his life for his country, his government, and his people. The photo collection of his son, Vue. Chahue (Ber C.).

Lt. Col. of all Hmong ethnic groups serving in MR-II included the following leaders and officers:

Vang Neng, Vang Koua, Blong Thao, Youa True Vang, Mua Kao, Chong Koua Vue, Mua Seng, Yang Chue, Neng Youa Vang, Youa Vang Kao, Vang Yee, You True Vang, Moua Thong, Ly Nou, Neng Yi Yang, Chong Neng Vang, Xainou Vang, Cha Ly, Chong Toua Yang, Ly Neng, Lyblong Pacha, Seumphan, Ly Yeu (died in Denver, USA), Tou Vang Yang (graduated from Law School in Vientiane, now lives in France), and Thao Na. There were many more Lieutenant Colonels in MR-II, whose names escaped the author's memory.

SYSTEM OF COMMAND OF MR-II (1951-1964)

MR-II military command system was organized as follows:

PRIOR TO 1961

Battalions BV21, BV22, BV23, BV24, and BV25 were stationed in Xieng Khouang Province, while battalionsBV 26, BV27, BV28 were stationed in Houaphan Province. In addition, there were also several commando battalions and village military guard units operating in MR-II.

AFTER 1964

Military Thai instructors provided training to Lao troops in MR-II and created two SGU battalions, one to secure Xieng Khouang Province and the other one, to secure Houaphan Province. The first group included SGU 201, 202, 203 through 209, and the second group consisted of SGU battalions 226, 227, and 228.

AFTER THE LOSS OF PHOU PHA THEE (LS85)

Starting in 1970, troops previously stationed in Houaphan Province were moved to Xieng Khouang Province. They were split into t, and 28 (8 regiments), I included regiments 21, 22, 23, 24, 25, 26, 27, and 28 (8 regiments) and was put under the command of Col. Douangta. In 1972, Col. Vang Geu was the Commander of Division II, which was about to attack the Plain of Jars but had to stop short because of the Agreement signed between the US and North Vietnam in Paris in 1973.

The MR-II field commanding officers are listed below with years of assignment:

- Col. Vang Geu, Commander of Regiment 21 during 1970-1971 and Commander of Division II during 1972-1973
- Col. Ly Nou, Commander of Regiment 22 during 1970-1972. He died in the Vieng Xay re-education camp in Houaphan Province.

- Col. Song Leng Xiong, Commander of Regiment 23, during 1970-1971. He was replaced by Lt. Col. Vang Youa during 1971-1972. After he was injured, Col. Vang Youa was replaced by Col. Ly Teng during 1972-75.
- Lt. Col. Moua Kao, Commander of Regiment 24 during 1970-1973.
- Lt. Col. Vang Koua, Commander of Regiment 25 during 1970-1973.
- Col. Ly Lao, Commander of Regiment 26 during 1970-1973.
- Lt. Col. Chong Koua Vue, Commander of Regiment 27 stationed at Muang Mork (LS46) during 1973-1975, could not leave Laos and died there.
- Col. Cheu Pao Mua, Commander of Regiment 28, stationed at Bouam Long (LS32) during 1970-1975. In 1976, he returned to the battlefield with his troops but died in the forest in Laos in 1994.

Col. Vang Geu served as the chief of MR-II's Development Office during 1973-1975. During 1973-1975, Col. Moua Sue was the Commander of Division II, with Lt. Col. Vang Nieng as his deputy. The regiment's command center was located at Sala Phou Khoune, at the junction of Highways 13 and 7.

During 1973-1974, under the two-faction coalition government, soldiers were dismissed and allowed to learn to be self-sufficient, performing businesses, and getting professional and educational training. MR-II military forces were reduced following cuts in US assistance programs, and so was the hope for freedom. The Pathet Lao took advantage of the situation and brought in the North Vietnamese to help them destroy all agreements, as the US had to withdraw from the Indochina battlefield for the following reasons:

- Public protestations were held in the US to show their opposition to the continuation of the war in Indochina
- Red China and the Soviet Union were engaged in border disputes and some fighting
- Russia increased the delivery of ultra-modern weapons to North Vietnam to help them fight back against the US. (In 1971, US President Nixon decided to mine Haiphong harbor and send more troops to Vietnam).

The US withdrawal led to many significant changes. It allowed Red China to become the main problem-solver in Southeast Asia and signaled the dissolution of the communist world as we used to know it. It sent out a clear message to the communist world that the US would never get involved in Indochina's affairs again. As a result, North Vietnam was quick to make new plans to conquer Indochina in a way that would prevent any international intervention. They played the new game and used their military forces to gain absolute power and leave no other way out to the Lao coalition government. They gave Kaysone Phomvihane the authority to sign an agreement allowing the North Vietnamese full control in all areas, leading to the arrest, detention and death of several hundred thousand of Indochinese in deadly re-education camps. All this was because Laos had limited resources, was a small country, and had practically no means to defend itself.

Col. Ly Pao

He followed Lt. Col. Touya as commander

of battalion II, stationed in the Plain of Jars

in 1957. He lead his battalion to escape onMay 18, 1959 to North Vietnam. Lt. Col. Vang, Geu's photos collection and see in source of The Unforgettable Laos.

CHAPTER 7

THE FIGHT AGAINST NORTH VIETNAM

During 1959-1972 communist North Vietnam did not implement the agreement that was signed and instead used the Lao territory as a path to fighting war in South-Vietnam, supported the Lao communists in fiercely attacking military posts of the neutral Lao Government (presided by Prince Souvanna Phouma) in MR-II, MR-III and MR-IV. This is was partly due to the drastic increase in modern weaponry provided by the Soviet Union to North-Vietnam for use in the Indochina war. This included heavy tanks, light and heavy transportation vehicles, anti-aircraft guns, artilleries of all calibers (86 mm, 122 mm, 130 mm), 122 mm rockets, and movable anti-aircraft missile systems equipped with 12.8 mm, 14.6 mm, 25 mm, 37 mm, 57 mm, and 76 mm guns, and MIG aircraft for the air defense of North-Vietnam and the air fight against the US. The US had to drop bombs on all the roads originating from the China Sea near Hai-Phong and Hanoi. The enemy was equipped with SAM (soil-to-air missiles), which made their military and weaponry power many times stronger than the fighting power of the allies. As a result, MR-II and the rest of the country came under heavy attack from North Vietnam.

At that time, MR-II had almost two divisions (about 10,000 soldiers) that were assigned for the protection of Xieng Khouang and Houaphan Provinces. All the changes mentioned earlier made it critical for the MR-II Commander to try his best to control communist North Vietnam's expansion. Maj. Gen. Vang Pao and military officers in all Lao military regions had to realign the structure of the Royal Lao Army starting in 1970. The kingdom of Laos was divided into five military regions, each of which was equipped with one division, for a total of five divisions countrywide, all receiving support from the US. When it was realized that the enemy had several times more troops and more weapons than the allies, the Vientiane Government had to ask for air support from the US to continually drop bombs on enemy positions and conduct air operations until 1973.

When Gen. Vang Pao received extra air support from the US for MR-II, he decided to lay out plans to launch the second attack against the Plain of Jars. The plan was code-named "Honor Recovery" Plan. Gen. Vang Pao asked for military support from Thailand for operations in the Long Cheng area because most of the MR-II troops were already busy on the front line. Starting in June 1969, the General's plan of attack was as follows:

o Front I: push the enemy from Samthong to Louang Mat, Ban Na, Phou Xeu, and Muang Phanh and ultimately attack the Plain of Jars,
o Front II: push the enemy toward Muang Soui and after seizing Muang Soui, cleanse the Lat Bouak area -- west of the Plain of Jars and communist command center.

16

The attack of Muang Soui this time around caused the loss of two courageous pilots, Capt. Ly Lue and Lt. Lor Neng. Ly Lue was the one who gave a lot of hope to Maj. Gen. Vang Pao. He received support from B-52's, F-4's, Fantom F111, A1E and T-28's that made joint sorties to protect his flights; he also got the support from the Thai Army who came to the rescue. The overall attack got fairly good results in that the allies were able to seize the Plain of Jars; destroy artilleries, tanks, ammunition stocks and several thousand of enemy soldiers; use the Plain of Jars as a site of celebration for the 1970 Hmong New Year. Gen. Vang Pao and the Thai military officers laid out firm plans to protect the Plain of Jars, coded-named Plans 163 and 114, including the following troop deployments:

- One Thai battalion to seize Phou Teung and dig a hiding ground hole.
- One battalion to protect Phou Keng and dig a hiding ground hole.
    One Thai battalion to capture Phu Xeu and dig a hiding ground hole.
- OneThai battalion to seize Phou Khae, set up four 155 mm artilleries and four 105 mm artilleries.
- One Thai regiment to station in Muang Phanh, mid-way between Phou Keng and Phou Xeu, with the mission to set the four mountain ranges listed above as support bases.
- One artillery battalion with four 105 mm and four 155 mm guns to station in Muang Phanh and ready to defend allies's positions in the Plain of Jars.
- Assign two MR-II Hmong battalions to locate enemy targets, monitor enemy mouvements and coordinate air and artilleries operations.
- Station one MR-II Hmong battalion on top of Phou Houat to protect the roads leading to Khang Khay and Lat Bouak.

Photo #112. *B-52 dropping bombs on enemy positions. Lt. Col. Vang, Geu's photos collection and see in source of The Unforgettable Laos.*

From January to March 1971, the weather started to be cloudy and limited the efficiency of the allies' air strikes, which in turn made it easier for the enemy to move their vehicles and their troops around. This allowed the enemy to heavily attack the allies everywhere on the ground around the Plain of Jars, including the Hmong troops who monitored their movements. They started attacking all the allies' mountain positions simultaneously, firing artillery shells and launching rockets to every corner of the battlefield, making it impossible for the allies to regroup.

Once the enemy seized several important mountain posts, they started attacking the Thai positions in the Plain of Jars, recaptured that whole area, and pushed the allies out to Long Cheng, making it an abandoned site during the entire 1971 year.

Photo #113. *US F-4 Jet providing air support to the Vientiane government and dropping bombs on North-Vietnamese positions Lt. Col. Vang, Geu's photos collection and see in source of The Unforgettable Laos.*

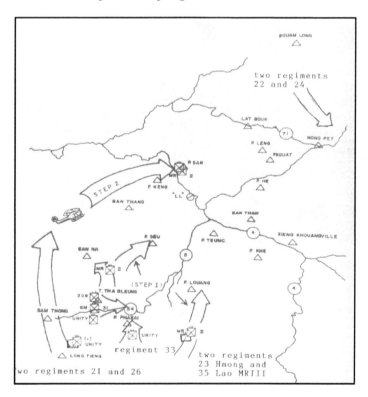

Map #114. *"Honor Restoration" War to recapture positions that fell into North-Vietnam's hands started in July 1969, led to the New Year celebration in May 1970, and seized again by*

the enemy in March 1971. Lt. Col. Vang, Geu's photos collection and see in source of The Unforgettable Laos.

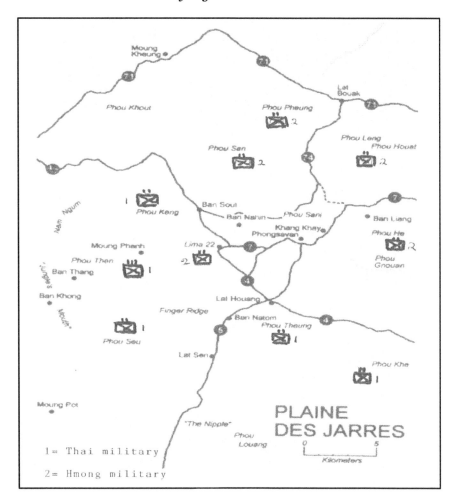

Map #115. *Position layout for the defense of the Plain of Jars in 1970/1971. Battalions #2 were Hmong troops, and Battalions and Regiments on front line. #1 were Thai troops in the rear. Enemy sent two Divisions 312 and 316 attacked the Plain of Jars and were about to seize Long Cheng that was saved at the last minute by heavy B52 bombing. Long Cheng was saved but stayed vacant for quite some time. Lt. Col. Vang, Geu's photos collection and see in source of The Unforgettable Laos.*

North Vietnam used two divisions to attack the Plain of Jars. More than 12,000 troops Division 316 and one artillery regiment, equipped with tanks, started their attack from Ban Bane, moving along Highway 7, and then attacked Phou Houat, Phou Keng and the Plain of Jars. Division 312 and several Datcong (dare-devil) battalions moved out from Xieng Khouang along Highway 4, and attacked Phou Teung and Phou Khae. Once they captured the Plain of Jars, the enemy began their cleansing operation of the allied troops —most of whom were Thai soldiers, who did not know their way out and had to fight for their lives and/or get injured. By the beginning of March 1971, once the allies left the Plain of Jars, the enemy pushed them toward Long Cheng, hoping to seize that military camp. Their plan of attack of Long Cheng (see Maps #122 and 113) was as follows:

19

- Division 316 and one dare-devil battalion attacked from Ban Na (LS15), along the Nam Chong Creek, heading toward the foothill of Phou Pha Thao to cut their eastern supply line. The allies were closely watching the enemy's movement. When the enemy reached the Nam Chong Creek and were about to climb Mount Pha Thao on their way to Sam Thong, Gen. Vang Pao and Mr. Jerry Daniels asked for two B-52 aircrafts to fly in and drop CBU bombs on North-Vietnam's Division 316, and almost eradicating the whole division.

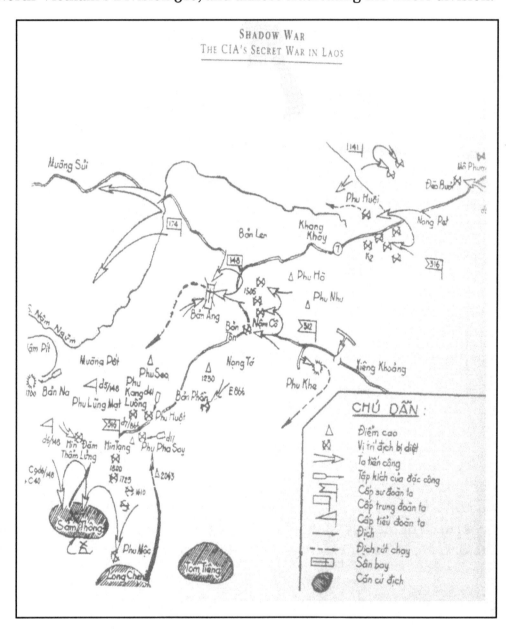

Map #116. North-Vietnam attacked all Gen. Vang Pao's and Thai troops at the Plain of Jars in February 1971 then pursued the Hmong and Thai troops to Long Cheng but B52 struck them and save Long Tieng. Lt. Col. Vang, Geu's photos collection and see in source of The Unforgettable Laos.

Nam Chong was a creek that flows along the foothill of Phou Pha Thao and Phou Pha Chon on its way to its junction with the Nam Ngum River. Without the B-52 and F4 dropping bombs on the enemy, Long Cheng would have certainly been los because the enemy had deployed two army contingents to the area. The more important unit of the two was Division 316, which severely suffered from B-52 bombing while on its way to Sam Thong, trying to cut the allies' supply line. A high mountain range sits on the western part of the Sam Thong-Long Cheng area and offers many hiding sites. Had the enemy been able to capture this area, it would have been hard to fight it back. Besides, the allies did not have a strong defensive base. Indeed, it B-52 bombing was very timely in cutting off enemy troops.

Division 312 and several dare-devil battalions were split into two groups as follows:

o The first group with heavy weapons and tanks moved in the middle, from Lat Sene-Ban Pha to Phou Louang Matt and to Ban Hinh Tang (LS74).
o The second group was on the allies' trail, pushing them from Pa Dong (LS05) to Phou Bia, then to Pha Khao (LS14), and finally to Long Cheng.

Part of Division 312 troopers, with tanks and heavy 130 mm, 122 mm,, and 86 mm heavy artilleries, were pushing from the Plain of Jars, heading toward Hine Tang, Phou Pha Xay, Nam Pha, and Pha Khao. They were about to reach Nam Pha when T-28 aircraft and F4 and F111 jets dropped bombs on them. Only one company survived the air raid and was able to reach the top of Phou Rassavang. Another Vietnamese battalion reached Mount Appolo, located on the east side of Long Cheng. The allies fought with that battalion for almost one mont and then left the area because the expected support coming from Sam Thong never arrived. As a result, Long Cheng remained safe.

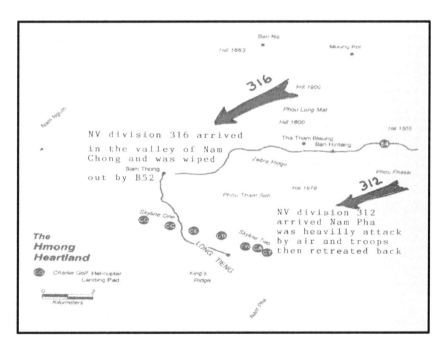

Map #117. *North Vietnam sent Divisions 316 and 312 to attack Long Cheng and wipe out the Hmong in Military Region II, but when Division 316 arrived at the valley of Nam Chong west of Samthong, B52 wiped itout and saved Long Tieng until May 1975. Division 312 arrived at N; Sky Rider was also bombed by F4, Sky Rider, and T28. It had to retreat back and sent only guerrillas to attack Long Cheng, which remained an empty town all year in 1971. Lt. Col. Vang, Geu's photos collection and see in source of The Unforgettable Laos.*

Regiment 174 was made up of Pa Chai troopers, and Regiment 141 consisted of mixed North Vietnamese ethnics. Both regiments were assigned the protection of the newly captured Plain of Jars from Gen. Vang Pao's troops. Air operations inflicted very heavy damages to the enemy and constituted a source of satisfaction for the allies, as long as they knew how to use those resources and had a good execution plan The enemy was afraid of B-52's, F111's, and bomb dropping by F4's, Sky Riders, A1E's and T-28's. As a result, their plan to capture Long Cheng failed to materialize. The enemy then deployed guerilla raiders from Regiment 866 to destroy several allies' positions around Long Cheng. These raiders were heavily repulsed each time, and finally retreated. 1971 was the year when the Long Cheng residents had to immigrate to Vientiane, Na Sou, and Ban Sone, leaving Long Cheng as a ghost town during most of that year.

Photo #118. The allied troops seized Phou Keng Mountain, southwest of the Plain of Jars in early 1970 but lost it back to the enemy in March 1971. Lt. Col. Vang, Geu's photos collection and see in source of The Unforgettable Laos.

Photo #119 (left). Rice bags captured at the Plain of Jars in 1970.

Photo #120 (right). North-Vietnam's 122 mm artillery captured in 1970 Lt. Col. Vang, Geu's photos collection and see in source of The Unforgettable Laos.

Photo #121. *North-Vietnam's AK guns captured in 1970 Lt. Col. Vang, Geu's photos collection and see in source of The Unforgettable Laos.*

Photo: Hugh Macleod/IRIN

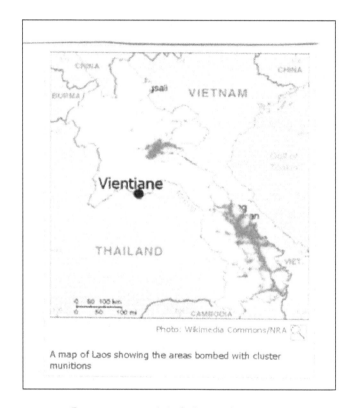

Photo: Wikimedia Commons/NRA

A map of Laos showing the areas bombed with cluster munitions

Photo #122 (left). *CBU bombs dropped from the air.*

Photo #123 (right). *Red spots refer to the most heavily bombarded areas in MR-II, MR-III and MR-IV during 1968-1972. Lt. Col. Vang, Geu's photos collection and see in source of The Unforgettable Laos.*

Lt. Col. Xainou Vang, Khon 22, Special Commando, SGU and Airborne Leader and his team caught Viet Cong in the Ho Chi Minh trails. He was able to place them in security placement and then shipped them to military secured placement in Vientiane, Laos from 1963 through 1974. This is a special intensive mission that he and his team had to evacuate at the frontier line. It was ordered and authorized by General Vang, Pao and CIA Leaders along with The Royal King Chao Sisa Vatthana in region two in Laos.

Lt. Col.'s daughter-in-law, Ka Thao, aka Mrs. Chongwa Vang's photo collection.

PLAN TO RECONQUER THE PLAIN OF JARS

This was Gen. Vang Pao's third plan to recapture the Plain of Jars. In July 1971, Gen. Vang Pao sent Regiments 21 and 26 by helicopter to Lat Bouak to attack the enemy's position at Song Hat, Muang Kheung, west of the Plain of Jars. He also sent Regiments 22 and 24 to join Regiment 28 at Bouam Long (LS32) by helicopter, with the mission to regain Lat Bouak and cut the enemy's supply line. After landing on the ground, Regiments 21 and 26 fought with the enemy for about three weeks and then ran into problems—many of their troopers developed blistering feet and could not walk. The causes of the blistering were unknown, some of which might include the following:

o   Troopers were wearing shoes made in Taiwan that might have chemically contaminated rubber components. Those not wearing the same Taiwanese shoes appeared not to have any blisters and no other problems.
o   In retrospective, these blisters might have been caused by the remains of the bombs that were dropped all over around the Plain of Jars. Maybe, the bombs contained chemical elements that caused the blistering. Regiments 21 and 26 soldiers used to walk along areas subject to heavy precipitations that made shoes wet. The Plain of Jars was probably the most intensely bombarded region in the whole world.

For those reasons, Regiments 21 and 26 had to pull out of the area. Many of the soldiers were pursued by tanks, and some of them drowned in the Nam Ngum River –this was during the rain, and some of them drowned in the Nam Ngum River –this was during the rainy season, with fast flowing flows and under heavy tank pursuit. To evade the tanks, some had to cross the river and drowned. Once Regiments 21 and 26 retreated, Regiments 22 and 24 were the subject of heavy enemy attacks and had to retreat to Bouam Long.

THE FOURTH PLAIN OF JARS ATTACK BY GEN. VANG PAO

In June 1972, Gen.Vang Pao sent Division II, along with one Thai regiment and two Lao regiments from MR-III (Regiments 33 and 35), to attack the enemy in the Plain of Jars. The mission of the Thai regiment was to be ready to reoccupy the newly recaptured positions. Division II made the following deployments:

- o Regiments 21, 23, 26 and 35 to enter Khang Kho (LS204), push the enemy toward Lat Sene and ultimately recapture the Plain of Jars.
- o Regiment 33 to seize Phou Pha Xay.
- o Regiments 22 and 24 to cut off enemy supply lines along Highway 7 between Kahng Khay and Ban Bane (Muang Kham).

Those operations had not yet allowed the allies to recapture the Plain of Jars; they only involved attacking several enemy positions around the Plain of Jars. The operations were called off due to the cease-fire agreement signed by the US and North-Vietnam in Paris, France on January 27, 1973. From that point on, Division II Commander got the order to assure security at Sala Phou Khoune Camp, at the junction of Highways 12 (heading to Vientiane) and 7 (heading to Phou Nong Si, the Plain of Jars, and North-Vietnam). From Division II, one regiment was assigned the mission to control the area between Ban Na (LS15), Phou Pha Xay, Pa Dong (LS05), and Khang Kho (LS204); two regiments to secure Bouam Long Camp (LS32); and one regiment, to secure Muang Mork (LS46). The overall objective was then to protect the allies-occupied territories from enemy penetration. No matter how the protection was performed, it was still useless because once the US and North-Vietnam signed their cease-fire agreement, the Royal Lao Army ran out of supporters

***Photo #124**. Ban Sone near LS272 in 1973*

Lt. Col. Vang, Geu's photos collection and see in source of The Unforgettable Laos.

3

When the situation became more insecure, the North Vietnamese and Lao communist troops took advantage of it by attacking several Vientiane military positions, including the command center of Division II at Sala Phou Khoune, Muang Mork and many positions around Long Cheng. When the Division II command center was seized by the enemy, Gen.Vang Pao decided to go and meet with Prince Souvanna Phouma at his residence in Vientiane. As soon as he showed up, the prince yelled at him, *"Vang Pao, you really like fighting the war?"* Gen. Vang Pao answered, *"I would like to return my general's hat and my stars to you; I'm asking you to accept my resignation."* He pulled his hat from his head, his two stars from his epaulets, and put them down on the table in front of the Prime Minister, and then walked away to get on board his car and drive to the Wattai Airport en route to Long Cheng.

This incident happened on March 9, 1975, It was reported later that Prince Souvanna Phouma sent an aide to try to get Gen. Vang Pao back to meet with him, but it was too late. On March 12, 1975 Gen. Vang Pao flew to Louang Prabang for an audience with King Savang Vatthana in his palace, seeking his advice out of concern for the country and its population. Gen. Vang Pao said, *"I'm here to seek an audience with Your Majesty and find out what you would order me to do to address the serious situation we are facing."* The king answered, *"I do not need anything else; I only need this house to live in and this piece of land to grow rice!"* Gen. Vang Pao and I (who accompanied him on this trip) clearly heard his statement. I patted the back of Gen. Vang Pao to suggest no further conversation—just leave and go back to Long Cheng.

On second thought, it could be seen that people all over the country, including police, military and civilian authorities of all ranks, the public at large and even His Majesty the king, did not fully understand the communist doctrine and how bad it really was. It was reported that in 1973 the Lao communists had invited His Majesty the king and several Vientiane leaders to pay a visit to the Vieng Xay Lao communist command center, and welcomed them with great honors. King Sisavang Vatthana even went on to admit that the Lao communists respected him more than the Vientaine faction.

Furthermore, it appeared that many Vientiane leaders very surprisingly also believed the same way in the Lao communist game play, and refused to recognize that communism was against royal dynasties, and was after leaders, capitalists, religious and political parties. As far as the communists were concerned, the only thing that counted was their central committee which detained all decisive power. Only when people had a chance to observe communist practices did they get a good flavor of what those practices really meant. By that time, it was too late to fix anything. Students and national employees organized public demonstrations against the rightist leaders --their own elders—and forced them to flee the country as political refugees. In the end, many of those short-sighted individuals also had to run behind the old leaders and their family elders, seeking refuge status in foreign countries. Gen. Bounpone Mart-Thepharat, Royal Lao Army Commander-in-Chief, was also lured into believing in the communist doctrine. After leading his staff into attending informational meetings at the Chinamo Camp, he and 46 thousand of his soldiers ended up in communist re-education camps. Gen. Bounpone and members of the royal family were also lured into going to the Vieng Xay re-education center, Houaphan Province where they died.

Photo #125. *H.M. King Savang Vatthana on his visit to the communist town of Vieng Xay in 1973*

Lt. Col. Vang, Geu's photos collection and see in source of The Unforgettable Laos.

Photo #126. *North-Vietnamese attacked and wiped out Division II headquarters at Sala Phoukhoun in March 1975. Lt. Col. Vang, Geu's photos collection and see in source of The Unforgettable Laos.*

Please read the book on the Vientiane leaders' fates at the Vieng Xay Camp, Houaphan Province and see for yourselves how much suffering was involved. You should read the book, "Get to the Trunk, Destroy the Roots –The Fall from Monarchy to Socialism", written by former Col. Khamphan Thammakhanti. His wife, daughter and son-in-law can still make that book available to readers across the world. Col. Khamphan's daughter, Nang Chanh Vannarath, can be contacted at 7321 SE 20th Ave., Portland, OR 97202-6211.

Col. Khamphan was released from the Vieng Xay prison and came to the USA in 1990. He passed away at the age of 74 in Portland, OR on August 26, 2004. *(Thank you, Christopher Kremmer, for telling us about the book).*

CHAPTER 8

LEAVING MILITARY REGION II AND LAOS

On January 27, 1973, an accord was signed to stop the war between the US and North-Vietnam. Present at the signing were Henry Kissinger and William Rogers, representing the USA; and Le Duc Tho, Ms. Ngyuen Thi Binh, Tran Van Lam, and Ms. Ngyuen Dui Trin, representing North-Vietnam.

Photo #127. North Vietnam's delegation to the Paris Peace Conference on January 27, 1973. From left to right: Ms. Nguyen Thi Bin, Ms. Duy Trinh, and Tran Van Lan.

Lt. Col. Vang, Geu's photos collection and see in source of The Unforgettable Laos.

The peace agreement was very damaging to the US in every aspect, including political and military. It signaled the greatest defeat ever seen before in the US and Laos history. At that time, North Vietnam only had a population of 15 million (less than 30 million for both the North and South) and was one of the poorest countries in the world. By comparison, the US had a population of over 300 million, was the most develNorth Vietnamin the world, and was a superpower. The US hadSouth Vietnamrom Vietnam as a loser, scrambling to get out at the last minute and had to leave everything behind. By contrast, North Vietnam continued to attack the US allies (Cambodia, South Vietnam, and Laos) very methodically, step by step, without any concern for the US and the agreements signed in 1954, 1962, and 1973.

Therefore, the Vietnam War was a war that deserves to be analyzed in more detail as lessons learned for Lao, Cambodians, and Vietnamese. It appeared that Henry Kissinger's visit to Laos and South Vietnam on February 9, 1973, was just to tell the Lao rightists to surrender to the

7

Communists because the US had to pull out of Laos, Cambodia, and South Vietnam –countries that fought with the US, believing that the US was a superpower and had a good exit plan. However, the US had no choice but to leave Indochina because Soviet Russia was strongly supporting North Vietnam. However, the US had no choice but to leave Indochina because Soviet Russia was strongly supporting North Vietnam. However, the US had no choice but to leave Indochina because Soviet Russia was strongly supporting North Vietnam.

After witnessing those changes, Gen. Vang Pao called for a meeting of several MR-II high-ranking military officers. The following options were discussed at the meeting:

1. Retreat to the jungle and continue the fight to avoid being taken prisoners and seeing the Vientiane rightists killed like animals because they were the losers. It was determined that this option was not feasible and would not work because the North Vietnamese and the Lao communists would eradicate the Hmong first and then the pro-Vientiane Lao and the communist followers. The Vietnamese wanted to take over Laos as their colony. This option would certainly not be safe to implement.

2. Seize Sayabouri Province and use it as a command center. If the enemy does not choose to attack the area, try to develop it. If not, be prepared to fight back because Sayabouri is close to Thailand allows for war war communication between the two countries because Thailand is not a communist country and used to be an ally in the Vietnam War. This alternative was not found to be safe either, because no less than 70 percent of the population of Sayabouri Province were pro-communist.

3. Ask for asylum in Thailand, waiting for the right time to come back to Laos. For sure, Thailand does not have any land to spare for use as a long-term residence area for refugees from Laos. The chance of success of this option was also very dim because of the many potential political issues that may arise that would be difficult to resolve.

4. Ask for support from the US and admission that this fight was part of the US policy to curb communist expansion to Southeast Asia and the rest of the world. Perhaps, the US might be able to help us, but we need to check further with their Embassy.

On May 10, 1975, Gen. Vang Pao invited the US Ambassador to a consultation meeting. At the time, the US Ambassador to Laos was Charles S. Whitehouse, and the US military adviser working with Gen. Vang Pao was Jerry Daniels. Once the US Ambassador arrived at the meeting room, Gen. Vang Pao explained that given the current developments, the MR-II who had been fighting for years head and shoulders alongside the US were likely going to be harmed by the winning communists. The US Ambassador asked Gen. Vang Pao, "How many military officers are in harm way?" The General took some time to think and then said, "About 3,500." The US Ambassador immediately reacted, "OK. I will find an aircraft from Thailand to pick them up. We need to talk some more about this."

As the meeting note-taker, Gen. Vang Pao sent me to Oudone, Thailand on May 10, 1975 to bring US helicopters in to transport the 3,500 military officers mentioned earlier to the US Ambassador. We also ordered more lights be installed along the runways, as the US military planes would only fly in at night. When I arrived in Oudone, the US officials decided to use C-130, C-46 and C-47 aircrafts instead. As a result, I had to stay in Oudone and never had a chance to see Long Cheng again since that time. I had to go and greet people that were flown in from Long Cheng, and took them to their assigned dwelling units at the Nam Phong Refugee Camp.

Each dwelling unit was equipped with a nice kitchen. In less than a month, all the units were full of refugees. It took three and half days during May 11-14, 1975, to transport all of Gen. Vang Pao's people to Namphong Camp in the Province of Khone Ken, Thailand. Once the planes stopped airlifting, many Hmong who were left behind searched for other ways to leave MR-II for Thailand. Many other people, including parents, relatives, assistants, nieces and nephews followed suite in large numbers by cars, walking across mountains and jungles, heading toward the Laos-Thailand border line near Nongkhay, Thabor, Leui, Phayao, and many other sites to the north and the south. The Hmong and Lao people from MR-II fled to Thabor, Nongkhay, and Namphong Camp. Those from MR-I (Louang Prabang, Sayabouri and Louang Namtha) fled to Nane, Changwath Leui and Chanwath Phayao. The border of Thailand was flooded with Hmong and Lao refugees fleeing from their country.

The refugee population quickly grew in size and soon found nowhere to stay, creating security problems for Thailand, which then ordered its border closed. Later on, the Thai and US governments opened several more refugee camps while also forcing many Lao leaders to leave Thailand for a third country in early June 1975. In November 1975, Namphong Camp started to close its doors to refugees. In 1976, the camp was entirely closed and the refugees who used to live there were transferred to the newly-created Vinai Camp. At Vinai Camp, Hmong and Lao refugees came from Thabor, Nongkhai, and Nam Phong Camps. When people lived together under a not-so-well-organized housing authority and with interferences from scores of bad guys, several issues arose that pushed the Thai government to move the lowland Lao refugees to the Na Pho Camp, Thailand.

In February 1976, the US began to grant entry permits to Lao and Hmong people who had worked for USAID and the CIA. Later on, churches in the US helped in securing entry visas to the US for Christian families from Laos and those who served in the Vietnam War. The US continued to allow those refugees to come to the US until 2006.

May the Lord bless the US and several other countries who loved and cared for refugees from Laos who had just lost their country, had no shelters, were desperate, disappointed, not used to the situation they were going through, were deprived of their roots, and had to leave their families and close relatives because of tragic life changes.

JERRY DANIELS

Jerry Daniels was an agent of the US Central Intelligence Agency (CIA) who came to help MR-II fight against the communists. He had worked alongside Gen. Vang Pao from 1968 until 1975 under the war nickname of "Hog" (wild pig). During 1971-1972, Jerry Daniels managed all military assistance programs to MR-II. From 1973 to May 1975, he oversaw post-war economic development in the field of social affairs, agriculture and cattle raising –buying cattle from Thailand and giving them to local residents to grow. He created several development centers in MR-II, including Nam Goua, Nam Pha, Phak Khae, Nam Mo, Thong Mieng and Muang Decha. In addition, he started implementing several projects involving tree plantation, growing medicinal and other types of plants.

When the war raged in MR-II, people had to immigrate to Thailand. During 1975-1980, Jerry Daniels coordinated food assistance programs to MR-II refugees at Nam Phong and Vinai camps. He helped the MR-II refugees find opportunities to immigrate to the US. On April 28, 1982, Jerry Daniels passed away at his Bangkok, Thailand residence. An official announcement was made about his death and his body was brought back to the US for burial in Montana in mid-1982.

The good deeds of Jerry Daniels and his dedication earned him great respect from the MR-II people. He will be remembered for ever by those he supported and became friend with. [*May his soul rest in peace in Heaven!]*

Photo #128. *Phou Koum's airfield (LS50) between Xieng Khouang Province and Houaphan Province fell into enemy hands in 1969. It served as a behind-the-line airfield. Photos by National Geographic, 1973 and see in source of The Unforgettable Laos.*

Lt. Col. Vang, Geu's photos collections and see in source of The Unforgettable Laos.

Photo #129. *Gen. Vang Pao (in the middle), Col. Vang Geu (right with a watch) and Thai and US experts.*

Photo #130. *Gen. Vang Pao, Col. Vang Geu, and Jerry Daniels on their visit to agricultural projects in Thailand, were being briefed by Thai agricultural expert Souvicha in 1973 in Chiang Mai. Lt. Col. Vang, Geu's photos collections and see in source of The Unforgettable Laos.*

Lt. Col. Vang, Geu's photos collections and see in source of The Unforgettable Laos.

Photo #131. *Souvicha Riranprouk, Thai agricultural research expert, spent time in MR-II working on projects sponsored by Col. Vang Geu and Gen. Vang Pao.*

Photo #132. *From L to R: A Thai mineral expert, Gen. Vang Pao, Dr. Souchit Riramprouk, Col. Tou Feu (the first Hmong who graduated with a Masters degree in Political Science from a US university), and Lt. Col. Thao Na (MR-II construction project manager). Photo taken in 1975. Lt. Col. Vang, Geu's photos collections and see in source of The Unforgettable Laos.*

Photo #133. *Jerry Daniels, Col. Vang Geu and Moua Kao in 1973. Lt. Col. Vang, Geu's photos collections and see in source of The Unforgettable Laos.*

LARRY WOODSON

Larry D. Woodson was one of the volunteers from International Voluntary Services (IVS) from Kansas State who came to help Laos. He used to write, "I arrived in Laos in August of 1964 and was assigned, as a foreign volunteer teacher, to teach at the Luang Prabang's school and help School Principal Taio Chanthavaddy taking care of school supplies, building repairs, agricultural programs and, in the summer, organizing various sports activities, because I played tennis and taught English."

In 1966, IVS invited Larry Woodson to serve as deputy project manager for educational programs in many Lao provinces. Furthermore, he also taught English at the Lycee (high school) and the German Technical School in Vientiane until 1969, with a contract extension every two years.

In 1969, he was promoted to the position of Volunteers Program Manager working at the Sisavangvong University in Dong Dok near Vientiane, with the task of recruiting English teachers and other language instructors.

In 1971, he was hired by USAID as an education counselor for refugees, working in the Laos Ministry of Education's Primary Education Department. He traveled everywhere to each and every refugee resettlement site from north to south to look at the educational needs of each village in terms of school supplies, teachers, students, classrooms, blackboards, desks, chairs, etc. All told, this might have involved no less than 19,000 students who were in need of teachers and schools. He set up about 4,000 additional classrooms.

Photo #134. –*A burnt-down school in MR-II. Larry Woodson ordered helicopters to bring in wood repair material. Lt. Col. Vang, Geu's photos collections and see in source of* The Unforgettable Laos.

Photo # 135. *Civilian workers carrying in wood repair material to rebuiid a school that was burnt down by the enemy. Larry Woodson was the main sponsor.for this program, using US HT 34 helicopters. Lt. Col. Vang, Geu's photos collections and see in source of* The Unforgettable Laos.

In 1974, Larry Woodson was tasked by the US Ambassador to facilitate agricultural and livestock programs in MR-II. He traveled several times to Long Cheng to coordinate the delivery of domestic animals to the Hmong and Lao population in that region (including swine, water buffalos, and cows) at the request of Gen. Vang Pao. Yang Yee served as his counterpart on this project, buying cattle and delivering them to several MR-II sites.

Larry Woodson had those cattles delivered to Bouam Long (LS32), north of the Plain of Jars, and to Long Cheng's farmers. These animals were to be raised by local farmers as part of a post-war program designed to help local residents become self-sufficient during times of lesser foreign assistance. Due to the changes in the political climate, Larry Woodson had to leave Long Cheng one Friday and then leave Laos altogether. He was sure Long Cheng would be captured the following Wednesday. Three days later, the USAID compound in Vientiane was also damaged.

Photo #136. Finally, many children were able to go back to school thanks to the US material assistance coordinated by Jerry Woodson. [Thank you very much, Jerry!]. Lt. Col. Vang, Geu's photos collections and see in source of The Unforgettable Laos.

Photo #137. Larry Woodson and his friends. From left to right: Col. Vang Youa, Mua Dang, Pahom Sundara, Dr. Louat, Graham Hunter (an Australian), Larry Woodson (US IVS) & many unknown girls residents of LS 37, Muong Phoune near Vang Vieng. Lt. Col. Vang, Geu's photos collections and see in source of The Unforgettable Laos.

[Larry Woodson was an American volunteer that I knew well. He spoke Lao very well, was a hard worker, and delivered what he promised. Most importantly, he dared to risk his life by

15

volunteering to help the Lao people during high-risk wartime. May God bless that man who loved and cared for Lao people of all ethnic groups.]

CHAPTER 9

QUESTIONS & ANSWERS ABOUT THE

INDOCHINA WAR

BASIC CAUSES OF THE INDOCHINA WAR

There were many factors that caused the Indochina War, including colonization by the Western World. Great Britain controlled and/or exercised deep influence in many Asian countries, and France took over the Indochina countries of Cambodia, Laos, and Vietnam as either colonies or protectorates. The French and the Siamese used the Mekong River as the borderline for administrative purposes, leaving territories on the right bank of the river under Siamese control and the left bank territories under the control of the French (and the Vietnamese, who wanted to be the masters of the three Indochina countries). Following the end of the Second World War II in 1946, the Siamese government under Prime Minister Pridi Phanomyong agreed to return the Lao provinces of Sayabouri and Champasak to the French basically to:

o Secure French support for Siam's admission as a member of the United Nations
o Eliminate any financial repayments for the damages caused by Siam during the war, and
o Maximize Siam's chance for massive assistance from the US.

As for the French, they resumed their power in Indochina and forced Siam to return the two provinces of Sayabouri and Champasak to Laos in 1946, territories that the Lao Issara and the Vietminh had been using as their regroupment zones in their fight against the French.

Before the colonial age, the Mekong River was flowing freely across the large Lao territory, as mentioned in many popular songs and poems. Foreign domination accelerated nationalist feelings and the thirst for independence of the people of Laos, Vietnam, and Cambodia. They were also encouraged by other countries to move in that direction for the sake of human rights and individual freedom. As a result, a large part of the population stood up to fight against the French right at the start of the Second World War II in order to recover independence from France. The Lao national rebellion movement joined forces with similar movements in neighboring countries of Vietnam and China, trying to secure military assistance and troops from those countries. In the end, those programs became national debts and obligations that were extremely difficult to repay and made our country the slave of the donor countries, adding pain to injuries.

The French regime had positive and negative impacts, but in retrospect, one was always wondering why the Lao did not learn from their fight against the French and use those lessons strategically and conceptually to their advantage. Wouldn't that be a better way out than an armed fight? In time of changes, there are always pluses and minuses. We need to gage which ways hold the most promises before deciding to move in the most favorable direction. Transformations always take time and require patience before showing any results. We should not use resentment and reactive mood if we want to avoid being taken advantage of by ill-intentioned people.

An armed fight made us the servants of countries that provided assistance to us and used a regime that we did not fully understand, like the Lao communist party. As a result, the Lao communists brought in a new administrative system. They also made our country a neo-colony of communist Vietnam, who came in to dominate us, took us back to the Dark Age, denied us freedom of speech, and shut our mouths so they could take away all our country's natural resources.

Ho Chi Minh, founder of communist North Vietnam, used to make a statement at a Vietminh party meeting in 1929, "We accepted to be French servants, but we have to be prepared to be the Lao and Khmer bosses in Indochina." Ho Chi Minh studied communism in France and underwent additional training in Russia. Once he became a communist expert, he returned to Thailand to begin the fight to push the French out of Indochina. At that time, Thailand adopted an anti-French position and gave Ho Chi Minh a good chance to start his fight for independence in Thailand. The timing was right as it coincided with the start of World War II initiated by Hitler in Europe. In Asia, Japan also rose up to free itself from western influence. This was a good opportunity for Ho Chi Minh to receive arms and ammunitions from the US and get ready to fight Japan alongside the US. When Japan lost the war, it also left several types of weapons with Ho Chi Minh and Thailand for use in national liberation fights.

Right before the start of World War II, Russia also underwent deep political changes. The communist party headed by Lenin, who led the revolution against the former tsarist regime and killed all the members of the Russian royal family except for a small girl who was able to escape, paved the way for Ho Chi Minh. In early 1945, once he was well equipped with weapons, Ho Chi Minh resolutely began his fight against the French, who were then heavily attacked and pushed around by the Germans.

THE NEW WORLD AFTER WORLD WAR II

The end of World War II marked the beginning of the communist war that split the world into two camps: the eastern camp and the western camp.

- o The eastern camp consisted of pro-communist countries, including Soviet Russia, Red China, and several other communist countries.
- o The Western camp, led by the US and its allies in Europe, consisted of free democratic countries that were well united until the loss of Dien-Bien-Phu, when several international conflicts arose.

In 1949, the pro-communist Chinese won their internal fight against the nationalist Chinese. They put the entire country of China under a communist regime led by Mao Zedong that was receiving assistance from Russia. In 1950, the Korean War started, prompting the US to deploy armed forces to assist free South Korea fighting communist expansion. Korea was then divided into two parts:

- **North Korea,** under a communist regime backed by Red China and Russia
- **South Korea,** a democratic country with strong backing from the US

Ho Chi Minh joined the Communist World in 1951. He sent many divisions of North-Vietnamese troops for military training along the borderline of Laos, Vietnam, and China. This caused the West (USA and France) to be worried about the expansion of communism into southeast-Asia (Thailand, Vietnam, Laos, Cambodia, etc.).

In 1951, Indochinese communists interfered in many ways in the internal affairs of Laos, over and under the table, including pulling Prince Souphanouvong into their camp. Dwight Eisenhower, who became the US President in 1953, was very concerned about the situation in Asia. He once declared, "If we lose Laos, it would be as if we lost the entire south-east Asia." He joined hands with France's President, Gen. Charles de Gaulle, in developing a plan of defense against communist expansion, setting up the military camp of Dien-Bien-Phu at a critical location between China and Laos in early 1952 as a strong signal to the communist side. The French dedicated a lot of efforts in the establishment of Dien-Bien-Phu, and deployed no less than 30,000 regular troops and several thousands of regional guards to that camp and the surrounding valley areas. The idea was to lure communist troops up in the higher elevations and have them fight from there because it was easier to attack them that way, especially dropping bombs on them. This was not something that the communists would like to do, as they usually carried heavy equipment and have not used that attack strategy very often.

In December 1952, North Vietnam did everything it could to help the Lao Issara capture Samneua and Phongsaly Provinces, believing that these provinces used to be the Lao Issara strongholds. In reality, what they did was to send troops to encircle the Dien-Bien-Phu base and cut the French reinforcement and support line as part of the overall strategy for China to attack from the north and North Vietnam to attack from the south. The US and France agreed that France should be deploying troops and weapons to reinforce the local forces around Dien-Bien-Phu and that the US would be providing air support. So, France did the troop deployment between early November 1953 and January 1954, but the US didn't do what they had agreed to do and, instead, sided with Ho Chi Minh. The US was talked out of helping France fight the Vietminh because that would be against the US policy of not helping an old colonial power (France) regain its old colonial territory (Vietnam). Therefore, the US agreed with Ho Chi Minh to start negotiations in Geneva, Switzerland, on May 21, 1954.

The Vietminh took advantage of the situation and started attacking Dien-Bien-Phu lost on May 7, 1954, three weeks before the scheduled Geneva negotiation date. The US decision to get involved was uncertain because they underestimated Ho Chi Minh and were not yet aware that he was an executive member of the international communist party. The fall of Dien-Bien-Phu made France very unhappy with the US, who then refused to sign the Indochina peace accords as planned for July 20, 1954. This situation caused France to change its strategy and collaborate with the communists. As a result, several Frenchmen ended up spying and looking for signals on the US strategy and feeding them to the Vietnamese communists.

Furthermore, the US generated fear of communism in many countries around the globe --in Asia, Europe, and Latin America-- and indirectly pushed many of those countries to collaborate with the communists. The political situation in the US and other relatively nearby countries like Cuba, Nicaragua, and Argentina was in turmoil; many issues also surfaced in Europe. This prompted US President Kennedy to begin an overseas war in the Indochina peninsula instead of allowing one to occur around the US or in the US itself. The US did not need to win the war; it was more interested in testing its new weapons on the communists and getting a feel for how destructive such a fight would be. Two good examples included the battles of Khe-Sanh in the end of 1967 and Hue on February 27, 1968, which the US qualified as "hopeless fights".

As a result, the US political situation changed drastically. Because of those changes, Gen. Vang Pao and the US forbid French aircrafts or Frenchmen to come to Long Cheng or MR-II. The US didn't allow any French newsmen in Hue, South-Vietnam either.

After the communist North Vietnam's victory at Dien-Bien-Phu, Vietnam became a two-part country –the North and the South.

NORTH-VIETNAM

The communist party took the opportunity to infiltrate very dangerously into South Vietnam and forced the US to come out and monitor the situation on the spot. This led to other events, including the coup d'état mounted by Kong Lae in Vientiane, Laos. The Geneva Accords of 1954 forbid all foreign interferences in the kingdom of Laos, and the French themselves had assured Laos that whenever communist Vietnam was to disregard those Accords, they would be the first country to come to Laos' rescue immediately.

After Kong Lae mounted his coup d'état, North Vietnam smartly allowed him to pick Prince Souvanna Phouma –who had just been named Laos Ambassador to France not long before—as the new Prime Minister of the Laos government. The prince was married to Aline Allard, a half-French lady born in Laos, and was the Lao leader that the French trusted the most. When Souvanna Phouma proclaimed Laos' policy of neutrality, the French were flabbergasted and chose not to help Laos anymore. Prince Souvanna Phouma then turned to Red China, North Vietnam, Russia, Vietnam, Russia, and the communist world for help. Those countries openly sent in weapons, war materials, and North-Vietnamese and North Vietnamese troops to help the new Laos revolutionary government in Vientiane. Between the start of the coup d'état and Kong Lae's retreat to the Plain of Jars, huge Russian Ilyushin jets continuously flew in to drop supplies at the Wattai Airport, Kasy, Muang Soui, and the Plain of Jars a hundred times a day, from morning to sunset.

Once they witnessed those activities, the US decided to provide military assistance to Prince Boun-Oum Na Champasak and Gen. Phoumi Nosavan. This led to direct US field participation in an attempt to control communist expansion to South Vietnam and Southeast Asia. US President Kenney decided to take part in the Indochina war from 1963 on, a war referred to as the "10,000-day war". This turned out to be the longest war fought by the US in its history. This was a war where you heard a lot of gunshots but saw nobody. The jungle was dense and full of wild animals. The weather was also different than in the US.

In 1970, Cambodia's King Sihanouk had to seek refuge in China because of Gen. Lon Nol's coup d'état and the fact that the US and South Vietnam needed Gen. Lon Nol's help. Sihanouk proclaimed Cambodian neutrality but Cambodia had to allow passage trails and hiding spots to North Vietnamese troops on their way to South Vietnam. Both Sihanouk and Souvanna Phouma adopted the same policy. Therefore, when Gen. Kouprasith Abhay attacked Vientiane after Kong Lae mounted his coup d'état, Prince Souvanna fled to Cambodia.

SOUTH-VIETNAM

South Vietnam became a free country after the French retreat in 1954, although there were still quite a few Frenchmen left behind, mainly businessmen. Eventually, those tradesmen also had to leave south-Vietnam little by little, causing some concerns to several Vietnamese leaders and prompting various kinds of appeals and negotiations. In the end, a coup d'état took place. The country had to request assistance from the US to counter communist expansion to South Vietnam. This was the main reason for the start of the Indochina war.

In 1969, Soviet Russia and Red China had a border fight along their areas. Between 1951 and 1969, the Indochina Communist Party (ICP) rarely did anything openly, but after the US President Nixon's visit to China on February 21, 1972 the ICP started playing a key role in several important decisions, including the appointment of Kaysone Phomvihane as Secretary General of the Lao Communist Party, leaving Prince Souphanouvong as leader by name only, without any real power. Prince Souphanouvong's own son was killed by Lao communists in Samneua, Houaphan Province, with the Hmong being blamed as the killers.

WHY DID THE US LEAVE INDOCHINA?

In fact, the US forces did not lose the Vietnam War. President Nixon made in chapter 8, page 219 of his Memoirs, "Why the North won the Vietnam war?" the following statements, "*We lost the war because of our own people. Ho Chi Minh was just the one that reaped the benefits.*" This was really true because of the unexpected changes in the US political scenery punctuated by student and public heavy demonstrations against the government in 1965 and 1966. In 1972, those demonstrations had to be harshly controlled by police forces, causing the death of several demonstrating students in Tennessee and Ohio. The Watergate scandal forced President Nixon to leave office in 1974 and be replaced by Vice-President Ford. These events prompted the US to spend more attention to its internal affairs, instead of Vietnam affairs, that occurred far away and had less of an immediate impact on the US. Hence, Indochina easily went under North-Vietnam's control without any choice.

Photo #138. *President Nixon met with Chairman Mao Ze Dong in Bejing in 1972 (after USSR-China border conflict in 1969). Source. Photo by Sovfoto/UIG via Getty Images and See in reference page.*

In 1967, communist Vietnam attacked the entire kingdom of Laos and South-Vietnam. A French journalist met with Gen. Vo Nguyen Giap (North-Vietnam's military tactical commander) and asked him, *"America is a powerful nation; how do you feel about fighting against America?"* Gen. Giap replied, *"A second Dien-Bien-Phu in South-Vietnam is unavoidable."* The French journalist had no further questions, took off and went on to meet with Gen. Westmoreland, US Military Commander in South-Vietnam. He asked the US General, "What do you think about Gen. Vo Nguyen Giap's statement that 'A second Dien-Bien-Phu is bound to occur in South-Vietnam'?" Gen. Westmoreland replied, *"I don't know. Go and ask my deputy-Commander in Hue."* The French journalist wanted to go to Hue, but the US would not allow any French journalists in for security reason. After the French journalist left, Gen. Westmoreland called a meeting with his senior staff to discuss Gen. Giap's hints about a second Dien-Bien-Phu battle in South-Vietnam.

How would that battle occur and where? The following were possible North-Vietnamese attack scenarios that were discussed.

o Deployment of troops from the China Sea. This scenario would be impossible because North-Vietnam did not have adequate Navy forces and were not ready for this type of attack from the sea. It would be tantamount to suicidal bees intentionally flying into a burning fireplace.

o eployment of troops across the demilitarized zone. This scenario was not any more feasible either, because the whole world would accuse North-Vietnam of invading South-Vietnam. Besides, North-Vietnam would have to use massive and well-equipped armed forces to have any chance to attack the allied forces in a region that was within the firing range of the US Navy ships operating in the China Sea. This scenario would be highly risky for North-Vietnam's army.

o Deployment of troops through the jungle along the Laos/Cambodia border to invade South-Vietnam. This was the option that North-Vietnam had and would probably like to use.

Following that meeting, the US commanders in South-Vietnam decided to establish the Khe-Sanh military base near Sepone and to close to the border between South and North Vietnam. Khe Sanh was a very well fortified camp with about 6,000 troopers and pro-US Montagnard soldiers deployed in the front line and South-Vietnamese soldiers in the middle. The whole base stretched over eight miles, packed with a series of interlinked posts to facilitate troop movements back toward the two square mile nucleus area. The US installed barbed wire fences all around and planned to add improvised explosive devices at selected spots as well. The whole complex, completed in the end of 1967, was equipped with electronic equipment capable of detecting the size of the invading troops and their movement.

The North-Vietnamese watched the construction of this base closely and developed a plan to attack it as soon as it was completed. Gen. Vo Nguyen Giap deployed an armed force of over 60,000 troopers (ten times more than the US-allied troops) for the Khe-Sanh attack. These troops first attacked the front line units stationed eight miles away from the central command center, and pushed them back four miles inside. The allied troops moved back and regrouped inside the 2-mile nucleus, under a plan to wait until the enemy reached the bombing target zone before ordering B-52's in. However, the enemy's attack was too strong, the US had B-52's dropping bombs immediately by waves of one B-52 after the other.

After the bombing, the US troops knew exactly the enemy's status thanks to the electronic sensors that were put in place. Because of the heavy losses his troops suffered at Khe-Sanh and to distract attention, Gen. Vo Nguyen Giap ordered the communist attack on Hue during New-Year holidays, causing serious damages to both sides.

In April 1968, the fighting still continued at Khe-Sanh through artillery firing. The US dispatched helicopters to round up all the allied troops and announced that the Khe-Sanh base has been seized by the communists. Several helicopters were shut down during the air evacuation operation. Gen. Vo Nguyen Giap learned very painful lessons from this battle. Of the 60,000 troops, only 10,000 survived, some of them badly injured.

After that, the French journalist came back to see Gen. Vo Nguyen Giap and asked him again, "Why didn't you ask for support from China like you did for Dien-Bien-Phu? Why did let so many Vietnamese soldiers die?" Gen. Giap replied, "I didn't want to ask for Chinese help because, wherever they went, Chinese would be born there." He didn't say anything more.

The North-Vietnamese communists, who were not able to take advantage of their number superiority in the battle of Khe-Sanh, implemented a new strategy that relied on using South-Vietnam's recruits dressed in black (not green) uniform. As a result, many people got the news that the fighters who died in the battlefields of Hue and Ban Me Le on February 27, 1968 New-Year Day were all wearing black uniforms. They accused the US for killing Vietnamese civilians, and branded the US troops stationed in Vietnam as murderers of civilians. Many US citizens did not fully understand the new ploy used by the communists. Jane Fonda was one of those who helped promote the communist plan and misled US laymen, students and long-haired hippies who were holding demonstrations against the government and against continuation of the war in Vietnam.

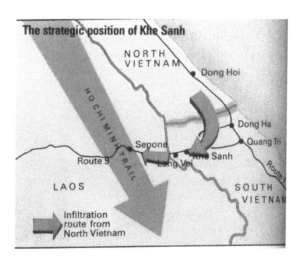

Map #139. *Ho Chi Minh Trail to South-Vietnam (1967-1968). North Vietnam sent more than 60,000 troops to attack Khe Sanh, but only 10,000 of those survived that battle, handicapped or badly wounded. Lt. Col. Vang, Geu's map information and see source in The Unforgettable Laos.*

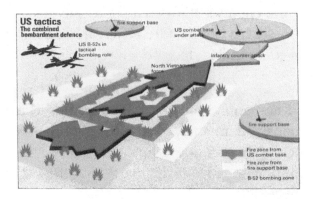 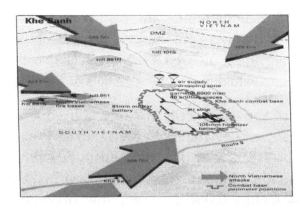

***Photos #140** (left) **and 141**(right). Defense line around Khe-Sanh in late 1967. Source: "Vietnam. The history and the tactics") source, see in The Unforgettable Laos.*

The US ended up losing an internal political war that led to the inglorious return of the US soldiers who fought in Vietnam. Normally, every activity should be directed at counteracting the enemy's strategy. However, in this field, the allies did not fully understand the strategy that was often used in hunting wild animals. Normally, the buck never comes out first in the open field; only the doe and the baby deer do. A novice and inexperienced hunter would tend to shoot the female deer or the young deer first, thus allowing the male deer to flee for safety. The Vietnamese soldier is like the male deer and the US soldier deployed to Vietnam is like the novice hunter, who shoots the doe and the baby deer first.

The communists liked to use children to plant bombs, and gave women a role to play in a war that was fought using all kinds of tactics, some of which fell under the psychological warfare portfolio. They used the words "people troops" and "people army" in that general context. In addition, the communists liked to use common citizens as human shield because they knew that the US would not shoot at unarmed people. The US presence in Vietnam was only of a supportive and defensive nature, with a lot to lose and nothing to gain. The plus sign was to split the communist world and generate new thinking. Currently, most of the communist world has changed a lot, with some communist countries changing faster than others. Changes that occurred in Russia and mainland China are good examples. It was only fair that the US assigned itself the task of controlling the situation in a world that was being affected by communist expansion and was unable to defend itself. Laos, Thailand, Cambodia, and South Vietnam were among those countries needing help. Absent a world superpower, this world of ours would be insecure because many countries cannot defend themselves.

The mainland China-Soviet Russia border conflict gave an opportunity for communist Vietnam to receive all kinds of weapons from Russia for use in their fight against the US. As a result, North Vietnam became a pro-Soviet country, which prompted Mao Zedong to ask for continued US presence in Indochina until 1972 and to state he would be open for a meeting with President Nixon.

In 1972, several Neo Lao Hak Xath leaders at the ministerial level had told Vientiane leaders, "Our feet are floating in the air with nothing to stand on. We need to help each other!" Phagna Touby Lyfoung and Gen. Vang Pao were both aware of the situation but failed to pay enough attention to it, because, so far, what the Pathet Lao or the Lao communists said has always been mostly misleading and/or unreliable. In 1974, Gen. Vang Pao was invited to a meeting at the royal palace in Louang Prabang. At that meeting, Prince Souphanouvong handed out a note to Gen. Vang Pao's personal security guard and told him, "Please give this note to Gen. Vang Pao." The note read, "Request a personal meeting with you, General, to discuss the downtrend slide of our country." But Gen. Vang Pao remained silent and did not pay any attention to the message. Based on his experience, the Pathet Lao never executed what was discussed or agreed to in written documents. They only misled people and executed North-Vietnam's policy.

— ***Photo # 142**. A Thai Dam woman doing excavation work on the road leading to Dien-Bien-Phu in 1954. . Lt. Col. Vang, Geu's photos collections and information and see source in The Unforgettable Laos.*

—

PERSONAL APPEAL FROM SOUPHANOUVONG

(Prior to his death, written in 1993)

Reference: *Stalking the Elephant King,* by Christopher Kremmer

[Christopher Kremmer was an Australian journalist who was interested in Southeast Asian and had written several books on the war in Vietnam and Laos. Even after the US had left Vietnam, Laos, and Cambodia behind to face their own destinies under communist control, he still maintained that interest, especially in the Laos situation. He tried many times to come and see for himself what it was like but has not been able to penetrate the bamboo wall that the Lao communists erected in secret. After the collapse of the communist regimes in Europe, Lao communist leaders had to open the door for foreign assistance to pour in. Australia was one of the donor countries. The Lao communist leaders were then not able to continue to prevent Australian journalists from visiting Laos. As a result, Christopher Kremmer was able to enter Laos in the end of 1993].

His main objective was to find out more about the fate of H.M. the King and his family, who had disappeared in 1976. Using his journalist connections, he was able to meet with Prince Souphanouvong, who was then gravely ill and under treatment at his residence at Phone Sa-Aath. On that occasion, Prince Souphanouvong provided details on his relationships with Vietnam and asked to issue his final message to all the Lao natives in the following paragraphs.

"Because I worshipped woman's beauty, I became deaf and blind throughout my whole life. It's only until now that I realize it was a big mistake of mine. I didn't think that the Vietnamese had such a secret plan to destroy my country and my countrymen. During all the time that I collaborated with the Vietminh in the fight for independence, we had agreed that once the fight ended, the Vietnamese would go back to Vietnam and that Lao would go back to Laos, irrespective of the fact that we have a Vietnam-Laos friendship treaty in place.

"I do not know when they were going to cremate my body, but I know that everything they have done to my country would not be erased after I stopped breathing and after my body is cremated. Up to now, I have not been able to speak up, only keep everything in the back of my mind. Therefore, in view of the currently dangerous situation in my country, I would like to appeal to all my countrymen, including women, men, nieces and nephews of all Lao ethnic groups, and elders who are still healthy, to unanimously forgive me for all the mistakes that I committed toward our Lao country and our Lao people.

"Now, I'm no longer a patriot and someone who is looking for things that are beneficial to my country because I had been betrayed. Once you folks have a chance to listen to or read my appeal, please take your thinking in a new direction in order to defend your country and the natural resources of the population, and most importantly, maintain your "Lao roots" pride forever.

"My dear countrymen, especially those of you, brothers, sisters, and nieces and nephews living abroad who sincerely love your country and your race, can see far and are well-educated, remember that your patriotism is deep and, please, don't let your country disappear. For those of you who live inside the country, you must adjust yourselves, love each other, move together in a new direction, and, more importantly, follow the lead of your relatives who live abroad. If you understand correctly the situation in our country and listen to my appeal, you will have a stable and honorable future. Before I die, I would like to leave this appeal with you all. Please, be patient and keep fighting hard. I am convinced that our country will survive and remain Laos forever."

Photo #143 (left). *Tiao Souphanouvong not long before he passed away.*

Photo #144 (right). *Taio Souphanouvong and his wife, Mom Viengkham, on the day of their wedding in Nha-Tranh on January 19, 1938. Mom Viengkham (nee Nguyen Thi Kinam) was an educated Vietnamese lady. Lt. Col. Vang, Geu's collected news information and see source in The Unforgettable Laos.*

PHOUMI VONGVICHIT

Phoumi Vongvichit was born on May 6, 1909, and died on July 1, 1994. He fought as a true nationalist for Laos' independence from 1945 to 1975 alongside communist North Vietnam. He did remove a wooden plow from the people's necks but soon replaced it with a heavier steel plow. That's how things are today when communist Viet Nam is controlling everything in Laos. He signed the agreement that led to the formation of the third Lao coalition government in 1973, together with Ngone Sananikone, a fake agreement that could not be used by the Lao people —only by the Vietnamese communists. Kaysone Phomvihane later signed a treaty that allowed for Vietnam to come in and rule Laos for 25 years on July 18, 1977, a treaty that may be extended for unlimited, consecutive 10-year terms.

Photo #145. *Phoumi Vongvichit and his wife. Photo taken in 1979 in Vientiane. Lt. Col. Vang, Geu's collected news information and see source in The Unforgettable Laos.*

CHAPTER 10

COMMUNISTS' SECRET AND

MANIPULATIVE PLAN

SHORT-TERM PLAN TO CATCH LAOS

The communists tried to encourage the Lao people to create a basis to fight their leaders. They must help and stay close to those Lao leaders they have picked that held grudges against their own leaders. The hand-picked individuals became permanent members of the central Lao communist party and were taught how to fight and to conduct themselves as true communists when taking actions. For example, good candidates included those who were mad because their sisters, brothers, parents, sons or relatives got killed or detained by their enemy; and those who were in difficulty but were very ambitious. Those folks were easy to approach and infiltrate, because they believed in the ads and took the call for struggle very seriously. The messages were also delivered to the rural population who lacked contacts with the government. This was done by dispatching teams of data gatherers to the field to collect information, stay close to the local residents and talk to them or pay them to do things that were not allowed by the government. Being on the opposition's side, the communists provided weapons for the fight. When the fight started, damages started piling up and created more intense hate within the community. At that point, the communists sent in supporting troops and took over as planned.

The cease-fire negotiations that took place on January 27, 1973, in Paris between the US and North Vietnam took place without the attendance of Laos, North Vietnam's collaborator. The Lao communists didn't have the right to attend, and had to wait for instructions from North-Vietnam and for that country to share some of its benefits. However, with North-Vietnam's victory, the benefit that Lao communists got this time was only an opportunity to deliver their country on a golden plate to their superiors, in accordance with the plan laid out by Ho Chi Minh, the founder of the Indochina Communist Party. This was some form of debt repayment for the blood of North Vietnamese soldiers who died in Laos while fighting for the red Laos. North Vietnam then violated the July 20, 1954, and July 23, 1962 cease-fire agreements that prohibited foreign troops from interfering in the internal affairs of neutral Laos. North-Vietnam invaded Laos openly without any fear of and any concern for the rest of the world.

[Please read the plan to dissolve the Vientiane faction by the Lao communists, the close first-hand servants of North Vietnam. This plan created dissension within the Lao community; it formed the basis for the North Vietnamese to take over Laos as its neo-colony].

Prince Souvanna Phouma was like a soccer player who abandoned his original team and joined a new one. But he didn't know the game plan of the new team. He just thought that, as a royal prince, he could do anything he wanted. This was an out-of-date thinking, because the world has evolved and is now under two political regimes: democratic regime and communist regime. Lao communists were going after the princes and the kings. They didn't like the old Laos' three elephant head flag that stood for the three Lao princes, and replaced it with a red flag with hammer crossed with a sickle –the current Laos' flag.

Photo #146. *The flag of the Laos PDR shown next to the flag of the Indochina Communist Party. The Laos' flag with a "Ka Deuane" (moon) logo was first introduced on December 2, 1975. Lt. Col. Vang, Geu's collected news information and see source in The Unforgettable Laos.*

see more source in:
https://www.facebook.com/permalink.php?story_fbid=pfbido2UaoRyBaFSv8VV1uqQTeXa5Ng
YM7J6AHYELgmS3EgGpLiZ8RRMQSFDwGnSq9o7VzSl&id=100063462529798

Once Prince Souvanna Phouma decided to join hands with the communists, he lost all credit and meanings, and just became a tool that served the communists' policy and interests. An old Lao proverb used to say, "United we survive, parting ways we die." This was really true. Prince Souvanna Phouma pulled himself away from the Vientiane faction to rally with Lao leaders who were closely knitted with communist North-Vietnam --Kaysone Phomvihane, Kham-Ouan Boupha and Phoumi Vongvichit, the keys that allowed communism to open the door to Laos. The most glaring evidence applied to Tiao Souvanna Phouma and Tiao Souphanouvong, two princely brothers with high education from France, definitely classified among the Lao elite, who initiated the fight to recover independence from France. After their deaths, none of them got any single statue cast and shown in a public place to memorize their role in Laos' history. Only statues of Kaysone Phomvihane, the "born in North-Vietnam and grown in Laos" leader can be seen today. *[According to reliable sources, Kaysone's father was a Vietnamese whom the French sent to Laos as a teacher; he brought his son Kaysone with him]*. This was because the Indochina Communist Party (ICP) said so. ICP ordered that monuments be built to honor Kaysone as a national hero, because he was the one who signed the friendship treaty between communist Vietnam and communist Laos on July 18, 1977 that allowed communist Vietnam to control Laos for 25 years (until 2002) with unlimited 10-year extensions after that.

The Lao communist party has many army generals, and many educated and capable cabinet ministers. Early in the game, none of those, however, were named Minister of Justice. That cabinet

4

position went instead to Kham-Ouane Boupha, a man highly regarded by Kaysone Phomvihane because he used to act like "a submissive Minister of Defense" to him. This appointment was made when the Lao communists had gained full power and was part of their plan to dismantle the Vientiane faction. The Minister of Justice in effect had full power over decisions regarding death penalties. He had the authority to sentence anybody to death in a one party regime, with no room for appeal. Please read Gen. Kham-Ouan Boupha's statements in the section, *"How to keep the Champa flower blooming."*

Gen. Kham-Ouan might have been a victim of North-Vietnam's tactics based on his tricky plan to attract high-ranking Lao officials away from their jobs and get them executed at the Vieng Xay re-education camp. The same plan also pushed a lot of people to immigrate overseas. Gen. Kham-Ouan was worried when he saw people become poorer and deprived of leaders, education, skill, and expertise to the point that the whole country of Laos is now rated one of the poorest countries in the world. Furthermore, Laos is now also a Vietnam's follower, and is allowing a lot of Vietnamese in. With no work to do, Lao natives have to look for jobs, sell their bodies abroad, and get married with Vietnamese and citizens from neighboring countries in order to survive. As more and more Lao people immigrate overseas, more and more Vietnamese are coming in to occupy lands for free (or buy them at very low costs). Foreign contractors in every field are pouring in to work on our natural resources that will likely entirely evaporate in a not too distant future.

LONG-TERM PLAN TO COLONIZE LAOS

In the end of 1981, I had a chance to interview a Lao refugee family who just arrived in the USA. The conversation went as follows.

- "When did your family immigrate to Thailand?"
- "About five months ago."
- "How come you were able to come to the US so fast?"
- "Because our children sponsored us. I also used to serve in the Royal Lao Army"
- "Why did you take so long to leave? Why didn't you come in 1975?"
- "We were dying to leave, but we didn't know the language, had nobody to show us the way, and no one to rely on. Finally, we realized we couldn't live on when there was no freedom; we were under constant surveillance and bullied all the time. They said that we 'Patikane' have no right to be Lao and continue to own what we used to own. All those things, they said, we inherited them because we were 'selling our country' and serving capitalist interests."
- "Why aren't you the owner of your possessions?"
- "The pro-Vietminh Lao communists are in full control. Everything belongs to the State. They keep saying we were CIA agents. That's why we decided to leave. It's better to die somewhere else, rather than being harassed all the time."

According to the news, many North-Vietnam-instigated measures have taken place, including moving the Vietnam/Laos border line 20 kilometers westward *(from the original border line)*, and multiple development plans involving road construction, lumber cutting, starting new villages, displacing residents to make room for new Vietnamese military bases or new Vietnamese civilian dwellings, prohibiting Lao citizens to walk by the new construction sites, etc. These measures are part of the long-range plan to permanently occupy Laos.

As a result, all those children born after the signing of the 25-year Vietnam-Lao friendship treaty by Kaysone Phomvihane will be half-Vietnamese kids who would have been fully trained in communist doctrines and ready to actively administer Laos as a new province of communist Vietnam. Before long, the history, customs, traditions and beliefs of the Lao people would be gone for sure, making the Lao a people without country, subject to constant pressure and under the control of the lone communist party.

These are the reasons that prompted many Lao citizens to leave their country and test their luck somewhere else in an effort to rebuild a new --albeit highly uncertain-- life abroad. Communist Vietnam is in control of all the armed forces, leaving the Laos PDR no armies and no heavy weapons to defend itself, except for local security guards and policemen equipped only with Ak 47 guns with a shooting range of less than 25 yards, and small hand guns. A Lao proverb read, "If you trust the Vietnamese, you will lose your crops." Souphanouvong and Souvanna Phouma trusted the Vietnamese. Those two Lao leaders disappeared from the scene in 1975.

Photo #147. *North-Vietnam's plan and tactics was to invade Laos in three phases, including (1) controlling mountainous and rural areas and population, (2) taking over villages and roads and creating disturbances, and (3) using invading military forces to reap victory and setting up permanent bases in Laos. Lt. Col. Vang, Geu's collected news information and see source in The Unforgettable Laos.*

Map #148. *This map shows how communist Vietnam is implementing their assimilation plan. Red zones have been fully assimilated, dark blue zones are being equipped with permanent constructions, and white zones are military bases and living areas of communist Vietnamese. The Lao people are not allowed in any of those areas since 1965. Lt. Col. Vang, Geu's collected news information and see source in The Unforgettable Laos.*

PLAN TO ASSUME POWER BY FORCES

The agreement signed between the US and North-Vietnam in Paris on 27 January 1973 allowed North-Vietnam to redeploy its army and regain control over Laos, Cambodia and South-Vietnam very easily. In mid-1974, Cambodia fell completely under the North-Vietnam's control.

In February 1975, the US and South-Vietnam forces fled South-Vietnam in disarray. In May 1975, Laos also fell completely under the control of the Lao and North-Vietnamese communists. Hundreds of thousands of Lao left their country or were sent to the re-education camp of Vieng Xay in Houaphan Province. The MR-II troops were flown to Oudone, Thailand, with the last flight ending on May 14, 1975 at aroung 11 a.m.

In the Paris Agreement, the two Lao factions agreed to delineate their respective territories, but the Lao communists used the Agreement as a mechanism to attack the rightist Lao troops who had no means to defend themselves since the US had already withdrawn their troops. North-Vietnam also took advantage of the situation and deployed their armed forces equipped with all kinds of weapons from the Plain of Jars to the Sala Phou Khoune's steel bridge, to Nam Link, to Hine Heup, to That Lath and then back to MR-II through Na Sou and Ban Sone to cut the support line of the MR-II troops stationed in Long Cheng. In the north, the enemy moved its troops from Ban Na to Phou Louang Matt and then to Sam Thong and Ban Hine Tang, getting ready to attack Long Cheng anytime. They were waiting for the right time to catch all the fish in the same net, and tried to avoid sending out an early wrong signal that would give people an excuse to run away.

At that time, Sisouk Nachampasak was still officially Laos' Minister of Defense. Had any fighting occur, the communist side would have been blamed by the whole free world for violating the signed agreement. The Lao communists were the ones with an edge, because they had several divisions of North-Vietnamese troops to support them. They could take over anytime they wished; although they felt they needed to use some political tactics to first incite the laymen people, students, and civilian employees to organize public demonstrations. The Vientiane faction had to find a way to cool down those demonstrations. As it turned out, this was instead a better chance for the Lao communists to attack the rightist faction, after accusing them of manslaughter before the International Court of Justice. The communist-backed demonstrations ended up forcing the rightists to decide to leave the country. The Lao communists then rounded up all the Vientiane's cabinet ministers, army officers, policemen and national employees who could not quite read the communist tactics, and sent them to the re-education camp of Vieng Xay, Houaphan Province. Of the 46,000 or so that were sent to the camp, a large number of detainees died there.

In 1979, when China attached Vietnam, a small group of political detainees were released from Vieng Xay, many of them with health and emotional problems. These events that involved so much hardship inflicted to other human beings was foretold in a prediction made way back in the Buddhist year of 2500, *"Ogres will come out and eat the Lao. The lucky ones will survive by seeking shelter under banyan trees."* This means that the survivors were the lucky ones who went abroad and escaped being killed or tortured by the communists.

PROS AND CONS OF SELF-EXILE

Gen. Vang Pao and many leaders have decided to leave MR-II and the kingdom of Laos. Advantages and disadvantages of such a decision are discussed below.

ADVANTAGES

The most obvious advantage was the absence of the bloodshed for both sides that has been avoided, because MR-II and the rest of the kingdom of Laos had already lost a great number of people between 1945 and 1975 due the battles that the communist Vietnamese fought in Laos. In addition to human losses, the abundant natural resources in those areas have also been significantly destroyed more than in any other country in the entire world because of military operations.

The following excerpts from Gen. Thonglith Chokbengboun's speech delivered after his arrival in a foreign country further described the turbulent situation.

"The agents of the Vietnamese communists used deep tactics to incite the members of the 21-Gang Organization to rise and chase the rightist leaders away from their positions. If the rightist party had used armed forces to counter the Organization, the Lao communists would for sure have referred this case to the International Court of Justice, claiming that the Lao rightists' had murdered people because the 21-Gang Organization included students and national employees mixed with several Lao communist leaders. If fighting had occurred at that time, there would have been no opportunities to immigrate to a developed country and to see the truth behind the Lao communists' strategy."

We want to congratulate Gen. Thonglith. He was a good high-ranking army officer who has learned the tactics used by the Lao communists, and deserved our full respect. We also are thankful for those highly ethical and compassionate countries that welcomed Lao refugees to their lands and cared for them, especially the USA who let in more refugees from MR-II and the kingdom of Laos than any other country, gave them the chance to restart a new life, learn new things, and allowed their children and grand-children to get a decent education. We wish to congratulate many Lao leaders who provided a bridge for our compatriots to cross and avoid becoming the victims of the communist regime. Leaders like Gen. Thonglith and Gen. Vang Pao clearly understood the gravity of the situation. They made the right decisions "to immigrate overseas to remove themselves from constant Lao communists' harassment."

DISADVANTAGES

The primary disadvantage rested with being away from your native country, your relatives and your close friends, all of which created a feeling of deep and unexpected sadness. We immigrants felt homesick; we no longer have a country of our own to speak of, and can no longer practice our customs and speak our traditional language. We have to start everything a new. The older folks are especially disappointed and sad because they are no longer qualified to do their old jobs and have no more opportunities to educate themselves. They felt bad about leaving their country in the exclusive hands of the Lao communist party. This is a party that did not implement the 18-point agreement it has signed with the rightist party; continued to infringe upon the rights of the Lao population of all ethnic groups that still live in Laos, constantly threatening them, creating internal family and community dissentions, looking for opportunities to using them as tools to dismantle the Lao society, and making false charges that are later used as the basis for incriminating individuals suspected of collaborating with the rightist group.

Furthermore, the Lao communist party had killed many Lao ethnic people, including the Hmong who went into hiding in the jungle and did not dare to come out and cooperate with the Lao communist party for fear of being killed or sent for an indefinite period to a re-education camp, away from the outside world and their close families. The Lao communist party does not have a religion and does not accept any moral guilt –just power. Their search for the ethnic groups hiding in the jungle was just an excuse; their main objective was to give their agents a chance to pilfer unashamedly everything they could find, e.g., cutting trees, collecting mining products, taking ownerships of productive lands, etc. This was the main reason for the ethnic groups to flee in the jungle or to look for a safe place to live.

In 2006, thousands of ethnic highland Hmong fled Laos and headed out to Ban Hoeui Nam Khao with the hope to escape an authoritarian regime backed by the Vietnamese that killed the Lao people and/or forced them to leave for another country. The 5,000 Lao Hmong who left Laos then were forced by the Thai authorities to go back to Laos on December 28, 2009 and resettle at Ban Phone Kham, Borikhamxay Province. Nobody knows about their latest fate. The properties of those refugees, including houses and lands, were all repossessed and retained as public properties. They were not returned to their original owners, who were not given the right to reclaim.

Photo #149. *The Hmong people were heading to Thailand in 1975, following Gen. Vang Pao's foot steps. Everybody had to walk on bare foot to maintain silence and to feel safe.   Lt. Col. Vang, Geu's collected news information and see source in The Unforgettable Laos.*

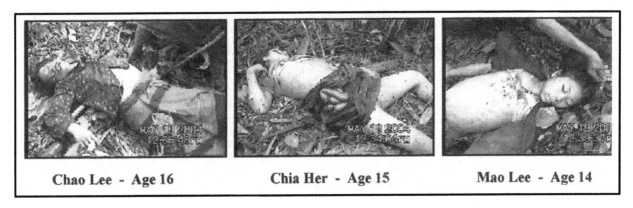

Chao Lee - Age 16   Chia Her - Age 15   Mao Lee - Age 14

Photo #150. *Female teen-agers were raped and killed like animals by the communists in 2004. (These pictures were taken by Fact Finding Commission from France and made available on the Internet.)*

_Photo #151__. Hmong refugees from MR-II using a small boat to cross the Mekong River at great risk. Many of them got drowned due to accidents of different natures, including boat sinking due to mis maneuvers, unfamiliarity with boat ride, losing equilibrium while standing on a moving boat, getting shot at, running into turbulent eddies, jumping in an overloaded boat, etc. Many people were still waiting for this boat to go back and pick them up. Many innocent children, women, and men got killed along the way to Thailand refugees camps while they were traveling from deep jungles from Laos from 1975 through 2002. Some of them die with hunger, shelter, and sickness along the way. Some of them were not able to escape so they were forced to go back to Laos and got reeducated in different camps in Laos. The most important part was that the survivors at wild potatoes, wild vegetables and wild animals while they escaped to Thailand. Lt. Col. Vang, Geu's collected news information and see source in The Unforgettable Laos._

CHAPTER 11

COMPOSITION OF VARIOUS LAO GOVERNMENT CABINETS

From 1893 to 1949, Laos was a French colony. On May 7, 1954 the French lost Dien-Bien-Phu, pulled out their armed forces from Indochina, and later granted independence to Laos, Cambodia and Vietnam. Despite being independent, those three countries became the theater of continuing interference by Communist North-Vietnam. When the French were in control of Indochina, they did not pay much attention to the development of Laos, which was treated as a remote secondary territory, with roads and highways hard to build and maintain because of the high altitudes involved. Laos had no access to the ocean, blocked mostly as it is by high mountain ranges. The French picked Vientiane as a small trading center to relay merchandises to Thailand. They also picked Luang Prabang as the royal residence for the Lao king who served as advisor to the French on an as-needed basis.

The French selected Seno as the main airbase in southern Laos. For northern Laos, they picked the Plain of Jars and Phongsaly. They divided Laos in two parts: Northern Laos and Southern Laos. They treated all three parts of Vietnam (Tonkin, Annam and Cochinchine) as an important business territory. Their main command center was Hanoi, North-Vietnam with Cap Saint Jacques, South-Vietnam was back-up. They had planned on making these two commercial centers look like Paris, but ran out of time.

When Laos was granted independence by the French in 1954, the kingdom of Laos was subdivided into twelve provinces. In 1962, more provinces were added for a total of 18. Today, the Lao

People's Democratic Republic has 17 provinces, including Phongsaly, Luang Namtha, Bokeo, Oudomsay, Luang Prabang, Houaphanh, Xieng Khouang, Sayaboury, Vientiane, Vientiane City, Borikhamsay, Kham Mouane, Savannakhet, Saravane, Sekong, Champasak, and Attapeu. [The province of Sedone was reshaped by the Lao Communists).

In 1945, the main Lao leader engaged in the fight to regain Laos' independence from France was Tiao Phetsarath. Because of that fight, the French realigned their role of administrator of Laos to that of defender of Laos (against neighboring Thailand). On August 30, 1945, King Sisavangvong proclaimed Laos' independence under French supervision. In September 1945, the Lao Issara Movement expressed its dissatisfaction with the proclamation made (with French support) by the king.

On October 12, 1945, Tiao Chao Phetsarath announced the formation of a united Lao government in Vientiane, with the following cabinet members:

Khammao Vilay	Prime Minister and Minister of Foreign Affairs
Tiao Souvanna Phoumma	Minister of Public Works
Tiao Somsanith	Minister of the Interior and Justice
Katay Don-Sasourith	Minister of Finances
Nhouy Abhay	Minister of Education
Tiao Souphanouvong	Minister of Defense and Telecommunication
Oune Sananikone	Minister of Economic Affairs
Ouneheuane Norasing	Minister of Justice
Sing Ratanasamay	Vice-Minister of Defense
Keuang Pathoumsath	Vice-Minister of Economic Affairs
Tham Saygnasithsena	Vice-Minister of Foreign Affairs

On October 20, 1945, the government led by Tiao Phetsarath announced the dethroning of King Sisavangvong and put the king in detention. On October 30, 1945, Tiao Souphanouvong announced the formation of a revolutionary group to join hands with Ho Chi Minh to fight against King Sisavangvong's government. On April 15, 1946 (Buddhist Year 2488) the French regained control of Laos and forced the Lao Issara Movement to seek refuge in Thailand. The Lao Issara Movement then set up a Lao government in exile in Thailand, consisting of the following cabinet members:

Khammao Vilay	Prime Minister
Katay Don-Sasourith	Minister of Information & Propaganda
Tiao Khamtanh	Minister of Financial Affairs
Tiao Souvanna Phouma	Minister of Public Works
Tiao Souphanouvong	Minister of Defense and Military Affairs

Cabinet members not listed above included Tiao Somsanith and Leuam Insisiengmai).

On January 27, 1946 Touby Lyfoung, Tougeu Lyfoung and Chao Saykham Southakakoumane (governor of Xieng Khouang) liberated Xieng Khouang from the Lao Issara and the Vietminh, who seized Xieng Khouang less than two months ago on December 28, 1945. On April 25, 1946 the French and their Lao rightist supporters regained Vientiane. The Lao Issara leaders from all over Laos opted to cross the Mekong River into Thailand. During one of those escapes, Tiao

Souphanouvong got injured from the French air gun fire while crossing the Mekong River from Thakhek to Thailand. When he recovered from his injury, Tiao Souphanouvong fled into the jungle and eventually reported back to his commanding team, the Vietnamese Communist Party (which sent him to Thakhek in the first place in 1945).

On August 27, 1946, the French signed an agreement granting independence to Laos with King Sisavangvong, who had been trying to bring all Lao ethnic groups under the same umbrella. The king was prepared to adopt a new constitution calling for the election of provincial representatives, and to oversee a Lao administrative system that relied on French support for national defense and economic development. At the same time, the kingdom of Thailand also reached an agreement with France on returning Sayaboury and Champasak provinces to Laos.

On December 12, 1946, elections were held to select provincial representatives to work on the draft constitution. The final version of the Kingdom of Laos' Constitution was adopted and publicly announced on May 27, 1947. In August 1947, national elections were held nationwide to elect representatives according to the new Constitution. King Sisavangvong named Prince Souvanna Phouma as Prime Minister for a one-year term. (TouLia Lyfoung was the first elected Hmong representative from Xieng Khouang).

1ST ROYAL LAO GOVERNMENT

The first Lao Government under H.M. King Sisavangvong and appointed per Royal Lao Decree #148 dated July 10, 1947 was in power from March 15, 1947 to March 24, 1948. . Its members were:

Tiao Souvannarath	Prime Minister, Minister of Interior and Minister of Defense
Tiao Kindavong	Minister of Economic Affairs
Outhong Souvannavong	Minister of Finance
Phoui Sananikone	Minister of Education
Kou Abhay	Minister of Justice and Religion Affairs

Per Royal Lao Decree #3 dated March 4, 1948 this government was modified as follows:

Tiao Souvannarath	Prime Minister
Tiao Kindavong	Minister of Defense
Outhong Souvannavong	Minister of the Interior
Leuam Insisiengmay	Minister of Finances

Kou Voravong	Minister of Public Works, Justice and Religious Affairs
Bong Souvannavong	Minister of Economic Affairs
Kou Abhay	Minister of Education and Public Health

Their mission ended with the general elections of the National Assembly members on December 7, 1947 that led to the formation of a new government.

2ND ROYAL LAO GOVERNMENT

Royal Lao decree # 38 dated March 21, 1948 set the terms for the second Lao government from March 25, 1948 to February 24, 1948. Cabinet members of this second Lao government were:

Tiao Boun Oum NaChampasak	Prime Minister and Minister of Defense
Phao Panya	Minister of Finances
Leuam Insisiengmay	Minister of the Interior and Public Works
Nhouy Abhay	Minister of Education, Health, Religion and Information

In 1949, Kaysone Phomvihane announced the creation of the Lao Issara Movement while Ho Chi Minh formed the Indochina Communist Party in North-Vietnam. On July 19, 1949 granted independence to Laos within the confine of the French Union. On October 24, 1949 the Lao Issara Movement announced from abroad the dissolution of the "Lao Penh Lao" Party. Some members of that party returned to Laos to join hands with the Royal Lao Government, and others opted to join Kaysone Phomvihane's Lao Issara Movement supported by the Vietminh. On February 27, 1950 Phoui Sananikone was named Prime Minister of the third Lao Government.

3RD ROYAL LAO GOVERNMENT

Royal decree #34, dated February 28, 1950 set the terms of the Third Lao Government from February 24, 1950 to October 15, 1951. The cabinet members were:

Phoui Sananikone	Prime Minister and Minister of Defense
Outhong Souvannavong	Minister of Foreign and Education
Khammao Vilay	Minister of Justice and Social Welfare
Kou Voravong	Minister of the Interior and Religious Affairs

Phao Panya	Minister of Finances
Leuam Insixiengmay	Minister of Economic Affairs
Tiao Souvannaphoumma	Minister of Public Works, Transportation, Planning, Communication, Information and Propaganda

Its terms ended with the election of the new members of the National Assembly on November 2, 1951 most of whom supported Prince Souvanna Phouma. During August 13-15, 1950 the Lao Communist Party (LCP) led by Prince Souphanouvong, and Kaysone Phomvihane held their first party meeting. Souphanouvong was the president of the party and Kaysone Phomvihane was the Defense Minister for the LCP, which was under the Indochina Communist Party (ICP) headed by Ho Chi Minh. In 1951, Ho Chi Minh ordered big changes everywhere in the three Indochina countries (Laos, Cambodia and Vietnam). On November 21, 1951 Prince Souvanna Phouma formed the fourth Lao Government.

4TH ROYAL LAO GOVERNMENT

Royal Lao Decree #286 dated December 23, 1951 set the terms for the Fourth Lao Government from November 21, 1951 to October 20, 1954. Cabinet members included:

Tiao Souvanna Phoumma	Prime Minister and Minister of Public Works, Transportation, Planning & Post-Office
Phoui Sananikone	Minister of Defense, Interior, Youth and Sport
Khammao Vilay Welfare	Minister of Justice, Religious Affairs, Health and Human
Nhouy Abhay	Minister of Foreign Affairs, Education and Information
Katay Don-Sasourith	Minister of Finances and Economics Affairs
Pheng Phongsavanh	Minister of the Interior
Ngone Sananikone	Minister of Economic Affairs

The composition of this government was revised twice per Royal Decrees #13 dated May 8, 1953, and Decree #104 dated March 18, 1954.

This government resigned to allow for the formation of a new government in accordance with the Accords signed by nine countries on July 20, 1954 in Geneva. After the signing of the Geneva Accords, the Lao Communist Party loudly proclaimed that the Indochina Communist Party had won a decisive battle. They then used military forces to attack the army of the Vientiane party, which they vilified as the servants of the French imperialists. On September 19, 1954 Kou Voravong, Minister of Defense of the Royal Lao Government and one of the Vientiane faction's representatives at the signing of the Geneva Accords on July 20, 1954 was murdered while having dinner at Phoui Sananikone's residence.

On November 27, 1954 Katay Don Sasorith formed the fifth Lao Government.

5TH ROYAL LAO GOVERNMENT

Royal Decree #397 dated November 29, 1954 set the terms of the Fifth Royal Lao Government from November 25, 1954 to February 13, 1956. The members of this government were:

Katay Done-Sasorith	Prime Minister and Minister of the Interior and Justice
Tiao Souvannaphoumma	Vice-Prime Minister and Minister of Defense
Phoui Sananikone	Vice-Prime Minister and Minister of Foreign Affairs
Nhouy Abhay	Minister of Education
Khammao Vilay	Minister of Religious Affairs
Leuam Insixiengmay	Minister of Finance
Pheng Phongsavanh	Minister of Public Works, Planning, Transportation & Communication
Ngone Sananikone	Minister of Commerce, Industries, Sport and Youth
Dr. Thongdy Sounthonevichith	Minister of Agriculture and Veterinary
Dr. Oudom Souvannavong	Minister of Health and Propaganda
Ounheuane Norasing	Vice-Minister of the Interior
Phouangphet Panareth	Vice-Minister of Finance

On December 1, 1954 Prime Minister Katay Done Sasorith called for a meeting of the two Lao factions to discuss national unification. His representative at the meeting was Dr. Thongdy, while the Lao Communist Party was represented by Phoumi Vongvichit. The meeting was first held in the Plain of Jars and failed to reach any agreement because the LCP acted too much like the winners. The second meeting was again held at the Plain of Jars, this time with Ounheuane Norasing as head of the Vientiane team, and Phoumi Vongvichit as head of the LCP team. The meeting still produced no results. The third meeting was held later in Vientiane, with Nhouy Abhay as head of the Vientiane team and Phoumi Vongvichit as head of the LCP team. Again, there was nothing positive to report from that meeting. The fourth meeting was also held in Vientiane, with Tane-

Chounlamountri acting as Vientiane team leader and Phoumi Vongvichit as LCP team leader. This fourth meeting was not any more successful than the previous three.

Because of this lack of progress, Crown Prince Sisavang Vatthana proposed a meeting of the top leaders of the Lao two factions in Rangoon, Burma scheduled for January 6, 1955. The Vientiane team leader was Katay Done Sasorith and the LCP team leader was Prince Souphanouvong. This meeting in Burma led nowhere because the LCP stood by their original winner's position. On January 21, 1955 the Katay Done Sasorith government ordered the Royal Lao Army to attack LCP military bases in Houaphan and Phongsaly Provinces and other bases. This motivated even stronger reaction from the LCP. On March 22, 1955 the LCP announced they have changed their name from Neo Lao Hak Xat to Khana Phathet Lao. On December 19, 1955 Laos became a member of the United Nations. On December 25, 1955, elections were held in the liberated zones of Laos.

6TH ROYAL LAO GOVERNMENT

According to Royal Decree #76 of March 21, 1956, the following served duty from March 21, 1956 to July 23, 1957 in the sixth Lao Government:

Tiao Souvanna Phouma	Prime Minister and Minister of Foreign, Defense & Public Works
Katay Don-Sasourith	Vice-Prime Minister
Nhouy Abhay	Minister of the Interior and Social Welfare
Leuam Insixiengmay	Minister of Finance, Economics, and Planning
Ngone Sananikone	Minister of Education
Ounheuane Norasing	Minister of Justice and Religious Affairs
Dr. Oudom Souvannavong	Minister of Health
Tiao Souphanouvong	Minister of Constructions and Rural Development
Phoumi Vongvichit	Minister of Religious Affairs
Tiao Souk Bouavong	Minister of Public Works and Transportation
Dr. Thongdee Sounthonevichit	Minister of Post-Office and Telecommunication
Tiao Somsanith	Minister of the Interior and Social Welfare
Chao Nith Nokham	Vice-Minister of Finances
Nouphat Chounlamany	Vice-Minister of Economy
Bouasy	Vice-Minister assigned to Prime Minister's Office
Thong Southivongnorath	Vice-Minister assigned to Prime Minister's Office
Nou-Ing Ratanavong	Vice-Minister of Justice

This Government was approved by the members of the 3rd National Assembly elected on December 24, 1955. Their term ended when an agreement was reached to form the "Lao Huam Lao" (Lao United) government. During January 6-14, 1956 the LCP announced the creation of an army dedicated to the liberation of the country. On March 6, 1956, Prince Souvanna Phouma was asked to form a new government. On September 29, 1956 the King's Council approved the unification of the two Lao factions. On December 28, 1956 the Vientiane Government and the LCP verbally agreed to form a coalition government and to put the two LCP-controlled provinces back under the control of the coalition government. On November 2, 1957 the two Lao factions signed an agreement to create a joint government on November 19, 1957.

7TH ROYAL LAO GOVERNMENT

By the Royal Decree # 163 dated August 9, 1957 the seventh Lao government served duties from July 23, 1957 to November 18, 1957. It consisted of the following cabinet members:

Tiao Souvanna Phouma   Prime Minister and Minister of Defense

Katay Dounesasorith   Minister of the Interior, Economics and Social Welfare

Phoui Sananikone   Minister of Foreign Affairs & Public Works

Leuam Insixiengmay   Minister of Finances, Justice and Religious Affairs

Nhouy Abhay   Minister of Education

Dr. Oudom Souvannavong   Minister of Health, Post-Office & Telecommunication

The 7th Lao Government resigned to pave the way for the formation of the Coalition Government on November 18, 1957.

8TH ROYAL LAO GOVERNMENT

There was no Royal Decree issued, but this Coalition Government last from November 18, 1957 to July 23, 1958. Cabinet members were:

Tiao Souvanna Phouma Prime Minister and Minister of Post Office, Telecom and Public Works

Katay Done-Sasorith   Minister of the Interior and Public Welfare

Phoui Sananikone   Minister of Foreign Affairs

Nhoui Abhay   Minister of Education

Leuam Insixiengmay   Minister of Finances

Ounheuane Norasing	Minister of Economic Affairs
Tiao Souk Vongsak	Minister of Public Works
Dr. Oudom Souvanavong	Minister of Public Health
Tiao Souphanouvong	Minister of Planning, Reconstruction, & Rural Development
Phoumi Vongvichit	Minister of Religious Affairs
Ngone Sananikone	Minister of Defense
Dr. Thongdee Sounthonevichit	Minister of Justice
Tiao Somsanit	Vice-Minister of the Interior
Chao Nith Nokham	Vice-Minister of Finances
Nouphath Chounlamany	Vice-Minister of Economic Affairs
Bouasy	Vice-Minister of Public Construction & Transportation

Their term ended after "Phak Kao Na" and "Phak Pathet Lao" joined together to form the "Lao Hom Lao" party following the new national elections, which the Neo Lao Hak Xat party participated in. Phoui Sananikone's political party, which became the majority party in the National Assembly, cast their votes to terminate the Coalition Government on July 23, 1958.

In early 1957, Capt. Kong Lae was appointed lead officer for the training of the special, dare-devil units of the Royal Lao Army at the Chinaimo Camp. He used that opportunity to systematically go and chat with Tiao Souphanouvong at his Nam Pasak residence every evening.

Tiao Souphanouvong referred to him as an individual with sharp teeth and nails, easy to curb, and very reliable. At that time, none of the Vientiane leaders paid any attention to Capt. Kong Lae.

On May 4, 1958 decision was made to elect additional national representatives. The Vientiane party and the Pathet Lao both announced the names of candidates for their respective party and were actively engaged in pre-election campaigns. June 10, 1958 was the vote casting day. Phagna Touby Lyfoung was one of those who got elected that day. On July 19, 1958 the International Control Commission (ICC) ended their control mission in Laos; members of the ICC then went back to their respective countries. On July 22, 1958 the government led by Prince Souvanna Phouma was dissolved as a result of the cut in all assistance programs by the US —who did not appreciate the presence of communist cabinet members in that Lao government. On August 18, 1958 Phoui Sananikone set up a new government without any Lao communist participation.

9TH ROYAL LAO GOVERNMENT

By Royal Decree #206 dated August 18, 1958 the following cabinet members served duties from August 18 1958, to December 30, 1959.

Phoui Sananikone   Prime Minister and Minister of Planning, Public Construction and Communication

Katay Done Sasorith   Vice-Prime Minister and Minister of Defense and V.A. Affairs

Bong Souvannavong   Minister of Education, Public Health, Religion Affairs

Khamphan Panya   Minister of Foreign Affairs

Inpeng Sourignathay   Minister of Justice

Sisouk Nachampasak   Minister of Public Information and Propaganda

Leuam Rasasombath   Minister of Finances and Economics Affairs

Pane Sisouphanthong   Vice-Minister of Public Constructions

Tane Chounlamontry   Vice-Minister of Public Health

Liap Somphounphakdee   Vice-Minister of Veteran Affairs

Khoragnok Souvannavong Vice-Minister of Defense

This Government was reshaped the first time on March 24, 1959 when it was conferred a one-year term of absolute executive power per Royal Decree #36 dated March 24, 1959. The cabinet's composition was as follows:

Phoui Sananikone   Prime Minister and Minister of Planning and Public Welfare

Katay Dounsasourith   Vice-Prime Minister and Minister of the Interior

Bong Souvannavong   Minister of Tele-communication and Fine Arts

Khamphan Panya   Minister of Foreign Affairs, Education, Public Information and Propaganda

Leuam Insixiengmay   Minister of Finances and Economics Affairs

Gen. Sounthone Pathammavong, Minister of Defense and Veterans Affairs

Sisouk Nachampasak   Minister of Public Information, Propaganda, Sports and Youth

Inpeng Sourignathay   Vice-Minister of Education

Pane Sisouphanthong	Vice-Minister of Public Constructions and Transportation
Tane Chounlamountri	Vice-Minister of Justices Affairs
Liap Phisaychoumphon	Vice-Minister of Agriculture and Forestry
Khoragnok Souvannavong	Vice-Minister of Interior and Religious Affairs
Col. Phoumi Nosavanh	Vice-Minister of Defense and Veteran Affairs
Lt. Col. Oudone Sananikone	Vice-Minister of Public Welfare

The second reshaping of the Phoui Sananikone's government took place following a disagreement between members of the Committee for the Defense of the National Interests ("Comite pour la Defense des Interets Nationaux", CDIN) and members of the Phoui Sananikone's political party. The disagreement was related to the term extension of the third National Assembly members.

Photo #152. *Lt. Col. Tou Ya, commander of the second battalion of the Lao communists stationed at the Plain of Jars in 1957 during the first coalition government. On May 18, 1959 Tou Ya led from the Plain of Jars and ordered the destruction of the bridge over the Nam Tom Rivernear Ban Phone on Highway 4 between the Plain of Jars and the town of Xieng Khouang. He knew this bridge very well and still got into an accident and died at the site in 1961. It is important to note that his driver, who was a Vietnamese, survived the accident. In 1961, following the political changes that took place between the French war and the US war in Indochina, several politicians and military officers broke ranks to join hands with Gen. Vang Pao and the Vientiane government. Lt. Col. Tou Ya's death might have been politically motivated because North-Vietnam was known for not allowing too many defections. On page 96 of the book, "Tou Ya Sai Chu, A Great Man from Lane Xang", one could read, "After learning*

about Tou Ya's death, Gen. Vang Pao ordered his troops to cease fire temporarily in the memory of the deceased, and stated he was deeply saddened by the death of Mr. Tou Ya, who was a very competent army officer and well respected by the Hmong people." Lt. Col. Vang, Geu's collected news information and see source in The Unforgettable Laos.

Royal Decree # 398 dated December 14, 1959 listed the following cabinet members:

Phoui Sananikone	Prime Minister and Minister of Foreign, Defense, Rural Development, Public Construction, Propaganda, Sports, and Youth
Katay Don-Sasorith	Vice-Prime Minister and Minister of the Interior, Religion & Justice.
Leuam Insixiengmay	Minister of Education, Public Health & Public Welfare
Tiao Somsanith	Minister of Finance & Planning
Chao Nith Nokham	Minister of Economics Affairs
Khoragnok Souvannavong	Vice-Minister of the Interior
Pane Sisouphanthong	Vice-Minister of Justice
Khoun-One	Vive-Minister assigned to Prime Minister's Office
Khamking Souvanlasy	Vice-Minister assigned to Prime Minister's Office

In December 1959, this government was dissolved because of its inability to control the political situation, and the emerging influence of the CDIN Committee that heavily attacked Phoui Sananikone. CDIN members, under the leadership of Gen. Sounthone Pathammavong, mounted a coup d'etat and asked Kou Abhay to form an interim government tasked with making preparations for the 4th national elections.

Many noteworthy events also occurred. On May 7, 1959 the government ordered that the two Pathet Lao battalions stationed in Samneua and Xieng Khouang Provinces be combined with the rest of the Royal Lao Army. The Pathet Lao disagreed with the order, forcing Gen. Ouan Rattikoun to fly to the Plain of Jars and try to reach understanding with the Pathet Lao battalion there. But the general was stopped and asked at gun point not to meet with anybody. The general had to fly back to Vientiane and ordered the forces under his control to lay siege to the Pathet Lao battalion at the Plain of Jars led by Lt. Col. Tou Ya.

On May 17, 1959 the two Pathet Lao battalions sent a fake promise to collaborate with the Vientiane faction within the next 24 hours. In the evening of May 18, 1959 heavy rainfall occurred and the following morning, the whole camp previously occupied by the Pathet Lao troops had been entirely vacated. Gen. Ouan Rattikoun ordered his Vientiane troops to chase the fleeing Pathet Lao in two directions, toward Paksane and toward Ban Bane, but to no avail. He then ordered Maj.

Vang Pao to put Hmong troops in the pursuit. The leader of the pursuing team was Capt. Lee Pao. His unit caught up with the fleeing Pathet Lao near Muang Mork and engaged in a light fire arm exchange in which the commander of Pathet Lao Battalion 2, Tou Ya, got shot in the leg. Voices of crying teenagers and women were heard, prompting Capt. Lee Pao to contact Maj. Vang Pao for more orders. Maj. Vang Pao ordered Capt. Lee Pao to stop the attack and let the enemy walk away.

On May 25, 1959 the Pathet Lao leaders were detained on order from the Phoui Sananikone's government at the police camp of Phone Kheng because they had refused to combine their troops with the Royal Lao Army and, instead, let them escape.

On August 4, 1959 the government declared an emergency situation throughout the country. On October 29, 1959 King Sisavang Vong passed away and Crown Prince Sisavang Vatthana was asked to take over the vacant royal seat.

In late 1959, Capt. Kong Lae was named commander of the second battalion of parachutists of the Royal Lao Army stationed at Wattai, Vientiane. The government was under Phoui Sananikone as Prime Minister. Laos was receiving some military training assistance from the US.

In around December 1959, the Phoui Sananikone government was pressured by the Royal Lao Army to resign. On January 21, 1960 Kou Abhay formed an interim government to allow for new, nationwide elections open to all political parties.

10TH ROYAL LAO GOVERNMENT

By the Royal Decree #403 dated March 8, 1960 the following cabinet members served duties from March 7, 1960 to May 30, 1960:

Kou Abhay	Prime Minister
Nhouy Abhay	Vice-Prime Minister and Minister of Education and Youth
Ngone Sananikone	Minister of Justice and Religious Affairs
Khamphanh Panya	Minister of Foreign Affairs
Nouphat Chounlamany	Minister of Propaganda & Public Welfare
Tiao Somsanith	Minister of the Interior
Gen. Phoumi Nosavanh	Minister of Defense and Veteran Affairs
Tiao Souvath Saygnavong	Minister of Public Health
Oudong Souvannavong	Minister of Public Works
Leuam Rasasombath	Minister of Finances and Economics

Their term of duties ended after the election of the 4th Congressional Representatives. On April 24, 1960 the election results showed that the newly elected representatives were exclusively from the Vientiane faction. The majority of the votes were casted for the CDIN party led by Tiao Somsanith, who then was automatically assigned the task of forming the next government.

11TH ROYAL LAO GOVERNMENT

Royal Decree #151 dated April 6, 1960 gave the authority to Tiao Somsanith to form the government with cabinet members listed below. The term of duties was from April 5, 1960 to August 9, 1960.

Tiao Somsanith	Prime Minister; Minister of Interior, Administration Development
Khamphan Panya	Minister of Foreign Affairs
Gen. Phoumi Nosavanh	Minister of Defense and Veteran Affairs
Inpeng Sourignatay	Minister of Finances and Planning
Ngone Sananikone	Minister of Justice and Religious Affairs
Leuam Insixiengmay	Minister of Propaganda and Socail Welfare
Nith Singharath	Minister of Public Works, Telecommunication & Transportation
Keo Viphakone	Minister of Economics & Rural Development Affairs
Nhoui Abhay	Minister of Education & Arts
Koukeo Saycocie	Minister of Public Health
Phouangphet Phanareth	Vice-Minister of Finances and Planning
Ou Voravong	Vice-Minister of Public Works
Bouavanh Norasing	Vice- Minister of Justice and Religious Affairs
Touby Lyfoung	Vice-Minister of Propaganda and Social Welfare

This government decided to appoint Souvanna Phouma as Lao Ambassador to France. On May 23, 1960 at midnight, all the Pathet Lao political prisoners detained at the camp of Phone Kheng very easily escaped, led by the main prison guard. This was the time when the Cabinet members were busy with the funeral of King Sisavang Vong in Louang Prabang and then were dismissed following the coup d'etat in Vientiane mounted by Capt. Kong Lae, who then asked Prince Souvanna Phouma to form a new government.

Capt. Kong Lae mounted a coup d'etat and formed a neutralist government. On August 9, 1960 Capt. Kong Lae mounted a coup d'etat against the Royal Lao Government led by Tiao Somsanith and Gen. Phoumi Nosavan. Capt. Kong Lae took that opportunity to bring in Pathet Lao troops and several battalions of communist North-Vietnamese to protect Vientiane, along with his own revolutionary troops.

KONGLAE'S REVOULTIONARY GOVERNMENT

Tiao Souvanna Phouma	Prime Minister and Minister of Foreign, Defense, Veteran.
Touby Lyfoung	Minister of Justice, Religious Affairs and Information
Kinim Pholsena	Minister of Interior, Sports and Youth
Khamsouk Keola	Minister of Health, Education, Social Welfare and Rural Development
Khamking Souvanlasy	Minister of Finances and Economy
Khamsing Ngonevorarath	Minister of Public Works
Tiao Boun-Om Nachampasak	Vice-Minister of Defense and Veteran Affairs
Tiao Sisoumang Sisaleumsak	Vice-Minister of Rural Development and Social Welfare

Prince Souvanna Phouma sent Gen. Amkha Soukhavong and Phagna Touby Lyfoung as his representatives to Xieng Khouang that ended up being detained by Maj. Vang Pao. On August 12, 1960 Kong Lae sent a helicopter to Ban Na Nhang, near Muang Kasy to pick the five Lao communist leaders, who just escaped from jail, and have them serve as cabinet members in the new neutralist Souvanna Phouma's government. The five Pathet leaders were Nouhak Phoumsavanh, Phoune Sipraseuth, Sisana Sisane, Singkapo Sikhot-Chounlamany and Phoumi Vongvichit. (Reference: Phoumi Vongvichit's Memoirs, page 143). On August 15, 1960 Gen. Phoumi Nosavan announced the formation of a counter-coup d'etat government in Savannakhet to stand up against Kong Lae's revolutionary government in Vientiane. On August 16, 1960 Capt. Kong Lae asked Prince Souvanna Phouma to form Laos' third neutralist government.

12TH ROYAL LAO GOVERNMENT (NEUTRALIST)

Because H.M. the King did not endorse the revolutionary government that he just formed, Prince Souvanna Phouma reached an agreement with the counter-revolutionary government led by Gen. Phoumi Nosavan to form another government, this time including both the revolutionary and the counter-revolutionary groups. Royal Decree #220 dated August 31, 1960 confirmed the following cabinet members of the 12th government that served duties from August 31, 1960 to October 9, 1960:

Tiao Souvannaphoumma	Prime Minister and Minister of Foreign Affairs, Defense and Veteran Affairs
Gen. Phoumi Nosavanh	Vice-Prime Minister and Minister of Interior and Religious Affairs
Nhoui Abhay	Minister of Education and Fine Arts
Leuam Insixiengmay	Minister of Economic Affairs
Inpeng Souriyathay	Minister of Finance
Ou Voravong	Minister of Post Office & Telecommunication
Kinim Phounsena	Minister of Information and Propaganda
Khamsouk Keola	Minister of Public Health
Touby Lyfoung	Minister of Justice
Khamsing Ngonevorarath	Minister of Public Works and Transportation
Gen. Ouane Ratikoun	Vice-Minister of Defense and Veteran Affairs
Khamking Souvanlasy	Vice-Minister of Foreign Affairs
Tiao Sisoumang Sisaleumsak	Vice-Minister of Rural Development Affairs
Tiao BounOm Nachampasak	Vice- Minister of Interior and Religious Affairs

The counter-coup group did not participate in this government, which was later dissolved after Prince Boun-Oum Nachampasak mounted his coup d'etat. On September 10, 1960, Gen. Phoumi Nosavan and Prince Boun-Oum Nachampasak gathered more than half of the national representatives and opened a National Assembly session in Savannakhet that voted to dismiss Prince Souvanna Phouma's government. On October 10, 1960 Gen. Kouprasith Abhay mounted an attack to liberate the city of Vientiane, but was not successful because of the strong defense put up by the communist troops. Prince Souvanna Phouma had to fly out to Phnom-Penh after relinquishing his prime ministership to Kinim Pholsena and Gen. Southone Pathammavong.

In the military and other fronts, in early September 1960, the Souvanna Phouma's government announced its cooperation with the Neo Lao Hat Xat and allowed the Pathet Lao to set their headquarters in Samneua, Houaphan Province. On October 13, 1960, Soviet Russia opened its embassy in Vientiane. On November 22, 1960 Prince Souvanna Phouma asked that Soviet Russia provide military and economic assistance to his neutralist government. On November 28, 1960 the counter-coup troops under the command of Gen. Phoumi Nosavan attacked the front line of Capt. Kong Lae's forces. During December 13-16, 1960 the Gen. Phoumi Nosavan's troops attacked and liberated the city of Vientiane. A new government was then formed. *[Phoumi Vongvichit in his Memoirs noted that, "We did not want to cause any damages to the population and the city of Vientiane and thus decided to move the battle field to the Plain of Jars").*

13TH ROYAL LAO GOVERNMENT

This government was created per Royal Decree #283 dated December 14, 1960 and stayed in office from December 13, 1960 to April 23, 1962. It put the Kong Le's revolutionary group to rest, but did not receive the needed votes of confidence from the members of the National Assembly until after the liberation of the city of Vientiane, as stated in Royal Decree #1 dated March 5, 1961. The cabinet members are listed below.

Tiao BounOum Nachampasak	Prime Minister and Minister of Foreign Affairs
Gen. Phoumi Nosavan Affairs	Vice-Prime Minister and Minister of Defense, Veteran and National Security
Bouavan Norasing	Minister of Justice, Information, and Propaganda Affairs
Leuam Insixiengmay	Minister of Interior Affairs
Phouangphet Phanareth	Minister of Finances and Planning
Touby Lyfoung	Minister of Public Health and Social Welfare
Ngone Sananikone	Minister of Economy
Tiao BounOm Nachampasak	Minister of Religious Affairs
Tiao Sisouk Nachampasak	Minister of the Prime Minister's Office
Khamphan Panya	Minister of Public Works, Telecom & Post Office
Nhoui Abhay	Minister of Education
Tiao Sopsaysanath	Vice-Minister of Foreign Affairs
Bounthong Voravong	Vice-Minister of Veteran Affairs
Bounlap Nhouyvanisvong	Vice-Minister of Economic Affairs
Phouangkeo Phanareth	Vice-Minister of Public Works

This government was dissolved to allow for the formation of a tri-party government. Prime Minister Tiao Boun-Oum Nachampasak had to resign to make this happen.

Once the counter-coup group liberated the city of Vientiane, troops under Capt. Kong Lae's command retreated from Vientiane along highway 13 heading toward Phone Hong, Vang Vieng, Kasy, Sala Phoukhoune, and the Plain of Jars. When they reached Muang Soui on December 25,

1960 they received food supplies and military equipments dropped from Russian airplanes between Kasy and Muang Soui. Once Kong Lae has regrouped his troops, he started attacking the rightist forces at Ban Bane, Muang Kham and the Plain of Jars, using military support from the North-Vietnamese communists.

On December 30, 1960 Maj. Vang Pao, commander of the rightist troops protecting the Plain of Jars, received some air reinforcements from Gen. Phoumi Nosavan but did not have the time to use them.

On December 31, 1960 the Kong Lae's troops, combined with North-Vietnamese communists, easily seized the Plain of Jars and Xieng Khouang. On February 11, 1961 Prince Souvanna Phouma flew back to Laos and landed in Khang Khay, Xieng Khouang Province, to join hands with the Lao communists and North-Vietnamese communists who had just captured and were in full control of the Plain of Jars.

The capture of the province of Xieng Khouang by the Kong Lae's troops led to dangerous changes. The people in those two provinces parted ways and/or became enemies as a result of the fight between the three Lao factions –leftists, neutralists and rightists. In the end, the leftists were fighting the neutralists, bringing in Vietnamese communists to slaughter the Lao people. Furthermore, the whole country was also divided into three territories answering separately to the rightists, the leftists, or the neutralists. The Lao people lost all their freedom because of mutual mistrust and total lack of confidence as a result of the Vietnamese communists' incitement.

On February 24, 1961 Prince Souvanna Phouma flew back to Cambodia as he felt that the situation was not safe yet for him to stay in Laos, due to the ongoing fighting in all corners of Xieng Khouang and Houaphan Provinces between the rightists, the neutralists, the Pathet Lao and the Vietnamese communists. On May 8, 1961 the International Control Commission (ICC) consisting of representatives of India, Canada and Poland came back to resume its duties in Laos. On May 11, 1961, the ICC announced the cease-fire.

On May 16, 1961 a negotiation meeting was held in Geneva, Switzerland. On June 22, 1961 the three Lao princes –neutralist Souvanna Phouma, rightist Boun-Oum Nachampasak and leftist Souphanouvong-- met in Zurich, Switzerland. They continued their discussions on the formation of a three-faction Lao government until June 12, 1962 at several meeting sites including Hine Heup, Plain of Jars and Zurich. When they failed to reach any agreement, North-Vietnamese and Pathet Lao troops strongly attacked Luang Namtha Province.

In May 1962, the US sent their military forces to Thailand to control the communist expansion into southeast-Asia. On June 23, 1962 the second Lao coalition government was formed. On July 23, 1962 representatives of the three Lao factions met in Geneva, Switzerland to support Laos' neutrality. At that meeting, Boun-Oum Nachampasak, Souvanna Phouma and Souphanouvong were represented by Phoui Sananikone, Kinim Pholsena, and Phoumi Vongvichit respectively. One of the agreements reached was to have all the foreign troops leave Laos completely. That agreement did not prevent the Vietnamese communists to beef up their troops in Laos.

14TH LAO THREE-PARTY GOVERNMENT

The Lao Coalition Government was reshaped five times per Royal Decree #219 dated March 23, 1962 due to the peace agreements reached in Geneva. The cabinet members served their duties from March 23, 1962 to June 1974.

Tiao Souvanna Phouma	Prime Minister and Minister of Defense, and Veteran and Rural Development Affairs
Tiao Souphanouvong	Vice-Prime Minister and Minister of Economy and Planning
Gen. Phoumi Nosavanh	Vice- Prime Minister and Minister of Finances
Pheng Phongsavanh	Minister of the Interior and Social Welfare
Phoumi Vongvichit	Minister of Information, Propaganda & Tourism
Leuam Insixiengmay	Minister of Education, Arts & Youth Affairs
Bounthan Songvilay	Minister of Religious Affairs
Tiao Sisoumang Sisaleumsak	Minister of Post Office & Telecommunication
Ngone Sananikone	Minister of Public Works & Transportation
Khamsouk Keola	Minister of Public Health
Khoun-One Voravong	Minister of Justice
Kinim Phounsena	Minister of Foreign Affairs
Keo Viphakone	Vice-Minister of Social Welfare
Bounthong Voravong	Vice-Minister of Arts, Sport, & Youth Affairs
Khamfeuane Tounalom	Vice-Minister of Economics & Planning Affairs
Tiao Souk Vongsak	Vice Minister of Public Construction & Transportation
Gen. Heuane Mongkhonvilay	Vice-Minister of Veteran Affairs
Khampheng Bouppha	Vice-Minister of Rural Development

In November 1962, following an internal disagreement between neutralist Capt. Kong Le and neutralist Deuan Sounarath, the neutralist forces stationed at the Plain of Jars split into two neutralist groups. [In his book on the Phuan history, Chao Khamlouang Nokham wrote on page 232, "Gen. Kong Le started noticing the feet of the snake and the snake then started eating the feet of the hen"]. Tiao Souphanouvong picked Col. Deuan Sounarath to replace Kong Le. As a result, the neutralist troops fell into pieces.

Photo #153. *The three Lao princes (from left to right: Chao Boun-Om Nachampasak, Taio Souvanna Phouma and Tiao Souphanouvong .In 1962, the three princes divided Laos into three parties —rightist, neutralist, and leftist—that fought against each other. In the end, Laos fell to North-Vietnam and the Lao monarchy came to an end in 1975.   Lt. Col. Vang, Geu's collected news information and see source in The Unforgettable Laos.*

see source: https://www.alamy.com/prince-souphanouvong-july-13-1909-january-9-1995-along-with-his-half-brother-prince-souvanna-phouma-october-7-1901-january-10-1984-and-prince-boun-oum-of-champasak-december-12-1912-march-17-1980-were-known-as-the-three-princes-each-represented-respectively-the-communist-pro-vietnam-neutralist-and-royalist-political-factions-in-laos-in-the-1950s-and-60s-image344255930.html

During 1962-1963, Gen. Vang Pao's command center located at Padong (LS05) was heavily attacked by the Vietnamese communists. In 1963, Pathet Lao troops combined with North-Vietnamse troops attacked the neutralist troops of Kong Le and pushed them out of the Plain of Jars toward Muang Phann. On February 12, 1963 Col. Ketsana Vongsouvan, Kong Le's chief of staff, was murdered at the Plain of Jars.

Photo #154. *The three Lao princes signed an agreement on June 22, 1961. From left to right: Chao Boun-Oum, Phoumi Vongvichit, Tiao Souvanna Phouma, and Tiao Souphanouvong. Lt. Col. Vang, Geu's collected news information and see source in The Unforgettable Laos.*

Photo #155. *Capt. Kong Lae, Col. Kettsana Vongsouvan (the 3rd person to the left of Kong Lae and his right hand man who was assassinated in the Plain of Jars in 1964 by Col. Thao Deuane Sounnarath and the Communist Pathet Lao) and Col. Deuane (the last person to the right). Lt. Col. Vang, Geu's collected news information andsee source in The Unforgettable Laos.*

On April 1, 1964 (Buddhist Year 2507) Kinim Pholsena, Minister of Foreign Affairs and the neutralist signer of the 1962 Geneva agreement on behalf of Prince Souvanna Phouma, was murdered on April 1, 1964 (Buddhist year 2507) by his personal guard, Sergeant Saykong, as he was coming home in the That Dam neighborhood from a dinner party. He was replaced as

Minister of Foreign Affairs by Khamsouk Keola. On April 12, 1964 Police Chief Khanthi Siphanthong, a pro-leftist neutralist, was murdered at his home in the Saylom neighborhood, Vientiane. This assassination lifted the neutralist issues one notch further.

In 1965, the Kong Lae's troops retreated from Muang Phann to Muang Soui, Xieng Khouang Province. In 1967, they then moved from Muang Soui to Kasy, Vientiane Province. Later on, having nowhere else to go, Kong Lae chose to go abroad, leaving his neutralist troops all scattered around, some in Vang Vieng, and some in the city of Vientiane. Soon afterwards, Kong Lae's neutralist troops literally disappeared from the scene. The assassination of Kinim Pholsena caused the split within the coalition government, and compelled all the Pathet Lao leaders to go back to Samneua. As a result, Prince Souvanna Phouma had to reshape his government for a total of five times.

Lt. Col. Vang, Geu's collected news information and see source in The Unforgettable Laos.

Photo #156. *Gen. Kong Lae met with Gen. Vang Pao in 1967*

FIRST GOVERNMENT RESHAPE

The reshape, made at the request of the Kouprasith Abhay's revolutionary group and effective May 22, 1963 involved the following changes:

1. Pheng Phongsavanh served as acting minister for Kinim Pholsena;
2. Gen. Soukan Vilayhong (new cabinet member) took over Gen. Heuane Mongkholvilay's position of vice-minister of Veteran Affairs;
3. Outhong Souvannavong (new cabinet member) took over Khamsouk Keola's position of Minister of Public Health;
4. Tiao Sisoumang Sisaleumsak took over Phoumi Vongvichit's position; and
5. Ngone Sananikone took over Tiao Souphanouvong's position of vice-Prime Minister.

SECOND GOVERNMENT RESHAPE

1. Bouavanh Norasing took over Khoun-One Voravong's position of Minister of Justice;
2. Ounheuane Norasing took over Bounthan's position of Minister of Religious Affairs;

3. Tay Keoluangkhot took over Bounthong Voravong's position of Minister of Education, Sports and Youth Affairs; and

4. Tiao Sisouk Nachampasak took over Phouangphet Phanareth's position of Minister of Finances.

On April 16, 1964 the three Lao factions resumed their talks on the coalition government.

On April 19, 1964 Gen. Kouprasith Abhay and Gen. Siho Lanphouthakun mounted a military coup against Prince Souvanna Phouma's interim coalition government and demanded that this government put a higher priority on resolving the country's economic and social problems. Their coup d'état was not very productive because foreign countries stood by Laos' neutrality status and, instead, exerted a lot of pressure on the coup d'etat instigators to return the power back to Tiao Souvanna Phouma's government. Power was indeed restored to Prince Souvanna Phouma so that he could resume his Prime Minister function and put his government back in action on April 23, 1964.

In early June 1964, the Vientiane government ordered heavy air bombardment by T-28 aircrafts on Pathet Lao and North-Vietnam's military command centers in the Plain of Jars area. In September 1964, the three Lao factions opened another series of negotiation meetings in Paris without much success.

On February 5, 1965 Gen. Kouprasith Abhay and rightist high-ranking military officers mounted a coup d'état to chase deputy-Prime Minister Phoumi Nosavan, National Coordination Department Director Gen. Siho Lanphouthakun, and Lao Air Forces commander Gen. Thao Ma to Thailand. After reaching Thailand, these three individuals sought and got political refugee status from the Thai government.

On April 17, 1966, Gen. Siho met with a priest in Thailand to ask him for protective amulets and then surrendered himself to the Laos authorities in Pakse. He was then sent for detention at the Phou Khao Khouay prison where he was later killed while attempting to evade on September 4, 1966. Nobody paid any attention to his death.

Center: RLAF commander Thao Ma with U.S. Ambassador William Sullivan, 1965. (Robert Tyrrell)

Photo #157. *Gen. Thao Ma and US Ambassador William Sullivan*

source: https://www.unforgettable-laos.com/governing-system-in-m-rii/4-3-administrative-system/

THIRD GOVERNMENT RESHAPE

On March 10, 1965 (Buddhist year 2508), Souvanna Phouma revised his Government as follows:

1. Leuam Insixiengmay took over Phoumi Nosavanh's position as Vice Prime-Minister;
2. Sisouk Nachampasak took over Phoumi Nosavanh's position as Minister of Finances;
3. Ouneheuane Norasing took over Bouavanh Norasing's position as Minister of Justice; and
4. Souvanna Phouma took over the position of Minister of Foreign Affairs from Pheng Phongsavanh.

FOURTH GOVERNMENT RESHAPE

Following the demand of the provincial representatives, on September 6, 1965 Souvanna Phouma had to revise his government as follows:

1. Inpeng Sourignatay, former vice-president of the National Assembly, took over Ounheuane Norasing's position as Minister of Justice;
2. Tiao Boun-Om Nachampasak took over Ounheuan Norasing's position as Minister of Religious Affairs;
3. Taykeo Luangkhot changed from Minister of Education to Minister of Public Health in replacement of Outhong Souvannavong who became President of the National Assembly;
4. Souvanna Phouma accepted Khampheng Boupha's resignation; and
5. Souvanna Phouma added the position of Minister of Rural Development to his current positions.

In October 1973, Gen. Thao Ma went to Wattai and used one of the T-28 aircrafts at the airport to drop bombs on the Chinaimo and Phone Kheng military camps for revenge. Gen. Kouprasith was able to escape the bombing at the last minute. After dropping bombs, Gen. Thao Ma flew back to the Wattai Airport to reload more bombs on the aircraft. As his plane hit the air strip, its landing gear got stuck, forcing the pilot to use emergency landing procedures that failed. Gen. Thao Ma was seriously injured, captured and carried to the headquarters of Gen. Kouprasith, who then killed him in front of several witnesses.

1966 was the year Lyteck Ly Nhia Vue got his law degree from a French university. As Gen. Vang Pao needed a staff member with good education to help him, he invited Lyteck to come and work as ethnic group administration and legal affairs. Lyteck, however, chose to go back and work at the Ministry of the Interior in Vientiane. He either did not feel comfortable working with the ethnic minorities and the military, or maybe he had a different career plan. In the end, in 1975, Lyteck was arrested and put in detention in Vieng Xay, Houaphan Province, where he was killed not long afterward. When they were working in Vientiane, Lyteck and Yang Dao ran into several problems. Both were well-educated but lacked cooperation and understanding skills. Lyteck had worked longer as a civil servant than Yang Dao, as Gen. Vang Pao picked Yang Dao who just completed his university level education to be a member of the three-faction Joint Political Committee in 1973.

FIFTH GOVERNMENT RESHUFFLE

This reshape, effective March 6, 1967, involved the following changes of duties:

1. Dr. Khamphay Abhay became the Minister of Public Health;
2. Houmphan Saygnasith became vice-Minister of Finances & Economy;
3. Souk Ouplavan became Vice-Minister of Rural Development;
4. Lien Pravongviengkham became Vice-Minister of Education, Youth, Sports and Arts; and
5. Sisoumang Sisaleumsak became Minister of Education, Youth, Sports and Arts; and

After all of these five changes, the Souvanna Phouma's 14th government consisted of the following cabinet members:

Tiao Souvanna Phouma	Prime Minister and Minister of Defense, Veterans, Foreign Affairs and Rural Development
Tiao Souphanouvong	Vice-Prime Minister and Minister of Economy & Planning
Leuam Insixiengmay	Vice-Prime Minister and Minister of Education, Sports, Youth, Arts
Pheng Phongsavanh	Minister of the Interior and Social Welfare
Sisouk Nachampasak	Minister of Finances
Inpeng Sourignatay	Minister of Justice
Phoumi Vongvichith	Minister of Information, Propaganda, & Tourism
Tiao Sisoumang Sisaleumsak	Minister of Post Office, Telecommunication & Health
Ngone Sananikone	Minister of Public Works and Transportation
Tiao Boun-Om Nachampasak	Minister of Religious Affairs
Keo Viphakone	Vice-Minister of Social Welfare
Khamfeuane Tounalom	Vice-Minister of Economy & Planning
Tiao Souk Vongsak	Vice-Minister of Public Works and Transportation
Soukane Vilaysane	Vice-Minister of Veteran Affairs
Souk Ouplavanh	Vice-Minister of Rural Development
Khamphay Abhay	Vice-Minister of Public Health

Houmphan Saignasith — Vice-Minister of Finances

Lien Pravongviengkham — Vice-Minister of Education, Arts, Sports and Youth

CHAPTER 12

LAST MINUTES CHAOTIC DEVELOPMENTS

In 1967, after the completion of the Radar Station at Phou Pha Thee, the US began to lead air strikes over North-Vietnam around the Hanoi area. Earlier that year, North-Vietnamese troops supported the Pathet Lao by attacking military bases in all the Lao provinces. Many of the bases under the command of Gen. Vang Pao were captured by the enemy. The southern part of Laos, including Saravan, Attopeu and half of Savannakhet Province were all lost to the enemy.

During March 10-11, 1968 Phou Pha Thee (LS85) was attacked and captured by the enemy, along with 90 percent of the Houaphan Province's territory. The enemy consisted mostly of Chinese ethnic troopers, while the North-Vietnamese communist troops attacked Khe-Sanh (South-Vietnam) and Hue (Central Vietnam). Phou Pha Thee was a very critical strategic site because of its radar installation that guided all the air operations over North-Vietnam, including keeping track of the pilots who were shot down in North-Vietnam. This was the reason why North-Vietnam had to eradicate that base at all cost.

THE LOSS OF PHOU PHA THEE

The loss of Phou Pha Thee was a sign of weakness of the US and the Vientiane government because the base has not been as well equipped as it should have been. When it was under enemy attack, the base lacked reinforcement and air support, and had to assure its own defense to death.

This was an open door for the invaders to penetrate and attack the whole country before reaching South-Vietnam, and capturing Attopeu, the south-eastern part of Pakse Province, and the entire Savannakhet Province.

During these attacks, the Royal Lao Army took several hundred of Vietnamese prisoners. On October 13, 1967, when Prince Souvanna Phouma was attending a United Nations session in New-York, USA he publically accused North-Vietnam of invading Laos and asked for international assistance, but the UN did nothing to address the situation. When he came back to Vientiane, the prince also invited international journalists to interview North-Vietnamese prisoners and broadcast the news to the entire world.

During the last part of 1967 and beginning of 1968, South-Vietnam was heavily attacked by communist North-Vietnam. In early 1969, several sites in Xieng Khouang and the south of Laos were lost to the enemy, including 100 percent of Houaphan Province; 70 percent of the south-east part of Savannakhet Province; the entire town of Paksong, and 100 percent of the eastern part of Pakse Province. More than 1.5 million rural area people (out of a total population of slightly over 3 million) left their native regions and moved to urban centers or other provinces, because of the insecurity brought about by North-Vietnamese invasion.

In mid-1969, rightist troops in military regions II, III and IV went back to the front line to attack the enemy, trying to recapture several areas within their territories with US air support and Thai ground troop support. However, they have not been able to keep the sites they have recaptured for very long, and had to cede them back to the enemy. In MR-II and southern Laos, the Royal Lao Army tried unsuccessfully to liberate several sites in the provinces of Huaphan, Xieng Khouang, Savannakhet, Saravane, Attopeu, and Pakse. The enemy had a bigger army and was equipped with more modern weapons. All the Royal Lao Army could do was to gradually pull back, step by step, unable to defend any positions as it should. As soon as they seized a new position, the North-Vietnamese would immediately send in several divisions for defensive purposes.

The fighting in the Plain of Jars area and in northern Laos during the rainfall season was more advantageous for the allied troops because of the availability of air support. But the situation was reversed during the dry season, because the enemy was then able to move around more easily and could bring in any kind of weapons and vehicles.

In June 1970, the Vientiane government and the Lao communists started a new round of negotiations in the city of Vientiane to try to reunite the two factions. In February 1971, several divisions of South-Vietnamese were deployed to the Lamson area to attack North-Vietnam's supply line along the Ho Chi Minh trail (Doan 559) that crossed the town of Sepone on the eastern side of Savannakhet Province. This resulted in a very fierce fighting, heavy life casualties, and many soldiers taken in as prisoners. The South-Vietnamese troops stopped the fighting and returned to their bases.

On January 2, 1971 the North-Vietnamese and Pathet Lao troops attacked the MR-II command center of Long Cheng, but were pushed back to Muang Kheung and Lath Bouak.

In May 1971, the Pathet Lao called for another round of negotiations. As in the past, each time the Pathet Lao asked for negotiation time, they were only trying to buy time and lay out more plans of attack against the Vientiane side.

***Photo #158**. North-Vietnam's 122 mm Rocket provided by Soviet Russia with a 25 to 30-kilometer firing range*

Lt. Col. Vang, Geu's collected news information and see source in The Unforgettable Laos.

see : https://www.unforgettable-laos.com/the-end-of-the-war/5-2-last-minutes-chaotic-developpements/

In January 1972, new elections were held nationwide (mainly in Vientiane government controlled areas) to elect a new group of 59 national representatives. Only 18 of the former representatives got re-elected. Prince Souvanna Phouma was tasked with forming a new government that, at first, did not get the required number of approving votes from the National Assembly's members. The quorum requirement was later removed under strong pressure from the foreign ambassadors to Laos, especially the US Ambassador, who wished to see Prince Souvanna Phouma continuing to serve as Prime Minister.

In July 1972, the Souvanna Phouma-led government and the Pathet Lao opened new negotiations that remained fruitless regardless of the amount of the efforts involved, because final decision-making did not rest with the Lao communists. It had to fit with the tactics and long-term strategy of the North-Vietnamese who were the real bosses with full decision-making power as illustrated by the following events:

- In 1972, Tiao Souphanouvong's son was killed in Samneua, Houaphan Province. The highland Hmong were blamed for that killing.
- Also in 1972, Kaysone Phomvihane granted even more power to the Lao Communist Party and had it renamed "Phak Passa-Son" (People's Party). At that time, Tiao Souphavouvong had no power wrested in him at all. The communists Lao began to slowly understand that North-Vietnam had already swallowed Laos.

On September 22, 1972 the People's Party called for new negotiations without any strings attached. The timing was good for them, because of the many developments that limited the options open to the US –the main supporter of Laos. These impediments included the following:

- Public demonstrations in the USA against the Vietnam war
- Watergate scandal that affected President Nixon's leadership –five of his Republican staff members were arrested for breaking and entering into the Democratic National Committee headquarters at the Watergate complex), and
- Soviet support to North-Vietnam in modern weaponry and many other items that compelled the US to decide to unconditionally pull its troops out of Indochina.

In October 1972 the two Lao factions agreed to renew their negotiations on the formation of the third coalition government. A pro-Lao communist leader confided to his Vientiane counterparts, "We Lao no longer have any ground to rest our feet on. Let's help each other!" [I, too, have heard the same words used by a leftist cabinet member at Phagna Touby's residence, and told Maj. Gen. Vang Pao about it. The general said, "They have no ground to rest their feet, but we do."]

In 1973, the two Lao factions decided to jointly form the third coalition government. At that time, the neutralist party only existed by name, with Prince Souvanna Phouma as its sole member. The neutralist troops and Kong Lae had all but disappeared since 1967. The only actors left on the scene were the red Lao and the Vientiane rightists. The negotiations did not lead to any agreement because the Lao communists were using the "18 Provisions" strategy as an excuse. On February 9,

1973 US Secretary of State Kissinger visited Laos and told the rightist Lao leaders to sign the cease-fire agreement with the Lao communist leaders or else all the US assistance programs would be cut.

On February 21, 1973, the cease-fire came into effect. At that time the Vientiane faction did not agree with the following provisions, out the 18 proposed by the Lao communists:

- Use Vientiane and Louang Prabang as regrouping centers for the two factions,
- Allow the Lao communists to deploy several thousands of troopers to those two centers, and
- Remove all the Vientiane troops from those two centers.

The Vientiane faction also did not agree with the job assignments and the demarcation lines, because those were too much in the red faction's favor.

On September 14, 1973 the Vientiane and Lao People's Party agreed to form a coalition government for the third time, along with a joint political committee. This was the reason why Gen. Vang Pao picked at this sole discretion Yang Dao to be on that committee as a Hmong representative in the Vientiane faction. Before the selection, several high-ranking, foreign-educated civil servants disagreed with the selection of Yang Dao. They ran out of options in trying to convince Gen. Vang Pao about his selection, because the general strongly felt that Yang Dao's father had been fighting the Lao communists for a long time and had been very helpful to him. Besides, he also immigrated to Laos to stay away from the communist North-Vietnamese during the French war. Unfortunately, things did not pan out the way the general thought. For one thing, Yang Dao ungratefully and incorrectly spread the word that he was picked by H.M. King Sisavang Vatthana in 1973 to play an important role in the Joint Political Committee.

FORMATION OF THE TWO-FACTION COALITION GOVERNMENT

The formation of the two-faction coalition government in the kingdom of Laos in 1975 marked the end of the royal Lao dynasty and the beginning of the Lao People's Democratic Republic ("Sathanalat Paxathipatay Passa-Son Lao") controlled only by the Lao Communist Party (LCP). No one could do anything against LCP-issued orders but to execute them. Offenders were automatically sent to re-education camps for a full-cycle of comprehensive learning. However, once you got to those camps, you did not know when you would be going home again.

A good example is related to the case of Vice-Minister Thongsouk Saysangkhi, who submitted his resignation from office on August 26, 1990. The vice-minister felt that the communist regime misled the public and would not be able to successfully lead the country. He ended up being arrested and detained in a re-education camp without any chance to see his family and the outside world again. To this day, nobody knows his whereabouts and his fate.

All those situational changes caused a lot of unusual hardship to the population of the royal kingdom of Laos who supported the rightist Vientiane faction, especially those who were lured into re-education camps and had to go through untold emotional and physical pains. In his book, pages 234-235 in the Lao version and pages 264-265 in the English version, Col. Khamphan

Thammakhanti wrote that the rightist Lao got insulted, hit, accused of all kinds of false accusations, deprived of food and medical treatment, put on severe diet or hunger, ate food worse than animal food, performed forced labor, were punished for no real reasons, enchained with iron schackles, prevented from walking/running, fed with timed poison, left to die slowly, killed, shot by firing squad, detained in a room full of ticks and lice. Obviously, these were extremely harsh punishments.

END OF THE LAO MONARCHY

Photo #159. *The Three elephant head flag of the Royal Kingdom of Laos was put out of service at the end of 1975.Image by Kingdom of Laos. Source, see in reference page.*

Photo #160. *H. M. King Sisavangvong was born in 1885 and was in power from 1904 until his death on October 29, 1959 at his royal palace in Louang Prabang. He had 12 wives and 23 children. Source see in reference page.*

Photo #161. *Tiao Maha Ouparath Bounkhong was born on July 4, 1857 and died on July 26, 1920 in Vientiane. He was the father of Tiao Souvanna Phouma and Tiao Souphanouvong. He had 11 wives and 24 children (11 sons and 13 daughters). On October 7, 1901 and February 8, 1903 the French and the Siamese agreed to put the area on the right bank of the Mekong River under Siam's control and the area on the left bank under French's control. Tiao Bounkhong was strongly opposed to that decision. In 1946, Thailand returned Sayabouri and Champasak Provinces to Laos.source, photo by History of Laos and see in reference page.*

The Last King Sisavang Vatthana, Laos. 1959-1975. Photo by Elephant Story. See more source in reference page.

Photo #162 *(left). H.M. King Srisavang Vatthana, born in 1907 and died of an agonizing death in 1978 at the re-education camp of Viengsay, Houaphan Province in the hands of the red Lao and North-Vietnamese communists .* **Photo #163** *(right). Prince Tiao Boun-Oum Nachampasak was born in 1911 and died at Boulogne-Sur-Seine, France on March 18, 1980. Photo of The Khun Lo Dynasty GENEALOGY, source in reference page.*

Photo #164 *(left). Tiao Maha Ouprahat Phetsarath, born on February 1, 1890, sought refuge in Thailand from 1946 to 1957 for 11 years before returning to Laos. He died on October 14, 1959 in Laos. He was one of the Lao princes who tried hard to bring independence back to Laos but, at the time, there were still a lot of differences in the public opinion. In the end, Laos became a neo colonialist country as reflected in the current national flag.*

Photo #165 *(right). Tiao Souvanna Phouma was born in 1901 and died in 1984 in Vientiane. He was actively seeking a neutral role for the Lao people to play but ended up creating three internal factions that fought among themselves. He too ended up putting Laos regrettably and painfully in the hands of the communists during a sad episode of the Laos history. Lt. Col. Vang, Geu's photo collected. See more sources in the reference page.*

Photo #166. *Tiao Souphanouvong, born on July 13, 1909 in Vientiane, died on January 9, 1995 also in Vientiane (at Ban Phone Xa-Ath, Muang Sai-Setthathirat). He gave a note to Gen. Vang Pao in 1974 expressing his desire to meet with the General to discuss about the country's political situation.In his written memoirs, Chao Khamlouang Nokham wrote, "Tiao*

Souphanouvong was the Trojan horse that the Vietnamese communists used to conquer Laos as their neo-colony as part of the Indochina Federation and to create the new Laos PDR, because he owed them a blood debt for their fighting in Laos from 1954 to 1975." Lt. Col. Vang, Geu's photo collected. See more sources in the reference page.

CHAPTER 13

THE LAST LAO COALITION GOVERNMENT

Photo #167. *From left to right: Phagna Pheng Phongsavanh and H.E. Phoumi Vongvichit signed the agreement to create the third coalition government in Vientiane in 1973.* **source,** *see in The Unforgettable Laos. and* **see in reference page.**

15TH (LAST) LAO GOVERNMENT

This was the last leftist plus rightist coalition government formed after the two factions reached an agreement. It was in office from June 1974 to December 2, 1975.

In April 1974, every cabinet member of the coalition government was in office at his/her department as agreed. On May 24, 1974 the Joint Political Committee (JPC) voted to accept the draft 18 provisions as parts of the national policy. Early that year, in Cambodia, the Lon Nol government and its armed forces fell completely in the hands of the Khmer Rouge. Lon Nol had to immigrate to Thailand and from there to the USA, where he died shortly afterwards.

The composition of that 15th Coalition Lao Government, which consisted Neo Lao Hat Xath (NLH) and Vientiane (VTE) members, is shown below.

1. Gen. Singkapo Sikhoth-Chounlamany (NLH)   Minister of Public Works and Transportation
2. Ngone Sananikone (VTE)   Minister of Finances
3. Phoumi Vongvichit (NLH)   Minister of Foreign Affairs

4. Tiao Souvanna Phouma (VTE)	Prime Minister
5. Leuam Insixiengmai (VTE)	Vice-Prime Minister and Minister of Education, Sports, Arts and Youth,
6. Khamking Souvanlasy (1)	Minister of Justice
7. Maha Kou Souvanna-Methi (NLH) (2)	Minister of Religious Affairs
8. Dr. Khamphay Abhay (VTE)	Minister of Public Health
9. Somvang Sene-Sathit (NLH)	Vice-Minister of Justice
10. Chanthone Chantharansy (VTE)	Vice-Minister of Foreign Affairs
11. Dr. Khamlieng Pholsena (NLH)	Vice-Minister of Public Health
12. Kham-Ouane Boupha (NLH) (3)	Vice-Minister of Defense
13. Oune-Neua Phimmasone (NLH)	Vice-Minister of Ed. , Sports, Arts and Youth
14. Col. Deuane Sounalath (4)	Vice-Minister of the Interior
15. Bousbong Souvannavong (NLH)	Vice-Minister of Finances
16. Khampheng Boupha (NLH)	Minister of Post-Office and Telcommunication
17. Dr. Somphou Oudomvilay (VTE)	Vice-Minister of Economy and Planning
18. Touby Lyfoung (VTE)	Vice-Minister of Post-Office and Telecom.
19. Tiao Souk Vongsack (NLH)(5)	Minister of Inf., Propaganda & Tourism
20. Soukarn Vilaysane (VTE)	Minister of Social Welfare
21. Pheng Phongsavanh (VTE)	Minister of the Interior
22. Houmphan Saignasith (VTE)	Vice-Min. of Public Works & Transportation
23. Tiao Sisouk Nachampasak (VTE) (6)	Minister of Defense & Veteran Affairs
24. Ouday Souvannavong (VTE)	Vice-Min. of Info., Propaganda & Tourism
25. Soth Phet-rasy (NLH)(7)	Minister of Economy and Planning

Photo #168. Members of the two-faction Lao Coalition Government. (Numbers from 1 to 25 refer to the list provided above). Lt. Col. Vang, Geu's photo collection. Sources, The Unforgettable Laos.and see in reference page.

Notes:

(1) Khamking Souvanlasy, Pro-Vientiane

(2) Maha Kou Souvanna-Methi, President of the 21-Gang Organization that demonstrated against the Vientiane cabinet members

(3) Gen. Kham-Ouane Boupha, Lead Activist in bringing down the Vientiane government

(4) Col. Deuane Sounnalath forced Gen. Kong Le out of the Plain of Jars. He was the Commander of the 2nd Parachutist Battalion who helped Gen. Vang Pao and French troops push the Viet-Minh toward Nong Het; was injured at Ban Phounong, Xieng Khouang. He was a pro-NLH neutralist.

(5) Tiao Souk Bouavong once said, "Our feet are now floating above ground. We need to help each other."

(6) Tiao Sisouk Nachampasak immigrated to the USA and died in California in 1982 from heart attack

(7) Soth Phet-Rasy, Co-President of 21-Gang Organization.

JOINT POLITICAL COMMITTEE

The list of the members of the Joint Political Committee is shown below in a numbering order that matches the line up in Photo #169.

1. Souvan Sananikhom; 2. Bounthan; 3. Vannavong Lescure; 4. Taio Sisoumang Sisaleum-Sack; 5. Tiao Souphanouvong; 6. Khamsouk Keola; 7. Gen. Kham-Ouan Rattikoun; 8. Chao Sinh Sinhthavong; 9. Unknown; 10. Ee Pottaphany; 11. Khamfanh Nouangsavanh; 12. Unknown; 13. Khamla Kingsada; 14. Foung Lo; 15. Unknown; 16. Unknown; 17. Gen.

Houmphan Norasing; 18. Unknown; 19. Unknown; 20. Phom Bounlutay; 21. Unkown; 22. Pha Vongsay; 23. Unknown; 24. Ms. Phaiboun Pholsena; 25. Ms. Khamsouk Vongvichit; 26. Bounteng Insisiengmai; 27. Khamphan Simmalavong; 28. Yang Dao; 29. Unkown; 30. Khamleck Saignasith; 31. Vongsavanh Boutsavath; 32. Heng Saythavi; 33. Boun-Nak Souvannavong; 34. Salath Rajasak; 35. Houmpheng Soukhaseum; 36. Khampheng Saignasith; 37. Saisavang Chanthepa; 38. Viboun Abhay; 39. Siharath Phasouk; 40. Khamphan Mahachan; 41. Bouasy Sopha.

The list shown below is based on party affiliation of the members of the Joint Political Party.

VIENTIANE FACTION

1. Gen. Ouan Rattikoun
2. Gen. Houmphan Norasing
3. Tiao Siharath Phasouk
4. Souvan Sananikhom
5. Khamfanh Nouansavanh
6. Vannavong Lescure
7. Tiao Sisoumang Sisaleumsak
8. Heng Saythavi
9. Salat Rajasak
10. Khamla Kingsada
11. Bounteng Insisiengmai
12. Yang Dao
13. Bounthan Heuangpradith
14. Tai Sinh Sinthavong
15. Phom Bounlutay
16. Souvanny Phomphakdy

NEO LAO HAK XAT (Communist)

1. Tiao Souphanouvong
2. Chan Pao Vanthanouvong
3. Maha Khamphan Virachit
4. Khamsouk Keola
5. Lofoung Lo Blia Yao
6. Visith
7. Liane Lithideth
8. Thamsinh
9. Ms. Khamsouk Vongvichit
10. Ms. Phayboun Pholsena
11. La Sousavanh
12. Ee Bothphanith
13. Maha Boutdy
14. Sanan Southichack
15. Khamphan Simmalavong
16. Khamta Vongsouvan

The members of the Joint Political Party classified as non-affiliated elitists included the following:

1. Dr. Tane Phaphatsarang
2. Khamleck Saignasith
3. Khampheng Saignasith
4. Houmpheng Soukhaseum
5. Sisavang Chanthepha
6. Pha Vongsay
7. Vongsavanh Boutsavath
8. Sisouphan Manghala
9. Bounkhong Pradichit
10. Boun-Nak Souvannavong

Photo #169. *Members of the Joint Political Committee (numbered from 1 to 41 per the list above). The Unforgettable Laos. and see in reference page.*

June 3, 1974 was the day the last families of US military agents left Laos. August 1974 was the month anti-Vientiane government demonstrations were held by the members of the 21-Gang Organization.

On April 30, 1975 South-Vietnam completely fell in the hands of the North-Vietnamese communists, forcing several million of South-Vietnamese to flee to other countries like Thailand, Indonesia and The Philippines. During their exodus, many of them ran into all kinds of extremely pitiful and regrettable dangers, including shipwrecks, armed robberies, rapes, deprivation, etc.

Some of them even got killed or tortured inside and outside the country. South-Vietnamese deaths included over 254,300 who were killed in the battlefields, over 200,000 who died during the exodus, and about half a million of civilians who were tortured and killed by the North-Vietnamese communists.

In February 1975 the combined Neo Lao Hak Xat and North-Vietnamese forces more and more heavily attacked all the military strongholds of the Vientiane rightist army, in violation of all

the signed agreements. In March 1975, North-Vietnamese troops equipped with tanks, heavy weapons and anti-aircraft artillery attacked rightist positions along Highway 7 from the Plain of Jars to Highway 13 at Sala Phou Khoune. They captured the command center of MR-II's second division and headed toward the city of Vientiane.

On April 9, 1975 Gen. Vang Pao sought an audience with Prince Souvanna Phouma, Prime Minister of the Coalition Government, to consult with him about the increasingly stronger and more dreadful attacks that were taking place. He did not get any meaningful answer and had to return to Long Cheng empty-handed and disappointed. On April 11, 1975 Gen. Vang Pao went to seek advice from H.M. King Savang Vatthana and met with the same disappointing results.

On April 13, 1975 the Lao People's Democratic Republic (Lao PDR) dissolved the National Assembly and announced new general national elections. The political situation worsened after the Lao PDR forces, supported by the fully armed North-Vietnamese troops, captured the rightist limitary camps of Kasy and Vang Vieng. In May 1975, students, civil servants and members of the public led by the "21-Gang Organization" held loud demonstrations denouncing and calling for the resignation of the Vientiane rightist government. On May 14, 1975 the Neo Lao Hak Xat forces, combined with the North-Vietnamese troops, took over the entire military command center of MR-II. At that time, Gen. Vang Pao and his military commanders and their families had already left for the refugee camp of Nam Phong, Khon Kaen Province, Thailand. That same day, the entire USAID compound in Nahaidieo, Vientiane was destroyed by the 21-Gang Organization demonstrators. During 21-30 May 1975, those demonstrators negotiated the cut in US assistance with the US Embassy. They left the compound after an agreement was reached on May 30, 1975.

On July 7, 1975 the first fight between Thai and Lao PDR forces occurred on the Mekong River, upstream from Ban Sithan Tay. The next day, Royal Lao Army officers and rightist high-ranking policemen and civil servants were lured into attending a meeting at the Chinaimo Military Camp in Vientiane. Several thousand of them were later sent to the re-education camp (Jail) of Vieng Xay, Houaphan Province.

In August 1975 Gen. Kham-Ouan Boupha, a pro-Red communist vice-Minister of Defense, ordered his troops to seize power in Vientiane and all the Lao provinces. On August 23, 1975 the Lao communists indeed seized full power in the city of Vientiane. High-ranking civil servants, military officers and policemen were lured into the re-education camp of Vieng Xay, Houaphan Province where they were left to suffer from mental and physical abuses, hunger, poisoning, manslaughter, and medical mistreatment.

In volunteering for a re-education program, those Vientiane rightist volunteer-detainees acted out of selflessness and honesty toward their country. But in the end, they were misled by the communists, as part of a secret plan formulated by Kaysone Phomvihane and Gen. Kham-Ouan

8

Boupha, who faithfully implemented the Indochina Communist Party's strategy to reshape the mind of all the Lao ethnic groups. This was within their overall goal to occupy Laos and get rid of all the Lao rightists in an extremely inhumane and barbarous way –a tactic that deserves to be fully documented and recorded as a lesson learned. All those of us who have survived the ordeal ought to remember the sacrifices made by those courageous individuals deep in our hearts. May their soul and spirit rest in peace!

DEATH, LIFE AND JAIL SENTENCES

In September 1975, Lao People's Democratic Republic proceeded to arrest and issue death sentences to the following individuals:

1. Phoui Sananikone
2. Prince BounOum Namchampasak
3. Gen. Vang Pao
4. Gen. Koupasith Abhay
5. Gen. Oudone Sananikone
6. Gen. Thonglith Chokbengboun

Those sentenced to life sentences were:

1. Gen. Silak Pathammavong
2. Gen. Etam Singvongsa
3. Chao Sisouk NamChampasak
4. Ngone Sananikone
5. Chao Sopsaysana Southakakoumane

Twenty people (most of them army officers) were sentenced to 20-year prison terms were:

1. Khamdeng Sananikone
2. Khamsing Sananikone
3. Col. Sakoune Sananikone
4. Somphet Sothsavanh
5. Col. Heuang Siharath
6. Col. Phady
7. Col. Arya Phimmasone
8. Col. Hatsady Sinhsai
9. Col. Onh Sananikone
10. Bounmy Sananikone
11. Pol. Gen. Vattha Phanekham
12. Col. Loune Sisounoune
13. Gen. Souchay Vongsavanh
14. Gen. Bouathong Phothivongsa
15. Gen. Khamsy Sananikone
16. Gen. Khamhou Bouthsarath
17. Dr. Khamphay Abhay
18. Gen. Houmphanh Sayasith

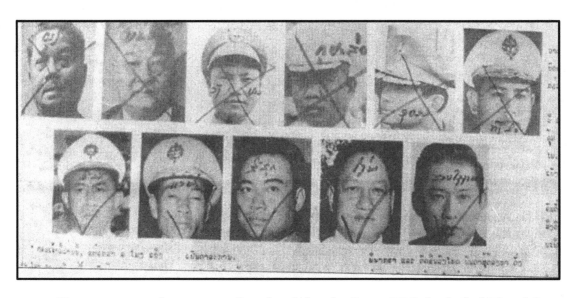

Photo #170. *Top row: people sentenced to death by the Laos PDR included Phoui Sananikone, Tiao Boun-Oum, Gen. Vang Pao, Gen. Kouprasith Abhay, Gen. Oudone Sananikone, Gen. Thonglith Chokbengboun. Bottom row: people sentenced to life terms included Gen. Silack Pathammavong, Gen. Ai-Tam Singvongsa, H.E. Sisouk Nachampasak, H.E. Ngone Sananikone and Sopsaysana Southakakoumane. Lt. Col. Vang, Geu's news documentation collections.* More source, check https://www.unforgettable-laos.com/the-end-of-the-war/5-3-the-last-lao-coalition-government/

During November 5-13, 1975 elections were held to elect regional representatives to serve as Lao PDR advisors. (Those elected appeared to be mostly former guerilla fighters with limited education. It was not clear in which advisory capacity they would be able to serve). This was actually part of a plan to elect communist Vietnamese and have them monitor the situation in Laos, looking for an excuse to send people to slow death re-education camps and make more room for Vietnamese to step in.

On November 17, 1975 the Laos-Thailand border was closed.

During November 20-23, 1975 Lao communists elected district and provincial administrators to expand the management circle, relying mostly on members of the Indochina Communist Party to fill all Lao PDR managerial positions in order to keep Laos for good. On November 28, 1975 the Lao Communist Party announced the dissolution of the democratic regime and changed it to the Lao PDR, moving from monarchy to communism.

During December 1-2, 1975 the leaders of the Lao Communist Party met in secret to develop plans to (1) dissolve the third coalition government led by Prince Souvanna Phouma as Prime Minister, (2) accept the abdication of King Sri Savang Vatthana, and (3) proclaim the formation of the Lao People's Democratic Republic, (LPDR).

On January 1, 1976 Thailand reopened its border at two locations to be used as entry and exit points. Border violators were subject to death penalty or jail detention. In January and February

1975, Kaysone Phomvihane was getting his orders from the Indochina Communist Party in Hanoi, North-Vietnam in performing his duties in Laos.

In May 1976, the LPRP met to formulate action plan to implement the Indochina Communist Party's instructions pertaining to Laos. These included arresting thousands of rightist leaders and civil servants who did not observe communist principles, and subjecting them to brain-wash and additional grass-root training. Some of the detainees were able to come home, partially disabled. Most of them never got home and just disappeared without their families ever knowing what really happened to them.

In February 1976, the US started admitting Lao refugees from the Soune Vinay camp to the USA. The first batch of refugees consisted of Lao individuals who used to work for a US agency like USAID, and/or served as language interpreters for the US during the war. The second batch consisted of Lao Christian refugee families sponsored by the US Christian organizations. The last batch was filled by military officers and soldiers who used to fight the communists alongside the US.

In July 1976, a severe drought in Laos drastically reduced rice harvest and other agricultural products. This weather condition has never been experienced before and caused severe public hardship.

On March 1, 1977 Lao Theung revolutionary Communist leader and Indochina Communist Party member Sithon Kommadan died of old age in Laos. Earlier that year, anti-Communist Government guerillas made their appearance near the city of Louang Prabang. The Lao communists surrounded the residence of former King Sisavang Vatthana, arrested him and his family, and sent them to an underground jail in Vieng Xay, Houaphan Province.

During March 19-20, 1977 the US sent in their first Missing in Action (MIA) Team for an inspection trip to Laos. In July 1977, a second year of drought continued to drastically reduce rice harvest and further exacerbated public hardship.

On July 18, 1977 Kaysone Phomvihane and Leduan, Secretary-General of the North-Vietnam Communist Party, agreed to sign a binding Laos-Vietnam friendship treaty that allowed Communist Vietnam to protect (and indirectly control) Laos for a 25 year term. The agreement may be extended for 10-year terms if agreed to by both parties. For all practical purposes, this was a life-long, no time agreement. As a result, Lao PDR had no need to maintain an army –just police teams and local security guards equipped only with AK 47 guns with a 25 yard shooting range and police handguns.

The Lao communists had to give up everything to North-Vietnam and let them issue orders approved by the Indochina Communist Party. North-Vietnam is the de facto boss of Laos and Cambodia because we owe North-Vietnam a blood debt.

AGREEMENT BETWEEN KAYSONE AND LE-DUAN

The special friendship and cooperation treaty between the Laos and North-Vietnamese Communists, represented respectively by LPDR Party's Secretary-General Kaysone Phomvihane and Vietnam Communist Party's Secretary-General Leduan, was signed on July 18, 1977. It called for a 25-year term that can be renewed for unlimited, consecutive 10-year terms if agreed to by both parties. For all practical purposes, this is an endless treaty that is highly disadvantageous to Laos because everything is now deceptively under Viet-Nam's control. The following paragraphs contain an unofficial translation of the treaty.

Recognizing the deep special Laos-Vietnam relationship in the fields of unshakable positive cooperation and close friendship between the Lao and Vietnamese people;

Recognizing the spirit of the extremely deep friendship between the Lao PDR and the Vietnam Communist Party, that was built over several decades of shared happiness and suffering,

Recognizing that our successful fight against an invading enemy, and our cooperation and mutual assistance are a precious foundation, a strong victory, a positive attitude, and a vigorous basis for the expansion of the Lao and Vietnamese revolution;

Recognizing that solid cooperation and long-term collaboration exist in all areas between Laos and Vietnam, including a strong national common desire;

Recognizing our two countries' long history of protecting national independence, democracy, freedom, the neutralism of the Far-Eastern countries in accordance with the interest of the rest of the world who is trying to fight imperialism and control old and neo-colonialism for the sake of freedom, national independence, democracy and social progress;

In full compliance with the Marx-Lenin doctrine, the true meaning of our national flags, the spirit of a truly nationalistic regime within proletarian internationalism, and our past efforts to safeguard and strengthen the special relationships between Laos and Vietnam, who used to cooperate in the fight for independence, in building and protecting our countries for years to come;

We agreed that independence, autonomy and legitimate leadership of the LPDR and Vietnam Communist Party, should form the basis for our two countries' common efforts in fighting imperialism and strengthening the special relationship between LPDR and Vietnam.

Based on the joint Laos-Vietnam declaration made on February 11, 1976, our common and sincere desire to maintain forever our long-term cooperation and mutual assistance in national development and protecting our peoples, our independence, peace, and freedom in both countries, the Far-East Asia and the rest of the world,

We have agreed with the following provisions:

Article 1 – The two parties agreed to make every effort to protect and expand the special relationship between Lao PDR and Vietnam, and will keep improving mutual confidence, long-term cooperation and assistance in all areas based on modern principles of ownership and equity; respect for independence, democracy, full territorial integrity, legitimate national interests, non-interferences in internal affairs; and make every effort to teach their party memberships, their armed forces, and their population to preserve and enhance the special relationship between Lao PDR and Vietnam, and to maintain it as a transparent and durable process.

Article 2 – Based on the understanding that the protection of national independence and the maintenance of national security are the sole responsibility of the country involved, the two parties promise to provide with utmost sincerity the mutual support and assistance needed to increase each country's capabilities to protect and maintain independence, democracy and complete territorial integrity, and protect the freedom of the work force from any tactics and dangerous actions perpetrated by imperialists and foreign trouble-makers.

Article 3 – As a means to facilitate mutual assistance, minimize potential problems, set the basis for full-fledge natural resources development, strengthen the country's infrastructure, improve permanent living conditions, the two countries will have to improve their cooperation as needed in modern society in order to reap mutual benefits in industry, forestry, agriculture, transportation, natural resources exploitation, regional economy, technology, etc. and do so with utmost sincerety. The two countries must help each other in training its labor force; exchanging experts in economics, culture, scientific fields; cooperating with each other in arts, education, health systems, news media —newspapers, radio, television, movie, gymnastics, and various fields of culture. Both sides have agreed to increase the frequency of professional meetings in disciplinary areas of interest to the two countries in order to discuss joint action programs and to exchange lessons learned in construction, economics, and cultures.

Article 4 – Both countries have decided to build the boundary line between Laos PDR and Vietnam as a long-lasting friendship boundary between two friendly countries in compliance with the Lao PDR -Vietnam treaty signed on July 18, 1977.

Article 5 – Both sides must respect and duly support the integrity of both countries. Both sides must come together to join forces with other communist countries to improve cooperation and mutual assistance in compliance with the Marx-Lenin doctrine and Proletarian Internationalism. Both sides must continually improve long-term cooperation and mutual assistance with Cambodia as a sister country, and based on full fairness, respect for independence, democratie and territorial integrity. The two sides must support southeast-Asian countries in maintaining their independence, freedom and cooperation with other countries in this part of the world. We must respect their independence, democratie, territorial integrity, avoid interference in their internal affairs, respect their equal rights, and look for fair and equitable mutual benefits. The two countries must support the fight of the people in Asia, Africa, and Latin America against imperialism, discrimination in order to maintain their independence, democracy, and social progress. Both sides must support labor unions and the labor force in capitalist countries in order to protect their democratic rights and social progress. Both sides must show we would do everything in our power to fulfill our duties and join in the global fight for democracy, national independence and socialism.

Article 6 – Both countries must be able to fairly exchange their opinions and points of view on matters of interest to the two countries and on various contemporary issues of mutual interest. This should be done through meetings between the leaders of the two countries, and/or official visits by national representatives, special envoys, or through diplomatic channels. Both sides will widen the cooperation between public organizations of both countries. Any issues related to the relationships between the two countries will be resolved through open and sincere negotiations in a frank and mutually respectable context.

Article 7 – This treaty will be effective from the day it is signed. The exchange of the signed documents will take place in Hanoi, the capital city of the Republic Democratic of Vietnam as soon as practical.

This treaty is valid for twenty-five (25) years and will be self-renewed for consecutive ten (10) year terms as long as one of the two parties involved does not express its desire to abolish the treaty to the other party in writing at least one year before its expiration date.

This treaty was prepared in Vientiane, the capital city of the Lao People's Democratic Republic on July 18, 1977 in two documents: one in Lao and the other, in Vietnamese. Both the Lao and the Vietnamese versions are of equal value.

Representing Laos PDR	Representing Vietnam Democratic Republic
Kaysone Phomvihane	Pham Van Dong
Prime Minister	Prime Minister

In 1978, the situation in Indochina became very intense because Soviet Russia lent their hands to help North-Vietnam attack southeast-Asia, causing China's great concern about south-China's security. This created the fight between China and Viet-Nam in 1979. Mainland China deployed several army divisions to attack North-Vietnam along their common borderline. The fighting spread almost as far as Hanoi, forcing North-Vietnam to recall several of their divisions back from their rear positions in Thailand, Cambodia and Laos in order to beef up their armed forces in North-Vietnam.

CHAPTER 14

LAOS' NATIONAL DEFENSE STRUCTURE

Once the French granted independence to the kingdom of Laos, the country formed a government and created the Royal Lao Army (RLA) for defense purposes. Gen. Sounthone Pathammavong was the first Commander-in-chief of RLA, with Col. Phoumi Nosavan as his deputy as well as chief of the military staff. Gen. Ouane Rattikoune was the next Commander-in-chief, with Gen. Amkha Soukhavong as his deputy. This was the time Capt. Kong Le mounted his coup d'état on August 9, 1960. Gen. Amkha Soukhavong was dispatched by Prince Souvanna Phouma to collect rice food supplies in Xieng Khouang to feed the troops in Vientiane, but was detained by Maj. Vang Pao in the Plain of Jars and was delivered to Gen. Phoumi Nosavan in Savannakhet.

After Gen. Phoumi Nosavan liberated Vientiane on December 16, 1960, Gen. Bounleuth Sanichanh became the third Commander-in-chief of RLA, with Gen. Phoumi Nosavan as his deputy. The National Coordination Directorate ("Direction Nationale de Coordination, DNC") was the created to serve as the central government agency. On April 19, 1964 following the coup d'etat mounted by Gen. Kouprasith Abhay and Gen. Siho Lamphouthakoun, Gen. Ouane Ratikoun came back to serve as RLA Commander-in-chief for the second time. In order to stay in the loop, Gen. Phoumi Nosavan still served as RLA deputy Commander-in-chief.

In 1965, Gen. Kouprasith Abhay mounted a coup d'etat and forced Gen. Phoumi Nosavan, Gen. Siho Lamphouthakoun and Gen. Thao Ma to flee to Thailand.

In 1966, Gen. Ouane Ratikoun retired from the RLA and was replaced by Gen. Bounpone Makthepharath as RLA Commander-in-chief, with Gen. Kouprasith Abhay as his deputy until 1975 –the year the Lao communists took power.

When Laos regained its independence from France, it was subdivided into 12 provinces as follows: Phongsaly, Louang Namtha, Louang Prabang, Houaphan, Sayabouri, Vientiane, Xieng Khouang, Khammouane, Savannakhet, Saravan, Champasak and Attopeu. In 1956, Laos had only four military regions (MRs) as listed below with their respective provincial coverage:

- o MR-I : Phongsaly, Louang Namtha, Louang Prabang, Sayabouri
- o MR-II: Houaphan, Xieng Khouang, Vientiane
- o MR-III: Khammouane, Savannakhet, Saravane
- o MR-IV: Champasak, Attopeu

Each Military Region had a regional military commander and appropriate number of troops to ensure the defense of the region and to provide support to other MR's as needed. There were five military regions as listed below with headquarters location and provinces covered:

- o MR-I (Louang Prabang): Phongsaly, Louang Namtha, Louang Prabang, Sayabouri
- o MR-II (Long Cheng): Houaphan and Xieng Khouang

- MR-III (Savannakhet): Khammouane, Savannakhet, Saravane
- MR-IV (Pakse): Champasak, Attopeu
- MR-V (Chinaimo, Vientiane): Vientiane province and Vientiane Metropolitan Area

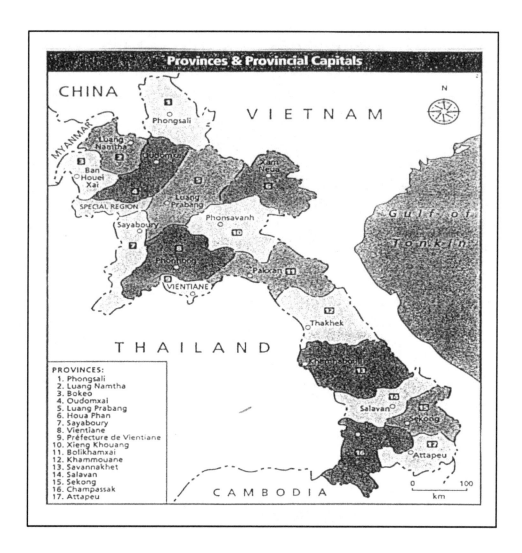

Photo #171. *After the Laos PDR came to power in 1975, Laos was sub-divided into 17 provinces (including the Vientiane Metropolitan area)*

see : https://www.unforgettable-laos.com/governing-system-in-m-rii/4-7-laos-national-defense-structure/

Each MR had the task of supporting other MR's on an as-needed basis. For example, MR-I, MR-II and MR-IV had to deploy troops to support MR-V many times. Likewise, in 1970, 1971 and 1972 MR-II had to deploy troops to support MR-I, MR-III and MR-IV many times also, although its main priority rested with its own MR, which was in the front line of the capital city of Vientiane. The loss of MR-II to the enemy could only mean the unavoidable loss of the entire kingdom of Laos. This was the reason why North-Vietnam had always deployed massive troops to attack MR-II.

16

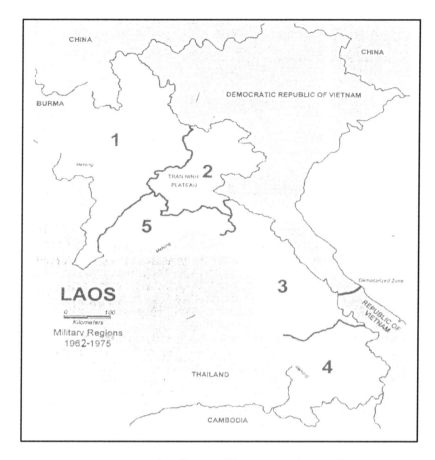

Map #172. *The five Military Regions of Laos*

source: https://www.unforgettable-laos.com/governing-system-in-m-rii/4-7-laos-national-defense-structure/

Laos was at the front end of the communists' infiltration line into southeast-Asia. The US was particularly concerned about Laos' security, because this was a small country that could not defend itself against communist invasion. Therefore, the Royal Lao Government had to cooperate with the US in the defense arena because communist North-Vietnam (1) violated the 1954 Geneva Accord signed by 13 countries that recognized Laos' independence, (2) had been using Laos as a place for hiding, training and moving its troops to attack South-Vietnam, and (3) openly took part in post-Kong Le's coup d'etat activities that preceded the war between the US and North-Vietnam. The US involvement had led to several developments in Indochina, including the change to a communist regime and the multi-million refugee exodus.

MILITARY REGION I (MR-I)

Photo #172 shows the five MR's sub-divisions in 1963. MR-I consisted of the following provinces: Phongsaly, Louang Namtha, Sayabouri and Louang Prabang. The civilian population in this MR-I was pro-leftist, more so than in any other MR's because of the many heavy attacks that went on in the northern and eastern part of the region. MR-I lost Nam Bark Camp and the whole Phongsaly province since 1962 and its northeastern part close to Houaphan Province since 1965. Communist infiltration in this region started as early as during the French war and peaked during the US intervention in the Indochina war.

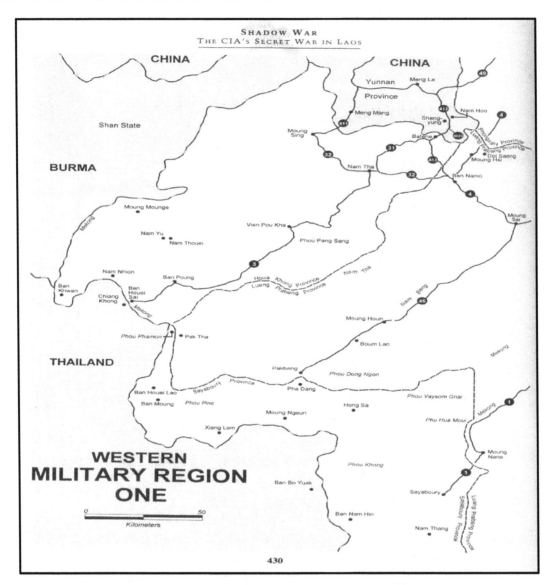

Map #173. Military Region I, Western Region

sources:

https://www.unforgettable-laos.com/governing-system-in-m-rii/4-7-laos-national-defense-structure/

After the end of the war in 1975, refugees from MR-I into Thailand accounted for the second largest refugee contingent from the entire country of Laos. The commander of MR-I was Maj. Gen. Tiao Sayavong, with Brig. Gen. Chao Vannaseng as his deputy. MR-I troops were part of Division I and comprised of five regiments [or GM]: 11, 12, 13, 14, and 15. Each regiment consisted of five battalions:

GM-11: 111, 112, 113, 114, and 115; GM-12: 121, 122, 123, 124, and 125; GM-13: 131, 132, 133, 134, and 135; GM-14: 141, 142, 143, 144, and 145; GM-15: 151, 152, 153, 154, and 155.

One battalion was comprised of five companies: Companies 1111, 1112, 1113, 1114 and 1115; Companies 1121, 1122, 1123, 1124, and 1125; Companies 1131, 1132, 1133, 1134, and 1135; Companies 1141, 1142, 1143, 1144, and 1145; and Companies 1151, 1152, 1153, 1154, and 1155. There is no information available on MR-I troop composition after February 1974.

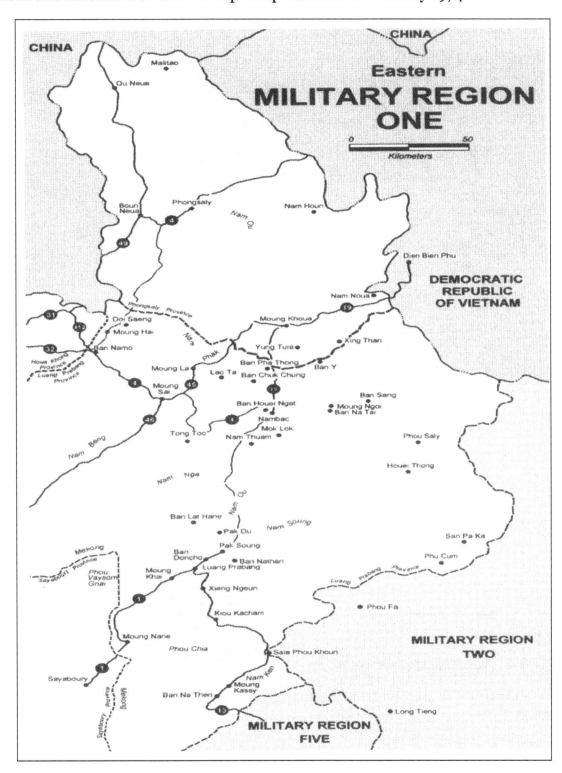

Map #174. *Military Region I, Eastern Region*

source: https://www.unforgettable-laos.com/governing-system-in-m-rii/4-7-laos-national-defense-structure/

Map #175. *Military Region II*

source: https://www.unforgettable-laos.com/governing-system-in-m-rii/4-7-laos-national-defense-structure/

MR-II was created in 1962 and covered Xieng Khouang and Houaphan Provinces. This MR had the longest border line with North-Vietnam than any other MR's and also sustained the heaviest enemy attacks, considering that the headquarters of the Lao Communist Party was located in Samneua. This important war zone created the highest threat to North-Vietnam because it was close to Hanoi, its capital city, and was in the front line of Laos's royal and administrative capitals of Louang Prabang and Vientiane respectively. As mentioned earlier, loosing MR-II would be militarily and politically like losing the whole country. This explained the heavy attacks this MR-II had to sustain over the years. The headquarters of MR-II was located at Long Cheng. Its commander was Maj. Gen. Vang Pao, assisted by two deputy-commanders, Brig. Gen. Tia Monivong (lowland Lao) and Col. Neng Chu Thao (Lao Hmong).

In 1960, MR-II troops were less than 10 regiments strong, compared to the 40 regiments of Vietnamese and Lao communists used in the invasion of the Laos kingdom. In 1970, Gen. Vang Pao reorganized those 10 regiments into one division consisting of 8 regiments: GM21, 22, 23, 24, 25, 26, 27, and 28. Each regiment was made up of 4 battalions and one commanding battalion. Each battalion had 4 companies and one commanding company.

One regiment comprised five batallions: GM 21: 211, 212, 213, 214, 215; GM 22: 221, 222, 223, 224, 225; GM 23: 231, 232, 233, 234, 235; GM 24: 241, 242, 243, 244, 245; GM 25: 251, 252, 253, 254, 255; GM 26: 261, 262, 263, 264, 265; GM 27: 271, 272, 273, 274, 275; and GM28: 281, 282, 283, 284, 285.

One battalion comprised of five companies: Companies 2111, 2112, 2113, 2114, 2115; Companies 2211, 2212, 2213, 2214, 2215; Companies 2311, 2312, 2313, 2314, 2315; Companies 2411, 2412, 2413, 2414, 2415; and Companies 2511, 2512, 2513, 2514, 2515

One Division of the Royal Thai Army came to help MR-II in 1967.

All those troops were funded under US assistance, which ended in 1973.

In February 1974, troops in the five military regions of Laos amounted to only 52,329, compared to 33,115 Lao communist and 40,000 North-Vietnamese troops –a total of 73,115. In 1974, MR-II had less than 12 regiments --GM 21 to GM 28 that were reshaped as GI 201 to GI 212. On May 22, 1974, the lack of US assistance compelled Gen Vang Pao to modify his plans, including (1) demobilizing some of his troops and send them to learn how to farm and breed animals, do business, or attend school, and (2) put the remaining 5,000 troopers on the Royal Lao Army's payroll. All these changes reflected the weaknesses of the Vientiane's faction and were taken advantage of by the Lao communists who attacked GI 212 at Bouam Long and GI 211 at Muang Mork. Because military losses to the enemy throughout the country in 1975 were very heavy, due to the US's unexpected and sudden retreat from Indochina, the military officers and recruits from those two camps fled into the forest but were later surrounded by the Lao and Vietnamese communists and executed.

MILITARY REGION III (MR-III)

In 1962, Military Region III was comprised of the following provinces: Khammouane, Savannakhet, and Saravane. This was the region through which North-Vietnam built the Ho Chi Minh Doan trail toward South-Vietnam. For that reason, MR-III was the most heavily bombarded region of all five Lao MR's by the US Air Forces. Conversely, North-Vietnam also used the most sophisticated weaponry they could find to protect the Ho Chi Ming trail –not the usual weaponry used in the Second World War. Their anti-aircraft artillery was ultra-modern and consisted of surface-to-air missiles (SAM) and weapons with firing ranges even greater than the US firing ranges. Although the US air operations were more to advantageous to the US, they were still very risky to the US Air Forces.

Map #176. *Military Region III.*

source: https://www.unforgettable-laos.com/governing-system-in-m-rii/4-7-laos-national-defense-structure/

MR-III's headquarters was located in Savannakhet. The MR-III's commander was Gen. Nouphet Daoheuang –who was later lured into the re-education camp in Vieng Xay, Houaphan

Province and died in the hands of the Lao communists and the North-Vietnamese in a very atrocious way. His deputy was Brig. Gen. Khong Vong-Norath. MR-III's armed forces consisted of Division III, which included five regiments: GM 31, 32, 33, 34, and 35. Each of the GM had five battalions –4 fighter battalions and 1 commanding battalion. Each battalion had 4 fighter companies and 1 commanding company. No data on the changes that took place in 1974 are available.

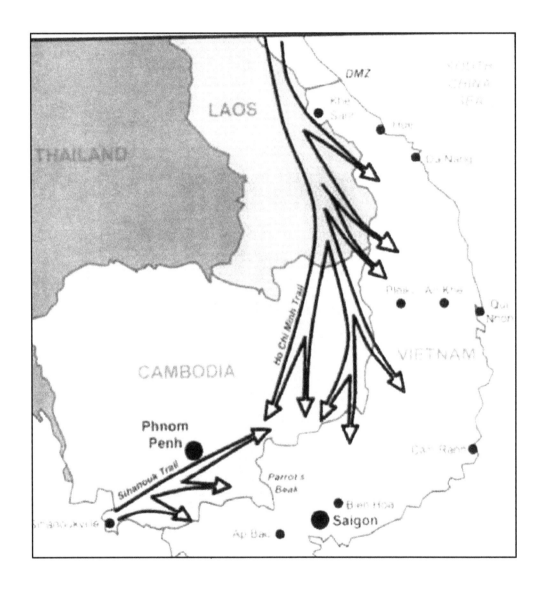

Map #177. *The Ho-Chi-Minh Trail to South-Vietnam Went Through MR-III*

source: https://www.unforgettable-laos.com/governing-system-in-m-rii/4-7-laos-national-defense-structure/

In 1972, MR-III deployed Regiments 33 and 35 to help MR-II attack the Plain of Jars. Their deployment was cut short by the cease-fire agreement, forcing the two regiments to return to their bases without any fighting. Several Thai regiments reinforced Military Region III in their fight against the Communists.

MILITARY REGION IV (MR-IV)

Map #178. *Military Region IV*

source: https://www.unforgettable-laos.com/governing-system-in-m-rii/4-7-laos-national-defense-structure/

MR-IV covered the provinces of Sekong, Champasak, Attapeu and Sedone with common border lines with Cambodia to the south, and with South-Vietnam to the east. Between 1959 and

1970, King Sihanouk did not get along too well with the US. As a result, Cambodia had to let part of its territory be used as a hiding place by North-Vietnam and as training facilities by the Viet-Cong —a group of South-Vietnamese fighting against their own country. This strange situation had forced the US to directly attack Cambodia on many occasions. Sihanouk declared he was neutral, but that neutrality was not in itself very helpful because it allowed North-Vietnam to make heavier attacks on South-Vietnam. As the Cambodian border area with South-Vietnam was under heavy US air strickes, the Vietnamese communists expanded their occupation of MR-III and MR-IV and then further increased their fighting intensity.

During 1963-1972, MR-III had to call for the assistance of Royal Thai Army regiments. Most of the MR's in Laos lost about 60 percent of their territories to the communists, especially in MR-III's eastern part and MR-IV's high mountain range of Paksong. MR-IV's headquarters was in Pakse. Its commander was Gen. Soutchay Vongsavanh, whose deputy was Col. Khamsouk Soratsaphak. (Gen. Soutchay Vongsavanh later immigrated to the US.)

MR-III's armed forces, Division IV, consisted of five regiments (GM): GM 41, 42, 43, 44, and 45. Each regiment was comprised of five battalions: 411, 412, 413, 414, and 415; 421, 422, 423, 424, and 425; 431, 432, 433, 434, and 435; 441, 442, 443, 444, and 445; 451, 452, 453, 454, and 455. One bataillon had five companies: Companies 4111, 4112, 4113, 4114, and 4115; Companies 4211, 4212, 4213, 4214, and 4215; Companies 4311, 4312, 4313, 4314, and 5315; Companies 4411, 4412, 4413, 4414, and 4415; and Companies 4511, 4512, 4513, 4514, and 4515.

One division of Thai troops fought with Military Region IV since 1967. No information is available on the changes that took place after the reunification of two Lao political factions.

MILITARY REGION V (MR-V)

In 1963, Military Region V consisted of Vientiane Province and the Vientiane Metropolitan area, the heart of the country which was always subject to constant, hard to predict political changes and the most difficult Lao region to defend. This was also the area, along with Louang Prabang, that the communists demanded to be treated as a regrouping center for the two Lao factions and devoid of any rightist troops. MR-V faced no military fighting. At that time, the enemy troop movements varied from one MR to the next, and thus required different types of military defensive operations.

MR-V's hedquarters was located at the Chinaimo Camp and under the command of Maj. Gen. Thonglith Chok-Bengboun, and his deputy, Brig. Gen. Atsaphanhthong Pathammavong. (Gen. Thonglith died at 5:30 a.m. on July 10, 2007 in France). MR-V's armed forces, Division V, included 5 regiments: GM 51, 52, 53, 54 and 55. Each regiment consisted of five battalions, and each battalion had five companies. No information is available on the changes that took place after the political reunification of 1974.

Remarks

1. MR-I and MR-V covered the royal city of Luang Prabang and the capital city of Vientiane respectively --cities treated by the two Lao political parties (Royal Lao Government Party and Lao Communist Party) as neutral, reunification zones during 1962 - 1975. These two cities did not experience too many military activities, but a lot of political conflicts

originated by the foreign embassies. They also produced more refugees than any other MR's.

2. Starting in 1975, the Laos PDR was subdivided into 17 provinces as follows: Phongsaly, Louang Namtha, Bokeo, Oudomsay, Louang Prabang, Houaphan, Sayabouri, Vientiane, Vientiane Metropolitan, Xieng Khouang, Borikhamsay, Khammouane, Savannakhet, Saravane, Sekong, Champasak, and Attopeu.

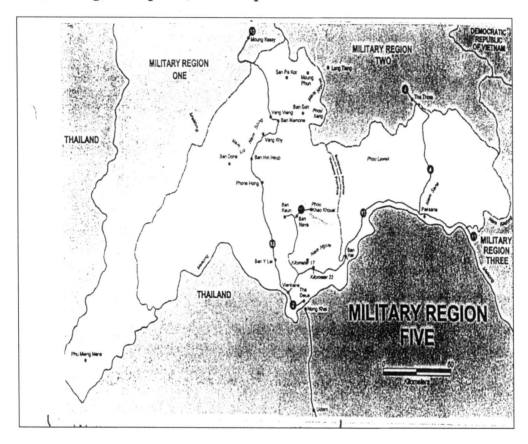

Map #179. *Military Region V*

source: https://www.unforgettable-laos.com/governing-system-in-m-rii/4-7-laos-national-defense-structure/

26

CHAPTER 15

NATIONAL EDUCATION AND PUBLIC HEALTH

NATIONAL EDUCATION

Before the French administration, Laos did not have public schools and government-paid teachers. The Lao people then relied on the temples as a place to learn. At that time, over 90 percent of the population diid not know how to write Lao; only those who had been in monkhood knew how to read and write Lao. Furthermore, there was a total lack of teaching equipment --only charcoal and paint were used to write on palm leaves. Those who were able to get an education were the ones rich enough to pay for tutors. The lack of education was a definite reason why earlier social development in Laos had been very slow, and why the country did not have too many professional experts. Under the French administration, some progress was achieved in the field of public education because the French created many public schools in the urban areas (and none in the rural areas). In most cases, the French brought in Vietnamese teachers to do the teaching as there were a lot more Vietnamese students than Lao students.

Schools in Laos were limited to primary schools –no high school yet. Only kids from wealthy families or civil servants working for the French had access to school. In the rural area, there was no way to go to school at all. Even if you could start primary school, once you graduated, you would still have to have a lot of money to be able to attend high school in Hanoi, North-Vietnam. From the start of the French administration until 1954, only about 30 percent of the Lao population got any form of education. In most cases, only schools from grade 1 to 3 were available in Lao. In higher grade classes, all the lessons were given in French. After 1956, the Lao government started getting some financial assistance from the US and began to build more schools in urban centers and several rural locations, thus allowing more Lao children to go to school. At that point, the percentage of people with reading proficiency rose to 70 percent. We then started seeing professional specialists in education, medical services, agriculture, veterinary, construction, finances and economics, business, administration, etc.

In 1973, at the signing of the "Lao Huam Lao" (Lao Coalition) agreement, the whole country was hoping to see an end to the long internal fighting and the various political parties joining hands, becoming united, co-existing peacefully, building and developing the country to be on a par with other countries. Unfortunately, good luck was still not at hand. What we saw was instead another disturbed and widely split country in an even worse condition than what we used to see before in our history. This was the product of the misleading political tactics used by the Lao communists, the followers of the Indochina Communist Party, who violated the agreement and brought in the new communist regime ruled by a single party, creating big turmoil and leading to the arrest of all the rightist leaders, educated people, civil servants, and military and police officers. Some of those who understood the situation chose to flee to foreign countries, based on their previous bad experiences or just to avoid being falsely accused of wrongdoing by the communists.

Those who stayed behind were mostly those who did not know where to go. They ended up losing all their rights to freedom under the regime of the Lao communists, who did not have any religion, ignored karma, and blindly practiced dictatorship.

The Indochina Communist Party had a plan to indirectly swallow Laos based on the irresponsibility of the red Lao who joined the rank of the communist Vietnamese and asked for their support so they could become leaders in their own country. But, as it turned out, those red Lao ended up being the puppets that killed the Lao people in a most painful way.

In 2005, the communist Vietnamese expanded the teaching of the Vietnamese language to Laos and had almost every Lao family fly the Lao red flag and the communist flag (red background flag with hammer and sickle). Pretty soon, those who do not speak Vietnamese may not have a job to do, and Laos might become one of the Vietnam's provinces under the sole control of the Indochina Communist Party. Laos would then be a neo-colony of communist North-Vietnam, a member of Indochina People's Federation.

MINISTRY OF EDUCATION

During 1973 – 1975, the Ministry of Education was headed by Phagna Sayaphet Champhone Leuam Insisiengmay, and the Director General of Education was Mr. Khamkhing Souvanlasy.

Photo #180 (left). *Phagna Saiyaphet Champhone Leuam Insixiengmai, Minister of Education, Arts and Youth.*

Photo #181 (right). *Mr. Khamkhing Souvanlasy, Director-General of Education*

see source: https://www.unforgettable-laos.com/governing-system-in-m-rii/4-1-educations/

PUBLIC HEALTH

In the past, Lao medical practioners relied on traditional, root-based medicine to treat sick people. Those medicinal roots were dug from plants grown in the forest or from house-grown plants. In some areas, shamans and spiritual healers, who could recite magic formulae to cure patients and get rid of evil spirits, were fairly popular. In neighborhoods that observed Buddhism, monks would normally spray holy water to beef up patients' morale. Traditional Lao people did not know how to practice hygiene and usually were not very healthy, and were physically weak. One of the most common diseases was malaria, a fever caused by mosquito and other insect bites, bad drinking water and unhealthy environment.

Typically, a Lao native would be prone to all kinds of sicknesses that prevented full body development, normal weight, decent height, and competitive sportmanship. The Lao men would get married at an early age and would generally not care too well for their wives. Kids usually grew up unattended, mentally and physically unchallenged, and ended up being unhealthy and not very smart. Life expectancy was relatively short. Some improvements took place under the French administration, especially in the fields of education and public health, with enough medicines, physicians, nurses, surgeons, hospitals, and modern facilities to treat patients.

In 1920, hospital facilities were only available in large cities like Vientiane (Mahosot Hospital), Savannakhet, Louang Prabang, and Xieng Khouang. But there was only one hospital in each of those cities, with limited medical supplies, surgical equipment, and medical specialists. There were only a handful of pharmacies around, and most of them had very little medicine to offer.

In 1954, medical care improved somewhat, thanks to the medical graduates from other countries who came back to practice medicine in their native country. In 1955, the French and US governments provided modern medical equipment to support their troops fighting the Indochina war, making it also easier to treat local patients.

In 1960, the French and the US opened medical training programs for nurses and physicians, and started building hospitals and medical schools at several locations in Laos. Unfortunately, many of those facilities were destroyed during the internal war. The Sene-Souk (Happiness) Hospital in Samthong, Xieng Khouang Province was a good example of a multi-million dollar, fully-equipped hospital built by the US. This hospital was capable of treating no less than one hundred patients per day. When Sam Thong was captured by the enemy in 1969, the whole hospital was left behind and eventually was fully demolished.

CHAPTER 16

WHO FORMULATED LAOS' POLITICS?

In 1973, a US expert came for a visit to Laos and went in to meet with the Director of the Ministry of the Interior in Vientiane after making several field trips around the city, especially to development, education, and training project centers. He was most interested in Laos' management style. The first question he asked was, "Do the Lao people have a dream?" The Director answered, "The Lao do not dream during the day-time, just at night-time." Having heard that answer, the US expert stayed mum.

Questions and answers are very important. If the person asking the question is not familiar with the background of the other person he/she is talking to, sometimes his/her question may be misinterpreted and/or completely misunderstood. The expert's question may be related to the Lao people's hope but if the Director provided a direct answer without first thinking about the real meaning of the question, this might get the inquirer confused, lead him to think in a different direction, or make him feel uncomfortable or uneasy. Obviously, the expert did not get the kind of answer he was expecting, hence his complete silent reaction.

In this case, the situation might somewhat special. The answerer might have been a little bit witty and did not want to give a simple, straight answer because he felt bad that most of the Lao people did not really dream about becoming better persons. Their only dream occurs at night, like all purely natural dreams.

Be as it may, most of the Lao civil servants were not highly educated people and, as such, did not fully understand political nuances, rarely did any research of their own, and did not always follow up with internal and external developments. The changes that occurred over time, the knowledge base and the Lao culture are hard to understand because of prolonged internal fighting, limited national leadership by people with only a mild education level that blindly applied foreign rules, exercised dictatorial control, and rose to power through party or family affiliation. All this, in addition to the variety of ethnic groups in existence, made it difficult for the country to stay united and work for national rather than personal interests.

The outcome was instead more internal conflicts and continuing insecurity that had last for hundreds of years. Throughout our history, the Lao princes had been asking for Burmese, Cambodian, Thai, and Vietnamese's support in their fights against their own compatriots. In the end, Laos became a broken country, and its people became foreigners in their own land. Before long, Laos could become a foreign country's property, because right now more than three tenths of the country is already practically in the hands of North-Vietnam. A good example is the Ho Chi Minh trail that ran along the Lao-Vietnam border toward South-Vietnam. Today, the width of that trail has been expanded westward, at least 20 kilometers into parts of Laos without anybody being officially informed about it or saying anything against it, because the Lao communists owed a blood debt to North-Vietnam.

The loss of the territory and population of Laos was caused by the Lao leaders' lack of political judgment and hint, statesmanship, and societal skills. Most of the Lao political leaders tend to use the power of their party for their own benefits, without thinking about the potential impacts on their compatriots and their country. A good example was the Kong Le's coup d'etat on August 9, 1960 that indirectly benefitted the Souphanouvong-led communist regime. Kong Le also had to asking for North-Vietnamese troops to help him attack the Royal Lao Army. His action caused havoc within the Royal Lao Army and resulted in a tri-party scission and fierce internal fighting. Princes Souvanna Phouma and Souphanouvong also used the same strategy of bringing in the communist regime to rule Laos by justifying to the outside world they had to do so to maintain neutrality −a neutrality than was 100 percent left-leaning.

After Lao fell under the communist regime, its new name was Lao PDR −Laos People's Democratic Republic. Princes Souvanna Phouma and Souphanouvong did not get any recognition from the LPDR, only Kaysone Phomvihane did. Because Kaysone was the real boss, a man with a Vietnamese father. He was born in Vietnam and brought by his father to Laos, where he grew up. Kaysone was a former French civil servant that committed a misdemeanor and went to seek shelter with Ho Chi Minh, who then trained him to be an anti-French fighter as an act of revenge for the French colonization. He was talking about removing French wooden yokes from the necks of the Lao people, but actually ended up replacing those with heavier, steel yokes. For all his accomplishments, Kaysone Phomvihane became very influential and a key member of the Indochina Communist Party (ICP). Princes Souvanna Phouma and Souphanouvong did none of those, were not classified as revolutionary fighters, did not have their names on the ICP list, and were not needed by the communists.

ປະທານ ໄກສອນ ພົມວິຫານ
ໃນຊຸມປີທ່ວງເຊັ້ນລູການດຳເນີນພາລະກິດປ່ຽນແປງໃໝ່

Photo #182. Kaysone Phomvihane, born on December 13, 1920; died on November 21, 1992 in Vientiane, Laos. As President of the Lao People's Democratic Republic since December 1975, he was the one who signed the treaty that put Laos under North-Vietnam's control from July 18, 1977 to present

Photo #183. Kaysone and Souphanouvong in 1950.

The one individual that got the highest grade from Kaysone Phomvihane was Gen. Kham-Ouane Boupha, a faithful follower who pulled the teeth and the nails of the rightists by using the 18-

provisions mini-agreement signed in Vientiane in 1973 as a tool and a tactic to get the eyes and ears of many deceivable, opportunistic rightist leaders and have them participate in disturbing demonstrations to disrupt national unity. Violating the 1973 mini-agreements proved to be part of the tactics used by the Lao communists to implement North-Vietnam's plan to swallow Laos.

This violation did not seem to be of any concern to the countries that signed the previous three agreements in 1954, 1962 and 1973. Those countries did nothing to try to resolve the issues and/or monitor the evolving situation. On the contrary, they looked the other way and let the perpetrators proceed with their neo-colonization plan, which they did without any regards to the International Court of Justice. This allowed Kaysone Phomvihane to put Laos under Vietnam's control for 25 year terms that are renewable indefinitely by 10-year increments under a treaty that seemed to contain no way out. *[Since the treaty was first signed in 1977, the first 25-year term expired in 2002. The first 10-year extension will last until 2012. The second 10-year extension would be effective for the 2012-2022 timeframe].*

All the Lao natives should read and remember the role played by Gen. Kham-Ouan Boupha, who implemented the Indochina Communist Party's plan to destroy Laos and its people. The short-minded civil servants and the unprepared Lao students who supported Gen. Kham-Ouan Boupha at that time should have spent more time soul searching before jumping into action. Since mistakes are easy to make; it would be too late to run first and then think back later. And fixing past mistakes is next to impossible, because the people affected are your own fathers, mothers, leaders and your own country. Issues should have been resolved amicably by all those involved and within an appropriate nation-wide context.

You are invited to read all the writings of Gen. Kham-Ouane Boupha about the red Lao communists' victory of 1975 that were made public in 1995, 20 years after the death of Kaysone Phomvihane. You may be wondering whose victory he was talking about --Lao's victory or communist Vietnam's victory? Because of all of those activities, about one million of Lao had to leave the country, some of whom died during their journeys abroad, were killed by accident, and are now resettled in several parts of the world. Worse, about 46,000 rightist leaders were subject to mistreatments, got ferociously and barbarously killed at the re-education camp of Vieng Xay, Houaphan Province without any possible help from any court of justice.

Gen. Kham-Ouan Boupha wrote a book in 1995 entitled, "How to Maintain the Champa Flowers?" It is already too late, general! Kaysone Phomvihane had already signed off Laos for a 25-year control by communist Vietnam –enough time for mixed Vietnamese-Lao blood to grow and become the bosses of our entire country.

In their personal memoirs, many Lao leaders and foreigners in and out of the country have written about Lao historical events as part of their life experience. These documents should be to interest to the younger Lao readers in their research and fact-finding activities regarding the origins of Lao events. We, Lao natives, ought to know our country's history well and make every effort to prevent the bad side of history from repeating itself.

Please read the destruction plan written by Maha Kou Souvannamethi, Minister of Religious Affairs in the third Laos Coalition Government, and by Sanan Southichak. This is a suggestion made by Souvannarath Chindavong, who used to be lured into joining the 21-Gang Organization and ended up being very badly mistreated to almost the point of no return. He fortunately survived, and was later able to reveal the truth about the Lao communists implementing North-Vietnam's plans as to achieve victory, seek revenge, and gain power. As it turned out, all they did was only to serve the interests of the Vietnamese communists.

TACTICS OF THE 21-GANG ORGANIZATION

Peaceful changes were part of the new war that was very dangerous to the political party and the regime in power because it involved destroying the population, national independence and individual freedom without using armed forces but some tactics like the following:

1. Use socialistic tactics within the country to promote internal dissensions. Capitalists usually only mostly deal with people from the urban centers, and seldom with those from the rural areas.
2. Deal with each generation separately in order to create long-term splits and dig big holes from where to destroy the party and the regime;
3. Use all legal, illegal, open, and secret means to create every opportunity to act, including economic market, open cooperation with foreign countries, investments, etc.
4. Use all political, economic, and cultural and other measures to put pressure on the armed forces as needed in order to encourage and support internal rebellious groups;
5. Continue psychological warfare as a sharp weapon to make false accusations and create hopes, as well as creating a basis to attract and pay civil servants and the population for their blind support and their work for the regime, then introduce socialism to open their

eyes so they can see and understand a democratic regime that advocates many political parties and complicated procedures.

WHAT DID THOSE TACTICS DO?

- They destroyed national independence;
- They created new parties in each region and for each ethnic group;
- They created conflicts between ethnic groups who became mad at each other and disunited because of the provocative tactics;
- They brought a lot of dissensions in the religious circles as people who practiced Christianity were denied their citizen rights to becoming soldiers and working with the rest of the population on Christ's holy days.

ELIMINATION PLAN OF MAHA KOU AND SANAN SOUTHICHAK

Step 1. Use the 18 provision plan to dismantle the Vientiane faction by having members of the 21-Gang Organization infiltrate every political party, service department, ministerial and provincial office, public fraternity, etc. If this political plan is not successful, then openly (mis)use the law that guarantees individual rights.

Step 2. Organize public meetings, demonstrations, and protestations to destroy important Vientiane leaders (civil servants, military, police and businessmen).

Step 3. Force the Vientiane faction supporters who do not like freedom to leave the country

and those who support freedom to get trained on how to fight the Vientiane's army; confiscate weapons and keep them in designated arsenals; organize heavy demonstrations to dissolve the Vientiane regime starting from the village base-root, to the Muang and to the Khoueng level on August 23, 1975 at the That Louang fairgrounds in Vientiane.

Photo #26 *(right). Tougeu Lyfoung and his wife Sisamone.* Separate those who will serve duties from those who will not, and send those who will not to re-education camps under the pretext that they were opposed to the revolution. Keep them in detention in the liberated areas based on the principle that we need to destroy germs to save bodies. If they survive, they would be freed eventually. If not, they will be left suffering for the bad deeds they did for the country. If they survive for too long, they will be subject to harsher treatments, slowly poisoned to death, or killed. Slow poisoning could either ended with death or serious physical incapacitation. Train selected people from the re-education camps so they could come back and serve duties on a short or long-term basis as needed. Select the right people to train, recognizing that those who will go and work outside the camps will be better off than those who stay in the camps.

Photo # 184. Prisoners at the Vieng Xay Re-education Camp guarded by young women from the Communist Party

- see source: https://www.unforgettable-laos.com/6-the-conclusions/6-2-who-formulated-laos-politics/

The plan and strategy to eradicate the Vientiane civil servants, police, military, students and younger people shortly after the communist take-over had been successful. *[This was a military plan that also relied on the psychological warfare component].* Civil servants and members of the police and military had to be specifically instructed by higher ups to undergo hands-on field training in the formerly liberated zones. The destruction plan itself was in accordance with

Step-4, "How to destroy the Vientiane's military officers who do not like freedom".

Representatives of the 21-Gang Organization got trained in psychological warfare and were active in leading the implementation of the short (10-year) term elimination plan, *"Our agents work inside, the opposition works outside".* The new organization created to eliminate high-ranking officers of the Vientiane's army was called "Chaofa". According to the Laos' history, some fighting occurred at the early stage of the French administration because some of the Lao population did not want to pay taxes to the French. The highland Lao leader involved, Thao Pang Chay, felt that the revolt against the French was a dangerous fight that needed a psychological strategy. He then proclaimed he was a God-sent leader that no one could kill, regardless of the weapons used. In that context, the word "Chaofa" referred to a bullet-proof leader. The short-term implication of this plan was military in nature and directed at completely eliminating the Vientiane military for good, along with those who were not ready to join rank with the "Chaofa".

As for the elimination of the Vientiane youth and students, it had to be accomplished right after the change of regime took place. People who were used to prosperity must be eliminated. The process should be as follows: the Communist Party had to give orders to the youth and students of the RLG Party to join the military, serve as volunteers in the fight against the Chaofa, and be trained on the use of firearms. The Communist Party would provide these weapons and support military actions. Ammunitions for AK47 guns were directly supplied by higher ups, and consisted of powder-activated projectiles with only a 25 meter firing range. This gave the Chaofa troopers an edge over the local guards. In the end, the leadership brought the bodies of the young recruits who died in fighting the Chaofa rebels to the That Louang compound, exposed them to the public

4

eyes, and asked for public support for using stronger weapons in completely elimination the Chaofa rebels.

Modern weapons were used in the fighting, including chemical weapons. This was the last stage of the psychological warfare –destroy from inside out, use insiders to fight insiders. In the end, real military forces had to be used to destroy the Vientiane government as the last resource. *[Yes, in the end, they brought in Vietnamese to completely eliminate all the Lao people].*

Photo #26 *(right). Tougeu Lyfoung and his wife Sisamone* Destroy every organization in third countries that is against the Lao Communist Government.

A. Split intellectuals, exclude youth from established associations, and generate continuing dissensions;
B. Split distinguished community members;
C. After successfully destroying associations, use the association establishment to work in the interest of the Party and the State, going from small to large Lao associations created in foreign countries;
D. Destroy the individuals who got separated from their peers, keep them isolated and despised by their friends and acquaintances, using various tactics to prevent further social activities involvement.

Smeu Mouthalay was the leader of the 21-Gang Organizations attached to the Dong Dok Teachers Federation. At present, he is the special envoy of the Red Lao Government assigned with the task of ensuring the successful implementation of Step 5 in Europe and the USA. He was sent by the Red Lao Government to France to collaborate with Chansamone Voravong in trying to reach out to the Royal Lao family and eliminate the Sananikone family in France. Ngeun Samrith assumed the required liaison with the Laos Embassy in France.

Those working for the Red Lao Government in the USA included Khamxay Saysane, Col. Souvan Phansy, (the late) Col. Fongsamouth and Somchine Phixaygnavong.

The Lao and Vietnamese communists unexpectedly dissolved the Lao Coalition Government that was the last hope of the Lao people in 1975, thanks to the Lao communists' plan to sell their country.

THE 21-GANG ORGANIZATION

The 21-Gang Organization performed vital tasks for and operated as the strong horses of the revolutionary communist party in Vientiane in 1975 without any regard for the Pro-United Lao agreement. Traitors who sold their country to the Vietnamese communists are listed as follows:

1. Thao Boun Hen, student, holding big cash reward money bag
2. Bousbong Souvannavong, Secretary-General of the Coalition Government's Ministry of the Treasury (as a Red Lao member)
3. Unknown
4. Maha Kou Souvannamethi, Minister of Religious Affairs, Coalition Government (as a Red Lao member)

5

5. Thao Khamfanh, student
6. Thao Sanith, student, holding a big cash reward money chest
7. Unknown
8. Thao Kham Hoy, student; a critical member of the 21-Gang Organization, killed in a refugee camp in Thailand
9. Col. Cheng Sayavong (alias Seng-Aroun), got promoted to the rank of General by the Red Lao Government and later assigned to the Phu Doy Regional Development Center, Luang Namtha Province. *[Before joining the 21-Gang Organizations, Seng-Aroun used to be the boss of Thao Khamsay, the founder of the Free Democratic Movement in the US. That movement consisted of two sub-groups, one led by Pa Kao Heu and Mua Yia Long in Thailand, and other one, led by Thao Khamsay. This confusing situation made it tough to identify everybody on the photo].*
10. Soth Phetrasy, Minister of Economy, Lao Coalition Government (as a Red Lao member), and the main financial supporter of the traitor students
11. Colonel Phonexay (Red Lao member), and
12. Thao Khamsay Sourinhthone, student, an important member of the Organizations that created a lot of turmoil. A well-known Pakse native, he has resettled in Canada.

Photo #185.*Members of the Twenty-One Gang Organization behind the manifestations against the Royal Lao Government from 1974 to 1975. They drove many Laotians to immigrate to many other countries around the world.*

source: https://en.wikipedia.org/wiki/Laotian_Civil_War

and

https://www.unforgettable-laos.com/6-the-conclusions/6-2-who-formulated-laos-politics/

SECRET PLAN TO FORM THE LAO COALITION GOVERNMENT

Before they took power from the Vientiane Government in 1975, the Red Lao communists worked out the following secret plan at Vieng Xay, Houaphan Province:

1. Create an interim coalition government, with equal representation from each political faction, dissolve the National Assembly, set up the coalition government with Tiao Souphanouvong as President, and Tiao Souvanna Phouma as Prime Minister (as usual);
2. Set up a fake new constitution within the context of the 18 political provisions;
3. Set up fake borders to regroup and hide the (Vietnamese) troops;
4. Do everything to liberate and regain power from the Vientiane faction, using secret tactics and financial rewards to attract the population, students, business people, civil servants, military, police and have them serve as core leaders;
5. Close down all the institutional symbols (nation, religion, and royalty), change the national flag, change the leadership team in all ministerial departments, and change the name of the country to a people's republic;
6. Extend transformations until the ocean shore to the south is reached, then announce the country's membership of the Indochina Federation headquartered in Hanoi, North-Vietnam and its North-Vietnamese style of direct communist regime; and
7. Based on close cooperation between the three Indochina countries, continue to liberate other south-east Asian countries, especially those that share borders with the three Indochina countries.

PLANNED STRATEGIES FOR THE VIENTIANE FACTION AND VANG PAO

1. Send members to the Vientiane military, police and civil service for re-education training in the northern parts of Xieng Khouang and Houaphan provinces;
2. Put the military at the rank of lieutenant on life detention without possibility to ever come back home
3. Put the military between the ranks of lieutenant and captain in re-education camps for an indefinite period and have them serve as the slaves of the State for their entire life
4. Put the military between the ranks of major and colonel in re-education camps until the day they die; and
5. Execute all the Royal Lao Army generals and high-ranking Vientiane civil servants.

Planned Measures for the Vientiane Civilians

1. Assign Vientiane's civilians to national reconstruction projects once the war is over; and
2. Have them serve as slaves and carrier horses for the State (Communist Party) until their deaths.

Planned Measures for the Hmong

1. Use time wisely and make appropriate plan to eliminate all the Hmong people starting around 1979-1981 or in 1982. Pick the right time because the Hmong are very resentful and keep their resentments deep in their hearts for a long time;
2. Eliminate all the Hmong between the ages of 5 and 50. Hmong of this age range are like rotten meat; it does not matter how many times you wash that meat, it will still smell bad.

Re-education Strategies

1. Must perform auto-critique
2. Must be forced to continually perform self-blaming; must not be allowed to socialize
3. Must use people rights and interests as themes of their diatribes
4. Must treat the country as people's property, focus on people's wishes and hopes until they are met, and then put pressure on the people and remove all their rights.

Negotiation Strategies with the Vientiane Government

1. Accept their proposals if they agree to cooperate
2. During the cooperative execution phase, all parties should have equal rights
3. Once the rights and treatments are equal, use those rights and communist policies to modify and eventually destroy the initial agreements on a step by step basis. Do not refer to past agreements.

Revolutionist Tenets

1. A revolutionist must serve the people and the country until death
2. A revolutionist must be completely detached from his/her family and relatives
3. A revolutionist who is still worried about his/her family and relatives and is not up to his/her duties must be sent for additional re-education training.

The Economics of War

Money is powerful. Based on the example of the Soviet Secret Service (KGB), Lao Communists need to use spies to infiltrate non-communist communities and attract money from abroad. Internally, Lao Communists must force people to spend the State's money, the so-called "liberation funds."

Plan to Build Economic Bases Abroad

This plan involves sending Lao PDR representatives to serve in consulates, and crafty investors to secretly participate in investment projects such as coinage, office building, tobacco processing, sawmills, etc. in order to produce some income from buyers and other customers from nearby urban centers and rural areas. The plan also serves the purpose of inciting politicians of the country to get involved in creating dissensions everywhere around the world.

1975-1980 Plan to Eliminate the Royal Lao Government

Implement the Indochina Communist Party's strategy as the basis for re-educating the public, training people, and completely exterminating defeated troopers who are still hiding in the jungle. Use 1980 as the year to proclaim socialism and implement a new constitution that calls for North-Vietnam's control in every area, such as

- Country's work force created by the revolution (you have to be Vietnamese to qualify)
- Internal trade, to be treated as a State's business through the State-controlled cooperative system.

PERSONAL NOTES FROM SOUVANNARATH CHINDAVONG

[Souvannarath Chindavong was a member of the 21-Gang Organization and the right-hand man of both Samane Southichak and Maha Kou Souvan Namethi during 1971-1975. On September 29, 1975 he was arrested, handcuffed, and forced to walk from Ban Phanh Manh to KM 4 Loading Point near Vientiane. He was then sent to Nongdouang and locked in a cage for twenty-five days, guarded by the Communist Party Police (most of whom were women). He was accused of being anti-revolution and cooperating with the Lao Huam Sam Phan Association. On October 23, 1975 he was sent to Samkhae Prison (near Phonekheng). On February 16, 1976, he and several prisoners from Samkhae were sent to Phongsaly in northern Laos, near the border of China. Also sent with him was Thao Keo Phoum Phomdeth, who was a part of the Twenty-One Gang Organization. When they arrived at Phongsaly in northern Laos, Thao Keo learned that he had been misled and then fled to China. Three days later, Souvannarath saw three men being admitted to the re-education camp. One of them was Thao Keo; he and Capt. Somsy Narongsak were military officers from Chinaimo Military Camp. The two men were executed shortly after being recaptured.

In 1979, when fighting broke out between the Chinese and the Lao Communists along the border between China and Laos, the communists released some prisoners. Boutsaboung Souvannavong requested that Souvannarath Chindavong be allowed to return to work in Vientiane. Souvannarath did return to work, but then escaped to Thailand on June 30, 1979. On September 3, 1979 he immigrated to West Germany, but he now lives in San Diego, California, USA. His notes are a self-confession that he had worked with the Twenty-One Gang Organization, which was used by Mahakou. In the end, he was sent to learn how to use the nine-link chain at the re-education camp in Ban Po, Phongsaly Province. He recorded all this so that people know how badly he was mistreated by the Communists.]

In 1978, China's Ambassador to France in Paris contacted some Lao organizations to see if the Lao people needed help. An appointment was set for the meeting, and twenty groups of Lao showed up, all of them representing the Lao People. This confused the Chinese Ambassador who at first asked for only one group of Lao representatives. The attendees left and never returned again.

On July 22, 1978 the Lao Communists sided with North-Vietnam in their fight against China with respect to their differences over Cambodia.

In 1979, the Chinese attacked North-Vietnam on all fronts, an attack that convinced North-Vietnam to make slight changes to its policy of domination over Indochina. In January 1979, the Lao Communists hailed North-Vietnam's invasion of Cambodia and subsequently denounced China's punishment of Vietnamese Communists. In May 1979, the Chinese radio announced the formation of a Lao Socialist Party. The Lao Communists then accused China of training and arming anti-Lao Communist Government guerillas. In July, 1979, the purging of pro-Chinese elements in the Lao Communists Party (LPRP) led to defection of a number of middle-level cadres to China and many others country. One of the defectors was Tiao Souphanouvong's son. Then, the Lao Communists Government announced immediate suspension of the cooperation program with China.

In 1980, Anti- Lao Communist government resistance leaders announced formation of the Lao People's National Liberation United Front.

1981 was the first year of meeting of the foreign ministers of the three countries of Communist Indochina (Cambodia, Laos and Vietnam).

On January 10, 1984, Souvanna Phouma died in Vientiane at the age of eighty-two.

In 1986, Lor Faydang Lobliayao died in Laos.

On March 11, 1991 the Pathet Lao signed an agreement with Thailand on mutual withdrawal of troops from a disputed border village.

In 1992, Thailand closed the refugees Camp of Ban Vinai from Lao Communist agreed to open friendship with Thailand.

On January 9.1995 Souphanouvong died in Vientiane at the age of eighty-five. His wife Viengkham died on September 1, 2006 also at the age of eighty-five.

There are still many Red Lao strategic elements that have not yet been revealed. Those outlined above were typical and demonstrated how ferocious the Red Lao's policies used against the Lao and Lao Hmong people actually were.

CHAPTER 17

WHO/WHAT CREATED LAO ISSUES?

ORIGINS OF THE ISSUES

Why was Laos subject to so much bad luck and why did the Lao people caused themselves so much karma that kept coming back endlessly? I personally had ran into problems many times and believe that these issues stemmed from the lack of justice, slanted personal beliefs (caused by emotion and religion), lack of strong principles and legal foundations, shabby political regime, lack of education, lack of judgment, and too much willingness to execute foreigners' plan to control Laos without much after-thought and internal debate as to whether the end results would be good or bad

for Laos. Furthermore, Laos is a country that lacks internal and external links, does not have a good plan to create national unity, cooperative spirit, forgiveness, and sincerity. The Lao people tend to be rather selfish, and more inclined to meet personal goals than to reach out to their compatriots. Laos sits in the middle of more populous countries that at times are engaged in infiltration and interference to gain power, create dissensions in Laos, and make it difficult for the Lao people to control the situation and the security.

1. Hatred

One of the reasons for our problems is the hatred maintained by people who got tortured, mistreated and accused for no real reasons other than to satisfy the interests of the leaders or their followers. That emotional dislike could also be caused by rivalry contests between individuals, political parties and regimes.

Hatred could make the Lao people easy victims of foreigners who interfere in our internal affairs and do all they can to promote deadly and prolonged armed conflicts. Very little time was left for the Lao people to develop their country and themselves. Instead, parts and parcels of the Lao territory kept being pulled away, making our country smaller and smaller. As long as the Lao people do not register any victory, hatred will never go away. The Lao communists had not only a chance to wash their hatred for the Vientiane rightists, but they also delivered our country on a silver plate to the Vietnamese communists. The Lao communists' dealing with hatred can only be their road to karma; which surely would come back and haunt them. Only forgiveness could stop karma's vicious circle. One of the Lao proverbs said, "In order to protect the country, getting rid of hatred should be a personal, not a collective, action. Building national cooperation and unity is the key to leading the country on the road to prosperity; it is also a good example for others to follow."

2. Belief

Without mutual trust and mutual respect, our country can only be heading in an unstable and questionable direction, with ethnic groups running into differences in thinking, belief and social status. Social justice cannot exist without mutual trust and mutual respect.

2.1 Religion

Laos is a small country with a small population that practices many religions with different tenets. For example, one religion teaches the importance of karma, always do the good things, and abide by the law. However, another religion may rely on different, more Satanist precepts, associated with the promotion of rebellious attitudes and favoring bad deeds to reach success, acting like a bad guy to become the lead guy, killing people to go to heaven. These differences are indeed difficult to change.

2.2 Culture

Mutual respect is the most important feature of Lao culture. The Lao society does not allow for infringement of the Lao culture and always calls for mutual respect in all areas involving custom, sex, social status, etc. and with particular reference to speech, hand-shaking, palm to palm pressing and bowing, walking past an elder or high-ranking civil servants, etc. Some of those practices may be out-of-date and it is up to individuals to make an adjustment. As the world evolves, custom and culture should also evolve to keep pace as appropriate. The one thing we need to change is alcoholic drinking in public places or entertainment areas, something that society despises because it does not reflect a good education level and the currently accepted standards. We need to change our attitudes and practices to be on a par with civilization, meet with the standards that most of the world is in favor of, and be able to coexist. We should not act over-pretentiously or dress up ostentatiously. The Lao culture calls for greeting guests in a positive mood, when asking our nieces and nephews to join in at Lamvong round-dancing, or offering them to share drinks in good spirit. We should, however, stay within acceptable social standards and not overdo it. A drunk can tarnish culture, which is what the proverb "Attitude is the sign of lineage" has been telling us all along.

2.3 Language

Many languages are spoken in Laos, although Laotian is the national and official language. We also have many ethnic groups, each of which speaks their own language. One of the problems we face is language-related because our leadership has yet to institute a grass-root, nationwide education system. In some areas, local residents have to educate themselves. Not being able to understand each other could be erroneously interpreted as lack of interest, lead to the wrong, irresponsive responses, and generate a feeling of being ignored. People in that situation would be easy to be lured into supporting the wrong cause. In addition, linguistic nuances sometimes also lead to different meanings; and when you have to guess, chances are you may be guessing wrong. One of the Lao proverbs did state, "Language is the sign of nationality; education is the sign of success."

3. Lack of justice

The country's administration is not based on implementation of firm laws and regulations. Even if those existed, they were rarely applied or people did not know how to apply them. When justice really means equality, it creates unity and harmony. In Laos, justice is almost non-existent because of social classes, family relationships, status, and differences in education levels. This is an open door for the use of personal power. With the lack of justice, no rule of laws, no rigid application of rules and regulations, and no morality, social issues will arise because of the inexistence of individual rights. The communist regime is a regime that does not recognize personal values and, therefore, cannot be fully trusted.

4. Governing Regime

The three major regimes in effect are democracy, socialism (communism), and neutralism. The major characteristics of democratic and socialist regimes are as follows:

4.1 Democratic Regime

o   The supreme executive power rests with the people
o   Free elections are held, and voting is fair and equitable
o   People's freedom is guaranteed in the Constitution, and rights to freedom are implemented by the National Assembly and the courts of justice
o   The government must work in the best interests of the nation as a whole --not for any particular individual or political party
o   Even though the people have delegated executive duties to the government, they still have the right to express their pro and con opinions vis-à-vis the government's policies
o   When a conflict arises that may have an impact on the nation, the people should be part of resolution process using the majority rule as the deciding factor
o   Before the government starts implementing its executive power, it must first announce its policies to the people and closely follow those policies. If it no longer retains the people's support through a National Assembly's vote of confidence, the government should resign
o   All citizens have the right to elect a national representative through the popular voting process, using the majority rule to decide the election results. They have the right to express their opinions on any proposals to amend the Constitution. Absent a majority support, the proposal involved will be rejected.
o   Human rights are universally recognized as rights granted equally to all the citizens, regardless of their ethnic origins, sex, age, social class, etc.

4.2   Socialism (Communism)

Socialism and democracy are two different ideologies. Because it relies on political regime and economics, socialism only allows for one political party to control power and exert influence around the world during the entire 1900-1990 period. Part of the world's population has adopted communism as their favorite regime and seriously threatened the free world. The first politician who introduced communism was V. I. Lenin of Russia, and the philosopher/economist/sociologist who wrote the Communist Manifesto in 1948 was Karl Marx of Germany. Communism does not recognize religion and, hence, religion is not practiced in a communist country. It also limits human rights –private ownership is not allowed—and supports a "classless, egalitarian and stateless society". For all those reasons, many citizens of communist countries have immigrated to the "free" countries of the world. *[Those constraints have been relaxed quite a bit following the dissolution of the Soviet Union in 1985].*

5. Lack of Education

Laos has developed some form of education between the end of the Second World War and the beginning of the Vietnam War. In the security-safe zones, the US had provided some education funding. Because the country from north to south was involved in a long internal war, the Lao government did not have much capability to strengthen education. Many of the Lao kids did not get any education at all, cannot read or write, even in their own native languages. Therefore, they were not able to see for themselves whether the situation in their country was good or bad; they just could not do it. They only tend to run behind those who knew "how to speak nicely".

Some of the Lao people were lured by the communists into serving in high-ranking civil service positions, under one condition --they had to convert their constituents into supporters of the communist doctrine. Those peoples were happy to be serving in high positions and encourage their family members and relatives to support the communists without ever worrying about the impacts of their actions. As a Lao proverb put it, "They were blindfolded by their ranks." Ranks indeed make the uneducated folks ecstatic and crazy about their power, and push many of them to fight to in the battlefield, and pull the entire country down. This was the lessons the Lao people have learned times and times again.

6. Lack of roads and communication links

Laos is a poor country that is behind in all development areas, with high mountain ranges and mountain passes that are hard and take time to cross, usually by foot and on horse-back only. When the French took control over Laos, they tried to build several highways in the northern part of the country, e.g., Highways 1 through 7, Highway 13 from Louang Prabang to the south of the country. The middle and southern regions had also several highways, e.g., Highway 8 through 12. Drivable roads were generally limited to the flat areas. In most urban areas, the roads were very dusty, did not allow for high speed rides, and were full of potholes, especially during the rainy season. Finding a car to ride on was a challenge, except for high ranking individuals or foreigners. Gas was also hard to find and was fairly expensive because the Lao currency (kip) was of relatively little value on the international market as a result of the country's weak economic bases that supported the national bank.

The war against the French fought by the Indochinese nationalists contributed to the deterioration of the road conditions and security. Many highways in the north, central and south of the country were left without maintenance for a long time. When the US got involved in the fight against the communists during 1960-1975, they did not use the highways very much. Most of their supply operations were by air, which was a lot safer. For this reason, many high-ranking Lao officers did not attach much importance to the roads that were more often used as secret attack paths by the communists. Nevertheless, roads were a critical part of an attack plan, when moving troops in and out of the target area, and getting prepared for the defensive operation. The more familiar you are with the terrain and the road lay-out, the better chance you have to fight with the enemy.

SIGNS OF "BEHIND-THE-TIME" DEVELOPMENT

Countries that are behind in their development usually share the following features: lack of progress in public confidence and public administration; lack of education improvements, means of communication, political research activities, and economic development. Those countries are behind time, not prosperous, do not or cannot put a high priority to their national development plans, are not unified, are low spirited and full of self-serving egos, and lack long-range vision. Unfortunately, Laos is one of those countries that are the least developed nations in the world, struggling through several decades of internal fighting, and continuing to reshape its vision and its territorial borders. If the country can move in the right direction, the Lao people would certainly be happier and truly thankful to their leaders. But right now, things seem to be in turmoil. The more changes are taking place, the poorer the nation becomes and the more debt it owes. Thete is a staggering amount of money the country's leaders have borrowed from abroad for their own or their political party's benefits –not for the country's development.

Conducting exploratory research and motivating the people are most critical for the country. This is why we need to have leaders that are educated and experienced, have a long-range vision on the needs of the country, and know how to reach out to the people and get their support and cooperation. They need to generate new ideas, and secure investment capitals and adequate labor force. Even when we had good leaders, if the population was uneducated, unsupportive and uninterested, not much progress would be achieved. By the same token, an educated grass-root associated with bad leaders would also lead to the same dead-end situation. A successful family is one where the parents provide good examples to their children. A nation that is led by orderly leaders stands a good chance of becoming an orderly state. By the same token, a nation that consists of unruly, unlawful, and selfish people is likely to be insecure, impolite, unsociable, and unappealing to potential economic and social donor countries.

Furthermore, Laos is a country without direct access to the sea, a small territory surrounded by a lot bigger and more populous countries. It is full of high mountain ranges, including Phou Phathi, Phou Loei, Phou Bia, and Phou Paksong (Boleven Plateau). This is a country drained by the majestic Mekong River that runs from north to south, and many other smaller but still beautiful rivers like Nam Ou, Nam Seuang, Nam Khane, Nam Lik, and Nam Ngum in the northern Laos; Name Sane, Nam Kading, and Nam Theune in central Laos; and Nam Sebangfai, Nam Sechamphone, Nam Sebanghieng, Nam Sedone, and Nam Sekong in southern Laos. These streams all lead to the picturesque and attractive Khone Pha Pheng (Lee-Phee) Falls.

Laos has many very peaceful and relaxing areas in the northern and southern part of the country. The Paksong mountain range in particular is blessed with clean air and two seasons –a dry season (sometimes marked by forest fires) and a rainy season. The cold season is practically non-existent, except in the area between northern Xieng Khouang Province and Houaphan Province. The dry season begins in November and ends in June. The rainy season begins in June and continues until the end of October. The best and most enjoyable weather occurs between November and March, when flowers bloom, temperature is cool, air is clean, and many popular festivals are organized, including the Lao New Year and the Hmong New Year. Fruits are rather scarce during this cool period, except for oranges, pomelos, and peaches. You have to wait until the end of the raining season for the most common Lao fruits to appear. During the hot season, Asian people celebrate many entertaining activities nights and days; young women use this season to dress up very nicely.

Laos enjoys a warm and decent culture. If you understand the language, no matter where you are, you will always be greeted nicely. You do not have to look for a hotel, especially in rural areas. Sanitary conditions may not be good as expected, especially with regards to mosquitoes, drinking water, flies, and food. Living conditions in rural areas are usually not as modernized as what most foreign tourists would expect to see.

Countries with good religious practices and efficient political regime are normally prosperous and secured, regardless of their sizes. Good examples are Switzerland, Japan, South-Korea and Germany. Even if they sometimes faced armed conflicts, they still have found ways to improve themselves. By contrast, Laos is a beautiful country, enriched with tons of natural resources that, so far, seemed to have been ignored. What we tend to see is a remote country, not important enough to warrant serious attention until a wider regional war broke out. When the US started the Indochina War, it felt this was the right time for them to teach a lesson to an expanding enemy. This was a decision that translated into unprecedented and extremely heavy losses for the Lao people.

CHAPTER 18

LIFE OF LAO REFUGEES THIRD COUNTRIES

HOPELESS LIFE IN REFUGEE CAMPS

On May 10, 1975 the situation in Military Region II (MR-II) and the entire Laos took turns for the worse in a scary and unprecedented fashion, following the US unilateral decision to drop their assistance to the Vientiane faction. This left Laos without any source of military support in their fight against the Lao communists, who were strongly supported by the North-Vietnamese using weapons and ammunition received from the Soviet Union. As a result, the commander of MR-II decided to leave the area in order to prevent his people from being further punished and tortured by the Lao and Vietnamese communists. He did so because he did not see any other way out; everything looked blurry for him. Many other high-ranking military officers also fled to Thailand, leaving behind their troops, nieces and nephews, families and relatives, without any pre-planning activities.

Because of those intense developments, the US had to bring in C 130, C46 and C47 aircrafts to fly several Long Cheng trooper families out to the refugee camp of Nam Phong, Khone Kaeng Chanwath, Thailand. Those aircrafts were not able to carry everybody away, because not too many people were aware of that airlift option and the lead time was too short. Some of the would-be evacuees also lived some distance away from Long Cheng and could not come in within the allocated time frame. The air evacuation started on May 11, 1975 and ended at 11 a.m. on May 14, 1975 because by then the enemy had already completely surrounded Long Cheng. Once the airlift ended, thousands of military and civilians and their families left Long Cheng for Vientiane by roads or forest trails, trying to cross the river to Thailand to join their leaders and other family members that had been transported to Thailand before.

Gen. Vang Pao and Jerry Daniels boarded a USAID aircraft at the top of the Pharassavang mountain range, flew out behind the last C130 flight, landed at Muang Cha (LS113) and then flew to Nam Phong on a Porter aircraft. By the end of May 1975, the communists closed the road between Vientiane and Long Cheng and many other roads, and set up check-points to prevent all movements within the area. A group of Hmong on their way to Vientiane were shot by the Lao communists when they were about to cross the bridge over Nam Lik River. Several of them were killed or injured.

Civilians retreated to Ban Sone Na Sou, looking for new trails that would lead them through the jungle to Thailand. The Lao communists did all they could to discourage their flights, including setting up roadblocks or even killing some of the refugees. Despite all those threats, the flights to Thailand still continued unabated. By the end of May 1975, the refugee movement toward the Laos-Thailand border line was so intense that it began to create serious problems for the Thai and the Lao governments who then decided to close the border between the two countries. The Thai government also decided to send the Vientiane high-ranking military officers and leaders who were seeking refuge in Thailand to a third country.

Photo #186. Bodies of Hmong killed at the bridge over the Nam Lik River in May 1975. About 50 bodies were buried at Ban Na Sou by a USAID team led by Tong Voua Mua (who later died in South Carolina on March 14, 2010). see source: The Unforgettable Laos.

After the departure of the Vientiane leaders from Thailand, the influx of refugees from Laos to Thailand still continued without any changes. The Thai government had to set up centers to provide shelter to refugees from Laos, Cambodia and South-Vietnam at several locations including Nong Khay in Changwad Nane, Vinay, Phanom, and Napho. After closing the Nong Khay camp following repeated arsonist acts and several murder cases, the Thai government closed a few more refugee camp in the northern and southern parts of Thailand.

Photo #187. C130 aircrafts s began to pick up Gen. Vang Pao's people from Long Cheng on May 11, 1975

see source: *https://en.wikipedia.org/wiki/Long_Tieng*

18

and https://www.unforgettable-laos.com/the-end-of-the-war/5-4-life-of-refugees-from-laos-in-the-third-countries/

SAD AND PITIFUL LIFE OF MR-II REFUGEES TO THAILAND

Photo # 188. *The last C-130 flight out of Long Chieng at noon on May 14, 1975 brought a lot of tears from the Hmong people. The mountain in the background was Phou Prarasavang, the site of the royal resort. Gen. Vang Pao and Jerry Daniel flew out that same day..*

see in : https://www.unforgettable-laos.com/the-end-of-the-war/5-4-life-of-refugees-from-laos-in-the-third-countries/

The Hmong refugees had to go through dangerous deep jungles and high mountain ranges, mostly during night-time in order to avoid Lao communists' ambushes and gun shots. May Lo, the sister of Reverend Mang Her who now lives in Minnesota, once reported that she and sixty of her relatives spent weeks walking through the jungle before reaching Paksane, south of Vientiane, with the ultimate plan of crossing the Mekong River into Thailand. One morning, at dawn, they realized they were being completely surrounded by the Lao communists. Everybody was arrested. Each man had his hands tied to the back and all the men were tied together near a small but fairly deep creek, and then shot to death by the Lao Communists, with their dead bodies falling into the creek. The women and the children, on the other hand, were not tied but were bluntly hit on the back of the head with Ak47 butts and sent to die in the creek. As they were about to hit May Lo's head, she grabbed her 4-year old daughter and pressed her body against her chest. After the mother was hit, both she and her daughter fell into the creek. The Lao communists then left the site. The daughter kept grabbing her mother all day and all night.

The following morning, she was still lying on her mother, crying, and watching her mother while sitting on top of cadavers infested with flies. Half a day later, the mother regained consciousness but had a big head-ache and saw plenty of small maggots around her whole body.

19

She washed off the maggots and asked her daughter, "How many days was I dead?" The daughter said, "I am hungry and thirsty. I have not eaten anything for a long time." She hugged her daughter and looked around to see if there were other survivors. Apparently, no one else had survived. She was convinced God had saved her life so she could come back and take care of her daughter. She then took her daughter out of the creek. By coincidence, three Hmong refugees were walking by. She asked for their permission to walk with them toward the Thai border that same night. She reached Thailand in mid-1976 and was admitted to the hospital at Nong Khay refugee camp.

[I had a chance to interview May Lo at a psychiatric hospital in Minnesota where she was being treated for off-and-on neurologic problems. She said that sometimes she did not know what she was doing, and often crossed the streets without asking herself first whether there were any running cars or not. Sometimes, she also thought about the circumstances that preceded her husband's murder and cried without an end, caught in an extreme feeling of fear].

In addition to the mistreatments by the Lao communists, armed robberies were also frequent, perpetrated by Thai and Lao felons ready to carry out their crimes on the Hmong along both sides of the Mekong River and causing several deaths.

A Hmong once hired a Thai boat that operated like a fishing boat in the middle of the Mekong River from dawn to sunset. This was during the rainy month of June 1976, when he noticed more than 20 dead bodies floating down the river. He was told that floating dead bodies during 1975-1985 were frequent incidents. From 1985 onward, nobody knows how many of the same incidents were still happening.

American C-46 during final evacuation of Long Cheng, May 1975 (Roger Warner collection).

Photo # 189. *US C46 aircraft carrying Long Cheng people away in 1975. Photo courtesy Roger Va Geu.*

https://www.unforgettable-laos.com/the-end-of-the-war/5-4-life-of-refugees-from-laos-in-the-third-countries/

The US claimed that refugees that left their country after 1982 were "economic" refugees –not "political" refugees. This was not entirely true because some refugees had very little control over when they could or could not leave, especially the military units that operated away from the front line and were surrounded for a long time by the enemy without any chance to escape. The worst part of the exodus was coming from the mountain ranges down to the flat areas. The Hmong were dreadful about getting mosquito bites and being infected with malaria. Many of them had also been exposed to Agent Orange through direct rainfall exposure or drinking contaminated stream waters. The Lao communists had killed the Hmong without any sign of regret by dropping bombs, spraying chemical yellow rain or Agent Orange powders over every forest where the Hmong were.

Two Hmong refugees who made it to Nong Khay reported that they have seen the body of a recently deceased Hmong woman with a one-year old child sitting on the body and still feeding on the dead woman's breast, despite the fact that the body was already in an early decomposition stage. They wanted very much to help the baby but were afraid that if and when the baby cried, the enemy would be able to track them. Because of this exceedingly high risk, they were not able to do anything. This explained why Lao refugee families with babies used opium to put their kids to sleep before they walked past dangerous check-points, especially at night and along the Mekong River bank where the Lao communists were known to be watching the human traffic.

A Hmong Xyooj woman by the name of Nang Song, affected with insomnia and deep sadness, and unable to do or remember anything, was admitted to a psychiatric facility in Minnesota. After one week of treatment, she was able to sleep and eat a little. By coincidence, I was then working at the facility and had a chance to ask her about her past medical history. She told me that she left LS05 (Padong) by foot, walked through the forest up to Phoubia Mountain and down to Muang Omm and then past several other mountain ranges. After the two to three day walk from Muang Omm, her mother got sick and passed away. Next, her father died of malaria contracted through mosquito bites, leaving only her and a 12-year old sister. Nang Song, then 14 and a half, and her younger sister continued their journey in the company of other relatives. When they got close to the Phou Khao Khouai Mountain, they had to climb high mountain peaks and steep rocks —a very difficult and energy consuming exercise. Nobody but you can help yourself.

When they faced a 4 to 5 feet tall rock plate, she had her sister sit down so she could step on her sister's shoulders and then climb the rock. Once she was up, she pulled her sister up. Unfortunately, both of them had fever. As she lowered her hands and attempted to pull her sister up, she was not strong enough to do so. Everybody else was gone and there was nobody else to help them. She had to keep her sister hanging on her hands for a full day. Her sister grabbed her hands until she died on the spot. When she noticed her sister's hands were getting cold, she lowered her sister to the ground. Her sister did reach the ground but then did not move at all. She wanted to go down and help her, but realized she too was dead tired because of the fever and many days without food —just eating tree roots and leaves. After she swallowed some food and water (provided by other passing-by refugees) and had recovered some energy, she was able to sit up and continue her walk to safety. From that point on, each time she thought about her sister and her parents, she would become dizzy and fainted. These conditions have been affecting her for several years and pushed her to sign up at the hospital for treatment in 1985.

Regiment 28 stationed at Bouam Long (LS32) was under the command of Col. Cheu Pao Mua. An aircraft flew him in for a meeting and then flew him out to Thailand immediately, leaving all of his troopers behind. Later on, his troopers fled into the jungle. Many of them got ambushed, arrested, and killed barbarously. Some went in to surrender to the authorities and then completely disappeared from the scenery without anybody knowing much about their fate. According to those who survived, the people who surrendered were all killed, even when they were still very young.

The Bouam Long Camp was the MR-II front-line post located behind the enemy ranks, northwest of the Plain of Jars. The camp has been attacked many times by the Lao and Vietnamese communists without much success. Starting from 1961, the year the camp was created, the enemy had suffered very heavy losses each time they attacked the site. The camp was a deadly strategic site that pushed the Lao and Vietnamese communists to arrest and kill many Hmong, and to cry out loud that, "The Hmong have deeply buried black hearts that smell like rotten skirts. You can wash them as much you want, they will still smell bad."

[This was to be expected, because the Vietnamese and Lao communists put the lives of the Hmong below those of domesticated animals; everybody had to fend for himself/herself. The Hmong did not invade communist countries; the Vietnamese communists were the ones that invaded the Hmong and the Lao territory. We all had to stand up and fight off the destruction of the Lao nation and the Lao territory that we loved, a land that used to be a peaceful place for us to live our lives since childhood. When we were invaded, when our happiness and our nation were destroyed, we all had to be ready to risk our lives to avoid complete destruction].

Photo #190. *When refugees first arrived in the Camp in Thailand, many were sick and starving.*

see source: https://www.unforgettable-laos.com/the-end-of-the-war/5-4-life-of-refugees-from-laos-in-the-third-countries/

Photos #191 (left) and 192 (right). Hmong soldiers had to continue fighting in the jungle on a day to day basis in order to survive, avoid surrendering and/or cooperating with the communists, and being captured and killed like animals. Photo courtesy Fact Finding Commission, 2004.

HOPELESS LIFE IN REFUGEE CAMPS

There are good and bad things in the refugee camps.

- o The good things were that people had a shelter and a safe place to stay, without any life threat from the communists, in a place where there was enough to eat and to drink, and where people were under reasonably good cares from the Thai authorities from 1975 to 2006.
- o The bad things were related to physical confinement. Refugees had to stay in the camp, with limited opportunities to go outside (unless accompanied by a Thai official). Our activities were restricted, without any hope for any personal training and development. Politics were the main deciding factor for the fate of the Lao refugees, because there was no certainty as to whether they would go back to their countries or have a chance to resettle later in Thailand or in a third country.

Because of all those uncertainties, many Lao refugees lived under intense emotional pressure, got very nervous, lost their memories, and lived a shorter life. These emotions caused some people to go to jail or even to die because they were too strong. During the behind-the-wall life in the Thai refugee camps, many had secretly escaped the camps to go and live with their Thai relatives, and ended up being stuck in Thailand and given no more chance to go to a third country for lack of T-numbers. Some of those who were lucky enough to be sent to a third country ran into health problems and died during their sleep. Several thousands of Lao refugees stayed behind in Thailand, and were later moved from Nam Phong-Soune Vinay camp to Soune Tham Kha-Bork camp to Soune Houei Nam Khao in 2009.

Luck had allowed many of the Lao refugees to see light during their dreams, as many countries in the world threw their helpful hands in our direction and allowed many of us to start a new life in their countries from 1976 until 2009. But there were also thousands of refugees left behind at the Houei Nam Khao camp in Thailand, subject to many issues brought up by the Thai and Lao armies as part of their negotiations to get the refugees sent back to the Laos PDR. Of all refugees that came to Thailand, the Hmong were the ones that suffered the most. All of them were sent back to Laos PDR on December 28, 2009, more specifically to Ban Phone Thong, Borikhamsay Province.

Notes: Civil servants, military officers and highly educated leaders mostly ended up in France because of the more relaxed entry requirements used by the French Government in 1975. The US waited until 1976 to accept Lao refugees in the USA, claiming that there was still a US Embassy in Laos. They also only picked selected group of refugees, i.e., those working for USAID and/or serving as interpreters. The US Christians were next in welcoming Lao Christians into the USA. The last group that was admitted consisted of military officers, and soldiers and their families who were fighting in the Vietnam War on the US side. This explained the high number of military members among the Lao refugee population in the USA. Many Americans still consider the Hmong as stone-age people because of the long war in Laos.

Photo #193. *Fighting for survival, always on the move, and setting up traps. No matter how difficult and painful, one had to fight and die with honor to avoid being caught and savagely executed like animals by the enemy. Sleep where and when you can.*

see source: https://www.unforgettable-laos.com/6-the-conclusions/6-4-past-events-future-projections/

NOTES FROM COL. VANG NENG, HEAD OF BAN VINAY REFUGEE CAMP

Col. Vang Neng started serving as representative of the Soune Vinay's refugees in September 1979, replacing Col. Vang Yi who left for a third country (USA). This was a difficult and dangerous time as a result of the transfer of refugees from the Nong Khay and Nam Fong camps into the Soune Vinay camp. The Soune Vinay camp, which was originally created to accommodate only 12,000 refugees, then had to shelter 42,000 refugees. Because of the influx of refugees, the refugee camp was subdivided into seven zones, each headed by a representative lead and a management team. Zone 5 was originally reserved for lowland Lao refugees. Before long, conflicts soon surfaced between the lowland and the highland Lao refugees, created by misunderstanding from among the younger refugees. The camp management realized that the misunderstanding came from differences in customs and languages; it then moved Zone 5 refugees to the Na Pho camp, leaving Zone 5 facilities practically empty.

Despite that move, problems still lingered because of the presence of many ethnic groups, including friends, foes, and ill-intentioned elements. Drug trafficking and other illegal activities created bad reputation and insecurity, and led to the daily arrest of wrong-doers. Robberies and nighttime murders became alarming and very scary. Col. Vang Neng then decided to lay out protective plans for the camp to ensure its existence, including several committees: Central Committee, Zone Committees, Neighborhood Committees, and Building Committees. One building accommodated several families. The performance by each committee was not fully satisfactory because of the uncertainty surrounding the departure to third countries. Conflict resolution was also hard to perform and did not meet the need. As a result, changes were deemed necessary. Also, a request was submitted to the United Nations for funds to build work offices at Ban Vinay for the following officials/offices:

- o President or Refugee representative
- o Two vice-Presidents, and Secretary Team; financial committee; audit committee; committee in charge of arrivals, departures, birth, death; youth committees, and security committee.

The duties of the **Central Committee** were as follows:

1. Managing and solving problems of all the refugees in the camp
2. Contacting the Thai authorities and the refugees organizations
1. Developing security plan including security guards for every building
2. Contacting all religious and assistance organizations to seek help for the refugees
3. Developing plans for education, health, profession, and future career
4. Scheduling workshops to promote mutual understanding and orderly co-existence
5. Reviewing individual plans to resettle in a third country, and following up with refugees who have already left the refugee camp, and
6. Resolving miscellaneous issues in the refugee camp.

Photo #194. *Col. Vang Neng opened the ceremony of Hmong New Year 1979 at the refugee Camp at Ban Vinai. The first two persons behind him to his left were Maj. Vue Mai (who became the Camp Representative after Col. Vang Neng went to the US in 1984). Standing furtherto the left was Neng Lo Yang. In 1992 the Camp was closed. Vue Mai led some Hmong back to Laos and about three years later, completely disappeared from public view.*

see source:

https://www.unforgettable-laos.com/the-end-of-the-war/5-4-life-of-refugees-from-laos-in-the-third-countries/

The Clans Committee had the following duties involving the 18 Hmong Clans (Vang, Yang, Li, Xong, Reu, Mua, Khang, Kong, Thao, Pha, Thang, Veu, Lo, Tsheej, Song, etc. :

- o Serving as the clan's elder with full authority to resolve issues within the clan
- o Serving as member of the Central Committee as a representative of the clan
- o Resolving all the internal issues of the clan
- o Addressing wedding-related issues affecting members of the two clans involved
- o Helping in conflict resolution affecting other clans as requested

Photo #195. *Col. Vang Neng, refugee representative at the Ban Vinay Camp making a speech at a preparatory meeting in 1980, asking all his fellow refugees from Laos to care for each other during difficult and hopeless times.*

see source:

https://www.unforgettable-laos.com/the-end-of-the-war/5-4-life-of-refugees-from-laos-in-the-third-countries/

The Inspection Committee had very important tasks to perform such as:

- Inspecting all suspicious buildings and facilities and reporting back to the Central Commit

Tee

- Monitoring the behavior of the members of the Central Committee and various developments within the camp
- Tracking the performance of the Clans Committee to ensure fairness and equity

The Advisory Committee provided opinions on various issues that are affecting or are likely to affect the refugee camp. Members of this Committee were hand-picked by Col. Vang Neng from former members of the military, police, civil service and educated and experienced elite groups to develop plan and/or resolve issues. After forming this committee, Col. Vang Neng held a meeting to address the following three issues:

- Refugee arrival and departure
- Security surveillance and change of guards at each building
- Ensuring the security of the refugees

Col. Vang Neng explained, "We are refugees living in another country. Our lives have changed. We do not have the same freedom to do what we want to do as we did in Laos. If anyone breaks the rule, he/she should be punished according to the laws of the host country. We refugees have no special rights; we can only use our eyes to look. We must find ways to communicate so we can co-exist and understand each other as a group and survive until we reach the following two scenarios: go to a third country or return to Laos. The one who has the right to live in Thailand is only the one with the Thai nationality. Even the refugees' children who are born in a refugee camp are treated as foreigner —not as Thai citizens."

Once everybody knows that we refugees only have two options, we need to think and decide which of the two options to choose -- go to a third country or go back to Laos. Or, remain hopelessly in the refugee camp? Because of this, everyone needs to plan ahead and be ready, especially the young fellows. You must go to school, learn a profession, learn dancing and perform various sport and Hmong cultural activities, so you can take advantage of later when there is an opportunity to do so. Everybody has to be self-conscious and improve himself/herself before it's too late."

After Col. Vang Neng's speech, many asked questions and cried, because most of them were not educated and only fought under their leaders' orders. Without orders, they did not know the way out.

Furthermore, many religions were practiced in the refugee camps and made it difficult for people to understand each other and maintain a smooth relationship. I had the chance to explain to everybody that religion is their own choice. They may believe in any religion but should not impose their religious belief on others or associate that belief with human co-existence, public administration, or refugee organizations. They should keep it within their family or within their religious group. Our internal cooperation is another item that will benefit from foreign assistance. Internal conflict and mutal disputes in refugee organizations were the source of disunion and unproductive, damaging, and self-destructive results. Everybody should join hands to show their sincerity, openness, and cooperation, and achieve progress and security.

After the meeting, the committee activities, security inspection and surveillance resulted in a surprisingly high drop in assassinations, robberies and drug-trafficking. Everybody loved and understood his/her neighbors and was willing to do everything possible for the collective good in the refugee camp. All the problems were abated by almost 100 percent —a real accomplishment for the Soune Vinay's refugees. This corresponded to the appointment of the new Thai Refugee Camp Manager, Bandit Omthaisong --a highly-educated, generous, and skilled manager who liked to lean on the majority rule as a basis for decision-making. In order to enhance the refugees' unity, Mr. Bandith worked closely with Refugee Leader Vang Neng, often asking him about the various Lao events that created so many refugees. This used to be a topic of high interest to Thailand, a neighbor country to Laos.

Mr. Bandit did not only take care of the refugees, but he also invited the new Chanwad Governor Thongdam Banexung, the security chief, and the police officials to visit the refugees during the Hmong New-Year celebration (Kinh Chiang). On this occasion, Col. Vang Neng expressed his thanks to the King of Thailand, the Thai government, and the Thai people for allowing the Lao refugees to stay in their country. He talked in detail about the various actions that the Lao Communists --the protégés of the North-Vietnamese-- did to violate signed agreements, divide the Lao people, bring the Vietnamese communists in to fight the Vientiane faction and force them to flee abroad. He also mentioned about potential impacts to Thailand, because the Vietnamese communists were eager to expand their influence to the rest of southeast-Asia.

Col. Vang Neng's speech, made in 1979, convinced many Thai leaders to organize workshops to discuss the various events within their communities. They invited Col. Vang Neng to provide a briefing on the Lao historical events, including the violent communist tactics used against the Vientiane faction. The briefing was of great interest to the Director-General of the Thai Ministry of the Interior and the Director of the Thai Army's Psychological Operations Department Director who came for a visit to the Soune Vinay camp. Later on, the Thai Minister of the Interior himself made the trip, followed by over 100 deputy-governors, then all the Thai governors led by the Governor of Bangkok. The whole purpose for those site visits was to learn about the various events that took place in Laos in order to develop the proper defense plan for a country that was the next logical communist target in southeast-Asia.

Vang Neng clearly explained that the refugees asked for permission to stay in Thailand for some time waiting for the situation to improve in Laos. If possible, some of them would return to Laos, others would continue to go to a third country; those born in Thai refugee camps would keep their refugee status and not try to get Thai citizenship. When the provincial governors heard that statement, they felt pleased and applauded the speaker. Col. Vang Neng also added that regardless of how difficult life in refugee camps was, refugees had to try to be patient and wait for a chance to either go back to their country or go to a third country to restart a new and free life. The Thai governors were pleased with that statement as well. Those meetings helped strengthen the understanding of the governors and other officials of the refugee issue. Later on, officials from Chanwad Leui were invited to participate in sport events at the refugee camp. They then returned the favor and invited refugees to participate in a parade and sport competitions with the people of Chanwad Leui.

SURVEY OF HMONG REFUGEES ON THEIR PLAN AND VISION

The results of the survey revealed that most of the older and elder refugees would like to go back to their country of birth. Most of the young people, with some education and less than 45 years old, would like to go to a third country to start a new life, and not to go back to live a dangerous life under a communist regime that limits their freedom. As for Col. Vang Neng, who spoke as refugees' representative and had learned many good lessons, what he remembered most vividly was the fact that highland Lao Hmong wished to have open-minded leaders with a good leadership plan, a decision-making process based on majority count, and adequate home-work before execution time.

They did not want leaders who only relied on their power, were only interested in money, and only worked for their party associates. Instead, they wanted to work with, for, and under transparent leaders. Therefore, future Lao and Hmong leaders will have to train themselves very hard, get a good education in many fields, and build a good reputation.

In 1984, conflicts started to rise again at the Soune Vinay refugee camp as a result of the change in the Thai policy to get closer to the Laos PDR policy on border control regulation. Many interrelated and complicated issues forced many refugees to leave for a third country. Col. Vang Neng himself had no choice but to leave the refugee camp, because Thailand had opened the door for too much communist interference in Thailand.

CLOSURE OF REFUGEE CAMPS

Namphong and Nongkhai Refugee Camps, which were closed at the same time in 1976, transferred all their refugee population to the Vinai Refugee Camp. Soune Vinay itself also was closed in 1992 as a result of the change in policies between Thailand and Laos PDR. Several thousands of Hmong refugees were transferred from Vinay Camp to Na Pho Camp to undergo physical examinations and complete the paper work needed for transfer to a third country.

Notes. The closure of the Vinai Refugee Camp in 1992 resulted from the figth between Thai and Laos PDR armed forces around three villages along the Laos-Thailand border. Thailand lost those three villages to the Laos PDR in 1984. On December 12, 1987 and January 1, 1988 the fighting broke up again on Phousone Say Loumkao Mountain. Thai troops launched many successive attacks but were not able to make any head ways. They then rounded up several Hmong living in Thailand and Hmong refugees in Thai refugee camps to fight with them, and this time met with success. Lao PDR troops were about to mount counter-attacks when Thailand threatened to recruit more Hmong refugees to do the fighting, compelling the Laos PDR to stop the attacks and to offer to negotiate without pre-conditions.

The negotiations led to the closure of all the refugee camps in Thailand, including Soune Vinay Camp. Several thousand of Hmong refugees who did not wish to go to a third country went into hiding in the caves of Thamm Kabork under the care and protection of Headmonk Louang Pho Khouba. When the headmonk died in 2006, this camp was also closed. Thousands of refugees then moved to a third country, although a group of about 7,000 refugees went into hiding at the Ban Houei Nam Khao in 2007.

In 2006, the Thai authorities dug up the bodies of Hmong refugees who died during an armed ambush and were buried at the Thamm Kabork camp --about 500 of them. One of the bodies belonging to a woman who died almost a year ago looked still fairly fresh as if the woman had just died a few days ago. Later on, friends and relatives of the deceased Hmong wondered where those bodies were moved to. The Hmong living in the USA demanded answers to the same question, but to no avail because we were just immigrants who came here to ask for shelter.

CHAPTER 19

PAST EVENTS & FUTURE PROJECTIONS

In 1981, a Front for the Liberation of Laos was created under the leaderships of the following personalities: Inpeng Souryadhay, Tiao Sisouk NaChampasak, Ngone Sananikone, Khamphanh Panya, Kouprasith Abhay, Houmphanh Sayasith, Phoumi Nosavan, Vang Pao, and Chao Phaya Luang Outhong Souvanavong (President). In 1982, Tiao Sisouk NaChampasak died of a heart attack in California. , and Gen. Phoumi Nosavan died in Thailand of old age.

The Liberation Front sent many letters to the US Government and the United Nations asking them to help address the invasion of Laos by North-Vietnam, who killed innocent Lao people, and treated Laos as a colony. This action produced no results, because the foreign newsmen who went for site reporting in Laos were lied to and misled by the Lao communists, the North-Vietnamese's protégés. Those foreign reporters who came to collect information were only allowed to urban areas, not to rural or remote areas for security reasons. But in 2004, members of the Fact Finding Commission (FFC) were able to go to Laos and share the pictures they took with the rest of the world. Still, they could not do anything to control and/or punish communist North-Vietnam.

On December 10, 1989 Gen. Vang Pao announced the formation of a "Revolutionary Lao Government" in exile with the purpose of securing freedom for the people of Laos, especially the Hmong, but some US politicians framed the Hmong as terrorists. Gen. Vang Pao was arrested on June 4, 2007 and released on December 7, 2007, but his case was still pending. The case was reopened on May11, 2009, without any results. The hearing was rescheduled for October 5, 2009 when the case was dismissed for Gen. Vang Pao, with eleven other Hmong still waiting for their cases to be heard. *[Nine Hmong were arrested at the same time as Gen. Vang Pao, and two others were arrested later]*. The false incrimination and the lengthy court hearing took a toll on Gen. Vang Pao's health conditions.

This was an unfortunate instance where the US appeared to have opened the door to the communists to come in and created misunderstanding among US citizens. Two more important facts seemed to have been underestimated. First, people tend to forget that Laos had signed itself off to North-Vietnam's colonization for twenty-five years from 1977 to 2002, a contract that can be extended every ten years with no expiration date. Second, the killing of Hmong in Laos and the detention of 46,000 high-ranking military officers and civil servants in re-education camps still has yet to be addressed.

SUMMARY OF HOSTILITIES-RELATED HUMAN LOSSES

- 1945-1947: the Lao Issara rallied its supporters against the French to get rid of colonization. There were more than 10,000 deaths among the Lao, French and Vietnamese ranks, mostly in southern Laos and in the provinces of Vientiane, Xieng Khouang, Luang Prabang and Houa Phanh.

- 1953-1954: the war between the French and the Vietminh caused the loss of about 30,000 Lao citizens, mostly in the provinces of Phongsaly, Houaphanh, Xieng Khouang, Savannakhet, and Pakse. These were the sites of fierce battles with the Vietminh that were pushed away by the French guerillas.

- 1960: the Kong Lae's coup d'état in Vientiane caused several hundreds of military and civilian deaths in the capital city of Vientiane and in Xieng Khouang Province. That same year, when Gen. Phoumi Nosavan and his troops reoccupied Vientiane, almost one thousand Lao military and civilians died.

The fight against communist expansion into southeast-Asia caused the following losses:

- **Military Region I (MR-I)**

About 20,000 civilians and 25,000 military were killed, in addition to the loss of 70 percent of the territory to the North-Vietnamese enemy in the northern and eastern parts of MR-I, and the entire Phongsaly Province. Over 60 percent of the population of MR-I (Oudomsay, Louang Namtha, Louang Prabang and Sayabouri) was pro-communist because they did not have any other choice and had to lean to the left to survive.

- **Military Region II (MR-II)**

About 100,000 civilians were arrested, tortured and killed by the enemy, or died from air bombing; and about 50,000 military (70 percent highland Lao Hmong and 30 percent lowland Lao) were killed in the action. Several thousands of Thai troopers were also killed. Sixty percent of the territory was lost to the enemy. In 1967, a radar station was set up in Houaphan Province to guide air raids over Hanoi. Therefore, this province became the target of heavy attacks by North-Vietnam. Of all the Laos provinces, Xieng Khouang Province shared the longest borderline with North-Vietnam and was located the nearest to Hanoi. In addition, Houaphan and Xieng Khouang Provinces served as hiding and training sites for the North-Vietnamese troops, as command centers for the Lao communists, and as the defensive front line for the capital city of Vientiane and the royal city of Louang Prabang. For all these reasons, those two provinces were more heavily attacked by the North-Vietnamese than any other MR's.

- **Military Region III (MR-III)**

More than 100,000 civilians were killed by the enemy, arrested and tortured to death, or died from air-bombing –the heaviest casualties anywhere in the world since the Second World War. Military losses were over 50,000 in the provinces of Kham-Mouan, Savannakhet, and Saravan (which was totally occupied by the enemy since 1965 for use as part of the Ho Chi Minh trail). About 70 percent of the MR-III territory was lost to the enemy.

- ○ **Military Region IV (MR-IV)**

More than 60,000 Lao civilians and about 30,000 military were killed in MR-IV, an area used by the North-Vietnamese to hide their armed forces and send them to South-Vietnam. The communists had to cleanse all the Lao civilians from MR-IV to keep them away from military centers of the North-Vietnamese and their Viet-Cong allies. MR-IV had to fight very hard to protect itself and,

in the process, suffered formidable losses, especially in the high Boleven plateau and several eastern locations. It lost all its territory along the border with South-Vietnam and Cambodia, and had at times to ask for support from the Thai Army. About 60 percent of its territory was occupied by the enemy. The provinces of Sedone and Attopeu fell entirely in enemy hands in 1965.

- ○ **Military Region V (MR-V)**

This military region suffered the most chaotic situation of all MR's because of the influence of the internal and external political changes that took place. It was the site of many foreign embassies and the center of the Lao coalition government --not the site of too many armed conflicts but definitely the site of fierce political fighting. Because of the presence of the foreign embassies, the split between the three Lao factions was not too obvious, despite the fact that the leftists and neutralists used every possible tactic to eliminate the rightists. When the rightists were gone, the only faction left was the communist faction. This gave Kaysone Phomvihane, Secretary-General of the Lao Communist Party and member of the Indochina Communist Party since 1944, the opportunity to put Laos indefinitely under the control of the North-Vietnamese communists for 25 years followed by renewable 10-year terms. This was supposed to be a mere Laos-Vietnam Friendship Treaty, a treaty that actually left Laos with no power and no Army because the North-Vietnamese are now in charge of the country's defense. MR-V suffered no or very little, if any, civilian or military losses during the early stages of the fight against the communist armed forces. But once the Laos Communist Party took over power, MR-V was the MR that recorded the most civilian and military losses, based on the 40,000 rightists and neutralists who died at the Vieng Xay re-education camp. MR-V was full of civil servants, and an MR where the highest number of refugees originated from.

POPULATION MOVEMENTS

The power take-over by the Laos Communist Party in 1975 forced more than 600,000 Hmong that lived in northern Lao provinces to move as follows:

- ○ About 200,000 remained under the direct control of the Lao Communist Party, as some of the Hmong did fight alongside the Lao and North-Vietnamese communists between 1945 and 1975
- ○ More than 30,000 went into hiding in the forest to engage in guerilla fighting. For them, collaborating with the Laos PDR would not be safe, because they had been fighting them for a long time (from 1960 to 1975). As of 2010, only about 2,000 of those guerillas were still alive.

- About 100,000 tried to immigrate to Thailand, but never made it there. Some died of hunger, thirst, gun shots, armed robberies, exposure to yellow agent rain, drowning during Mekong River crossing, boat sinking, malaria, etc.
- About 200,000 survived and reached the Thai Mekong River bank and then went on to start a new life in a third country. Over 140,000 went to the USA, over 60,000 to France, French Guiana, Canada, Australia, England, and other countries. In 2008, several Hmong were still in Thailand, but in 2009 they were sent back to Laos PDR.
- Currently, there must be at least 400,000 in the USA, including the states of California, Minnesota, Wisconsin, North-Carolina, South-Carolina, Georgia, and other states. Most of the Hmong who had resettled in those states have had good opportunities to get an education, and become economically self-sufficient. This was a big improvement compared to when they first arrived and needed interpreters, social welfare, road guides, etc. because they did not understand and could not read English.

Photo #196. The war torn family system leaves only women behind to care for children. This picture was drawn by Ms. Halinka Luangpraseut, Khamchong Luangpraseuth's wife (who now lives in California, USA).

see source:

https://www.unforgettable-laos.com/6-the-conclusions/6-4-past-events-future-projections/

As for the lowland Lao, at least 600,000 of them, especially high-ranking military, police, and civilian personnel and their families, have resettled in several foreign countries. Almost 100,000 of them went to France and other European countries. Over 300,000 of lowland Lao, especially those who went to school in the USA or have fought in the US rank in the Indochina War, came to the USA with their families and started a new life mostly in the following states: Texas, California, Georgia, North-Carolina and South-Carolina. Since most of them were educated people, they faced less of a challenge in the new environment than the other Lao ethic groups. Finally, no less than

100,000 Lao refugees ended up in other countries like Canada, Australia, Thailand, Japan and the Middle East.

All told, it appeared that the lowland Lao refugees who resettled in the USA are better off than those who went to other foreign countries. Many of their children and grand-children were able to get higher education, and almost all the families are at fairly decent standard of living at the Lao society scale. By comparison, the highland Hmongs, on the other hand, are in a tighter situation. Most of them were not well-educated, having spent most of their lives fighting a lengthy war and not getting too many opportunities to develop themselves. This is why many Americans treated them as "stone age" people. In 2010, many of the Lao refugees who came to the USA have been in this country for a full 34 year period and appeared to have done reasonably well. Many have become specialists in several professional fields and have adapted themselves to a new live in a new country.

SHORT STORIES ABOUT EARLY HMONG AND LAO REFUGEES IN THE USA

1. A lowland Lao man, who drove his car past the traffic lights, got arrested by the police. He was asked, *"Can't you see? Why did you run through the red light?"* The man answered, *"No money, no country, thinking, thinking, no see!"* The police officer then asked for his address, told him to get on the police car, and drove him back to his apartment. The police officer went inside, looked at the refrigerator and the bedroom. He saw only two bottles of milk and some ice cubes in the refrigerator. He told the man to come with him to the Social Service office. When they got to the office, he asked the Social Service official to give the man several hundred dollars worth of food stamps. He then took the man to a grocery store, bought tens of food items, and brought the man back to his apartment to unload the groceries in the refrigerator. The man later confessed that when he got in the police car, he was scared to death because he was afraid he would be put into jail and forced to pay a fine. He had no money to pay for anything. In the end, he bowed to and saluted the devout police officer who was so compassionate toward a poor refugee. The man told his story with joy and tears flooding his cheeks. He now lives in Minnesota.

2. In 1976, a Hmong family was sponsored by a group of Christians to start a new life in the USA, doing farming and cattle breeding. The sponsors needed assistance in that field and believed, through some research, that the Hmong family would do just great in that type of activity. The Hmong family arrived in Iowa in February of that year, a frigid month for that state. They were greeted warmly and put in a house located about a mile from downtown, near a cornfield owned by local American farmers. The church's pastor took them inside the furnished house, put the light switch on to bring heat, and loaded the refrigerator with food. After handing the house keys to the family, he then left. This was on a Friday evening.

That Hmong family did not know how to light the fire-place, open the water faucets, cook food, or even open the fridge. All they could do was to sit around and wait for somebody (maybe an interpreter) to show up for a visit. The whole family waited and waited, with nothing to eat, from Friday evening to Sunday evening, when the wife of the pastor was the first person to drop by. She saw the family members all clustered together to stay warm, hungry and cold. When she opened the fridge and noticed that everything in there was left untouched, she realized the family did not know what to do at all. She then called for an interpreter from the Refugee Center.

The interpreter, a lowland Lao native, came and took care of everything. He then joked with the head of the Hmong family, "You are too stupid. This evening, I'm going to take your wife away." The highland Lao man was a very jealous person, and thought this was going to really happen. If it did, he wouldn't know what to do; he had no relatives nearby and couldn't even speak the language. So, in the evening, when the visitors were gone, he told his wife to hang a rope on the basement's ceiling, brought in a table, and had everybody –husband, wife and their three kids— climb on the table and lay their feet on it. He tied everybody's neck with the rope, beginning with his wife and moving on to the children. When he was tying the neck of his children, his wife quickly removed the rope from her neck and hid the rope in her hands. The husband tied his own neck and then kicked the table away to hang himself. The wife was able to untie the rope from the neck of one of her children and her husband. But she could not help her other two children before they were choked to death. The husband's neck was twisted badly, with the husband himself being unconscious. The wife ran out the door crying, and continued running barefoot on the snow toward the nearest neighbors' house to call for help. When the neighbors arrived, they could not save the life of two of the children. They were able to save the husband's life, and took him to the hospital. Ever since, he became physically weak and emotionally unstable.

The Christian sponsors later moved this Hmong family into town, closer to the other Hmong refugee families to allow for more social connections. They also discontinued their sponsorships of the Hmong families. *[The Hmong family referred to above came from the Soune Phayao refugee camp in northern Thailand designed to provide shelter to refugees from Sayabouri Province]*. Their main objective was to save Christian Hmongs, allow them to restart a new life and get to know Christ. This particular Hmong family came to the USA without much further thought and, besides, has not yet accepted Christ. Since their friends have left, they just wanted to follow them in order to stay away from the refugee camp uncertainty.

3. In 1979, the US Government provided funds to accept refugees who were members of the Vientiane faction's civil service, military and police, and used to fight the Indochina war against North-Vietnamese communists alongside the US. Those funds were limited to refugees from the Ban Vinay Refugee Camp, Thailand –not from any other refugee camps— and designed to cover bus expenses. But when the buses arrived at the Ban Vinay Camp, many refugees changed their mind about coming to the USA, thus leaving some room to accommodate refugees from other Northern Thailand camps such as Soune Phayao, Soune Nan, etc. Those refugees were not educated and used to live in rural areas, away from the cities and modern conveniences. The Lao Communists had plenty of time to lure, coerce and isolate them from the Vientiane faction's influence. Very few of them fought the communists in the ranks of the Vientiane faction. For all these reasons, the highland Lao Hmong had a lot of problems getting adjusted to a new life. Hence, the US policy to only accept refugees who used to be civil servants and police and military officers that fought the Indochina war with the US, especially those who immigrated to Thailand during 1975-1982. Despite that policy, the US was still accepting refugees until 2006, with those from the Tham Kabork Camp being the last batch of refugees admitted to the USA.

4. Reports on actions taken by the Lao PDR against the Vientiane faction and the cleansing of the highland Hmong who took refuge in the jungle were based on testimonies made by several people who were personally involved in the brutal actions committed by the Lao PSR at the re-education camps of Vieng Xay, Houaphan Province and many other locations. The decade-long incidents deserve to be recorded as lessons learned for the younger generation, because Laos is the middle of several countries who are interested in investing in our country. We have to recognize that Laos is sparsely populated, hard to protect, not fully secure, constantly faced with invasive border problems, and had been embroiled in a long and almost endless internal fighting. The last war might have ended, but another one may break out again in the future, as it is evident that the competition among our neighboring countries may not die down anytime soon. Everybody wants to start investing in Laos, but once they have done so, would refuse to leave, claiming they are Lao citizen because it is so easy to forge an identity in Laos.

Photo #197. *Col. Bill Lair and Gen. Vang Pao met in Saint-Paul, MN in 2008 to form the SGU Veteran Association in the United States*

see source:

https://www.unforgettable-laos.com/6-the-conclusions/6-4-past-events-future-projections/

and

other source: https://badgesboots.com/2013/05/17/bill-lair/

and

https://en.wikipedia.org/wiki/James_William_Lair

ARIYA LYFOUNG'S PERSONAL OPINIONS

I was honored by Col. Vang Geu's invitation to review his memoirs covering his military experience in MR-II and the historic role of the Hmong in the fight against the red communists in the kingdom of Laos, including (1) the fight alongside the French against the invading Vietnamese and red Lao troops, and (2) the fight alongside the US against the North-Vietnamese who infiltrated Laos territory and moved south to support the Viet-Cong in attacking free Vietnam and their US allies.

In either fight, the enemy was the same, the Soviet Union, who picked hypocritical, misleading, Machiavellian and over-ambitious communist North-Vietnamese leaders to lead communist expansion into southeast-Asia. The open public message was to liberate the people from an out-of-date French colonialism and an out-of-date US colonialism, and never to mention the ultimate aim of replacing those old regimes with a single party communist regime.

As soon as the Second World War ended, the cold war began between the capitalists (free world) and the communists (socialism). The free world was led by the US and the socialism, by the Soviet Union who believed the world community should only consist of the working class (represented by the hammer on the soviet flag) and the peasantry (represented by the sickle) –the only two classes that could lead to a human heaven. As for the other social classes like the former civil service, the Russian Orthodox Church, the elite, the businessmen, etc. they were considered public threats because they relied on wealth, social standing, racial origins, favoritism, and took advantage of the workers.

One could see that during the cold war, many people from communist countries fled from the human heaven of the working class to go to free world countries at great risk to their personal safety. They managed to defect past the Berlin Wall (the wall of shame or the iron curtain), swam out of China to the free area of Hong-Kong, and fled from the arenas of the Olympic Games to avoid living in the red hell. On the other hand, very few people, if any, fled from a "free" country to a communist country.

Our country of Laos went under the French protectorate starting from October 3, 1893, after having being a part of Siam since 1779. It was forced into becoming the fifth territory of the French Indochina, following the path taken by Cochinchina, Tonkin, Annam and Cambodia. All the five territories were placed under the control of the "Gouvernor General" of the French Indochina with offices in Hanoi and Saigon. Administrative power in each territory was delegated to the territorial "Resident Superieur", who in turn supervised the Lao provincial governors. The French divided Laos into 10 provinces, which are listed with the location of the governor offices as follows:

1. Houakhong (Houeisay)
2. Louang Prabang (Louang Prabang)
3. Phouan (Xieng Khouang)
4. Houaphan (Samneua)
5. Vientiane (Vientiane)
6. Kham-Mouane (Thakhek)

7Savannakhet (Savannakhet)

7. Saravan (Saravan)
8. Champasak (Pakse)
9. Attopeu (Muang Mai)

The "Resident Superieur" located in the capital city of Vientiane was represented in each of those 10 provinces by a French "Commissaire". In special regions such as Muang Sing (Houakhong Province), Paklay (Louang Prabang Province) and Sepone (Savannakhet Province), the local French "Commissaire" was represented by a Delegate for those specific sub-provincial territories. The French also created a command center for the fifth military territory in Phongsaly.

When Laos was part of Siam, there was no education system. Those who wished to study had to enter monkhood where, in addition to religion, they could also learn Lao, Sanskrit, and Pali; how to do sculpture, prepare traditional health recipes, work with gunpowder, build fireworks or scented candles, etc. Only members of the royal family had an opportunity to go and study in Bangkok.

Under the French administration, schools were built in larger towns. Rural families who wished to see their children receive an education and later increase their social status had to send them to stay with relatives, acquaintances, civil servants, monks that they knew in those towns.

My mentioning the education system was based on the fact that the lack of national development was mostly due to the lack of education and lack of knowledge, especially in the psychological field. This was an area where the communist North-Vietnamese were known to have disseminated all kind of misleading propaganda because they were eager to use messages from hell. Furthermore, they had been trained by the Soviet Union whose Red Army had captured many Nazi (extremely rightist) experts and had them develop messages that work well for the extremely leftist communist regime. Do not forget that over six million of Jews in Europe had been eliminated by Nazi Germany because of the use of a propaganda that considerably stretched the truth about the Jews.

A 23-year period separated the 1870 French-Prussian war from the 1893 French's occupation of Laos. After the French occupied Laos for 21 years, the First World War broke out in 1914. After 46 years of French occupation of Laos, the Second World War erupted in 1939. During thos e three wars, the French suffered almost 2.5 million military casualties in addition to unspecified civilian casualties and property losses.

Because of two factors alone –lack of education in Laos and wars that took place in the invaders' environment—one could state that development had practically been non-existent in Laos. Even after the Second World War, when the wounds have not yet been healed, the French on their own ran into the Indochina war where the communist world came to the support of the Viet-Minh. Therefore, the next components of the Laos economic development plan – agricultural products to feed the factories and the processing factories themselves—never saw the light of the day. All we saw was an agriculture only designed to meet domestic needs, a system that proved to be inadequate and had to be supplemented by imports from Thailand. When the Indochina war started, we began to see some development taking place, but fueled by foreign investors and bankers who were willing to take a chance in investing in a politically unstable country.

In addition to the lack of basic manufacturing tools and investors, the next missing ingredient was the lack of skilled work force. In general, the Lao people do not like to work like a "coolie". Besides, many of our male bachelors mostly spent their time serving in the army and protecting our nation against the communist invasion. In 1963, the Royal Lao Government (mainly under

Gen. Phoumi Nosavan) was completing the construction of a war monument (Anousavary) to commemorate the army veterans and the victims of war who spilled their blood to protect our precious nation. The construction was marred by the coup d'etat carried out by Gen. Kouprasith Abhay (that forced Gen. Phoumi Nosavan to seek refuge in Thailand) and was only completed later. Currently, the Lao communists renamed this high profile building as Victory Gate (Patousay).

After some thought, the use of the communist regime in the Lao society does not seem to match reality at all. This is a new rope communist North-Vietnam wanted to use to tie the entire Lao people, once they have killed their parents and forced their relatives out of the country, and appointed their comrades, the Lao Revolutionary Party, on the driver seat. These are the people who only know how to nod and impose restrictions on their compatriots, on order from their bosses in Hanoi. The Lao people have to find ways to speak up and cough up loudly. The minute they raised any voice, they would be accused of being anti-party and anti-State. The new country leaders pretend they are clever, foresighted, and were able to beat the US capitalists and the Lao traitors. Based on some considerations, the US found it necessary to sign the Indochina cease-fire agreement at the Playel Room in Paris on January 27, 1973. Article 20, section 7 of the agreement clearly referred to Laos and Cambodia. The US then moved their troops and most of their funds from the Seventh Fleet to the Sixth Fleet in the Mediterranean Sea to protect the wells of the Middle East Oil –the blood of the Western World—right before the Yom Kippur war during October 6-24, 1973.

Please excuse me for any errors in my write-up and thank you in advance for that. [Please read the biography of Ariya Lyfoung in Chapter 20].

OTHER PERSONAL OPINIONS

Issues usually arise when small fish became the victims of big fish. However, in the ocean, small fish are clever. When big fish swim in to eat them, they massively gather together and form a dark cloud like a small mountain to mislead the big fish and make the big fish believe they (the small fish) are bigger. This is how small fish can get away from the big fish. This strategy works and saves the small fish from becoming bait.

Dr. Khamphay Abhay once wrote about actual historical events and the current Lao situation. He said not to "forget number 75 in the Lao history", because that was the year of major catastrophe and dissolution of the entire Lao nation marked by the move from the democratic regime to the dictatorial regime of the Lao PDR.

The changes between various eras and regimes will occur over and over again over time. Nothing will last forever. The colonization war to assume power and economic gains only last so long, followed by the Second World War that liberated all the colonized countries. The communist (revolutionary) regime went through many transformations after the end of the Indochina war between the US and communist Vietnam. Soviet Russia evolved, and so did mainland China. Smaller countries like Laos and Vietnam are also likely to change before long. All those changes have minuses and pluses. I will not elaborate on the minuses, because they are now part of the past. I would, however, make some predictions of my own on likely future changes.

I believe that Laos will no doubt undergo changes in the near future, in the form of a new nation with more educated people who can speak many languages and know how to connect with the rest of the world. Laos will be the center of communication for Asian countries and a rest area for the people of the world, especially for Asians. Future Lao citizens will consist mostly of people of mixed nationalities born in the country and abroad.

The changes that took place in Laos in 1975 gave the Lao people the chance to go and study overseas in great numbers, because the Lao government usually does not have the means to send so many students overseas. The new generation of Lao from inside and outside of the country will earn their rights to become the country's leaders, armed with intelligence and long-term 21st century like vision.

[This is consistent with the views expressed by Tiao Souphanouvong before he passed away in 1995, when he said that the best direction for the country to take is the direction that matches with the views of the younger Lao born overseas. He predicted that if they understand the country's challenges and were given the chance to take the lead as he suggested, the Lao people will live a stable and honorable life].

Every part of the world is likely to keep changing, and it appears almost certain that mainland China will soon become Asia's umbrella thanks to its economic progress and its huge population. The Chinese umbrella is likely to stand alongside the US umbrella to guarantee southeast-Asian countries' independence and freedom. As long as China and the US see eye to eye, southeast Asia will likely continue to see peace and prosperity.

This is indeed our hope as our country steps into the 21st century, the era of technology and modern Laos' transformation.

CHAPTER 20

SELECTED BIOGRAPHIES

1. 12CHAO SAYKHAM SOUTHAKAKOUMANE

Chao Saykham Southakakoumane was born in 1918, the son of Chao Sayavong and Mrs. Douangdy from the Muang Phuan principality. He had 12 siblings: Chao Xoua, Chao Ouane, Chao Pheng, Chao Damdouane, Chao Souvath, Chao Sithavong, Chao Sisouphanh, Chao Saykham, Chao Sonh, Chao Siphay, Chao Atao and Chao Phengdy.

see source:

https://ancestors.familysearch.org/en/LK2S-2N7/chao-saykham-saignavongs-1918-1977

Chao Saykham went to high school in Vietnam and graduated from the law school in Vientiane. In 1945, he was sent to Nonghet, Xieng Khouang Province by the French to be the Naikong (district chief) with administrative control over the Hmong people in that district. This gave him a chance to get better acquainted with the Hmong and their culture.

On March 9, 1945 Japanese invaded Laos. Chao Saykham had to retreat in the mountain, along with some French and under the protection of the Hmong led by Tasseng Touby. Thanks to his good relationship with the Hmong and his strong support for their causes, Chao Saykham was safe from any injuries caused by the Lao Issara and the Japanese. During all this time, a young man by the name of Vang Pao served as an informant for Touby, Chao Saykham and the French in the Nonghet area, collecting information and delivering messages.

On August 14, 1945 the Japanese lost the war and left behind some of their war tools to the Pathet Lao and the Viet Minh to turn against the French for decolonization. This forced the French to send more war material to their allies, which in turn allowed Chao Saykham and Touby to seek and gain more support from the Hmong in their fight against the Lao Issara and Vietminh.

On November 28, 1945 the Lao Issara and the Vietminh occupied the town of Xieng Khouang. On January 25, 1946 Chao Saykham and Touby Lyfoung led many troopers, most of them Hmong, in retaking Xieng Khouang from the Lao Issara and the Vietminh. Not long afterwards, Chao Saykham was promoted to the rank of Oupahat and named Chaokhoueng of Xieng Khouang Province, and Touby Lyfoung became the chief of the first Hmong district created in Laos. Through continued close collaboration between those two individuals, Chao Saykham was able to remain the Governor of Xieng Khouang until 1975.

On December 31, 1960 Chao Saykham and his high-ranking civilian staff left Xieng Khouang to set up a temporary provincial office in Savannakhet, working side by side with the Government established to counter Kong Le's Coup d'état. This last until 1961 and gave a chance for Chao Saykham, who knew Col. Vang Pao very well, to recommend that General Phoumi Nosavan and Chao Boun Oum select Col. Vang Pao as the Military Commander of Xieng Khouang.

In 1962, Chao Saykham, with the support from Col. Vang Pao, recommended the creation of Military Region II to Gen. Phoumi Nosavan and Chao Boun Oum. That same year, Chao Saykham moved his temporary provincial office from Savannakhet into a building next to the Ministry of the Interior in Vientiane where it functioned as a behind-the-front line support office until 1965. During that period of continued political turmoil, Chao Saykham remained the major representative of the people of Military Region II, always trying to ensure good cooperation and understanding between the neutral Lao government headed by the three princes, and Gen. Vang Pao.

In 1965, once Gen. Vang Pao completed the construction of a new provincial headquarters office in Samthong, Chao Saykham transferred his behind-the-front staff from Vientiane to that new building. That same year, Gen. Kouprasith Abhay led a coup d'état that removed Gen. Phoumi Nosavan from office. Gen. Vang Pao was about to come to Gen. Phoumi's rescue but decided not to do so given the lack of support from Chao Saykham and the US officials.

In 1966, when the injured Gen. Vang Pao was under treatment abroad, some misunderstanding surfaced between the Seng Ly and Seng Vang families. Chao Saykham and Touby Lyfoung, who knew each other very well, worked together to resolve the problem and ended up with good results.

In 1969, when North-Vietnam took over Samthong, Chao Saykham temporarily moved his office to Vientiane and, by the end of the year moved that office to Nasou, Ban Sone. He paid frequent visits to all the centers where refugees from Xieng Khouang Province had resettled and, together with USAID officials, made sure that those refugees were appropriately taken care of. He continued to be always a good adviser to Gen. Vang Pao.

From 1973 to 1975, Chao Saykham and Gen. Vang Pao made every effort to visit all the Xieng Khouang refugee centers to brief about various improvement programs and the changes needed to move from a war context to a resettlement and self-improvement context. They had not much time to relax and take care of their own families; all they did was to fully dedicate themselves to the population. They deserved to be considered by everybody as an icon and be remembered forever for their good deeds. Nowadays, it is rather rare to find anybody who fulfills his/her responsibilities to their people the same way as the two of them did. On May 14, 1975 Chao Saykham was a refugee at Namphong, Thailand and in 1976, moved on to France. He died in Perpignan on December 5, 1977.

Family-wise, in 1948 Chao Saykham Southakakoumane was married with Nang Keo Oudone, a native of Savannakhet. They had 4 children together: Sodachanh, Moukdarone, Niramonh and Ladavanh. Nang Keo-Oudone died in an airplane accident at Seno Airport, Savannakhet Province on November 25, 1968.

2. PHAGNA DAMRONG LITHIKAY TOUBY LYFOUNG

see source:

https://www.lyfoung.com/2017/06/03/une-presentation-de-phagna-touby-lyfoung-par-tata-hli/

and

https://en.wikipedia.org/wiki/Touby_Lyfoung

Touby Lyfoung was born on August 13, 1919, in Phakkhae, Tasseng Phakboun, Naikong, the son of Lyfoung and Lo Mai (Lo Mai was the daughter of Kaitong Lo Blia yao.). When Touby was eight years old, his father picked Mr. Kham Manh to tutor his son. In 1929, Touby came to Xieng Khouang, where he remained until he completed elementary school. He then went to Vientiane to high school, but he became sick due to the Vientiane's high temperature and returned to Xieng Khouang. After he fully recovered, his father sent him for four years of school in Vinh and Hanoi, Vietnam. When he returned to Laos from Vietnam, he was able to speak many languages, including Lao, French, Chinese, and Vietnamese.

In 1939, he became the Tasseng of Keng Khouay, Nonghet district. On August 14, 1945 the Japanese invaded Laos. Touby led several Frenchmen and Chao Saykham into hiding in the forest around Nonghet. Once the Japanese retreated from Laos, Touby was promoted to the rank of "Nai Kong", Step 4 and replaced Chao Saykham as chief of Nonghet district. This allowed Chao

Saykham more time to cooperate with the French in dealing with the fight for independence initiated by the Lao Issara and the Vietminh.

On August 28, 1946, Touby was promoted as first chief of the newly-created Hmong district in Xieng Khouang Province ("Chaomuang Meo").

On May 1, 1949 Touby was promoted as deputy-Governor in charge of all the Hmong ethnics of Xieng Khouang Province, and was conferred the honorific title of Phagna Damrong Lithikay (the Preserver of High Quality and Honor) by King Sisavangvong. He also received several other medals of honor from the France and the Royal Lao Governments.

Phaya Damrong Lithikay Touby Lyfoung had three wives: Ntsuab, Nxhoo, and Xia. His first wife, Ntsuab, died of malaria in the jungle for lack of medicine when she was chased by Lao Issara, Viet Minh and Japanese troops. His children included:

o Sons: Ly Siblong, Ly Teng, Ly Touxa, Ly Tou Xoua, Ly Touvue, Ly Toulu, and
o Daughters: Ly Ly, Ly Xia, Ly Kao Ly, Ly Kao Hnub, Ly Kao Va, and Ly Kao Yer.

In 1958, Touby was elected as Xieng Khouang's provincial representative and then moved to Vientiane.

On April 6, 1960 Touby joined, as Minister of Information and Social Service, the 11th Royal Lao Government headed by Tiao Somsanith. From August 9, 1960 to October 9, 1960 Touby was a member of Prince Souvanna Phouma's Neutral Government, serving as Minister of Justice, Religious Affairs and Information. He was sent to the Plain of Jars to negotiate with Maj. Vang Pao, but Vang Pao detained him and then sent him to Chao Boun Oum and Gen. Phoumi Nosavan in Savannakhet.

On December 14, 1960 Touby was named Minister of Health and Social Service in the Counter-Coup d'état government headed by Prince Boun Oum, and remained in that position until 1962. In 1962, Touby was named Minister of Health in the tri-faction Government headed by Prince Souvanna Phouma.

On April 5, 1974 Touby was named Deputy-Minister of Post-Office and Tele-Communications in the two-faction (RLG party and the Lao Communist party) Coalition Government headed by Prince Souvanna Phouma.

On August 23, 1975 Touby was arrested by the Lao Communists and sent to prison at Vieng Xay, Houaphan Province. Vien Xay was the main center used by the Pathet Lao to "re-educate" and incarcerate Lao Rightist political prisoners. Touby wrote a letter to his wife in France telling her that "right now, I am fairly healthy and happy, and weighing no more than 40 kilograms." This was a secret and very important message, because when he was in Vientiane Touby never weighed less than 90 kilograms. After that letter, no more letters were received from him until 1978, when the news about his death spreaded around. According to former detainees who survived the Vieng Xay ordeal, Touby was badly tortured by the Red Lao Communists and executed by a firing squad.

3. MAJOR GENERAL VANG PAO

see in : https://en.wikipedia.org/wiki/Vang_Pao

Gen. Vang Pao was born on December 8, 1929 at Houei Khi Thao, Tasseng Keng Khouei, Muang Nonghet, Xieng Khouang Province, Laos. He received limited education during his childhood. In 1945, when the Japanese invaded Laos, Vang Pao was only 15 and volunteered to serve as an informant and delivered messages to the French, Touby Lyfoung and Chao Saykham. After he reached the legal adult age, he enlisted with the French Army and received various types of military training, namely

- ✓ Corporal and Corporal chief school in Louang Prabang
- ✓ Sergeant school in Vientiane, and
- ✓ Military Officer School in Dong Hene in 1951.

After his graduation in 1952 with the rank of Aspirant, he was sent for action in Muang Hiem, where his first wife died from malaria, leaving him four children to raise, including two sons and two daughters. In November 1952, Muang Hiem was attacked by the North-Vietnamese, forcing Vang Pao to retreat to the Plain of Jars. He was promoted to S/Lieutenant, and was remarried to a woman from the Xiong family. But not long after they arrived at the Plain of Jars, the couple separated.

In November 1953, he got married with Nang Ntxhiav Thao and was later promoted to the rank of Lieutenant, serving as deputy-commander of the Lao Hmong Air Force Regiment (GCMA) in the fight against the Vietminh in the Nonghet area. On November 16, 1953, Vang Pao was wounded at Phou Nong Sam Chae. After his recovery, he got promoted to the rank of Captain in the French and Lao Army.

In 1954, after the liberation of the Nonghet district, Capt. Vang Pao got promoted to the rank of Major and was reassigned to the garrison of Khang Khai, getting ready for a support mission to the French garrison of Dien-Bien-Phu. He was named Commander of the combined Lao, Hmong and French GCMA division of about 10,000 soldiers. By the end April 1954, Vang Pao and his troops started heading north and arrived at the Laos/Vietnam border when Dien-Bien-Phu was seized by the North-Vietnamese on May 7, 1954. He then pulled his troops back to Khang Khay and then to Nonghet.

In 1957, Maj. Vang Pao was assigned as the Commander of Lao and Hmong troops at Muang Peune, Houaphan Province by the two-party coalition Government. In 1958, he was on sent on discovery trips to two south-east Asian countries and returned to Khang Khay, Xieng Khouang Province.

On May 25 1959, Maj. Vang Pao ordered Capt. Ly Pao to lead one battalion in the pursuit of the Issara battalion commanded by Lt. Col. Tou Ya who escaped from the Plain of Jars one week earlier (May 18, 1959).

In 1960, Maj. Vang Pao was named Commander of the military airport at the Plain of Jars by Gen. Phoumi Nosavan and Gen. Ouan Ratikoune. Two weeks after Kong Le's Coup d'état in Vientiane, Maj. Vang Pao's assistant-Commander, Captain Boun Noi, attempted to assassinate him for political reasons. Major Vang Pao escaped safely and then regrouped the Hmong troopers to retake the Plain of Jars. In September 1960, Gen. Amkha Southavong was sent by Prince Souvanna Phouma to the Plain of Jars to collect food to supply the communist troops in Vientiane. Maj. Vang Pao arrested Gen. Amkha and flew him to the counter Coup d'état forces in Savannakhet. In mid-September, Prince Souvanna Phouma also dispatched Phagna Touby Lyfoung to Xieng Khouang to try to reach consensus with Maj. Vang Pao. Maj. Vang Pao arrested Phagna Touby Lyfoung and flew him to the counter Coup d'état forces Savannakhet.

In 1961, Maj. Vang Pao joined the US forces in fighting the Communist expansion in Laos and in Southeast Asia, which led to the US-Vietnam war. In 1961, he was promoted to Lt. Colonel; then in1962, to Colonel and was named commander of Military Region II (MR-II). In 1963, Col. Vang Pao was promoted to Brigadier General and retained the command of MR-II. In 1964, Brig. Gen. Vang Pao established his command headquarters and airbase at Long Cheng. In 1965, he directed construction of civilian administrative offices, a hospital, and a school at Samthong. He also had a royal resort built for the king at Long Cheng and invited him to visit MR-II. The king promoted Brig. Gen. Vang Pao to Major General and conferred him the honorific title of Phagna Norapamok (the courageous king tiger).

On May 14, 1975, Gen. Vang Pao was a refugee at the Namphong camp, Khone Kaen Province, Thailand. On June 2, 1975 he was pressured to leave Thailand for France, and then in July 5, 1975 arrived in the United States where he first took residence in Montana.

In 1981, Maj. Gen. Vang Pao joined a group of former Lao leaders in creating the United Lao National Liberation Front (ULNLF), along with Inpeng Souryathai, Chao Sisouk Nachampasak, Ngon Sananikone, Khamphan Panya, Kouprasith Abhay, Houmphan Saignasith and Gen. Phoumi Nosavan. In 1982, Gen. Vang Pao moved from Minnesota to California in order to improve communication while performing activities initiated by ULNLF led by Phagna Louang Outhong Souvannavong.

On June 4, 2007, Gen. Vang Pao was arrested on a political charge of fomenting a plan to bring down the Lao PDR government. On December 7, 2007 he was released for lack of evidence and insufficient proof. This case created serious dilemma for the US Administration, which also led the court decision to put the case on hold.

On May 11, 2009, Gen. Vang Pao went back to court but the hearing was rescheduled. At the October 5, 2009 hearing, the court was still unable to find sufficient of evidence to reach a judgment. Several primary witnesses were also not present, while over 10,000 Hmong protestors were hitting the street, claiming that Gen. Vang Pao had been falsely accused and that it "was part of a plan to open the door for Communists to create turmoil and misunderstanding in the US." In the end, the Vang Pao case was dismissed without prejudice. On December 22, 2009, Gen. Vang announced he would go to Laos, but the Lao PDR was quick at denying him entry into the country. On December 28, 2009 the Thai Government sent more than 5,000 Hmong refugees from the Houei Nam Khao refugee camp back to Laos, to be resettled in a new village located at Ban Phone Kham, Khammouane Province. According to the news media, these refugees were faced with many problems.

On June 19, 2010 Gen. Vang Pao's health started to deteriorate, with a failing heart that caused physical weaknesses. On July 1, he went to visit the Lao Hmong in Minnesota. On December 25, 2010 he went to Fresno to celebrate the Hmong New Year. Due to the cold weather, he got a lung infection and had to be hospitalized on December 26, 2010.

In the morning of January 6, 2011 Gen. Vang Pao died at the hospital in Clovis, CA. His body was transferred to the Clovis Community Center for the funeral rituals. During February 4-9, 2011, no less than 50,000 Hmong and Lao living in the US and other countries attended his funeral. This was the biggest funeral ever observed in Fresno, California.

4. PHAGNA TOULAPRASITH TOUGEU LYFOUNG

see

source:

http://hmonglessons.com/the-hmong/hmong-leaders/tou-geu-lyfoung-tub-ntxawg-lis-foom/

and'

https://soc.culture.hmong.narkive.com/H9rQz2gl/phaya-tougeu-lyfoung-passes-on

Phagna Tougeu Lyfoung was born on March 12, 1921 at Ban Nhot Kha Noi, Kong Nonghet, Xieng Khouang Province, Laos. He was the son of Mr. Lyfoung and Mrs. Va Yang. He completed primary school in Xieng Khouang; high school in Vinh (Vietnam); got an M.S. in Agriculture in Hanoi (Vietnam); and completed an advanced Law training program in Paris (France).

In 1949: he got married with Nang Sisamone Thammavong (the daughter of Nha Phor Thip Thammavong). They had seven children together.

1945-1946: Tougeu was a member of the French Resistance Group. On January 27, 1946 he participated in the recapture of the town of Xieng Khouang from the Lao Issara and the Vietminh, and helped set the basis for the town's security.

1948-1951: Tougeu served as a member of the Royal Advisory Council, providing advice to H.M. King Sisavangvong.

1951-1955: Tougeu was a member of the National Assembly as representative of Xieng Khouang Province.

1955-1956: Tougeu served as president of the Appeal Court and the Supreme Court of Justice of Laos.

1956-1957: Tougeu was a Lao member of the International Commission in Burma.

1960-1966: Tougeu served as Director-General of the Justice Department, President of the Appeal Court, Advisor to the Minister of Justice, and participated in a New-York meeting of the Committee for the Coordination of Investigations on the Lower Mekong River Basin.

In 1968: Tougeu was President of the Supreme Court of Justice and the King's legal representative.

In 1971: Tougeu was a delegation member of the French-speaking Legal commission meeting in Canada, and in 1974, a delegation member of the Lao commission on Family Defense Planning meeting in Tunisia.

Honorific Awards

- ✓ 1945: French Military Medal; Medal for Bravery from the Laos Royal Palace; Civil Award and Legion d'Honneur Medal from the French Government; and another Meritorious Award from the Royal Lao Government.
- ✓ 1972: Honorific title of Phagna Toula Prasith (One who performs legal functions with great success and extreme fairness) conferred by H.M. King Savang Vatthana. Phagna Tougeu Lyfoung was a high-ranking national official at the rank of Xanh Ek (Step 13+) at the Ministry of Justice.

In 1975, Tougeu Lyfoung sought political refugee status in France. He moved to the USA in 1992 and got naturalized US citizenship in 2004. He passed away on February 10, 2004 due to old age sickness.

5. COLONEL MESNIER

see source: https://www.unforgettable-laos.com/historical-of-events/part2/

and

http://www.unforgettable-laos.com/the-end-of-the-war/5-5-selected-biographies/

Born on May 25, 1926; got married with Francoise, and the father of three children. During 1944-1956, was a military commander leading guerilla troops in the northern Dordogne area, and fighting the Germans in Alsace and Germany.

During 1945-1947, was sent to Indochina. Before leaving France, Mesnier went to the cadet officer school at St. Cyr, : Coetquidam), 1330th Promotion, specializing in information gathering, parachute deployment, and behind-the-line defense. S/Lt. Mesnier went to Indochina after graduation.

During 1950-1952, Col. Mesnier was the Commander of the Nong troops in South-Vietnam. He served as Commander of the GCMA division until 1954. He came to visit Gen. Vang Pao in the USA twice, in 2008 and 2009. Col. Mesnier passed away on November 13, 2011 at his residence in Aix-En-Provence.

6. CAPTAIN (GEN.) KONG LAE

Captain Kong Lae was in the position of pie khah means he was not involved either pathet lao group nor royal king military group. His military group stayed in neutral position and chose not to support either both group during the Vietnam war aka lao civil war. His military group remain inactive in military services in Xieng Khouang province, Laos.

Kong Lae was born in 1934 in southern Laos from parents of Lao Theung ethnic. His father died in 1940. Kong Lae went to school in Savannakhet and, at the age of 17, enrolled in the French Army. He later went for training in parachute deployment, which he completed in 1953. Of the 21 graduating trainees, he was ranked 19th. He then went to work for Capt. Ouan Rattikoun in Louang Prabang. Kong Lae later attended several training programs abroad.

In 1957, Kong Lae served as instructor for the Commando elitist group at the Chinaimo garrison and had many opportunities to meet with Tiao Souphanouvong secretly every evening.

In early 1959, Kong Lae was named Commander of the second Parachutist battalion with Capt. Deuane Sounnarath as his deputy, dealing with training and US assistance.

On August 9, 1960, Kong Lae mounted a coup d'état to bring down the government headed by Tiao Somsanith, with Gen. Phoumi Nosavan as deputy-prime minister. On November 27, 1962 Kong Lae was appointed chief of the new army (nominally the merged armies of the neutralist, communist and rightist factions) and later exceptionally promoted to the rank of Brigadier General by the Neutralist Government headed by Souvanna Phouma.

In 1965, Kong Lae moved his troops from Military Region II to Kasy and Vang Vieng. He was later expelled from Laos to Thailand, then to France. Kong Lae died in France on Jan. 7, 2014 at 7 AM.

7. POL. MAJ. HANG DOUA

(As personally recounted to Col. Geu Vang, the author).

On May 28, 1958 Hang Doua, as an active police officer, was sent to the Police Academy School at Done Tieuo, Vientiane, Laos. After graduation in May 1959, he returned to duties in Phonesavanh, Xieng Khouang Province.

In 1961, after the Kong Lae's coup d'état, Hang Doua was transferred to Tha Linh Noi Camp, where in mid-1961, he was promoted by Maj. Vang Pao as the deputy Commander of Tha Linh Noi battalion.

In 1962, Hang Doua was sent to Sanh Chor (LS02) and then to Pak Kha-Na Xieng (LS181—Zone 6A) where he served as a military officer until October 1969.

In 1968, Hang Doua received staff officer training in military strategies provided by Thai instructors.

During 1969-1970 Hang Doua was sent by the National Police Department for international police training in data collection at the police academy in Malaysia.

During 1970-1971, was promoted to the position of Police Commander of Muang Vang Say, with commanding office in Long Cheng.

During 1971-1972, was sent for training at the Police Academy in Vientiane and promoted to the rank of Police Major per Royal ordnance signed by King Sisavang Vatthana. After graduation, he returned to his Long Cheng duty station.

In 1973, he was sent for training in police data gathering at the Police Academy in Vientiane. He then returned to his Long Cheng duty station and served there until 1975. Due to the political changes, he later immigrated as a refugee to the USA where he still lives today as a duly naturalized US citizen.

8. NHALOUANG BOUNCHAN VOUTHISOMBATH

(former Muang Kham district chief and deputy-Governor of Xieng Khouang Province)

source: https://www.unforgettable-laos.com/the-end-of-the-war/5-5-selected-biographies/

Born on December 27, 1927 (but the date of birth shown on the birth certificate was November 2, 1928) at Ban Tong, Tasseng Kham, Muang Kham, Xieng Khouang Province. Bounchan attended primary school in Xieng Khouang. In 1945, he attended grade 6 in Xieng Khouang, along with Lytou Lyfoung.

Professionally, on September 1, 1945 became a school teacher in Xieng Khouang. By the end of October 1945, was transferred as school teacher to Muang Soui to replace Chao Som Nokham. Two to three days after his arrival at Muang Soui, the Lao Issara troops (from Tiao Phetsarath's army) that deposed the ruling king in Louang Prabang reached Muang Soui, arrested Mr. Bounchan and took him with them on their way to capturing Xieng Khouang on November 28, 1945. Not long afterwards, French troops, with Touby Lyfoung and Chao Saykham Southakakoumane in their ranks, retook the town of Xieng Khouang and forced the Lao Issara troops to leave town on January 27, 1946. Phagna Touby spent about three days fighting around Xieng Khouang, and forced the Lao Issara battalion to retreat toward Tha Vieng. The troops led by Phagna Touby and Chao Saykham consisted mostly of Hmong and some lowland Lao ethnics recruits.

In 1946, Bounchanh served as a district officer at Ban Houei Kham, a Vietnamese village located on Highway 7 between Khang Khay and Phonesavanh. The Muang Perk district chief at the time was Mr. Khampheng, who was later replaced by Mr. Van Tanovan.

In 1947, after getting married at Lat Houang, Mr. Bounchanh was transferred to the district office of Muang Kham, where he worked for two years under district chief Bounmy Thipphavong (Col. Sisavath's father). During 1948-1950, he went to Vientiane to attend law school during the morning and work at the Prime Minister's office in the afternoon. In 1949, the Prime Minister was Chao Boun Oum NaChampasak, and the Secretary General of the Prime Minister's office was Mr. Bouasy, a Xieng Khouang native.

In 1950, after graduation from the law school, he tried to fly to the Plain of Jars on an Air Azur airplane but the plane could not land because of foggy conditions. The plane flew on to Hanoi, Vietnam where the passengers spent the night in a hotel courtesy the airline company. The airplane landed safely at the Plain of Jars airport the following morning. In 1950, Khammanh Vorasane, a native of Phone Thong, replaced Mr. Bounmy as district chief of Muang Kham.

On January 9, 1958 Bounchan was named deputy-district chief of Muang Kham.

In 1974 Gen. Vang Pao and Chaokhoueng Chao Saykham Southakakoumane took Mr. Bounchan with them to attend a Baci ceremony for His Majesty the King in Louang Prabang. Mr. Bounchanh was conferred the honorific title of Nai Phia by King Savang Vatthana.

In April 1975, the Government named Bounchan and Mouachia Chongtouamoua as deputy-governors of Xieng Khouang following the unexpected political changes that took place in Laos. The US completely pulled out of Indochina, cutting all assistance programs to the Vientiane government.

In May 1975, North Vietnamese and Neo Lao troops moved along Highway 13 toward Ban Sone on their way to Long Cheng. Gen. Vang Pao asked for US airplanes to fly his military and administrative staff out of Long Cheng and take them to the old military garrison of Nam Phong, Khone Kene Changwath, Thailand. The refugees later moved from Namphong to the Refugee Camp of Pak Soume, Lei Changwath. In 1976, Mr. Bounchanh took a flight from Bangkok to France where he still lives up to now.

During the time of extreme political turmoil, Mr. Bounchan and his family were faced with many difficulties. From 1960 to 1975, Mr. Bounchan was happy to work with Gen. Vang Pao and his lowland Lao and Hmong staff. He felt very grateful to the General for taking good care of his aides and their families when Kong Le brought in North-Vietnamese troops to occupy and eventually destroy Xieng Khouang. The whole political regime was altered due to the communists' intervention; Xieng Khouang supporters of the right wing government had to seek political refuge abroad (mostly in the USA), following Gen. Vang Pao's footsteps. They survived all kind of ordeal to this day, thanks to the General's good deeds.

9. Chaomuang Laothai Va Lue Vang

see in

source: https://www.unforgettable-laos.com/the-end-of-the-war/5-5-selected-biographies/

Lao Thai Vang was born on May 1, 1942 in Muang Hong Nonh, Houa Phanh Province. In 1948, he went to school in Sam Neua. In 1953, at the age of 12, he enrolled as an ADC (Auto-Defense Chock) soldier with the French operating in the Phou Pha Thee area. [His younger brother, Maj. Kia Tou Va Lue Vang, eventually became the Commander of the company assigned to defend Phou Pha Thee, an army unit that expanded to a battalion size during the war supported by the US]. On January 1, 1959 at the age of 18, he served as an official of the Department of the Interior, Houaphan Province desk. Six months later, Governor Thongsavath named him deputy-district chief of Muang Sone, near the triangular border of Xieng Khouang, Luang Prabang, and Houaphan.

In 1960, the Kong Le's coup d'état in Vientiane led to the Communist invasion of Houaphan Province and the loss of several territories to the Communists, forcing Maj. Kia Tou Va Lue Vang to bring in one Royal Lao Army company and three ADC companies to fight the enemy until October 1961. Gen. Vang Pao ordered all the administrative, military and police officials, who had been involved in the fight against the Communists, to regroup at the garrison of Hoeui Tom, Xieng Khouang Province, near Sa-Arn Creek and the town of Houa Muang, Houa Phanh Province. Maj. Kia Tou was ordered to go back and reclaim Phou Pha Thee; and Col. Sisouvanh was instructed to retake Mouang Peune at all cost.

On February 2, 1962 Maj. Kia Tou regained control of Phou Pha Thee. Gen. Vang Pao dispatched Col Tong Va Lor and an inspection team to Phou Pha Thee to reassess the camp's situation and set up a special Guerrilla Unit (SGU). Everybody agreed to have Chaomuang Lao Thai Va Lue acting as the Commander of Battalion 1301 operating in military Zone 13A at Houei Kham Moune, northeast of Phou Pha Thee (LS 85).

In 1965, the Ministry of the Interior issued an order for Chaomuang Lao Thai Lue Vang to serve as the district chief of Muang Hong Nonh, Houaphan Province, in addition to his duties as Commander of Battalion 1301.

55

In February 1968, the Communists furiously attacked the whole Houaphan region, putting Phou Pha Thee and several other posts back in the hands of North-Vietnamese communists. Thousands of soldiers and ordinary citizens had to move as refugees to Phou Herr (LS 255), Xieng Khouang Province, south of Muang Desa and Muang Cha.

In 1969, Chaomuang Lao Thai Lue Vang resigned from his position of military commander, keeping only his civilian (district chief) position. Several thousands of families from Houaphan Province have joined him as refugees at Muang Nonh. Chaomuang Lao Thai Lue Vang went as a refugee to the United States, and now resides in Minnesota.

10.   LT. COL. CHONG NENG VANG

Lt. Col. Chong Neng Vang served in the military from 1961- 1973 in region two, at the M-24 department at the ho chi minh trail. There were many actions taken at the frontier line by his team and him. Lt. Col. Chong Neng Vang was assigned to handle duty in military action from 1961 through 1970 in Moung Nhanh and Moung Mor in Xieng Khouang Province and was on duty in the plain of jars areas and other zones in the ho chi minh trail under the region two in Laos. In 1970 through 1971, he completed the SGU military training in Phitsanulok, Thailand by CIA and Royal Thai Military training. He was a very intellectual man in leadership and Hmong cultural clan leadership in civil liberty manner in the Hmogn society in Laos. He was a county commissioner in Moung Nqa Moung Mor in Xieng Khouang province from the mid 60's through the early 70.s. He sacrificed his life for his country, peoples and the government during this war in laos. Mrs. Ka Thao aka Mrs. Chongwa Vang's photo collection.

11. **LT. COL. XAINOU VANG**

   Lt. Col. Xainou Vang was a former private French and Lao Language School Teacher in Bolikhamxay province, Laos. He graduated with the Language Educational Instructor in French and Lao Language School and taught from 1957-1961. He was fluent in Hmong, Laotian, Thai, and French. Lt. Col. Xainou Vang completed commando intensive training in Phitsanulok, Thailand from 1961-1963 under the CIA and Royal Thai commando intensive training. After completing this special intensive training, Lt. Col. was assigned to work as a special commando leader in region two under General Vang, Pao in Laos in khon Group 22 in military region two, Laos. From 1964-1974, He was assigned to handle all the different major crisis tasks in region two in different zones at the frontier line in the Ho Chi Minh trail areas in Xieng Khouang province, Laos. He had three major projects such as the Commando intensive Unit project, the sniper team duty plan in actions in the deep jungle, and the airborne intensive duty plan in actions with the Royal Lao King Military team from Luang Prabang province and the General Vang, Pao region two military project in Xieng Khouang province combine. He had special skills and a special strategic plan to support his team and educated his team with many action plans in the frontier line for many years. They were a very successful team. Ka Thao aka Mrs. Chongwa Vang's photo collection

12.   MAJOR MA TONG SEE YANG

Major Ma Tong See Yang Tong See Yang, was in military training from 1966-1967 in region two, Laos. He was assigned to handle assignments under Lt. Col. Vang, Thai in Moung Nqha zoning areas and Flat Nontah Kouh areas from 1967- 1969. 1969-1970 in Bolikhamxay province, of the region two military projects in Laos. he completed his special Commando intensive training in Phet Nong Ta Kouh, Thailand. From 1970 to 1974, Ma was assigned to handle the intensive commando and airborne duties in military projects under Lt. Col. Xainou Vang, khon 22 group, in region two, Laos. Ka Thao aka Mrs. Chong Wang Vang's photo collection

13.   CAPTAIN XAY VANG

Captain Xay Vang was a military officer in region 2, Khet 10 B, in Meung Nqha, 1963-1965. Xay was promoted to a SGU officer as a Lieutenant and was the Financing Department Officer in branch 204 in Long Cheng, Laos from 1965 to 1968. Xay Vang then was a Sergeant 1968-1970. Captain Xay Vang then was a Captain from 1970-1974 and was transferred to be responsible for the Military Operational Radar Specialist leader in region two in Vientiane, Laos. Captain Xay's photo collection

14.   CAPTAIN JOUA LOR VANG

Captain Joua Lor Vang was trained to be a SGU military Officer in 1963-1964 and was assigned to work under Lt. Col. Chong Neng Vang's team from 1964-1973 at the Ho Chi Minh's trail Khon. M 24. Interviewed with information by Captain Xay Vang. Cha kee Vang, son of Captain Joua Lor Vang photo collection.

15.   MAJOR TONG KHUE VANG

Major Tong Khue Vang participated in the SGU military training in Phitsanulok, Thailand, 1963-1964. He served in the region 2 military frontier line from 1965 through 1974 in region two, Laos. Captain Tong Lou photo collection

16.   CAPTAIN NAO LUE VANG

Captain Nao Lue Vang, was in the military region two and was in the Khon 23 branch, Kheio Lao company3 from 1961-1975, in region two, Laos. Captain Tong Lou Vang's photo collection

17.   CAPTAIN PA CHAI VANG

Captain Pa Chai Vang was in the military region two from 1960-1968 in Meoung Nqah, Bolikhamxay province. He then was assigned to work in the military as Neo Lao Ban-sa-kah, Long Cheng, Laos from 1968-1974. Captain Tong Lou Vang's photo collection

18. CAPTAIN KAO (PA ZE) VANG

Captain Kao (Pa Ze) Vang was trained as the Telegram/radio Operator in the military in region two by CIA from 1962-1963 in Phitsanulok, Thailand and was assigned to work at this task in region two in Long Cheng and other frontier line zones, Laos from 1963-1974. Captain Tong Lou Vang's photo collection

19. T28 PILOT AIR FORCES CAPTAIN VANG BEE

see in source:

https://www.unforgettable-laos.com/the-end-of-the-war/5-5-selected-biographies/

Air Forces Capt. Vang Bee was born on October 15, 1944 at Ban Pou, Tasseng Tham Tap, Muang Ngad, Xieng Khouang Province, Laos. He had ten siblings (five brothers and five sisters), all of whom have resettled in the US. When he was eight or nine, he used to watch French planes flying back and forth in the air above his village on their way to fighting the Vietminh at Dien Bien Phu. The elders used to comment that such frequent air traffic was a sure omen of instability and insecurity. During 1956-1957, Vang Bee attended school in Muang Ngan and was taught by a Lao teacher. Not long after that, the country was in political turmoil because the Lao Huam Lao, the Pathet Lao, and the Vientiane Government got into deep fighting following the Kong Le's coup d'état in Vientiane. Vang Bee was missing school because of security concerns. He soon decided to continue his studies at Long Cheng where the US started providing assistance to Military Region II (MR-II).

In 1963, Vang Be went back to attend school in Vientiane, but ran into several difficulties as he was living away from his parents. He then decided to return to Long Cheng and went to work for the Lao Ethnic's Radio Station until 1966. The Communists then attacked many government posts from north to south, increasing the intensity of the overall situation. The MR-II Commander needed airplane pilots to engage in air battles for obvious strategic reasons. Therefore, Gen. Vang Pao ordered recruitment of young Hmong men for training as T-28 pilots. Many of them did respond to the call, spent time getting trained and reported back to duty in MR-II. The third promotion of T-28 pilots consisted of 11 men who got trained in Thailand, starting with Piper Cub 150, a small 2-passenger plane. Later, the training involved 4-passenger Cessna 180 planes. After they were proficient in flying those two types of planes, the trainees returned to Savannakhet, Laos.

In early 1970, Vang Bee received flight training on T41 or Cessna planes that landed on their front wheels like T-28 planes. All the Hmong pilot trainees were highly rated by their Thai and US instructors based on their capability to safely land and take off, especially considering that they only had a very short (Steep Turn) training in English in Vientiane. In 1970, Vang Bee went back to Thailand to get trained on T28 planes, dropping bombs in the battle field. In the final flying test, pilot Vang Bee came out first, followed by pilot Xiong Koua. Both of them received warm congratulations from the Commander of the Royal Lao Air Forces and the head US instructor in Oudone, Thailand. Nobody else had performed better than those two before.

In early 1971, Vang Bee returned to Long Cheng, which was a very dangerous military zone because it was equipped with the strongest anti-aircraft guns in the whole Indochina theater, especially in 1971 when the enemy mounted attacks on many fronts. Vang Bee flew countless number of missions without any break at the MR-II Commander's order. All the pilots responded to orders, not according to any set flying schedule, and thus ended up flying many more missions that those ever recorded in usual world flying mission statistics. One could safely state that no other pilots anywhere in the world had made more flights on a daily, monthly or yearly basis than the MR-II pilots. Vang Be added that the pilots from the third promotion inflicted the most damages to the enemy compared to pilots from the other promotions, having completely destroyed anti-aircraft guns everywhere. Pilot Vang Be was able to fly three types of aircrafts, T28, Cessna 180, and Baron for MR-II. Each and every flying mission was extremely dangerous because he was always fired at by anti-aircraft guns. Vang Be said he was just lucky and survived because time has not come yet for him to die.

In 1973, when his T-28 aircraft got shot shown at Muang Mork, pilot Vang Be had to jump off the aircraft. An Air American Chopper 96W came to his rescue and dropped a rope for Vang Bee to climb on and be pulled up to safety. He was waiting on the spot for almost three hours before being rescued. The enemy was aware of the situation but could not get there in time on foot. Pilot Vang Be got back to Long Cheng by dusk. He never complained about being tired, never refused to execute an order from his commander, never acted like a scared, pretentious, or selfish person, or like a bragger. He was true to himself, always delivered what he said he would do, and was driven by his love for his race and the country where he was born, grew up and lived in.

On April 5, 2008, pilot Vang Bee suffered from a serious illness. As of January 20, 2011, he still has not yet fully recovered. Capt. Pilote T28 Vang Bee died on September 6, 2013 in North Carolina, USA.

20.   ARYA LYFOUNG

see in

source:

https://www.unforgettable-laos.com/the-end-of-the-war/5-5-selected-biographies/

Arya Lyfoung was born on October 28, 1944 in Louang Prabang as the first son of Mr. Toulia Lyfoung and Tiao Khampheng Vongkot Rattana (daughter of Sathou Khammanh Vonkot Rattana, a member of Lao royal lineage). He has three brothers (one of whom was an adopted brother who died at the front line in the battle field of Nam Bark in 1964), and two adopted sisters (who now live in St. Petersburg, Florida, USA).

Attended high school grade 5 in Louang Prabang.

In March 1964, Aryaattended agricultural controller school in Phnom-Penh and in Preiek-Leap, Cambodia. He graduated with an advanced degree in agriculture in October 1968.

On March 2, 1968 joined the government service as Xanh Tho grade employee at the Department of Agricultural Development in Vientiane (working with Messrs. Bounnong Sipha, Oroth Chounlamountri, Souphan Savatdy, and Tiao Somsavath Vongkoth).

From January to May 1969, Arya served as program coordinator with a survey and data collection team from The Netherlands, working on financial assistance needed for the development of the Plain of Vientiane. He accompanied foreign experts on field trips to the Samthong-Long Cheng area. From August to December 1969, Arya received training in agricultural cooperatives at the International Agricultural Center in Tel-Aviv, Israel.

From May 1970 to September 1971: worked with Israeli experts at the Lao-Israel Agricultural Experimental Center at Hat Dork Keo.

From September to December 1971: received training in agricultural cooperatives at the Asian Agricultural Institute in Tokyo, Japan.

From January 1972 to December 1974: was named provincial Agricultural supervisor in Sayabouri, working closely on the Nam Tane- Muang Phieng Levee Project. In early 1973, Arya participated in the creation of the Muang Phieng's Agricultural Station.

In March 1973: he received a 5-week training in agricultural crop testing at the Biotrop Institute in Bogor, Indonesia. From March 1973 to April 1974: attended Post-graduate course in Comprehensive Rural Regional Development Planning in Rehovot, Israel. Arya returned to Hat Dork Keo Agricultural Station to work on formation of agricultural collectives for future ex-military officers.

From January 1975 to January 1976: reassigned to the National Rice Center as official responsible for purchase and storage of crude rice products from southern and northern Laos. Arya was sent on special training at the National Assembly and later, on hands-on field training at Tasseng Nasay, Muang Settha.

On January 10, 1976: made a personal decision to self-exile from his native country after noticing that the spirit of the Vientiane Accord and the actual day-to-day life had nothing in common. On May 24, 1976: left the refugee camp in the Nongkhay for Bangkok. On October 2, 1976: was sent to the political refugee center in Metz, France. In September 1976: was hired as an employee of Peugeot-Citroen's Gear Factory in Metz, France.

In April 1978: received training as refugee instructor in Marseilles. From May 1978 to September 1980: worked as Lao Refugee Instructor at two refugee centers in the Tarn region. In July 1978: received teacher training at Norsan-Aix-Blanc.

From September 1980 to February 1985: worked as deputy-manager, Center of Refugees from south-east Asia and the rest of the world, in Aude department.

From October 1985 to August 1986: received training in security surveillance at Penchard. From October 1986 to October 1991: served as security guard at the Union des Banques de Paris, and as security signal receiver at the Savings bank.

From October 1991 to November 1997: worked as a stage actor to explain security standards to visitors at the Euro Disney Center. Arya was named Security Instructor of the month of November 1994. From November 1997 to January 2003: asked for transfer to the Storage Department's reception desk. From January 2003 to May 2010: was transferred to the shipping department of expensive merchandises.

Ariya Lyfoung got married at Dong Dok on March 8, 1970 with Nang Bouakham Deovan, a teacher and the oldest daughter of School Principal Nhouy Deovan and his wife, Nang Phia Bounthan from Ban Sankhalok, Louang Prabang. Mr. Ariya and his wife have 4 children (3 daughters and one son), 4 grand-sons and another grand-daughter is due pretty soon. Hold French citizenship from September 1978 to date. Currently, lives in France.

21. NAIKONG PACHA LY LI YIA VUE

Pacha Ly was born on February 18, 1907 at Nonghet, Xieng Khouang Province, the only son of Mr. Li Vue and Mrs. Xia Thao. His father died when he was about one year-old. His mother remarried with a younger brother named Xay Xeu Liyia Vue. Pachaly Liyia Vue was raised by his step-father, along with 5 step-brothers and 4 step-sisters. He was a smart child, physically well-built, and good at playing traditional music. He could read and write Lao fairly well, and could speak French as well.

He was married three times with the following spouses:

1. Nang Chia Lo (who gave him seven children, including 4 sons and 3 daughters)
2. Nang Youa Thao (who brought along 1 son of hers, and gave Pachali 5 sons and 2 daughters)
3. Nang Ya Song (who gave him 9 children, including 7 sons and 2 daughters).

In 1945, Pacha Ly collaborated with Chao Saykham, Touby Lyfoung and Toulia Lyfoung in the fight against the Lao Issara, the Vietminh and the Japanese. In 1946, he participated in the liberation of the town of Xieng Khouang, the Plain of Jars, Louang Prabang (on May 13, 1946), and several locations along the Xieng Khouang-Vientiane border, including Sala Phoukhoune, Muang Phoune, Vang Vieng, and Ban Sone-Nasou. After the Lao Issara fled to Thailand, Pachaly went back to Xieng Khouang.

In 1947, Pacha Ly became the Naikong (district chief) of the Hmong residents in Xieng Khouang Province, including the following six Tassengs (counties): 1) Nok Kok, 2) Navang, 3) Muang Pha, 4) Pha Say, 5) Muang Pha, and 6) Muang Pain Pha (Lao Khamoui ethnic).

During 1953-1954 the Vietminh and the Lao Issara were fighting in the Plain of Jars and throughout the Xieng Khouang Province. Mr. Pacha Ly was assigned the responsibility to defend against and liberate the southern part of the province from the Viet Minh troops, support the French GCMA troops in the defense of the Plain of Jars, and send troops to harass the Vietminh at several sites, including the highway reach between the Plain of Jars and the town of Xieng Khouang, the road between Muang Phang and Muang Ngarn, the Tham Thao caves, and Nam Pee close to the town of Vinh in Annam.

Pacha Ly was a noted fighter during the French administration and was one of the leaders who performed their duties very well in favor of their constituents. He passed away on March 7, 1967 at Long Cheng at the age of 60. Many important figures attended his funeral, including Phagna Touby Lyfoung representing H.M. the King; Mr. Khamla Kingsada, director of Political Affairs; Mr. LyCheu Liyia Vue, a member of the National Assembly; Chao Saykham Sothakakoumane, Xieng Khouang Province Governor; Gen. Vang Pao, Commander of Military Region II; military, policy and administrative officers; the Honor Guard; and a mourning crowd of over 10,000 people.

As a son of Mr. Pacha Ly, I feel very appreciative of my father's actions and am grateful for the love he provided as a leader to his family and all his relatives. I feel it was my duty to write his biography. *[Thank you, Army Officer Ly Blong Liyia Vue!]*.

CHAPTER 21

OLD LAO POEMS/PROVERBS & PHOTOS OF RELEVANCE

This chapter is designed to provide the reader with a feel for the old Lao poems -- more so about what they mean than about how they sound—and some of the photos of significance to the Lao nation during 1960-1975.

Photo #198. *The Lao people are traditionally good, polite and courteous people*

see in source: *https://www.unforgettable-laos.com/the-end-of-the-war/5-6-old-lao-poemsproverbs-photos-of-relevance/poems/*

POEMS AND PROVERBS

Lao Nation

My country is called Muang Lao

It is a big country that stretches to the horizon

Crossed by the Mekong River and clean highways.

This is a large territory of our birth

We need to build the Lao nation and ensure its longevity

So that it does not lag behind

Lao Nationality

When you are born Lao, you have to help the Lao

As a Lao native, you have to be perseverant

Anything that the Lao stand for, you have to protect it fiercely

We are Lao, we need to love each other

And cooperate with each other for the good of the nation

Lao Natural Resources

Listen to the cries of the tigers, lions and elephants that resonate throughout the forests

You can also hear the clear calls of the birds

You can see all kinds of horse breeds

Some of them screaming loudly

You can see trees full of monkeys and gibbons

Jumping agilely from branch to branch

That Louang Monument

On the ground of the Sisattanak City

People were having more fun than in heaven

Especially under the clear sky after the end of the rainy season

During the 12th month of the year when everything is wide open

People flock in to offer prayers at the temple

Burning candles and incense sticks, and performing merit-making rituals

Rivers and Streams

Under a dark and cloudy sky

I watch the wide Mekong River bed

And only see the sky and feel the breeze

Some clouds are heavy and moving fast

Others are colorful and beautiful

Moving slowly over a wide space

I see boats moving up and down the river under the breeze

It was cool and refreshing

Education

In my school, we are all friends regardless of our ages

I always love them like my family members

I don't make noise when told so by the teacher.

My friends sit in rows; we don't talk loudly.

We are a group of real Lao

We have many schools and teachers who teach us well

How to write and read and deal with numbers

We learn many things.

I never miss school

Those who do not care and cannot read

Are like blind eyes that cannot see and tell you where to go.

Family

In my family, my sister and brother help my parents cook

When I hear my younger brother cries, asking for breast feeding from my mother

I go in and pick him up, like my mother would.

My sister and my mother are happy

I don't waste time walking around and playing

After dinner, I read and not play around like I used to.

Temple

My village has a temple where people come to listen to prayers on special Buddhist days

On the Phavet celebration day, a procession is organized

I really enjoy listening to the priests making their prayers

Telling us not to commit bad deeds

I listen with the adults and keep my tongue quiet

Love

When we are alone, life is very easy but not very happy

Living with a spouse is very happy but not easy

Life in rural areas means a lot of lively activities but no careers

Life in urban areas means careers but is not very lively.

Animal Voices

Birds are noisy; and dog barks are not worth paying attention to.

Proverbs

To marry a young wife is like taking care of nine old cows.

To marry an old wife is like taking care of nine mothers.

Hmong Proverbs

Txoj cai luaj txoj plaub hau, txhua leej txhua tus hla tsis dhau .

Yog ua raws kevcai mas txhaum loj txhaum me los yuav tsum kho.

(Laws are passed but not to be bypassed) by Xou Vang

source: see in reference

Ruaj cuag thaiv, thaiv cuag zeb ntsuab.

Hais dab tsis yuav tsum hais kom tawv hais kom ruaj.

(No man is better than his principles)

Attitudes to Avoid

by Xou Vang

source: see in reference

A daughter-in-law treats her mother-in-law like a deranged woman

A mother-in-law treats her daughter-in-law like a devil.

Differences between Men and Animals

Road equals Horses

Time equals Men

Photo #199. *The That Louang Monument in Vientiane, the center of annual, national, religious and cultural celebration every December.*

see in:

https://en.wikipedia.org/wiki/Buddhism_in_Laos

Photo #200. *The Plain of Jars in Xieng Khouang Province*

see in:

https://en.wikipedia.org/wiki/Plain_of_Jars

source:

https://laosliving.wordpress.com/wp-content/uploads/2013/06/political-map-of-laos-1.gif

In the kingdom of Laos there are many ethnic groups, including lowland Lao, Lao Theung, highland Lao or Hmong, Yao, Thai Dam, Thai Khao, etc. close to a total of 60 different groups but there are about 150 subgroup that was not recognized by the government in legal record within the ethnicity majority groups in Laos. . All of them were courageous and resolute people who fought against the communist expansion into southeast-Asia during the 1960-1975 war. The pictures shown below are excellent reminders of the colorful and elaborate dresses worn by Lao ethnic women during special occasions.

Hmong people in Xieng khoung province, Laos.

Photo #201.https://the-elephant-story.com/blogs/news/a-gold-medal-for-the-hmong-people

***Photo #202**. White Hmong women in their traditional clothings in the 60-70's in Xieng Khouang province, Laos.*. source:

Photo #203. *Beautiful Lao girls performing a well-wishing dance during the That Louang celebration in 1960. See source:* https://www.unforgettable-laos.com/the-end-of-the-war/5-6-old-lao-poemsproverbs-photos-of-relevance/photos-relevances

Laotian dancers. See source: https://www.everyculture.com/Ja-Ma/Laos.html

Thai Dam ladies.

Photo #204. *Two beautiful Phuan girls from Xieng Khouang posed for picture on the shore of theNam Ngum Reservoir in Vientiane Province in 1968. Gen. Vang Pao brought over 20,000 people from Xieng Khouangto resettle in the Tha Lath area, near the Nam Ngum Dam. See source in: The Unforgettable Laos.*

Photo #205. *Two beautiful Yao aka Mien girls in the late 1960's.*

see source in: The Unforgettable Laos.

Photo #206.*Two beautiful lowland Lao girls from the Vientiane area performing a cultural dance. See source: in The Unforgettable Laos.*

- **Photo #208** *Ladies with important roles in MR-II in line to welcome King Savang Vatthana in 1965. From left to right: 1. Mrs. Hang Sao, 2. Mrs. Thong Vong-Rasmi, 3. Mrs. Phanh Singharath, 4. Mrs. Vang Pao, 5. Mrs. Phimpha, 6. Mrs. Saykham Southakakoumane, 7. Mrs. Tougeu Lyfoung, 8. Mrs. Simh Vichit-Vongsa, 9. Mrs. Touby Lyfoung, 10. Unknown, 11. Mrs. Ly Sang, 12. Mrs. Tou Lu Mua and 13. Mrs. Mua Thong*

- see source:

TODAY'S HMONG FAMILIES OF NOTE

Photo #209 *(left). Yve Vang (or Vang Yia), the first highland Lao Hmong man who graduated with a Ph.D. in electrical engineering and his wife, Dr. Va Lyfoung, the first highland Lao Hmongwoman who got a doctorate degree in medicine.* **Lt. Col. Vang, Geu's photo collection.**

Photo #210. *Ariya Lyfoung and his wife, Nang Bouakham. Ariya helped write the Lao version of this book and provided the necessary supporting documents to enhance the book's objectivity and truthfulness. Lt. Col. Vang, Geu's photo collection.*

Photo #211. *Hmong leaders with critical roles in successfully facilitating Lao refugee resettlement in the northern US. From left to right: Tou Fu Vang, Vang Geu and Leng Wong (Leng Vang). Lt. Col. Vang, Geu's photo collection.*

THOSE WHO CREATED AND MADE IT POSSIBLE FOR MR-II TO SURVIVE UNTIL 1975

Photo #212. Gen. Phoumi Nosavan

Photo #213. Gen. Vang Pao

Photo #214. *Chaokhoueng Saykham Southakakoumane*

Photo #215. *Phagna Touby Lyfoung*

Photo 1964 L20A
Long Cheng

Group Standing from left to right:
1- Major Vue Mai, 2- Chertong Ly,3- Col. Naoyis Yang, 4- Col. Shoua Yang, 5-Naikong Nao Yeng Ly, 6- Col. Neng Chu
Thao, 7- Col. Tou Pao Ly, 8- Naikong Tong Pao Ly, 9- General Vang Pao, 10- Naikong Neng Thong Ly, 11- Naikong Nao Tou
Lor, 12- Col. Chong Koua Vue, 13- Xayshoua Yang, 14- Col. Cher Pao Moua
Group Sitting from left to right:
1- Major Lor Xeng (moved to KM 52 with Ly Teck in 1965), 2- Col. Naokao Lyfoung, 3- Major Tongsao Ly (died in LS 02),
4- Xiblong Lyfoung, 5- Col. Ly Xang Tong Pao, 6- Naikong Nao Pou Ly, 7- Capt. Nurse Yang Chong,
8- Col. JouaVa Ly.

see source: The Unforgettable Laos.

*The General from left to right: the two no hat # 1 Tiao BounOum Nachampassak # 2 Gen.
Phoumi Nosavanh. The second row with six Generals are: #1- Gen. Sourith Douunesasourith
#2-Gen. Oudone Sananikone #3- Gen. Koupasith Aphay #4-Gen. Ouane Rattikoune #5- Gen.
Sang Rattanasamay and #6- Gen. Kott Venevongsoth. The row with the 7 Generals: #1- Gen.
La pathammavong #2- Gen. Bounthieng Venevongsoth #3- Gen. Sing Rattanasamay #4- Gen.
Bounleuth Sanichanh #5- Gen. Houmphanh Norasing #6- Gen. Bounpone Mattheparath and
#7- Gen. Vang Pao. The row of the ladies from left to right: The first 6 ladies are #1-Mrs.
Bounmy the wife of Gen. Sourith Dounesasourith, #2-Mrs.Gen. Sang #3-Mrs Boutsayo wife of
Gen. Bounthieng Venevongsoth #5-Mrs. Gen. Bounleuth Sanichanh and #6-Mrs. Gen.
Houmphanh Norasing. Then the last four on front: #7-Mrs. Gen. Ouane Rattikoune, #8-Mrs.
Khambang Gen. Kouprasith Aphay #9-Mrs.Pheophanh wife of Gen. Bounpone Matttheparath
and # 10-Mrs. Bounsou the wife of Gen. Oudone Sananikone. She stands right on front of Gen.
Vang Pao and she passed away November 29, 2014 in France. see source: The Unforgettable
Laos.*

Picture in May 7, 1954, Day that the French lost Diem Bien Phu to the communist. Touby Lyfoung Family was refugee from Laos to Hanoi North Vietnam for safety in 1954. This picture was taking in Hanoi before returning to Laos after the Geniva Agreement in July 20, 1954 from left to right: The first lady was Kwm Chua the last wife of Mr. Lyfoung (Touby Lyfoung's step mother), The lady smiling was Mrs. Touby Lyfoung, the next man was Tougeu Lyfoung (Touby Lyfoung younger brother) the next lady was Mrs. Tougeu Lyfoung (Her Name was Sisamone she is Lao the daughter of Gna Pho Thip Thammavong) then Mr. Touby Lyfoung and Mr. Bounchanh Vouthisisombath (The Chao Muong he is Laotian). The lady next to Kwm Chua was Mrs. Col. Lyxiblong Lyfoung her name Nang Paib (Hmong lady) next Mrs. Col. Ly Nao Kao her name is Kwm Mim (she is Hmong) next Nang Mao song (She was the first Hmong lady who graduated nurse degree from Vientiane around 1956), The first two boys and two girls from left to right 1- Dr. Tou sua Lyfoung, 2- Medical Dr. Touxa Lyfoung, 3- Nang Va (first Hmong lady graduated from Medical Doctor and the last girl was Nang Song Yang (graduated from nurse degree in Vientiane 1956 lather she was married with principal Inspector School Ly Beu Buag Fwm. He was assassinated by the Neutral (Kong Lae party) in Vang Vieng Laos.

See source in: The Unforgettable Laos.

and

see in:

https://en.wikipedia.org/wiki/Touby_Lyfoung

Military Leaders and officers in action at the frontier line (Ho Chi Minh Trail), Laos and did a great plan in action:

Military Leaders and Officers in frontier line with great strategic plan:

Lt. Col. Xainou Vang and his team. The special "Khaomoundou" aka commando had many assignments and led his team in airborne duties through actions assigned to capture Vietcon soldiers in the deep jungle in the border line of Vietnam and Laos. Some special impossible mission in the action plan assigned to Lt. Col. Xainou and his special unit team deal with military actions with critical incidents. They were successful with many critical situations through the years due that he had special skills and strategic plans in action and along with the good leadership of the CIA teams and General Vang, Pao. Lt. Col. Xainou Vang has his team at the Ho Chi Minh Trail zone, border of Laos and Vietnam. His team dealt with critical situations and was successful done due to his special strategic plan in action based on the military plan from 1968-1972.

Ka Thao aka Mrs. Chongwa Vang, daughter in law 's photo collection.

*General Vang, Pao and other leaders were at the frontier line.*https://histclo.com/country/asia/laos/hist/lh-vnw.html

Major Tong Khue Vang, other military leaders and officers in the frontier line, 1968. Captain Tong Lou Vang's photo collection.

Captain Xay Vang and his military group evacuated the Moung Nqa areas near by The Plain of Jar, Xieng Khouang province caught Vietcom military officer, in Laos in 1968. Captain Xay Vang's photo collection.

preteen young military officers, region two, Laos during the vietnam era.

source: https://warontherocks.com/2017/02/the-secret-war-that-transformed-the-cia/

men who called themselves Chao Fa, fought against the Pathet Lao communist government after the country collapsed in 1975-present in the Jungle of Laos.

https://www.thecolumbiastar.com/articles/laos-strangely-wonderful-3/

The women of Military leaders and officer's responsibilities:

One of the most important task that these women at home support to Military leaders and officers were: processing dried foods, rice, and spices and sending them to Leaders and Officers when they have no food in the deep Jungle or high mountain zone of the frontier line for months and days. The Military Department in region two may not get food in time during an emergency crisis at the frontier line. The second most important tasks that these Hmong women leaders did was provide support systems to any low income and sick military women and children and refugees community members escape from other regions in Laos during this war in Long Cheng, Xieng Khoung province, Laos. Special thankful to skills women leaders like Lt. Col. Xainou Vang's wife and her team and Captain Xay's wife and her team. On a personal level, they also have to take

7

care of their family and relatives at the local community level,too. These women and children are the victims of war. They provided emergency shelter and food to disabled and aging populations who were victims of war,too.

PHOTO CREDITS

(By Order of Their Appearance in The Book)

Geu Vang Collection

Mr. Arnaud Lyfoung

Mr. Vang Xang

Personal account of Kaysone Phomvihane's activities during the war in Laos

"The CIA's Secret War in Laos", by Kenneth Conboy & James Morrison

Mr. Chong Tua Moua and Haze, *"Guerre Secrete en Indochine, 1950-1955"*, by Lt. Col Michel David

Roger Warner, *"Out of Laos"*)

Mrs. Tougeu Lyfoung

Mr. Yves Vang's Collection

Mai Paj Yang

Col. Max Messnier from France

Mr. Yang Lue

Mr. Pham Khamsouane, the son of Lt. Pham Van Duong

Book "Biography of Gen. Kong Le"

Col. Tom Lum

Somchay Siharath (Col. Phanh Siharath's daughter)

Larry Woodson

Mr. Noah Vang in Minnesota

Mr. Leng Wong in Minnesota.

Mr. Bounchanh from France

Xang Vang collection

Gale L. Morrison, *"The Sky Is Falling"*

Mr. Lao Thai Wa Lue Vang

Kaying Yang collection

John Pimlott, "Vietnam: the History and the Tactics"

Pilot Vang By

Pilot Vang Khang Collection

National Geographic 1974 vol.145 No1.

Shadow war. The CIA's Secret War in Laos," by Kenneth Conboy and James Morrison

"Souphanouvong," by Douangsay Luangphasy

Fact Finding Commission, France

Mr. Lue Yang

Col. Thao Bone Collection.

Noah Vang in MN collection

Book of Chao Boun Oum

Lt. Col. Tou Ya Noah Vang collection

Phoumi Vongvichit and his wife (from Phoumi's book of memoirs)

Col. Tom Lum US Military

Col. Vang Youa son

Mrs. Halinka Luangpraseut

Phonekeo Sayasane collection

Captain Xay Vang's collection

Captain Tong Lou Vang's collection

Vue,chahue (Ber C.). collection

Ka Thao aka Mrs. Chong Wa Vang collection

SOURCES

(Ho Chi Minh's photos)

https://www.google.com/search?sca_esv=861bfe30a48f43f8&sxsrf=ADLYWIK_q2UllSL0N3t9NcOH0rVFAJ_O7g:1724677866600&q=ho+chi+minh&udm=2&fbs=AEQNm0Aa4sjWe7Rqy32pFwRj0UkWd8nbOJfsBGGB5IQQO6L3J3ppPdoHI1O-XvbXbpNjYYwWUVH6qTfR1Lpek5F-7GS5CjYSAeMKk98Y0RKOczWs8CWw7lN9NlZQhd9LdmaGqzhMDhVc9if9h6eZ-m9bQOvCpcaUs2kavYjfxiUUwLUKKhg4-JlXE9Eup2n5heUmVYair56gpiuIzFbH9Jw8MdSPgzll4Q&sa=X&sqi=2&ved=2ahUKEwipz9zc3ZKIAxVomokEHUydBCoQtKgLegQIERAB&biw=1920&bih=911&dpr=1

(Tou By Lyfoung's photos)

https://www.google.com/search?q=Tou+By+Lyfoung&sca_esv=861bfe30a48f43f8&udm=2&biw=1920&bih=911&sxsrf=ADLYWIK87wCjeN3DTA8f1C7NdOY2c40t_Q%3A1724677871570&ei=737MZoqoIvibptQP5a_wyQw&ved=0ahUKEwjK24vf3ZKIAxX4jYkEHeUXPMkQ4dUDCBA&uact=5&oq=Tou+By+Lyfoung&gs_lp=Egxnd3Mtd2l6LXNlcnAiDlRvdSBCeSBMeWZvdW5nSOo5UJoFWN83cAJ4AJABABAZgBS6ABnwuqAQIyNLgBA8gBAPgBAZgCCCqACqwSoAgrCAgoQABiAB
BixAxhDGIoFwgIIEAAYgAQYsQPCAgUQABiABMICChAAGAEGEMYigXCAgcQIxgnGOoCwgIEECMYJ8ICCxAAGAEGLEDGIMBwgIJEAAYgAQYYGBgKmAMDiAYBkgcCMTCgB4Zh&sclient=gws-wiz-serp#vhid=-PA0UWFNvHIQnM&vssid=mosaic

(Hmong leader, Lao, and others photos)

https://www.google.com/search?q=Thai+Khao+Leaders+(from+left+to+right)%3A+Ong+Sang%2C+Ong+Dzeng+and+Ong+Dzin&oq=Thai+Khao+Leaders+(from+left+to+right)%3A+Ong+Sang%2C+Ong+Dzeng+and+Ong+Dzin&gs_lcrp=EgZjaHJvbWUyBggAEEUYODIBCDYwODZqMG05qAIIsAIB&sourceid=chrome&ie=UTF-8#vhid=AKsZC2MEXJYnMM&vssid=l

(Pop Buell from USAID's photos)

chrome-extension://efaidnbmnnnibpcajpcglclefindmkaj/https://pdf.usaid.gov/pdf_docs/Pnabz296.pdf

https://www.unforgettable-laos.com/historical-of-events/part2/

(La Peuples de la Montagne's photos)

https://www.google.com/search?q=la+peuples+de+la+montagne%2C+1960%2C+Laos&sca_esv=861bfe30a48f43f8&udm=2&biw=1920&bih=911&sxsrf=ADLYWIJgtQ-

oCwu_qegJpqcsHj2L_7MDMQ%3A1724679804332&ei=fIbMZrKBFKCzoPEPo_nZ4Ao&ved=0
ahUKEwiyr9r45JKIAxWgGTQIHaN8FtwQ4dUDCBA&uact=5&oq=la+peuples+de+la+montagn
e%2C+1960%2C+Laos&gs_lp=Egxnd3Mtd2l6LXNlcnAiJWxhIHBldXBsZXMgZGUgbGEgbW9u
dGFnbmUsIDE5NjAsIExhb3NIrhpQwwlY6BdwAXgAkAEAmAFBoAHdAqoBATa4AQPIAQD4A
QGYAgCgAgCYAwCIBgGSBwCgB44C&sclient=gws-wiz-serp

https://www.unforgettable-laos.com/historical-of-events/part2/

Photos of On July 19, 1949 King Sisavangvong signed the Treaty of "Independence within the French Union" with French President Vincent Aurio)

https://www.slideshare.net/slideshow/laospptx/265741668

(Civil governments and Military Leaders and Military sites photos)

https://www.unforgettable-laos.com/

(President Nixon meet with Chairman Mao photos)

https://www.google.com/search?q=President+Nixon+met+with+Chairman+Mao+Ze+Dong+in
+Bejing+in+1972+%28after+USSR-
China+border+conflict+in+1969%29.&sca_esv=b3631baa3837d75b&udm=2&biw=1920&bih=9
11&sxsrf=ADLYWIIFprz4_-QnfUgJ-hqXp-
pYrZfiaQ%3A1724685075053&ei=E5vMZrTwAtGcptQPqcuIkAs&ved=0ahUKEwjoxf3J-
JKIAxVRjokEHaklArIQ4dUDCBA&uact=5&oq=President+Nixon+met+with+Chairman+Mao+
Ze+Dong+in+Bejing+in+1972+%28after+USSR-
China+border+conflict+in+1969%29.&gs_lp=Egxnd3Mtd2l6LXNlcnAia1ByZXNpZGVudCBOaX
hvbiBtZXQgd2l0aCBDaGFpcm1hbiBNYW8gWmUgRG9uZyBpbiBCZWppbmcgaW4gMTk3MiAo
YWZ0ZXIgVVNTUi1DaGluYSBib3JkZXIgY29uZmxpY3QgaW4gMTk2OSku MgcQIxgnGOoCMgc
QIxgnGOoCMgcQIxgnGOoCMgcQIxgnGOoCMgcQIxgnGOoCMgcQIxgnGOoCMgcQIxgnGOoCM
gcQIxgnGOoCMgcQIxgnGOoCMgcQIxgnGOoCSJsiUPkWWPkWcAF4AJABABJgBAKABAKoBAL
gBA8gBAPgBAfgBApgCAaACB6gCCpgDB5IHATGgBwA&sclient=gws-wiz-
serp#vhid=jMNPOqHfKmBJRM&vssid=mosaic

https://www.insidehook.com/culture/nixon-met-mao

(Royal Lao Flag)

https://www.google.com/search?q=the+royal+lao+flag&sca_esv=b3631baa3837d75b&udm=2&biw=1920&bih=911&sxsrf=ADLYWIIeVrednShIBTbh35F5HWu7YulLAQ%3A1724685912138&ei=WJ7MZr6ECKioptQPlu6xwA4&ved=0ahUKEwi-kJHZ-5KIAxUomokEHRZ3DOgQ4dUDCBA&uact=5&oq=the+royal+lao+flag&gs_lp=Egxnd3Mtd2l6LXNlcnAiEnRoZSByb3lhbCBsYW8gZmxhZ0jhSFCTC1i1RnACeACQAQCYAU2gAYAJqgECMTm4AQPIAQD4AQGYAg-gAtoGqAIKwgIHECMYJxjqAsICBBAjGCfCAgUQABiABMICCBAAGIAEGLEDwgILEAAYgAQYsQMYgwHCAgoQABiABBhDGIoFwgIOEAAYgAQYsQMYgwEYigXCAgoQABiABBBixAxhDGIoFwgIEEAAYA5gDB-IDBRIBMSBAkgcCMTWgB4ZI&sclient=gws-wiz-serp#vhid=o3Ez2mUkH7jrNM&vssid=mosaic

(Photo of King Sisavang Vong)

https://www.alamy.com/laos-king-sisavang-vong-or-sisavangvong-1885-1959-of-the-kingdom-of-laos-detail-from-a-100-kip-banknote-from-1957-sisavang-phoulivong-or-sisavangvong-14-july-1885-29-october-1959-was-king-of-luang-phrabang-and-later-the-kingdom-of-laos-from-28-april-1904-until-his-death-on-20-october-1959-his-father-was-king-zakarine-and-his-mother-was-queen-thongsy-he-was-educated-at-lyce-chasseloup-laubat-saigon-and-at-lcole-coloniale-in-paris-he-was-known-as-a-playboy-king-with-up-to-50-children-by-as-many-as-15-wives-image344227329.html

(Photo of King Sisavang Vatthana)

https://the-elephant-story.com/blogs/news/the-princely-brawl-for-control-of-laos   Royal   King   Sisavang Vatthana photo)

(Photo of Tiao Boun-Oum Nachampasak)

https://www.youtube.com/watch?v=e3H90VZ30bs and. *Photo of The Khun Lo Dynasty GENEALOGY and https://www.royalark.net/Laos/champasa3.htm*

(Photo of Tiao Maha Ouparath Bounkhong)

ByHistoryofLaos

https://www.facebook.com/permalink.php/?story_fbid=3506907539426741&id=789193917864797&locale=he_IL

(The Royal Lao King and President Kennedy photos)

https://jfk.artifacts.archives.gov/people/2012/king-savang-vatthana

(Phetsarath Ratanavongsa photo)

https://en.wikipedia.org/wiki/Phetsarath_Ratanavongsa

(Prince of Laos- Souphanouvong)

https://en.wikipedia.org/wiki/Souphanouvong

(The Vientiane Agreement, 1973)

https://laonc.blogspot.com/2016/02/the-vientiane-agreement-1973-and.html

(the news photo of The black list of Laotian government officials)

https://www.unforgettable-laos.com/the-end-of-the-war/5-3-the-last-lao-coalition-government/

map:

chrome-extension://efaidnbmnnnibpcajpcglclefindmkaj/https://media.defense.gov/2019/Jul/02/2002153035/-1/-1/0/B_0156_CELESKI_SPECIAL_AIR_WARFARE_%20AND_THE_SECRET_WAR_IN_LAOS_AIR_COMMANDOS_1964_1975.PDF

https://laosliving.wordpress.com/wp-content/uploads/2013/06/political-map-of-laos-1.gif

https://www.commondreams.org/news/2008/08/22/film-reveals-cias-most-secret-place-earth

Hmong proverbs by Xou Vang and

see more: http://hmonglessons.com/the-hmong/hmong-language/hmong-proverbs/paaj-lug-paj-lus/

www.ingramcontent.com/pod-product-compliance
Lightning Source LLC
Chambersburg PA
CBHW060802290425
25833CB00074B/56